# TO COCAINE

Latin American Commodity Chains and the
Building of the World Economy, 1500–2000

Edited by Steven Topik, Carlos Marichal, and Zephyr Frank

DUKE UNIVERSITY PRESS
Durham and London 2006

Printed in the United States of America on acid-free paper ∞
Designed by Jennifer Hill
Typeset in Quadraat by Keystone Typesetting, Inc.
Library of Congress Cataloging-in-Publication Data
appear on the last printed page of this book.

Duke University Press gratefully acknowledges the support of the
Stanford School of Humanities and Sciences, which provided funds
toward the production of this book.

# FROM SILVER TO COCAINE

AMERICAN ENCOUNTERS/GLOBAL INTERACTIONS
*A Series Edited by Gilbert M. Joseph and Emily S. Rosenberg*

This series aims to stimulate critical perspectives and fresh interpretive frameworks for scholarship on the history of the imposing global presence of the United States. Its primary concerns include the deployment and contestation of power, the construction and deconstruction of cultural and political borders, the fluid meanings of intercultural encounters, and the complex interplay between the global and the local. American Encounters seeks to strengthen dialogue and collaboration between historians of U.S. international relations and area studies specialists.

The series encourages scholarship based on multi-archival historical research. At the same time, it supports a recognition of the representational character of all stories about the past and promotes critical inquiry into issues of subjectivity and narrative. In the process, American Encounters strives to understand the context in which meanings related to nations, cultures, and political economy are continually produced, challenged, and reshaped.

# FROM SILVER

# CONTENTS

# Commodity Chains in Theory
# and in Latin American History

Steven Topik, Carlos Marichal,
and Zephyr Frank

N
W E LATIN AMERICA HAS been actively engaged in global trade
S since a Genoese sailor with Portuguese cartographic and navi-
gational skills and experience sailing to Africa on Spanish
ships partially financed by Italian bankers reached what would be known
as the "New World."[1] A German named the new continent America, after
a Florentine who wrote in Latin. Although today many observers of the
world economy are fascinated by a package of transformations known
as "globalization," which they think was born in the post–Washington
Consensus era as a result of the application of new rules on trade and
finance, this volume stresses that forms of globalization have long existed. In fact, many students of international trade date the beginning of
the world economy to 1492 with the incorporation of the Americas.[2] Marx
and Engels eloquently noted this a century and a half ago: "The discovery
of America, the rounding of the Cape, opened up fresh ground for the
rising bourgeoisie. The East-Indian and Chinese markets, the colonisa-
tion of America [north and south], trade with the colonies, . . . gave to
commerce, to navigation, to industry, an impulse never before known."[3]
In contrast, researchers of a modern school date the intensification of
global trade and price convergence to the last quarter of the nineteenth
century.[4] Still others argue that, despite antecedents, the true age of globalization is actually the contemporary era.[5] In any case, it is clear that the
growing integration of the world economy has deep roots in history.

The essays in this volume explore the numerous and changing connections of Latin America with the rest of the world by looking at the complex networks of commodity trade and the chains that were created between producers and consumers over five centuries: some commodity chains, such as those of silver, sugar, and tobacco, began in the sixteenth century; those of others, such as bananas and rubber, started only at the end of the nineteenth century, and cocaine came into its own in the twentieth. Our studies are distinctive not only because we examine in detail the trajectories of twelve significant commodities that prospered at different times in the last five hundred years, but also because we use a commodity chain approach to investigate the relationships between producers, intermediaries, and consumers. Unlike some studies that concentrate on where—in which country or continent—in the chain the surplus is accumulated, we are also interested in the social and political consequences on both ends of the chain. And rather than pay attention primarily to the strategies of global firms, we are equally interested in the many other participants in the production, processing, and marketing of commodities.

We focus on the production of most of the important export goods within Latin America but then move on to follow the commodities to their domestic Latin American as well as European, North American, and Asian markets. This approach is consonant with a new and vigorous trend in world economic history which has focused attention on changing patterns of consumption over time and recognizes that value is created in the consumption and commercial spheres as well as in production. This expansive view allows for a more complete understanding of the full circle of supply and demand of many of the principal goods that human beings produce and consume.[6]

The idea that Latin America has been profoundly shaped by its relationship with the global economy is of long standing and well accepted.[7] But the nature and consequences of that relationship have been strenuously debated. Early on in Europeans' colonization of the Americas, mercantilist views prevailed.[8] The accumulation of natural resources, especially precious metals such as silver and gold, defined wealth. Investment of capital in technology, especially manufacturing, and increasing the employment level in these agrarian states was considered secondary. A complementary axiom was that the main purpose of colonies was to enrich the Iberian metropolises. Hence the imperial states of Spain and Portugal played central roles in directing their colonies' economies. They attempted to constrain colonial commerce through royal monopolies, regulations, and licenses in order to ensure control of commodity trade and fend off their English, French, and Dutch rivals. It is manifest that the welfare of the colonial subjects was considered less important than the benefits that accrued to the imperial centers.

Recent research, however, shows that Latin American producers were much more than simple marionettes set to dance by overseas commands and demands. They were not simply passive victims.[9] Often they played enterprising, defining, and even controlling roles. We do not assume that European players constituted the metropolis while Latin Americans were peripheral or semiperipheral. The chains were dynamic and the participants often changing. Mexican and Peruvian silver miners as well as Brazilian and Caribbean sugar growers applied some of the most advanced technologies to create some of the largest, most integrated manufactories of the world in the sixteenth to the eighteenth centuries, generating what were then several of the most valuable internationally traded commodities.

Silver and sugar bound together Europe, the Americas, Africa, and Asia, thereby fueling early globalization. This era is witnessed in our volume by four chapters on colonial exports and their international trajectories: Carlos Marichal writes on silver, which was not only a precious commodity but also the most widely used money of the ancien regime; David McCreery studies indigo and explains three competing chains of the most widely used dye in the world textile industry; Marichal adds a complementary essay on cochineal, the most expensive colonial dye; and Laura Nater analyzes the production and trade of tobacco in colonial Cuba. Generally speaking, the production and commerce of these valuable goods was more closely regulated by the Spanish crown than the commodity trade of other, rival European empires. In each of these cases, the leading export commodities from Spanish America were essentially luxury goods demanded by aristocrats, merchants, and political and ecclesiastical elites of ancien regime societies both in the Americas and in Europe.

With the rise of the Industrial Revolution and expanded long-distance trade, the liberal free trade theories of Adam Smith, David Ricardo, and Jean-Baptiste Say became popular. Mechanization of production and transportation as well as expanded use of steam, wind, and water power led to a new calculus of profitability. Rather than sell a little for a high price under the controlled markets of the mercantilist era, producers now found it more profitable to sell a lot for the low prices now possible, and indeed necessary, under conditions of intensified competition. Thus when the French, Spanish, and Portuguese colonies won their independence during the first two decades of the nineteenth century in what were, in effect, among the first national wars of liberation, free trade became an attractive alternative to mercantilism. "Free trade" had two conflicting meanings, however: initially it meant the power to trade freely with any partner of preference; later in the nineteenth century it came to mean duty-free trade.[10] Latin American nations thus became pioneers in the Third World in negotiating their positions within the world economy as independent national states. The new statesmen wanted to free themselves from Iberian economic as well as political control and succeeded. Domestic political elites adopted liberalism because it was an effective political and ideological instrument and because it promised increased prosperity. It accentuated civil society over the state, secular powers over religious, private property over communal or public property, rationality over tradition, the market over the state. In effect and paradoxically, liberalism was viewed as a theory of individualism that would at the same time maximize the collective good, as Adam Smith had suggested.[11] State building and economic development hence went hand in hand.

However, the transition to free trade and laissez faire government was much more difficult and much slower than it is often portrayed. It was certainly not simply an automatic reaction to swelling markets overseas. High transportation and transaction costs as well as spoilage in transit retarded both production and consumption. Commodity chains developed over time as actors in the Americas and Europe experimented. Political economy, the mix of politics and economics, colored reactions to mounting foreign demand for raw materials and a growing supply of industrialized ones. Responses varied according to country and time period.[12]

Many people opposed opening up the economy to countries overseas. Protectionism long vied with free trade throughout Latin America, and local political elites developed sophisticated economic discourses in favor of one or the other.[13] Dr. José Rodríguez de Francia's radical attempt to maintain insular self-sufficiency in Paraguay (1814–40) and Rafael Carrera's rule in Guatemala (1838–65) are perhaps among the best known. But protectionist lobbies exercised great weight in Brazil, Peru, and Mexico in the first decades after independence. Moreover, regional caudillos such as Argentina's Juan Facundo Quiroga, made famous by Domingo Sarmiento, also were key actors in the struggles to control economic resources. Prolonged political conflicts generated instability, which proved to be a great obstacle to economic development and investment. As a result, the performance of most of Latin America's exports was weak for almost three decades after independence.[14]

A first stage of export booms took place from mid-century and ran strong until the world economic crisis of 1873. Peruvian guano, Brazilian coffee, Argentine wool, and Mexican silver came to play dominant roles in international commodity markets. Subsequently, from the 1880s the export booms gained even greater strength as Chilean nitrates, Brazilian rubber, Argentine meat and wheat, Central American bananas, and Mexican copper fed into world trade.[15] But even states that have been extolled as models of free trade liberalism, such as Porfirio Díaz's Mexico and Republican Brazil, in fact maintained high tariffs and large economic roles and monopolies.[16] Nonetheless, Latin American policy makers continued to use the language of free trade; they urgently sought foreign commerce and investment.

Foreign markets became so attractive not just because of the seductiveness of the idea of free trade. The reality of the unprecedented expansion of the world economy beginning in the last quarter of the nineteenth century and continuing up to 1929 drew economic actors to the global economy. European and North American prosperity combined with institutional changes such as the widespread acceptance of the silver and gold standards, generalized recognition of contracts, growing respect for private property, and reduction in transportation costs to vastly increase demand for Latin American goods. Prosperity in Western Europe and the United States led for the first time to international mass markets of middle-class and even working-class consumers who previously had purchased only local goods. These transformations gave rise to remarkable booms in exports. The greater integration of the world economy meant that some of the exports of the boom were exotics, brought to Latin America from abroad. Sugar, which originated in monsoon southern Asia, is discussed by Horacio Crespo. Coffee, which began in Africa, is studied by Steven Topik and Mario Samper. Marcelo Bucheli and Ian Read examine bananas, which were cultivated first in South Asia.

Many of the products, however, were still indigenous, as they had been in the colonial period: henequen, analyzed by Allen Wells; cacao, which Mary Ann Mahony presents; rubber, discussed by Zephyr Frank and Aldo Musacchio; and fertilizers, examined by Rory Miller and Robert Greenhill. Cocaine, studied by Paul Gootenberg, is an industrial product based on an indigenous raw material, coca. Foreign demand for these products had a profound effect on the countries where they were produced, just as the Latin American exports profoundly affected the lives of European and North American consumers.

It would require the precipitous drop in international trade and capital flows during the Depression of the 1930s to generate new ways of understanding Latin America's relationship with the global economy.[17] The self-regulating market ceased to regulate itself. But as has been established by economic historians, domestic markets in most of Latin America had already expanded and diversified considerably under export-led growth.[18] Consequently, import substitution industrialization became increasingly attractive as a means of lessening reliance on imports. Politicized and radicalized urban workers and, in a few countries such as Mexico, peasants and even workers in the export sectors demanded greater economic and social participation by the state.[19] They sometimes attacked reliance on foreign markets and capital as imperialism.

After World War II, policy makers, politicians, and entrepreneurs in much of Latin America turned to developmentalist theories to justify the call for greater state intervention and more protection of nascent industries. These trends were rather typical of what was occurring in other parts of the world: for instance, World War II and immediate postwar periods were the golden age of state enterprises, capital controls, and protectionism. Domestic economic growth was given priority over traditional export-led models. Development economists such as Jonathan Levin, W. Arthur Lewis, and Celso Furtado focused on the supply side of economics rather than on demand, and won adepts among some sectors of political and entrepreneurial elites, while others were attracted by ideas based on Harold Innis's staples theory. An intermediary bridge was proposed by Albert Hirschman, who advanced the concept of linkages, in which foreign trade and industrialization were understood to be complementary.[20]

At the same time, a different, more revolutionary break with free trade liberalism known as dependency theory gained many adherents.[21] According to its most radical champions, the global market was an uneven playing field and the rules were rigged against Latin American exporters. Latin America would become impoverished if it went on exporting its natural resources cheaply, and the domestic class structure would create a *comprador* class that oversaw a "non-nation." The solution was autarky—a turn away from the global economy overseen by an economically active state. Other *dependentistas*, such as Brazil's future president Fernando Henrique Cardoso and his co-author, Enzo Faletto, suggested that some sort of development was possible within the world economy, but that it required considerable state involvement.[22] Immanuel Wallerstein expanded on this view in the formulation of world systems theory that posited a "semi-periphery" as intermediary between the developed metropolis and underdeveloped periphery, complicating the international chain.[23] However, the framework of analysis was the nation-state more than individual workers, entrepreneurs, firms, or sectors. All three visions tended to agree that national sovereignty and a more equitable distribution of wealth were better goals than the trade surplus, capital inflows, and gross indicators of national wealth stressed by champions of free trade liberalism.

As the heated import substitution industrialization of the post–World War II years began to falter in the 1960s and the revolution of rising expectations was dashed on the rocks of economic slowdown and corrupt, narrowly elitist governments, the nationalist import substitution industrialization model was attacked. Revolutionary movements drew their inspiration from Cuba, which underwent a brief attempt at autarky and a sustained massive redistribution of wealth under a command economy. Their Cold War antagonists, led by national militaries, bankers, industrialists, and U.S. counterrevolutionary institutions, imposed authoritarian regimes. They sometimes emphasized opening to private foreign investment, as in Chile and Argentina, or continued with a statist model but still based on foreign loans, mostly from multilateral lending agencies, as in Brazil. In Mexico, similarly, the 1970s marked the high point of state-led capitalism as the accumulation of a huge foreign debt allowed for the development of an enormous number of state enterprises.

The debt crisis of the 1980s represented a new watershed, as most governments in the region faced imminent bankruptcy. The international debt renegotiations in the following two decades were followed by a process of privatization of public enterprises while military regimes gradually relinquished control to civilians. The return to parliamentary government throughout the vast region was accompanied by the adoption of the socioeconomic policies that have been termed neoliberalism, which attempted to reduce the state's role in the economy and reduce tariffs as well as barriers to the entry of foreign capital. Advocates of lowered barriers to trade through such commercial regimes as the North American Free Trade Agreement (NAFTA) and the Free Trade Area of the Americas (FTAA) and openness to foreign investment once again emphasized the rationality and efficiency of markets.

This brief historical review clearly demonstrates that the various approaches that Latin Americans have taken to global trade at various times have diverged fundamentally over the appropriate role of the state, of the private sector, of foreign private and multilateral capital, as well as over the relative weight exports and imports should be given. Whether more emphasis should be accorded to the size of a country's gross national product (GNP) and productive capacity or to the distribution of wealth and power has been debated in the past, as it is today.

In this volume we attempt to open up new ways of looking at the complex and diverse long-run trajectories of economic activity in Latin America by focusing less on national economic policies than on the history proper of the leading export commodities over the long run. Most students of Latin American economies have used national analyses, whether they look at the aggregate economy, foreign trade, or the industrial sector.[24] This approach certainly has the advantage of enabling the researcher to identify the history of national policies in different economic fields. But the disadvantage is that such an analysis ignores the fact that economic activity transcends national frontiers and cannot be adequately understood only within the limits of political administrations and frontiers. In many cases the success or failure of a sector in one Latin American country—coffee in Brazil, for example—encouraged or discouraged production in competing Latin American countries. Decisions were based on the international dynamics (health) of a commodity chain, not simply on the autonomous plans of a national government.

Our volume departs from the usual national-case approach in key ways. To begin with, by analyzing the historical trajectories of major Latin American export commodities, we offer an innovative perspective that focuses on products rather than nations. Each of the essays in this volume argues that studying the interlocking processes of production, transport, commercialization, and consumption of export commodities requires an analysis that transcends national histories. Latin America has been closely linked to Europe and the United States by commodity chains that stretch back to the sixteenth century (for Europe) but have become progressively more important and complex over time.[25] Today there is virtually no agricultural, industrial, commercial, or financial activity that is not highly globalized. The contributions to this volume are valuable for illuminating the origins and historical paths of globalization.

However, studying the dynamics of commodity production, trade, and consumption does not imply ignoring states and societies. On the contrary, each essay attends to the way specific export sectors developed in Brazil, Chile, Cuba, Costa Rica, Guatemala, Mexico, and Peru, locating their place in the domestic society and political economy. We see markets not as natural laws that impose themselves on humans but rather as human constructs that are determined by social and political values and institutions.

The study of an export sector is not unusual in the literature, but analyzing in detail the trajectories of twelve Latin American commodity sectors over the long run has only rarely been done before.[26] The most effective way to do so was to call for the collaboration of an international group of historians, each of whom is an expert on one or more export commodities. This volume is the product of such a joint effort and therefore reflects not only a wealth of information on each of the stories told but also of the authors' personal reflections on the complex and diverse evolution of global trade over the centuries as seen from the vantage point of the links between Latin America and world markets.

More specifically, as economic historians interested in studying a common problem from a similar vantage point, we look at the complex interactions of supply and demand which determined the development and cycles of the major export commodities. Usually studies on Latin America have focused more on supply than on demand. They examine how the product is grown, harvested, processed, sent on a train to port, and then loaded on ships bound for other countries. The researcher, like the export merchant, stands on the dock waving goodbye without examining what happens to his shipment afterward, or even wondering why there was a market for it in the first place. Each of the essays of this volume pays attention to the degree to which international price trends and demands shaped the trajectories of commodity production in Latin America.

But contrary to traditional approaches, we argue that the international market was not an exogenous force on which Latin American producers had no influence. Export producers and traders did not just dance to whatever tune the anonymous global market played. We question the common view that they were victims or beneficiaries but had little to do with the market, as is implied in the popular term "commodity lottery." It is certainly true that the market power of different producers varied with their share of the market and the size of the global market as well as the nature of competing substitutable products.[27] For example, Brazilian rubber merchants had much more power to set prices, and even standards, in the world rubber market when they held a virtual monopoly. That power dropped sharply once southern Asian plantations flooded the market after 1912 and became insignificant once relatively inexpensive synthetics became available.

Similar stories on the complex interaction of supply and demand in the studies of silver, tobacco, indigo, sugar, cochineal, fertilizers, and henequen are found in our volume: specific attention is paid to the rise of competing non–Latin American producers, new cultivars, or synthetic substitutes which reduced Latin America's market share and usually also its market power. On the other hand, Latin American coffee, and Brazilian coffee in particular, continues to dominate the world market, and Mexico is the world's largest silver producer. Moreover, the domestic market for some of the products that lost international market share became more important in the twentieth century as a result of export-led growth and diversification, especially in the largest and richest countries. Consequently, an increasing share of production does not have to compete internationally and more of the final processing is undertaken within Latin America.

We have made an effort to understand the consumption of the products as well as their production and intermediation. We suggest that demand is related to more than just relative price. First, as the economist Jean-Baptiste Say said, supply creates its own demand, and that demand can take some interesting and peculiar forms. Second, the propensity to consume is as much a social issue as an economic one.[28] The goods produced in Latin America's tropical jungles or mild temperate zones connected with very different societies and different acts of consumption abroad. Those differences were partially inherent in the nature of the commodity. Some commodities, such as silver, henequen, and rubber, were raw materials for industrial production (though silver, along with gold, was a unique repository of value as coins). Others, such as cacao, coca, coffee, sugar, and tobacco, were stimulants that were consumed during social events. Cochineal, indigo, and fertilizers were inputs for the production or transformation of other goods. Bananas were initially a luxury food, a finished good. But the same commodity could vary enormously in its uses in response to the cost of production and the evolving nature of demand.

Although international goods link producers and consumers in an intimate way, that connection is usually opaque today and was much more so in the past. Growers and buyers thought little about the provenance or destination of their products. The two ends of the international market reacted to each other mostly through prices. But the fact that participants did not recognize the ironies in the drama they were performing should not keep us from appreciating them. One of the main contributions of this volume is understanding the interactions and relative power of different positions on a commodity chain even when the actors themselves did not perceive the larger script. For most of the last five hundred years global trade was characterized much more by heterogeneity, difference, than by homogeneity. International markets were far from uniform or consistent. They were marked by peaks and valleys, booms and busts, radical changes in prices and applications. But market forces did connect these diverse and distinctive characters and cultures.

Global trade created ironies of meaning in which producers and consumers understood the good exchanged in vastly distinct ways and the meanings and uses were transformed over time. Silver, which in the form of pesos became the world standard for value that linked the Americas, Europe, the Middle East, Africa, and Asia, had been valued by the Incas and Aztecs, but not as coins, since they used other instruments. From the sixteenth century to the late eighteenth, the silver bars and coins exported in huge quantities from the Americas supplied the rest of the world not only with its main source of metallic currency but also with a fundamental means of saving and displaying wealth. From the late nineteenth century, on the other hand, its use as money and wealth conservation diminished rapidly, and silver became increasingly an industrial input.

Other commodities underwent similar transformations. The chocolate that was reserved mainly for Aztec nobles, who drank it with chile, later became feminized as the beverage of the languishing Iberian nobility as they added sugar, and then yet later was infantilized as the Swiss turned it into a mass product that was every child's delight: milk chocolate. Tobacco, which was smoked by native North Americans and Caribbeans in religious and diplomatic ceremonies, came to serve as a major trade good used to purchase Africans to toil in slavery in the New World and later served as the foundation of massive multinational corporations. The sugar that sweetened the delightful chocolate for centuries was produced by the most bitter form of human slavery on large-scale plantation and mill complexes that some historians have considered the first factories. Rubber was made into balls used by Aztec and Mayan warriors for their ceremonial ball games, as objects of divination and of aristocratic and chivalric prowess. Much later it allowed dapper dandies in the United States to ride their swift newfangled modern bicycles without thinking of the sweating Indians and *seringueiros* who were laboriously tapping rubber trees in the sweltering Amazon to provide the raw material for their labor-saving tires. Coca, used for centuries as a stimulant in pre-Inca times, had been hierarchically regulated by the Incas. The Spanish world empire (built on forced labor in mines) was partly built on the spreading use and commercialization of coca, which was perfect for dampening fatigue and hunger. In the twentieth century it was transformed by the miracles of modern science into cocaine. At first a pain-killing medicine, then an ingredient in Coca-Cola, cocaine is today a recreational and status drug. And rather than building a state empire, the cocaine trade challenges national states while building *narcotraficante* empires. Cochineal, the magic dye from Mesoamerica, colored the beautiful tapestries that decorated the palaces of European nobility, such as Henry VIII's Hampton Court, and was also used for centuries to dye the most expensive textiles in Europe and the Near East until the arrival of synthetic dyes. From the late nineteenth century, this product came to be used for certain beverages and for the production of lipstick on a global scale.

Following the international link reveals not only that the products took on very different uses and meanings abroad; it also dramatizes the clash of social formations. French revolutionaries sat in Paris's Procope coffeehouse plotting their attack on the Bastille and sipped cup after cup of coffee while drafting the Rights of Man and debating the principles of liberty and equality. But most of them did not stop to think about freeing the slaves in the French colony of St-Domingue (today Haiti), whose toil provided them their leisure drink. This was not just a colonial circumstance. The beverage known as the bourgeois drink or the brew of business continued to be grown mostly by slaves for most of the nineteenth century.[29] The McCormick reaper/binder machine allowed farmers in the midwestern United States to greatly increase the scale and profitability of their family farms, tied to the world market by one of the world's densest railroad systems.[30] But the mechanization that saved labor for North American farmers was fueled by binder twine made of henequen grown in Mexico's Yucatán Peninsula. There Mayan peasants were virtually enslaved to labor endlessly to feed the labor-saving machines of the U.S. Midwest and its factories in the fields. Latin America's link to the global economy created conditions of combined and uneven development, but somewhat different from Leon Trotsky's vision.[31] The Latin American countries' development was combined because of the intimate links to foreign markets, capital, technology, and ideological currents driven by the world capitalist system. It was uneven because the social formation included sharply contrasting modes of production. Latin American states and economies did not simply follow the diffusionist model that predicted that they would follow in the footsteps of Great Britain and the United States.[32] Indeed, in many cases the path of (commodity) export-led growth demanded labor forms and a role for the state not proposed by classical economics.[33]

This story did not play out the same over all of Latin America. Over time the Latin American economies became increasingly capitalist, though that process varied from country to country, sector to sector, region to region. The "revolution on the Pampas" in Argentina clearly enriched rather than impoverished the workers in the wheat fields and slaughterhouses and the sheep herders, at least for several decades in the nineteenth century.[34] But that came only after the primitive accumulation of appropriating the land and driving out the native peoples who dwelled there in the cynically named "War of the Desert" in the 1870s and 1880s.[35] Coffee growers in Costa Rica and banana growers in Macondo, Colombia, for instance, enjoyed relative prosperity, as did some nitrate, copper, and silver miners in Chile and Peru.[36] Over time, the social formations of producers and consumers became more similar. Latin American production became more capitalist and less coercive, though even today coercion still exists, and shifts in labor practices did not always reflect gains for workers.[37]

Our analytical vehicle for connecting Latin American producers with consumers in Europe and the United States is the concept of the commodity chain which we complement with some of the insights of the French *filière* approach and the Spanish and Portuguese-American *circuito comercial* approach.[38] We have used "commodity chain" because it is well known in the literature. However, "chain" does imply a rigid, predetermined path in one direction, while *filière* (strand or line) is more contingent and subject to change, and *circuito comercial* speaks to a circuit that could be initiated or controlled at different points. Even a steel chain is malleable and links can be uncoupled and recoupled. It is not necessarily a center–periphery relationship. As the flow chart for coffee (Figure 1 in chapter 5) illustrates, different levels or actors in the "system" can interact with various other levels. The commodity chain's direction and path are not predetermined. Economic historians must continue to grapple with the question of why trade in commodities so often failed to generate long-term economic development and why the gains from the trade tended to be concentrated in Europe and later in the United States. In brief, this approach posits the commodity chain—defined as the production of tradable goods from their inception through their elaboration and transport to their final destination in the hands of consumers—as a basic instrument of analysis that can complement the more traditional country or regional studies.

By moving away from the strong claims of world systems theory regarding the systemic nature of trade between core and periphery, commodity chain theory provides a more flexible and empirically satisfactory model with which to explain global trade. In the new model, the location of production and the distribution of returns in commodity trade are no longer assumed, a priori, as a function of a core–periphery relationship. Rather, each commodity chain develops its own logic according to a much wider set of conditions: core economies sometimes export primary commodities to one another; peripheral economies sometimes import primary commodities from the core; depending on the complexity of the chain, there may be several intermediate steps in the production, processing, warehousing, shipping, and marketing of the commodity—all of which make it necessary to pay attention to what happens to commodities at each stage in the chain. Moreover, the nature of the relationships usually changes over time because of technological, ecological, and political modifications. Hence the bulk of market power rests with different actors along the chain at different times, in part depending on the dominant international trade regime at the time.[39] This approach makes us sensitive to the fact that there is not one world market; there are myriad and often segmented markets, and indeed, the same commodity may have numerous chains depending on its end use or destination.

Nonetheless, we should emphasize that our point of departure is different from some commodity chain analyses. Rather than assume that global trade is necessarily unfair and monopolistic, and tends to concentrate profits in the core rather than the periphery, we evaluate these assumptions empirically with respect to each commodity chain. We also do not assume that all parts of Latin America were or continue to be peripheral to the world system, particularly not to the specific commodity market we are studying. Frequently Latin Americans have been the price-makers and developed the cutting-edge production technology.

The great merit of the global commodity chain approach, as we see it, is in expanding the vision of economic historians and students of international relations in general to encompass both the production and consumption ends of commodity chains as well as the many intervening steps of processing, transportation, and marketing. As Paul Gootenberg observes in chapter 12, "this holistic view helps us to overcome traditional divides between 'internal' and 'external' factors and between 'economic' and 'noneconomic' factors in Latin American history, binaries shared by neoclassical and dependency perspectives."

Most of the contributors to this volume were trained primarily as historians, not as economists or economic sociologists. For this reason, the bulk of the contributors see the use of commodity chains more as a conceptual tool for understanding the complicated business of global trade than as a normative theory capable of generating refutable hypotheses.[40] That is, most of us see commodity chains as a way to integrate our analyses of local or national industries into broader questions of world trade and commodity markets by asserting that commodity production in Latin America is part of a larger tapestry of global commodity trade. In effect, what happens in habits of coffee consumption, in taste in clothing, drug use, or tire technology will ramify back into commodity chains in profound ways; conversely, changes in the quality or quantity of raw commodities can induce major transformations in consumption and use.[41] The concept allows us to step beyond our national or regional borders and address the place of Latin America in world markets, showing how changes at any point in the chain can have powerful effects up and down the line.

Latin America is famously diverse, and its economies are no exception. For this reason, we hesitate to venture strong claims about Latin America and global trade writ large. Each country, indeed each commodity, has its own unique history. Grand generalizations are hard to make and harder to substantiate. But our approach, we believe, allows us to make useful (if not perfect) bounded generalizations that are sensitive to product, time, and place. One goal of this volume is to provide students of Latin American and world economic and social history with an integrated series of essays that show a panorama of the common experience of the region in global trade and raise a broad range of methodological and empirical issues that require future exploration.

We have incurred many debts in the course of creating this book. Support from the Social Science History Institute (SSHI) at Stanford University allowed the editors and contributors to meet for a weekend conference in November 2001. Participants included Joseph Love, David Weiland, and Dennis Kortheuer, as well as Stephen Haber, Noel Maurer, Anne Hanley, Mike Tomz, Scott Wilson, Lyman Johnson, and David McCreery as discussants. The capable staff of SSHI, Scott Wilson and Marie Toney, ensured that the meeting went off without a hitch. A second meeting, in July 2002, at the International Economic History Congress in Buenos Aires, benefited from the incisive commentary of Sven Beckert and Rory Miller. Finally, at Stanford, Ian Read and Heather Flynn provided assistance in organizing and disseminating contributors' chapters to the far-flung participants in this venture, and Piotr Kosicki helped with the bibliographies. We thank the participants for their essays and comments, which helped guide us in this introduction and in this joint enterprise.

At these meetings we considered a number of unifying questions:

1 To what extent does the specific crop or mineral product determine its social and economic outcomes? Is botany or geology destiny?

2 What were the relative roles of producers, intermediaries, and consumers in creating global markets? Was global trade a zero-sum game, or could all participants win?

3 What were the relative roles of labor and technology (growing, processing, transporting, and marketing) in the chain? How did they change over time?

4 How important were class, ethnicity, gender, nationality, and racial divisions and unities in shaping production, marketing, and consumption?

5 How stable were commodity chains over time? What factors explained major shifts? How important were variations in prices, increased competition, the scale and scope of participating firms, changes in consumption patterns, and exhaustion of natural resources?

6 The international trade in the key commodities was conducted on different levels and with marked differences in degrees of competitiveness. How important were monopsonies and monopolies or cartels in the commerce of the export goods?

7 What were the relative weights of economic (market) forces and political (state) forces?

8 How important were regional, national, and international institutions and conventions in shaping chains and in determining which actors would most benefit and who created the institutions?

9 How central were commodity chains to the regional economies from social, economic, and political perspectives? What was the role of firms and cartels in making or distorting markets and in developing, diffusing, or monopolizing technology?

10 How important was the reigning international regime in which a product operated? How significant were colonialism, imperialism, and neoliberal regimes?

11 How did production and consumption interact? Did consumption generate or shape production as well as vice versa? That is, were the chains driven by producers or by buyers?

12 Did the crops encourage foreign or national investment and what difference did the investment make?

13 Were crops or mineral exports dictators of production processes or was the same product produced under different labor, property ownership, and processing regimes?

14 What were the ecological and social consequences of the crops or extractive products? How did they sustain or damage the environment and affect the distribution of land and wealth?

Each chapter examines a specific commodity. The chapters are organized roughly chronologically, according to when the commodity became prominent in the world economy. The first four chapters treat exports that rose to prominence under the Spanish colonial system, generally luxury products with a high value-to-weight ratio because of transportation bottlenecks and the small global consumer market: silver, indigo, cochineal, tobacco. Chapters 5–8 focus on commodities that became truly valuable in the nineteenth century in response to the emergence of mass markets in Europe and the United States for foodstuffs and industrialized goods: coffee (with an important history stretching back to the earliest years of European colonization), sugar, cacao, and bananas. Chapters 9–12 examine products that had widespread application as agricultural, industrial, or pharmaceutical inputs: nitrates, rubber, henequen, and coca.

The final chapter is an overview of the volume by the editors. We reflect upon the economic, social, political, and ecological lessons we learn from this commodity chain approach to Latin American history and their contribution to new forms of global history.

---

## NOTES

1 See Phillips and Phillips, *The Worlds of Christopher Columbus*.
2 Flynn and Giraldez, eds., *Metals and Mining in an Emerging Global Economy*; Frank, *Reorient*.
3 Marx and Engels, *The Communist Manifesto*, 80.
4 O'Rourke and Williamson, *Globalization and History*.
5 Bordo and Eichengreen, "Is Globalization Really Different than Globalization a Hundred Years Ago?"
6 An early and influential study is Mintz's *Sweetness and Power*; another outstanding example is Brewer and Porter, eds., *Consumption and the World of Goods*.
7 Studies that make this point include Bulmer-Thomas, *The Economic History of Latin America since Independence*; Haber, *How Latin America Fell Behind*; and Weaver, *Latin America in the World Economy*.
8 For a sophisticated analysis of mercantilism that looks beyond the fetish of bullionism, see Grenier, *L'économie d'Ancien Régime*.
9 See, for example, Stern, "Feudalism, Capitalism, and the World System in the Perspective of Latin America and the Caribbean."
10 Thanks to Rory Miller for this important point.
11 See Hale, *Mexican Liberalism in the Age of Mora* and *The Transformation of Liberalism in Late Nineteenth-Century Mexico*; González, *El liberalismo mexicano*; Romero, *Las ideas políticas en Argentina*; and Santos, *Ordem burguesa e liberalismo*.
12 The importance of national cultures for economic development, albeit for a much later period, is stressed by Porter, *The Competitive Advantage of Nations*.
13 The essential studies here are Gootenberg, *Between Silver and Guano* and *Imagining Development*.
14 See, for example, Burns, *The Poverty of Progress*; Luz, *A luta pela industrialização do Brasil*; and Bulmer-Thomas, *The Economic History of Latin America since Independence*.
15 The editors lament their inability to commission chapters on beef, copper, wheat, and wool, which were included in the original prospectus. See Bulmer-Thomas, *The Economic History of Latin America since Independence*, for a good overview of these commodities in Latin America.
16 Marichal and Topik, "The State and Economic Growth in Latin America"; Beatty, *Institutions and Investments*; Riguzzi, *¿Reprocidad imposible?*; Topik, *The Political Economy of the Brazilian State*. Gootenberg shows the innovative economic ideas espoused and occasionally practiced in nineteenth-century Peru in *Imagining Development*.
17 There certainly were numerous eloquent critics of free trade liberalism before 1930 and policies in contradiction, but only with the Depression was there a general consensus questioning free trade.
18 For discussions of pre-1930 industrialization see Cortés Conde and Hunt, eds.

The Latin American Economies; Haber, Industry and Underdevelopment; Stein, Brazilian Cotton Manufacture; Suzigan, Indústria brasileira; Topik, The Political Economy of the Brazilian State.

19  For studies of the political roles of export workers see Bergquist, Labor in Latin America, and O'Brien, The Revolutionary Mission.

20  Innis, Essays in Canadian Economic History; Hirschman, Journeys Towards Progress.

21  Frank, Capitalism and Underdevelopment in Latin America. For a collection of dependency studies see Chilcote, ed., The Struggle for Dependency and Beyond. Also see Love, Crafting the Third World. An inspiration, though not usually lumped with the dependency literature, is Wolf, Europe and the People without History.

22  Cardoso and Faletto, Capitalism and Development in Latin America.

23  Wallerstein, The Modern World-System.

24  For example, the important three-volume compilation edited by Thorp, An Economic History of Twentieth-Century Latin America.

25  See Topik and Wells, The Second Conquest of Latin America, for a discussion of the advantages of a commodity-based approach.

26  See Duncan and Rutledge, eds., Land and Labour in Latin America, for an important earlier study of several commodities. However, its emphasis was on land and labor, not markets. Bulmer-Thomas, The Economic History of Latin America since Independence, stresses the importance of the "commodity lottery" but looks at commodities more within their national contexts. Also, see the classic study by Jonathan Levin, The Export Economies.

27  See Porter, The Competitive Advantage of Nations, chap. 2, for a useful theoretical formulation of these issues.

28  For more on consumption as a social issue, see Appadurai, ed., The Social Life of Things; Bauer, Goods, Power, History; and Fine, The World of Consumption.

29  For the conception of coffee as a bourgeois drink see Jimenez, "The Capitalist Drink"; Schivelbusch, Tastes of Paradise; Habermas, The Structural Transformation of the Public Sphere.

30  See Cronon, "Nature's Metropolis."

31  Trotsky, The History of the Russian Revolution.

32  For a model diffusionist study see Rostow, The Stages of Economic Growth.

33  Gerschenkron, Economic Backwardness in Historical Perspective, following Trotsky, argued that backwardness had relative advantages, because stages of development could be skipped. However, he still had in mind an industrially based model. For studies on export-led growth see Cardoso and Faletto, Dependency and Development; Hirschman, Journeys towards Progress; Sunkel and Paz, El subdesarrollo latinoamericano y la teoría del desarrollo; Shaffer, Winners and Losers; and Huber and Safford, eds., Agrarian Structure and Political Power.

34  See Scobbie, Revolution on the Pampas; Cortés Conde, The First Stages of Modernization in Spanish America; Díaz Alejandro, Ensayos sobre la historia económica argentina; and Hilda Sábato, Agrarian Capitalism and the World Market, 103.

35  For comparisons of Argentine wheat and beef development with those of North America see Adelman, Frontier Development; Slatta, Cowboys of the Americas; and Solberg, The Prairies and the Pampas.

36 See Samper, "The Historical Construction of Quality and Competitiveness." LeGrand's "Living in Macondo" modifies García Márquez's depiction of the Macondo banana economy in *One Hundred Years of Solitude.*

37 For example, see McCreery's discussion of the shift from state-directed coercion to market-driven necessity in Guatemala in the twentieth century in *Rural Guatemala.*

38 For an insightful comparison of the commodity chain and the filière approaches, see Raikes, Jensen, and Ponte, "Global Commodity Chain Analysis and the French Filière Approach." Commodity chains theory is in good measure an outgrowth of world systems analysis. But it also emerges from studies of the dynamics of modern transnational production and trade. The filière approach has been developed by French scholars to apply to agrarian commodity production in empirical cases.

39 For a discussion of international regimes, see Krasner, *The Third World against Global Liberalism*, and Smith, Solinger, and Topik, *States and Sovereignty in the Global Economy.*

40 We are responding to an apt criticism by Stephen Haber made at Stanford's Social Science History Institute.

41 Thus our definition of a commodity chain differs from Talbot's in "The Struggle for Control of a Commodity Chain," where he views it as "a network of labor and product processes whose end result is a finished export commodity," without taking the interaction with consumer demand into account.

---

**BIBLIOGRAPHY**

Adelman, Jeremy. *Frontier Development: Land, Labour, and Capital on the Wheatlands of Argentina and Canada, 1890–1914.* Oxford: Clarendon, 1994.

Appadurai, Arjun, ed. *The Social Life of Things: Commodities in Cultural Perspective.* New York: Cambridge University Press, 1986.

Bauer, Arnold. *Goods, Power, History.* Cambridge: Cambridge University Press, 2001.

Beatty, Edward. *Institutions and Investments: The Political Basis of Industrialization in Mexico before 1911.* Stanford: Stanford University Press, 2001.

Bergquist, Charles. *Labor in Latin America: Comparative Essays on Chile, Argentina, Venezuela, and Colombia.* Stanford: Stanford University Press, 1986.

Bordo, Michael D., and Barry Eichengreen. "Is Globalization Really Different than Globalization a Hundred Years Ago?" National Bureau of Economic Research, Working Paper 7195, June 1999.

Brewer, John, and Roy Porter, eds. *Consumption and the World of Goods.* London: Routledge, 1993.

Bulmer-Thomas, Victor. *The Economic History of Latin America since Independence.* New York: Cambridge University Press, 1993.

Burns, E. Bradford. *The Poverty of Progress: Latin America in the Nineteenth Century.* Berkeley: University of California Press, 1980.

Cardoso, Fernando Henrique, and Enzo Faletto. *Capitalism and Development in Latin America*. Trans. Marjory Mattingly Urquidi. Berkeley: University of California Press, 1979.

Chilcote, Ron, ed. *The Struggle for Dependency and Beyond*. New York: John Wiley, 1983.

Cortés Conde, Roberto. *The First Stages of Modernization in Spanish America*. Trans. Toby Talbot. New York: Harper & Row, 1974.

Cortés Conde, Roberto, and Shane Hunt, eds. *The Latin American Economies: Growth and Export Sector, 1890–1935*. New York: Holmes & Meier, 1985.

Cronon, William. *"Nature's Metropolis": Chicago and the Great West*. New York: W. W. Norton, 1991.

Díaz Alejandro, Carlos Federico. *Ensayos sobre la historia económica argentina*. Buenos Aires: Amorrortu, 1975.

Duncan, Kenneth, and Ian Rutledge, eds. *Labour in Latin America*. New York: Cambridge University Press, 1977.

Fine, Ben. *The World of Consumption*. London: Routledge, 2002.

Flynn, Dennis, and Arturo Giráldez, eds. *Metals and Monies in an Emerging Global Economy*. Brookfield, Vt.: Variorum, 1997.

Frank, Andre Gunder. *Capitalism and Underdevelopment in Latin America: Historical Studies of Chile and Brazil*. New York: Monthly Review Press, 1967.

——. *Reorient: The Global Economy in the Asian Age*. Berkeley: University of California Press, 1998.

Gereffi, Gary. "The Organization of Buyer-Driven Global Commodity Chains: How US Retailers Shape Overseas Production Networks." In Gary Gereffi and Miguel Korzeniewitz, eds., *Commodity Chains and Global Capitalism*. Westport, Conn.: Praeger, 1994.

Gerschenkron, Alexander. *Economic Backwardness in Historical Perspective*. Cambridge: Belknap Press of Harvard University Press, 1962.

Gibbon, Peter. "Upgrading Primary Production: A Global Commodity Chain Approach." *World Development* 29, no. 2 (2001): 345–62.

Gootenberg, Paul. *Between Silver and Guano: Commercial Policy and the State in Postindependence Peru*. Princeton: Princeton University Press, 1989.

——. *Imagining Development: Economic Ideas in Peru's Fictitious Prosperity of Guano, 1840–1880*. Berkeley: University of California Press, 1993.

Grenier, Jean-Yves. *L'économie d'Ancien Régime: Un monde de l'échange et l'incertitude*. Paris: Éditions Albin Michel, 1996.

Guilherme dos Santos, Wanderly. *Ordem burguesa e liberalismo político*. São Paulo: Duas Cidades, 1978.

Haber, Stephen. *How Latin America Fell Behind: Essays in the Economic History of Brazil and Mexico, 1800–1914*. Stanford: Stanford University Press, 1997.

——. *Industry and Underdevelopment: The Industrialization of Mexico, 1890–1940*. Stanford: Stanford University Press, 1989.

Habermas, Jürgen. *The Structural Transformation of the Public Sphere: An Inquiry into Bourgeois Society*. Trans. Thomas Burger and Frederick Lawrence. Cambridge: MIT Press, 1989.

Hale, Charles. *Mexican Liberalism in the Age of Mora*. New Haven: Yale University Press, 1968.

——. *The Transformation of Liberalism in Late Nineteenth-Century Mexico*. Princeton: Princeton University Press, 1989.

Heroles González, Jesús Reyes. *El liberalismo mexicano*. Mexico City: Fondo de Cultura Económica, 1974.

Hirschman, Albert. *Journeys Towards Progress: Studies of Economic Policy Making in Latin America*. Westport, Conn.: Greenwood, 1965.

Hopkins, Terence K., and Immanuel Wallerstein. "Commodity Chains in the World Economy Prior to 1800." *Review* 10, no. 1 (1986): 151–70.

Huber, Evelyne, and Frank Safford, eds. *Agrarian Structure and Political Power: Landlord and Peasant in the Making of Latin America*. Pittsburgh: University of Pittsburgh Press, 1995.

Innis, Harold A. *Essays in Canadian Economic History*. Toronto: University of Toronto Press, 1957.

Jimenez, Michael. "From Plantation to Cup: Coffee and Capitalism in the United States, 1830–1930." In William Roseberry et al., eds., *Coffee, Society, and Power in Latin America*. Baltimore: Johns Hopkins University Press, 1995.

Krasner, Stephen. *The Third World against Global Liberalism: A Structural Conflict*. Berkeley: University of California Press, 1985.

LeGrand, Catherine. "Living in Macondo." In Gil Joseph, Catherine LeGrand, and Ricardo Salvatorre, eds., *Close Encounters of Empire*. Durham: Duke University Press, 1998.

Levin, Jonathan. *The Export Economies: Their Patterns of Growth in Historical Perspective*. Cambridge: Harvard University Press, 1960.

Love, Joseph. *Crafting the Third World: Theorizing Underdevelopment in Romania and Brazil*. Stanford: Stanford University Press, 1996.

Marichal, Carlos, and Steven Topik. "The State and Economic Growth in Latin America: Brazil and Mexico, Nineteenth and Early Twentieth Centuries." In Alice Teichova and Herbert Matias, eds., *Nation, State and the Economy in History*, 349–72. Cambridge: Cambridge University Press, 2003.

Marx, Karl, and Friedrich Engels. *The Communist Manifesto*. Middlesex, England: Penguin Books, 1967.

McCreery, David. *Rural Guatemala*. Stanford: Stanford University Press, 1994.

Mintz, Sidney. *Sweetness and Power: The Place of Sugar in Modern History*. New York: Viking, 1985.

O'Brien, Thomas. *The Revolutionary Mission: American Enterprise in Latin America, 1900–1945*. New York: Cambridge University Press, 1996.

O'Rourke, Kevin, and Jeffrey Williamson. *Globalization and History: The Evolution of a Nineteenth-Century Atlantic Economy.* Cambridge: MIT Press, 1999.

Phillips, William D., and Carla Rahn Phillips. *The Worlds of Christopher Columbus.* New York: Cambridge University Press, 1992.

Porter, Michael E. *The Competitive Advantage of Nations.* New York: Free Press, 1990.

Raikes, Philip; Michael Friis Jensen; and Stefano Ponte. "Global Commodity Chain Analysis and the French Filière Approach: Comparison and Critique." *Economy and Society* 29, no. 3 (August 2000): 390–417.

Riguzzi, Paolo. ¿Reprocidad imposible?: La politica del comercio entre México y Estados Unidos, 1857–1938. Mexico City: Instituto Mora, 2003.

Romero, José Luis. *Las ideas políticas en Argentina.* Mexico City: Fondo de Cultura Económica, 1956.

Rostow, Walt W. *The Stages of Economic Growth.* Cambridge: Cambridge University Press, 1960.

Sábato, Hilda. *Agrarian Capitalism and the World Market: Buenos Aires in the Pastoral Age, 1840–1890.* Albuquerque: University of New Mexico Press, 1990.

Samper, Mario. "The Historical Construction of Quality and Competitiveness: A Preliminary Discussion of Coffee Commodity Chains." In William Clarence-Smith and Steven Topik, eds., *The Global Coffee Economy in Africa, Asia and Latin America, 1500–1989.* New York: Cambridge University Press, 2003.

Sarmiento, Domingo. *Life in the Argentine Republic in the Days of the Tyrant.* Trans. Mrs. Horace Mann. New York: Collier Books [1868].

Schivelbusch, Wolfgang. *Tastes of Paradise: A Social History of Spices, Stimulants, and Intoxicants.* New York: Pantheon, 1992.

Scobbie, James. *Revolution on the Pampas.* Austin: University of Texas Press, 1964.

Shaffer, D. Michael. *Winners and Losers: How Sectors Shape the Developmental Prospects of States.* Ithaca: Cornell University Press, 1994.

Slatta, Richard. *Cowboys of the Americas.* New Haven: Yale University Press, 1990.

Smith, David A.; Dorothy J. Solinger; and Steven C. Topik. *States and Sovereignty in the Global Economy.* London: Routledge, 1999.

Solberg, Carl E. *The Prairies and the Pampas: Agrarian Policy in Canada and Argentina, 1880–1930.* Stanford: Stanford University Press, 1987.

Stein, Stanley. *The Brazilian Cotton Manufacture: Textile Enterprise in an Underdeveloped Area.* Cambridge: Harvard University Press, 1957.

Stern, Steve. "Feudalism, Capitalism, and the World System in the Perspective of Latin America and the Caribbean." In Frederick Cooper et al., eds., *Confronting Historical Paradigms: Labor and the Capitalist World System in Africa and Latin America,* 349–72. Madison: University of Wisconsin Press, 1993.

Sunkel, Oswaldo, and Pedro Paz. *El subdesarrollo latinoamericano y la teoría del desarrollo.* Mexico City: Siglo Veintiuno, 1970.

Suzigan, Wilson. *Indústria brasileira: Origem e desenvolvimento.* São Paulo: Brasiliense, 1986.

Talbot, John. "The Struggle for Control of a Commodity Chain: Instant Coffee from Latin America." *Latin American Research Review* 32, no. 2 (1997): 117–35.

——. "Where Does Your Coffee Dollar Go? The Division of Income and Surplus along the Coffee Commodity Chain." *Studies in Comparative International Development* 32, no. 1 (1997): 56–91.

Thorp, Rosemary, ed. *An Economic History of Twentieth-Century Latin America*. New York: Palgrave, 2000.

Topik, Steven. *The Political Economy of the Brazilian State, 1889–1930*. Austin: University of Texas Press, 1987.

Topik, Steven, and Allen Wells. *The Second Conquest of Latin America, 1850–1930: Coffee, Henequen, and Oil*. Austin: University of Texas Press, 1997.

Trotsky, Leon. *The History of the Russian Revolution*. Trans. Max Eastman. 1932. Ann Arbor: University of Michigan Press, 1961.

Vilela Luz, Nícea. *A luta pela industrialização do Brasil*. São Paulo: Alfa-Omega, 1975.

Wallerstein, Immanuel. *The Modern World-System: Capitalist Agriculture and the European World-Economy in the Sixteenth Century*. New York: Academic Press, 1974.

Weaver, Frederick Stirton. *Latin America in the World Economy*. Boulder: Westview, 2000.

Williams, Eric. *Capitalism and Slavery*. Chapel Hill: University of North Carolina Press, 1944.

Wolf, Eric. *Europe and the People without History*. Berkeley: University of California Press, 1982.

# 1

# The Spanish-American Silver Peso: Export Commodity and Global Money of the Ancien Regime, 1550–1800

Carlos Marichal

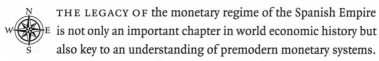 THE LEGACY OF the monetary regime of the Spanish Empire is not only an important chapter in world economic history but also key to an understanding of premodern monetary systems. The international diffusion of the Spanish-American silver peso between the sixteenth and eighteenth centuries transformed it into what could be termed an almost universal metallic money. The reasons for the global trade and circulation of this commodity money can be explained by the dynamics of supply and demand. On the supply side, the silver mines of Spanish America were the richest in the world and allowed for a voluminous and rising production of high-value bars and coins for several centuries. On the demand side, it is clear that silver and gold were long the most highly valued money commodities in ancien regime societies and economies, since metallic currencies tended to be dominant as media of exchange in a large range of transactions. In this regard, analysis of the extraordinary historical and geographical trajectories of the silver peso in the Americas, Europe, the Middle East, and Asia between the sixteenth and early nineteenth centuries can elucidate important aspects of premodern processes of globalization.

Indeed, historians have clearly linked silver to the origins of a world trading system from the sixteenth century.[1] As two researchers have argued: "Global trade emerged [in the late sixteenth century] when all important populated continents began to exchange products continuously—

both with each other directly and indirectly via other continents—and in values sufficient to generate crucial impacts on all the trading partners. . . . The singular product most responsible for the birth of world trade was silver."[2]

Certainly this hypothesis may appear debatable, since in fact such products as silk, salt, spices, and gold had already been traded for centuries across Europe, the Middle East, and Asia. But there is no doubt that it was not until the New World exports of silver and gold began to generate large transatlantic and transpacific trade flows that the full circle of global commerce was joined, making world trade a reality. Given the key role of precious metals as both commodities and money, it is not altogether surprising that they should have played such an important role initially and should have continued to do so for centuries.

Silver and gold coins have always competed with other monies but were the most esteemed in practically all ancient regime societies because they fulfilled the three traditional functions of money most effectively. Their durability and high unit value allowed them to serve as an excellent medium of exchange. In addition, their universal acceptance made them the measure of most units of account, since most metallic monies came to be measured by relative weight of silver or gold. Finally, as a store of value, silver and gold were highly prized, and therefore had universal demand. It is well known that a large variety of monies were circulating in the world in the period under consideration (1500–1800), including metallic currencies minted by states, commodity money in the shape of products (cotton, tobacco, cowry shells, cacao, etc.), and bills of exchange created by merchant bankers. The varied nature of monies meant that many clients placed a premium on a money with an intrinsically high metallic value and a relatively stable value. In many states silver and copper coins were systematically debased and hence soon lost their attraction for international trade. In a few cases such as China, where there had been a large circulation of official paper money, the paper currency could not be used outside the Chinese Empire. In other cases—in Europe, the Middle East, Africa, and Asia—private monies issued by merchants (whether bills or promissory notes or tokens) were extremely useful to square accounts on trade yet had a limited or specific circulation outside of certain markets.[3]

A premium, hence, tended to be placed on metallic currencies that were not debased. Indeed, perhaps the key reason for the international success of the Spanish-American silver peso was the fact that rising volume of production from the sixteenth century on was accompanied by maintenance of high quality, as assayers everywhere attested. Contemporary research testifies to this. Marie Thérèse Boyer-Xambeu and her colleagues concur, noting that "Spanish coins exercised their role as international monetary standard (reference point) all the better insofar as their quality and official exchange rates remained virtually fixed. This fixed value was absolute for the silver *real* from 1497 onwards and during three centuries."[4]

High-quality (almost pure) silver and gold coins had extraordinary demand among several groups, in particular (1) merchants involved in long-distance trade, (2) international merchant bankers who sought profits in arbitrage as a result of differentials in silver/gold ratios, (3) states that needed precious metals for their own coinage and for payment of armies, and (4) producers of commodities with high international demand. From the early sixteenth century to the early nineteenth, the Spanish crown controlled the territories with the richest mineral resources in precious metals, although it should be recalled that Spain did not have a monopoly on silver. For example, silver mines in Central Europe were highly productive in the late fifteenth and early sixteenth centuries. Similarly in Asia, Japan provided China and India with a large supply of silver from 1540 to 1640. Nonetheless, Spanish America produced more silver, on a more regular basis and for a longer time, than any other region of the world.

The present essay begins with a look at key factors in silver production in Spanish America during the colonial period, including location of mineral resources, capital, labor, and technology. A second section focuses on the production of money in the Spanish-American mints. The remainder of the essay deals with the international trade in silver during the colonial era, demonstrating that the demand for the silver peso as commodity money was a worldwide phenomenon: the export of silver pesos from Spanish America to Spain and Western Europe was only one stage in a complex trajectory of the circulation of this universal money of the ancien regime. Many silver coins and bars also went to the Baltics, Russia, the Ottoman Empire, India, and China, the latter two states absorbing the largest volumes of silver. The precious metals also traveled for centuries across the Pacific Ocean via the Manila galleon to the Philippines and hence to China. Finally, it should be recalled that there was also widespread use of silver coin within the Americas, both in Spanish America and in the thirteen Anglo-American colonies. In fact, the United States dollar can be considered a descendant of the long-famous and once-dominant Spanish-American silver peso.

## SILVER MINING: LABOR, CAPITAL, AND TECHNOLOGY

I have suggested that from the sixteenth century to the end of the eighteenth century, Spanish America provided the bulk of silver essential to the functioning of metallic monetary systems around the globe. According to the frequently cited estimates of the German scientist Alexander von Humboldt (published in 1811), total registered and unregistered silver production in the hemisphere between 1492 and 1803 probably surpassed four billion pesos.[5] More recent estimates coincide: Denis Flynn and Arturo Giráldez argue that "Spanish America was the source of approximately 150,000 tons of silver between 1500 and 1800, comprising perhaps 80 percent of world production."[6]

Spanish America and Brazil also produced a considerable volume of gold, but much less gold than silver and much less as a percentage of world production. During the sixteenth and seventeenth centuries the gold production of the western hemisphere represented only between 10 percent and 20 percent of world totals. The situation changed dramatically during the eighteenth century. For over fifty years (1720–70), Brazil was the world's largest producer and exporter of gold, providing close to 60 percent of global totals.[7] In itself, this Brazilian gold boom constitutes an important chapter in world monetary history, as it has been linked to the early adoption of the gold standard by Portugal and Great Britain in the eighteenth century. However, the emphasis of the present chapter is not on gold but on silver.

What explains the fact that Spanish America became the world's main supplier of silver so rapidly? A first explanation is simple enough: factor endowments. Several of the mountainous regions of Mexico and Peru, in particular, were among the richest in the world in minerals with high silver content. Moreover, the exploitation of these resources was not limited by significant constraints. The technology for extraction was relatively simple: mine tunnels were dug by pick and shovel, assisted by powder explosions to blow apart large rocks. The refining of the minerals was carried out by traditional smelting methods but increasingly with mercury amalgamation, as developed in the mid-sixteenth century in Mexico and subsequently applied in Peru.

Capital for investment in the mines was made available consistently by merchants and entrepreneurs willing to risk money in what promised to be an extremely lucrative business. Peter Bakewell, David Brading, Louisa Hoberman, and Frédérique Langue, among others, have published extremely detailed and stimulating historical studies on the merchant and mining elites that were active in dynamic mining regions such as Potosí, Zacatecas, and Guanajuato.[8] The rapidity with which the mining centers stimulated the development of regional economies and trade from the mid–sixteenth century was notable, as first demonstrated in a set of classic studies by Carlos Sempat Assadourian, which have given birth to an abundant historical literature.[9] Provisioning of the mines with mules, food, salt, powder, mercury, and other products soon transformed the economic landscape of highland regions of the viceroyalties of Peru and Mexico that profited from silver literally for centuries.

There were few labor constraints to the development of the mines. In the first place, it should be emphasized that the workforces required for the functioning of the silver mines were relatively small: the greatest silver mine of all time, that of Potosí in Upper Peru (today's Bolivia), produced large quantities of precious metals in the late sixteenth century with a total of some 13,000 forced laborers. Subsequently, wage laborers also were hired to carry out the exhausting work in the mines situated at over 12,000 feet above sea level. According to the careful research of Enrique Tandeter, approximately half of the laborers in eighteenth-century Potosí were free workers who received wages, but half remained forced laborers, recruited by the Spanish officials using the colonial system of the mita, which obliged many Peruvian peasant communities to provide men for diverse tasks for which they received virtually no pay.[10]

In Mexico, on the other hand, practically all mineworkers were paid from the mid–sixteenth century on. Nonetheless, in the eighteenth century, the total number of mineworkers in the most important silver producer, the viceroyalty of New Spain (Mexico), did not surpass 50,000 men, about 1 percent of the total population of this large territory. In 1790 the greatest silver mine of the viceroyalty, La Valenciana of Guanajuato, employed approximately 3,000 workers to produce more than 2 million pesos of silver per year.

In summary, in respect to resources, capital, technology, labor, and economic linkages, silver mining in Spanish America was a complex and quite sophisticated operation from the start. Moreover, in respect to profit/capital ratios, it was perhaps the world's most lucrative productive activity for decades, if not centuries. According to Flynn, the costs of production did tend to increase in relation to real value of silver production between 1540 and 1640, after which there was a three-decade decline in the industry. However, after 1670 many silver mining regions once again recovered and spurred production to new heights. By the end of the eighteenth century, Mexican mines were producing silver to the tune of some 20 million pesos per year, a higher average than at any time in the colonial era. And this was at a time when the prices of silver (in relation to the prices of other goods) were rising systematically, making it ever more profitable to exploit this mineral wealth.[11]

## THE PRODUCTION OF MONEY: MINTS, TAXES, AND PROFITS

One of the most striking features of the Spanish imperial monetary regime was the extraordinary stability of the standards and units of account of the metallic monetary system over a period of three centuries. Indeed, it was the high quality of the silver coins of the Spanish Empire that generated an intense and constant international demand for them. The monetary system of the Spanish monarchy was established by the monetary reform of 1497, which conserved the gold ducat as unit of account. But since gold had little circulation, the same reform conserved the silver *real* as standard money, valued at 34 *maravedís*; this ratio remained constant for over three centuries. This impressive continuity helps to explain the wide acceptance of the silver peso.[12]

Marc Flandreau has offered a possible explanation for the success of the silver peso as a kind of universal money in the early modern period, suggesting that its quality and stability in value could have made it, in effect, almost a perfect money commodity of the age.[13] The best coins in the ancien regime (such as the florin, ducat, and silver peso) were in much demand because of their quality (fineness), their standardized weight, and merchants' confidence in them. These characteristics were highly prized in a world where monetary circulation was basically metallic or in which letters of exchange were normally liquidated either by other bills or by metallic currency in silver or gold.

In the event, the most extensive state in Europe and the world, the Spanish Habsburg Empire, soon adopted the silver peso as standard currency. As the historian Guillermo Céspedes del Castillo has noted, by the mid-sixteenth century it is possible to note a tendency toward the

Royal mints in colonial Spanish America, 1535–1810

Havana
(1741)

Sto. Domingo
(1536)

Mexico
(1535)

Cartagena
(1620)

Guatemala
(1731)

Bogotá
(1620)

Popayán
(1749)

Lima
(1565 1a)
(1683 2a)

Potosí
(1572)

Santiago de Chile
(1743)

⊙ Mints with short duration
△ Mints which were permanent

consolidation of the silver peso, with a value of 272 maravedís, equal to 8 silver *reales*.[14] In Spanish America, as Roberto Cortés Conde and George McCandless observed, "the most common silver coins were the *real* and its multiples: the *real* of two (later the peseta), *real* of four (half peso), and *real* of eight (the peso, an ounce of silver). Fluctuating over time, between 16 and 17 silver pesos were equivalent to one gold peso (one ounce of gold)."[15]

One of the reasons for preserving the high quality of coins minted was the desire of the Spanish crown to systematically collect taxes on silver and gold production, avoiding evasion and debasement. Mints had to be places where miners and merchant bankers could take precious metals with confidence, and they had to be in major cities, where there was not likely to be a great deal of contraband. As a result, only a few mints were established in Spanish America: Mexico City (1535), Santo Domingo (1536), Lima (1565), Potosí (1572), Bogotá (1620), Santiago de Guatemala, then the capital of the captaincy general (1731), and Santiago de Chile (1743).

The norms of mintage varied over the centuries. The rather coarse techniques used in the sixteenth century stimulated much clipping of coins. Hence, silver pieces of eight were frequently cut literally into eight triangular pieces or, alternatively, into four pieces of two *reales* ("two bits") in the eighteenth century. It is extremely difficult to know exactly how much silver was exported from Spanish America in the form of coins and how much in bars or other forms, but over time, the volume of coins increased noticeably. Still in 1708, a French merchant captain noted after a visit to Mexico that he calculated that only half of the silver that went into the Mexico City mint was finally minted, as many traders preferred bars.[16] Such a fact reflected clearly the interchangeability of silver as money and commodity.

Subsequently, however, coinage clearly came to dominate. The new machinery put into the Mexico City mint in 1733 permitted the stamping of almost perfect coins at the same time as assay reached a point of near perfection. The Spanish crown preferred the new system, as it allowed for greater fiscal control. Mintage of coins increased from an annual average of 4 million pesos in 1691–1700 to over 9 million coins in the 1730s. And by the end of the century, the Mexico mint was producing 24 million silver pesos a year, as indicated in Table 1.[17]

The new monetary and minting policies of the Bourbon monarchy allowed for much closer state regulation and control, but the technical

Table 1

Annual number of silver pesos coined at mints in Spanish America, c. 1790 (estimated)

| Mints | Pesos |
|---|---|
| Mexico | 24,000,000 |
| Lima | 6,000,000 |
| Potosí | 4,600,000 |
| Santa Fe de Bogotá | 1,200,000 |
| Santiago de Chile | 1,000,000 |
| Popayán | 1,000,000 |
| Santiago da Guatemala | 200,000 |

Source: Alejandro de Humboldt, *Ensayo político sobre el reino de la Nueva España* (Mexico City: UNAM, 1991; original edition, Paris 1811).

improvements also reinforced the vast international demand for Mexican silver pesos. The importance of this particular mint for world economic history was registered by Humboldt on his visit there in 1803: "It is impossible to visit this building . . . without recalling that from it have come more than two billion pesos over the course of less than 300 years . . . and without reflecting on the powerful influence that these treasures have had on the destiny of the peoples of Europe."[18]

Control of mints was also important for maintaining the traditional revenue source of the colonial administrations, made up by a collection of mining taxes, the most important being the *diezmo minero*, a 10 percent duty levied on all silver produced. This tax was charged at the royal mints, where all silver from the viceroyalty was brought to be coined. While the direct tax on mine production was the single most important item among the varied list of exactions which fell upon Mexican and Peruvian silver, a close runner-up was income derived from seignorage (revenue from the minting of coins calculated as the difference between the face value of the coins and the value of the metal in them). Additional income was derived from the sale of the products of the state-owned mercury monopoly; mercury was an essential ingredient for colonial silver-refining processes, but the bulk of the income thus generated was shipped off to Spain to buy more mercury. The net revenue obtained in Bourbon Mexico from mining taxes—directly and indirectly—was close to 4 million pesos in the 1790s, approximately 26 percent of total net income of the viceregal government.[19]

Given such mining riches, it might be presumed that the colonies would have enjoyed widespread circulation of silver and gold currency, and that this would have served to buttress a dynamic credit system, with a presumably beneficial impact on all social and economic sectors. In fact, however, the actual circulation of metallic currency within both Spanish America and Brazil was fairly limited, a fact so paradoxical that it has provoked considerable debate among historians, hard put to explain the scarcity of cash in circulation within what were eminently silver- and gold-producing economies. Various arguments have been advanced to explain this situation, but the most important factors are clearly the following: (1) the extraction of large volumes of silver by the Spanish crown, which used it to pay for the administration of the imperial monarchy in the Americas, Europe, and the Philippines; (2) the use of silver by merchants to pay for the bulk of imports to Spanish America from the sixteenth to the early nineteenth centuries; (3) the international demand for the silver pesos both as currency and as commodity; (4) the demand generated by merchant bankers engaged in international arbitrage on silver.

The international diffusion of the silver peso was therefore impelled by a series of strong and dynamic forces. Its circulation was in fact worldwide, but for reasons of clarity I will offer a summary of the major geographic regions.

## RIVERS OF SILVER: THE EXPORT OF SILVER PESOS AND BARS TO EUROPE, 1550–1800

For over half a century historians have been debating the volume and cycles of the flows of silver and gold that crossed the Atlantic from the sixteenth to the eighteenth centuries. The modern discussion began with the classic study by Earl Hamilton, *American Treasure and the Price Revolution in Spain, 1501–1650*, published in 1934. Since then, dozens of essays and books have supported or argued against his central thesis, that the price revolution of the sixteenth century in Europe was caused largely by the influx of silver and gold from the Americas. Despite the enormous influence of this work, later studies have come to question the majority of Hamilton's propositions, and his study has been dismantled bit by bit.[20] With regard to the estimates of silver flows from the Americas to Europe, the new studies demonstrate that while Hamilton's figures were on the mark for the period 1550–1630, he underestimated trends in later

1. Annual shipments of precious metals from the Americas to Europe
(silver and gold, in tons), 1501–1800

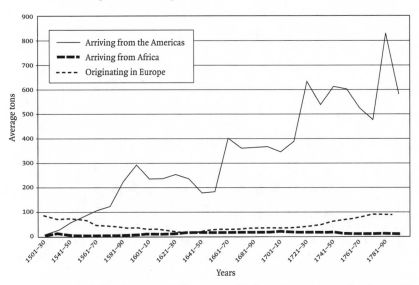

Source: Michel Morineau, *Incroyables gazettes et fabuleux métaux: Les retours des trésors améri-cains d'après les gazettes hollandaises, XVII–XVIIIᵉ siècles* (New York: Cambridge University Press, 1985), 578.

decades. Current research suggests that after 1630 shipments declined only during three decades and then resurged with force from 1670 on. Hence the theory of the long seventeenth-century depression was not entirely applicable to Spanish America.

The important study of Michel Morineau, *Incroyables gazettes et fabuleux métaux*, reconstructed the flows of silver not only to Seville but also to other European ports and demonstrated that the trends of silver exports (coins and bars) went upward from 1670 to 1810 (see Figure 1). Of all monies, silver pesos became the most widely circulating currency in the world. In his great study of the transatlantic circulation of American silver, Morineau pointed out that by the late sixteenth century, the silver peso had already found a fundamental niche in the monetary vocabularies of most European nations: among the most common terms used to describe the silver peso were "pieces of eight," *stuken van achten, pièces de huit réaux, pesos fuertes, piastres fortes, piastres,* and *patacones* (Figure 2).[21]

In Antwerp, under Spanish control and possibly the most important port and financial center of northern Europe in the mid–sixteenth century, the arrival of constantly increasing flows of American gold and

2. Value of exports of silver and gold from Spanish America and Brazil to Europe, 1701–1805 (millions of silver pesos)

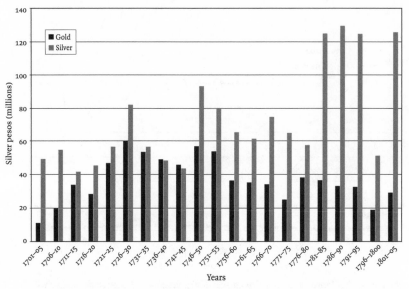

Source: Michel Morineau, *Incroyables gazettes et fabuleux métaux: Les retours des trésors améri-cains d'après les gazettes hollandaises, XVII–XVIIIᵉ siècles* (New York: Cambridge University Press, 1985), 483–84.

particularly of silver contributed to financial modernization. Such eco-nomic historians as Frank Spooner, Herman van der Wee, and Carlo Cipolla have emphasized the importance of the remittances in the takeoff of the stock market of Antwerp (1531), one of the earliest and most dynamic of northern Europe, where the precious metals served as basic support to the first international market of securities, a large part of the instruments negotiated being the famous *juros*, debt instruments of the Spanish monarchy, whose issue grew exponentially in the sixteenth cen-tury. As early as 1553, Thomas Gresham, financial expert and British envoy to Flanders, reported that in Antwerp the gold market was quite small because practically all mercantile transactions were carried out in Spanish silver *reales*.[22]

In the second half of the sixteenth century and the first decades of the seventeenth century, the shipments of silver were also fundamental to financing of the administration of the Habsburg Empire in Flanders and Germany, most particularly for the financing of armies and wars. It is impossible to conceive of alternative means of financing the military forces and imperial projects of Charles V, Philip II, and Philip III, at a time when the Spanish monarchy became the leading power in Europe. The silver peso became the coin of armies on the march through north-central Europe for decades, contributing notably to the circulation of this currency of Spanish-American origin in the Old World.[23]

The Spanish state hence contributed forcefully to the transformation of the silver peso into a universal currency. The fiscal transfers were highly cyclical during the sixteenth and seventeenth centuries. For instance, during the Thirty Years' War in Europe (1618–48), the Spanish crown obliged the American colonies to provide extraordinary sums, part in taxes and part in a combination of forced loans and interest-paying loans. The transfer in these decades of Peruvian silver to Spain (and hence to Spanish armies in Italy, Germany, and Flanders) was truly astonishing.[24] This trend continued in later periods as well. From the late seventeenth century, the Madrid officials required the Spanish-American viceroyalties to ship fiscal surplus both to the metropolis and elsewhere in the empire to sustain Spain's civil and, above all, military administrations. The money thus served to buttress the Spanish government in the Iberian Peninsula and in southern Italy, and also throughout the Americas, in the greater Caribbean, and in the Philippines.

During the eighteenth century, metropolitan exactions increased, reaching their peak at the end of the eighteenth century as the Spanish crown became involved in successive international wars against its great rivals, Great Britain (1763–67, 1779–83, 1796–1803) and France (1793–95, 1808–14). As a result, the demands of the Madrid treasury increased, and colonial administrators were instructed to remit as much fiscal surplus as possible. Bourbon Mexico alone was obliged to send 250 million silver pesos of net fiscal surplus abroad between 1760 and 1810.[25]

Of even greater importance than the shipments of silver from Spanish America to Europe and elsewhere on royal account were private remittances and payments which were basically tied to international mercantile transactions. Most imports to Spanish America were paid with silver and gold, which in turn became the chief exports of the colonies for three centuries. The merchandise sent to the Americas on the great convoys known as *flotas*, which left annually from Seville and later from Cadiz (from the mid-sixteenth century on) included mostly textiles from Italy, France, Flanders, and England, but also many other goods from Spain and other European countries. The legal trade was complemented by a flourishing transatlantic smuggling business, which surged in the second half of the seventeenth century. According to the historians Carlos

Malamud, Zacarías Moutoukias, and Michel Morineau, the French took over the bulk of the illegal trade in that period and drained off huge sums of American silver, which never passed through the Iberian Peninsula. One estimate is that in the 1680s France provided some 40 percent of the products destined for Spanish America, being followed in importance by Genoa, England, the Low Countries, and Hamburg.[26] The Dutch and British also participated actively in many of these transactions through their entrepôts in the Caribbean.

During the eighteenth century, the Spanish convoys returned to Europe from the colonies laden with the following products, in order of importance: silver, gold, tobacco, cochineal, indigo and other dyes, cocoa, hides, and a variety of additional primary commodities of less volume and value, such as quinine and vanilla. It is extremely difficult to ascertain the exact distribution of the silver throughout Europe, but numerous documents provide estimates. Among them is a report by a French merchant in Cadiz in 1686 who indicated that of the total of precious metals that had arrived directly in Spain, the French merchants had taken out 4.6 million silver pesos, the Genoese 4 million, the Dutch 3.3 million, the English 2 million, the Flemish 2 million, and merchants from Hamburg 1.3 million.[27]

Another important question is what happened to the silver coins once they entered into the circulation of currency in the various European countries? Recent estimates are that approximately one-third went to the mints of France, England, and Holland, where they were resmelted, although in some cases they were simply stamped over.[28] But another important portion of the silver was used for international trade with the Baltic states, Russia, the Middle East, India, and China.

Among the first scientific writers to attempt an overall estimate of precious metals exported from the Americas to Europe was Alexander von Humboldt in the early nineteenth century, after his five-year journey through the Americas (1798–1803). His calculations are still considered valuable indicators by such modern historians as John TePaske, who have specialized in the subject of the production and circulation of silver and gold in the early modern period. Moreover, the figures advanced by Humboldt provide evidence of the importance that he and his contemporaries attributed to these international flows of precious metals.

Humboldt, however, did not limit himself to global estimates or to the long-term flows of American silver and gold exported to Europe, for he also calculated the subsequent redistribution of the precious metals in other world regions. According to the German scientist, the total value of silver and gold coins that arrived in Europe from the Americas in the late eighteenth century was close to 43 million pesos per year, of which 4 million were redirected to trade with Russia, 4 million to trade in the Middle East, and 17.5 million to India and China by sea, mainly by way of the Cape of Good Hope. Summing up, Humboldt estimated that perhaps 18 million silver pesos were used for currency circulation within Europe (a large portion being smelted or restamped), but the rest of the silver was reexported.

In recent years, researchers have been reevaluating the old estimates. Among the most cited and provocative are those of the Swedish historian Artur Attman, who has argued that silver flows reflected the size of trade balances between world regions. Europe received an abundance of precious metals and was therefore in a position to cover its trade deficits with other regions by exporting silver and gold coins. According to his view, from the sixteenth century, three great zones enjoyed surpluses in their foreign trade as they exported more (nonmoney) commodities than they imported. These were the Scandinavian and Baltic countries, the Near East, and Asia (India and China). According to Attman, they balanced their trade with the import of precious metals, mainly in the form of bars and coins.[29]

Various specialized historical monographs demonstrate that at least from the sixteenth century, the export of Baltic timber, fish, furs, and other primary commodities to England and Central Europe generated a counterflow of silver.[30] Similarly, other studies indicate that there were important flows of silver or gold to the Ottoman Empire, although these were much less significant than the shipments that went by ocean to South Asia and China.[31] It is to the latter that we now turn our attention.

## THE ADVENTURES OF THE SILVER PESO
## IN CHINA AND INDIA

What factors explain the secular transfer of huge sums of silver to Asia? According to Charles Kindleberger, it was common in the Roman Empire to speak of Asia as the graveyard of silver from the West. Numerous authors in the Middle Ages and in the sixteenth century insisted that Asians, Chinese in particular, had a proclivity to hoard silver. Curiously enough, Charles Kindleberger accepted this proposition at face value and argued that in the early modern world, the difference between Europe and

Asia could be described as a contrast between Westerners (who exported silver and gold) as spenders and Easterners (who imported silver and gold) as hoarders.[32]

This traditional view has been rebutted by numerous studies of the Asian economies in the sixteenth, seventeenth, and eighteenth centuries, including their dynamic and complex monetary and credit systems, the nature of their international trade, and the links with other macroregions of the world economy. In 1982, in a now classic essay, William Atwell published pioneering estimates of the flows of silver to China in the long century 1530–1650. Atwell pointed out that by the sixteenth century, China under the Ming dynasty already had more than 100 million people, which made it the largest market in the world. The demand for silver as both commodity and currency was therefore enormous.[33] Other currencies were by then quite scarce. Gold did not circulate much for mercantile transactions. The paper money that had circulated abundantly in the Chinese Empire since the twelfth century was by then discredited. Copper money, which had also circulated widely and had been repeatedly debased, fell out of favor with traders, consumers, and the government itself. Atwell added that the notable increase of Chinese exports from the sixteenth century, among them raw silk, silk and cotton textiles, tea, porcelain, mercury, and precious stones, also generated much demand for silver as a commodity. Hence a large population and a growing economy inevitably created a large market for silver bars and coins, both serving as commodities and as money.[34]

Subsequently, the economic historians Richard von Glahn, Dennis O. Flynn, and Arturo Giráldez have argued that among the most important factors that contributed to the enormous increase in demand for silver were the monetary and fiscal policies of the Chinese state.[35] The adoption of new fiscal rules (particularly the Single Whip Tax Reform of the 1570s) which obliged Chinese peasants, artisans, and merchants to pay taxes in silver contributed forcefully to the new trend. As Flynn and Giráldez affirm, "such a massive shift in the demand for silver caused its value to soar. Using bimetallic ratios as an indicator, silver's value within China jumped to about double the levels prevalent in America, Japan, Europe and much of the rest of the world."[36] The change in the ratio of silver to gold in Chinese markets made it increasingly attractive to export silver to China and, inversely, to export gold. According to von Glahn, in the mid–sixteenth century the gold/silver ratio hovered around 1:11–12 in Europe, whereas it was 1:6 in China and approximately 1:8 in India.[37]

For European merchants engaged in international trade the potential profits to be obtained from arbitrage (based on the differential ratios between silver and gold in different markets) was therefore enormous. Not surprisingly, all the leading merchant bankers in Europe began accumulating large stocks of Spanish-American silver pesos with an eye to trade with China and India, where they could potentially obtain double profits on commodity trade and by speculating on the varying prices of money commodities.

European merchants were not the only entrepreneurs active in this lucrative double trade. Indeed, Japanese miners, merchants, and shippers were even more active in the sixteenth century. And between 1540 and 1640, Japan became the main supplier of silver for China, although by the mid–seventeenth century, the Japanese government was forced to call a halt to silver exports, as local mines had become virtually exhausted. By this time, differences in silver/gold ratios had diminished substantially, and as a result, profits on what was strictly the silver or money trade diminished. Nonetheless, throughout the seventeenth and eighteenth centuries, European merchants continued to find silver pesos to be in great demand in China. Moreover, several studies on the various East India companies (English, Dutch, and French) demonstrate that they continued to be active in the business of acquiring Spanish-American silver pesos for their abundant and diverse trade with China and India.

In an extraordinarily meticulous historical study of European commerce carried out in the port of Canton during the eighteenth century, Louis Dermigny was able to estimate the amount of silver coin used to pay for the acquisition of tea, silks, and other merchandise. The French, Danish, and Swedish traders active in Canton paid for their merchandise practically exclusively with silver pesos. Meanwhile, the Dutch and English merchants covered their acquisitions with a combination of commodities and silver.[38]

Apart from the large flows of silver that European merchants brought to China by eastern routes, an important flow of silver pesos also came via the Pacific. The shipments that arrived in the famous Manila Galleon brought approximately two million silver pesos a year from Mexico to the Philippines (and hence to Canton) from the late sixteenth century quite steadily until the early nineteenth century.[39] In the sixteenth and early seventeenth centuries, part of this silver did not originate in Mexican silver mines but in Potosí and other mines in Upper Peru. Ships with the precious metals would leave from the Peruvian port of Callao bound for Acapulco to connect with the arrival of the Manila Galleon, which brought many of the Chinese silks and other luxury items in much demand in the cities of the viceroyalty of Peru. Later, however, the Spanish crown drastically reduced the trade with Peru, allowing Mexican merchants to retain a monopoly on the transpacific trade.[40]

According to Dermigny, it may be estimated that over the course of the eighteenth century, approximately 500 million silver pesos entered China by both routes: somewhat less than 200 million via the Manila route and more than 300 million pesos from Europe on ships that made their way around the Cape of Good Hope and across the Indian Ocean. In other words, perhaps as much as a third of the total production of Mexican silver in that century would end up in Chinese markets.[41]

China was not the only Asian market with a strong demand for Spanish-American silver. An important historical literature on the international trade of India in the seventeenth and eighteenth centuries provides many insights on the role of precious metals in the expanding global trade of that era.[42] These studies document the importance and variety of Indian exports, including an enormous variety of cotton and silk textiles, as well as raw silk, from Bengal, Madras, and other regions, much of which were sent to Europe but also to many other markets, including the Levant and Southeast Asia. Some of these products were even reexported from Manila to Spanish America.[43] Most of these products were paid for with precious metals, and particularly with silver coins.

A classic study by K. N. Chaudhuri on the famous English East India Company opened this field of study and demonstrated that excellent company studies allowed for detailed reconstruction of the international trade of India.[44] Subsequently, Sushil Chaudhury carried on more detailed regional research on the role of both the British and Dutch East India companies' mercantile activities in Bengal, the most prosperous part of India in the seventeenth and eighteenth centuries. This research revealed the complexity of the exchange of silver for Indian textiles and raw silk. A part of the trade was carried on by Asian merchants who exported goods via West Asia to the Levant and Europe. Another part was conducted by the European companies via the ocean route around the Cape of Good Hope. But there was also a complex triangular trade between Europe, South Asia, and Southeast Asia. The Dutch merchants found that the producers of many spices in the Indonesian archipelago were excellent clients for the light and multicolored cotton textiles of Bengal. As a result, the Dutch East India Company would send cargoes of silver pesos to

Calcutta to pay for local cloth, which they later transshipped and re-exported to Southeast Asia in exchange for pepper and other spices.[45]

But why was there such great demand for silver in India? The economic historian Om Prakash offers various answers, citing the classic observation that precious metals arriving to India had "a thousand gates for their entry and none for their exit."[46] To begin, Prakash notes that silver was used to pay for cotton textile goods from India, which were in great demand in Europe before the Industrial Revolution because they were cheaper and more attractive than the competition. He notes that in order to keep up manufacturing production in Mughal India, much of the incoming silver was reinvested. But precious metals were also used for currency (with great demand among the larger Indian merchants and merchant bankers), for decoration of temples (just as in all Catholic Europe), and for women's ornaments.[47] The large consumption of silver and gold for women's jewelry was linked to a complex set of marriage dynamics in a society of multiple castes in which marital alliances had enormous importance for all social sectors.

Furthermore, in India as in China, silver was hoarded by individuals in many socioeconomic groups because it was one of the best and most secure ways of saving money. In an economy without deposit banking and with no savings accounts, hoarding (saving) silver was a "rational form of holding liquidity."[48] And given the large size of both the Indian and Chinese populations in the ancien regime, the market effects led to a very large and constant demand for silver, which continued, in fact, down into the early twentieth century.

## CIRCULATION OF SILVER PESOS IN THE AMERICAS: THE ANTECEDENTS OF THE DOLLAR

While our attention has been focused mainly on the international circulation of the silver peso, it should not be forgotten that circulation was also important within the Americas, since the silver peso was the most widely used monetary instrument for several centuries. Paradoxically, however, in the viceroyalties of Peru and Mexico colonial actors frequently and repeatedly protested that there was a paucity of silver coins. But how could silver be scarce in the land of silver? Historians have advanced several explanations for the relative scarcity of metallic currency in daily circulation through much of Spanish America from the late sixteenth to the late eighteenth centuries. To begin with, they have pointed to the very considerable export of precious metals to Spain and Portugal from the earliest days of colonization of the Americas. These exports included remittances by both merchants and the Spanish state, which suctioned off a large fiscal surplus. The state's share increased over time, reaching a peak in the eighteenth century. Between 1760 and 1810 the financial officers of the viceroyalty of New Spain (Mexico) transferred abroad an annual average of 5 million pesos, a sum equivalent to 2 percent of colonial Mexico's gross product each year.[49]

Moreover, within the colonies themselves, many silver and gold bars and coins were quickly retired from circulation and from local markets. This may be explained by the fact that heavy silver and gold stocks were held for long periods by the state as well as by corporations and rich individuals, although not mainly for the purpose of hoarding. The nature of the colonial economy and polity explains this accumulation of large stocks of silver and gold. All colonial tax administrations in the principal mining regions retired a significant portion of metallic currency from circulation in order to have reserves available when the warships sent from Seville arrived; this practice reduced costs caused by possible delays in loading them with the precious metals. Furthermore, private actors also accumulated huge stocks of precious metals and coins. From the sixteenth century until the end of the eighteenth century, the oligarchies of wealthy merchants in Mexico, Lima, Cartagena, Havana, Bahia, and Rio de Janeiro made it a point to concentrate large stocks of silver and gold in their firms, which they reserved for months in order to have sufficient funds to buy practically all the imported products sold at the great annual fairs held in each colony after the arrival of the convoy of ships from Spain or Portugal. Finally, the powerful ecclesiastical institutions in all of Spanish America and Brazil extracted large amounts of silver through tithes and other ecclesiastical taxes and hence accumulated important stocks of silver, which were used in part to ensure both future expenditures and the continuous flow of credit operations that ecclesiastical organizations realized on behalf of large property owners.

The fact that much silver and gold was exported or held outside of consumer markets for long periods may help to explain the relative stability of colonial prices over the long run. Despite high production of precious metals, coins were not abundant in domestic circulation. Therefore prices rose only slowly, except at times of agrarian and commercial crises. However, research on markets in Bourbon Mexico indicates a fairly sustained rise in the prices of basic agricultural commodities at the end of the eighteenth century.[50]

Ruggiero Romano and other specialists have explained the monetary paradox of these colonial societies by arguing that the metallic monetary system in Spanish America was basically controlled by elites. Hence monetary stocks (and wealth in general) were highly concentrated. The popular sectors suffered the consequences, for they had considerable difficulty in obtaining the silver coins they required both for payment of taxes and for mercantile transactions. Numerous ways were found to circumvent the shortages of fractional currency. A parallel monetary system developed which was based on nonmetallic monetary instruments, among them a great variety of tokens issued by merchants in cities, towns, and haciendas; these were generally known in Peru as *moneda de la tierra* and in Mexico as *tlacos*. The result was a dual monetary system which reflected the stratification of the economy and the society. On the one hand were small but powerful elites which included mine owners, great merchants, and large landowners, all highly monetized. On the other hand, most of the rest of society lived on the fringes of the monetary economy and had to get by from day to day with tokens issued by local merchants and on credit, also extended by merchants and landowners. Too often the result was debt peonage. The peasants who formed the bulk of the rural population in the viceroyalties of Mexico and Peru participated in the monetary economy but also engaged extensively in barter. Similarly, slaves in Brazil and throughout Spanish America had occasional access to metallic currency but on a very small scale. Clearly, this situation made for low levels of individual savings.

If we look beyond the mainland, we see that significant flows of silver pesos went to the islands of the Caribbean. It is well known that English and French pirates from the early seventeenth century risked their lives for the famous pieces of eight (*reales de a ocho*) of the Spanish naval convoys. Later, more stable trade networks and the establishment of naval squadrons transformed many of the islands in the West Indies into floating warehouses of European goods, which were exchanged for silver pesos through vast contraband networks.[51]

Parallel to this illegal commerce, legal trade between the Spanish-American ports on the Caribbean Sea also intensified, particularly in the eighteenth century. The trade between Caracas and Mexico, Cartagena and Havana, and Veracruz and Cuban ports was oiled fundamentally by the flow of silver pesos. Moreover, Mexico financed the administrations of Cuba, Santo Domingo, Puerto Rico, Trinidad, and Florida with regular transfers of silver.[52]

From the early eighteenth century a set of new actors became very active in the silver trade in the West Indies: the merchants and shippers of the thirteen Anglo-American colonies also created commercial channels throughout the islands, increasing their activities after independence in 1783. As a result, silver pesos began to circulate ever more widely and soon became among the most widely used metallic currency in many of the thirteen colonies. It was no surprise, therefore, that during the War of Independence (1776–83) the government of the Confederation of the United States should have adopted the silver peso as the metallic reserve for its new paper currency of dollars. The first issue of paper money specified that the bills were payable in "Spanish milled dollars," which actually meant Mexican silver pesos. Subsequently, the monetary law ratified by the U.S. Congress on April 2, 1792, established that the metallic currency would be the silver dollar and that it would be equal in value to the silver peso of eight *reales*. In fact, it may be recalled that, in practice and law, the Mexican silver peso remained legal tender in the United States until the mid–nineteenth century.

### THE SILVER PESO IN THE NINETEENTH CENTURY

It should be emphasized that after the independence of the Spanish-American states, the silver peso continued to be minted throughout large parts of the hemisphere during the nineteenth century and constituted the single most important export of Mexico and Bolivia for another eighty years. Nonetheless, the wars of independence of the Latin American states (1810–25) had wrought major changes. Each of the new governments in the region sought to affirm its monetary sovereignty, and, not surprisingly, the outcomes differed markedly from nation to nation and even from region to region.

Generally speaking, after 1825 those countries with the greatest wealth in silver continued on a metallic monetary standard, using the classic silver peso (*peso fuerte*) or some relatively close variation. Mexico, Peru, Chile, and Bolivia continued to mint silver pesos on a large scale throughout the nineteenth century. On the other hand, countries such as Brazil, Colombia, and Guatemala, which had important gold (but not silver) deposits, found it difficult to increase production and therefore sought alternative monetary solutions; Brazil, for instance, began to experiment with a paper money standard in the early nineteenth century, as did the Argentine Confederation.

Among the most important of the old silver-mining economies which continued to export silver pesos on a large scale, Mexico merits special attention. It continued to be the major supplier of silver coins to the world economy during the first three-quarters of the nineteenth century; in fact, until the 1880s, silver consistently represented close to 80 percent of total Mexican exports. The reasons for this continuity were closely linked to international markets for silver currency. In the first place, down to the 1870s there were important clients in Europe. Spain, France, Germany, and Italy, for example, all remained on bimetallic standards until the 1870s. After 1870, however, silver prices plummeted throughout Europe. In contrast, in Asia, and most particularly in China, the Mexican silver peso remained in heavy demand among traders even after the 1870s, because it continued to carry a premium in most local markets.[53] So attractive were these markets that silver miners in the United States successfully lobbied Washington to mint a new silver dollar, the American trade dollar, a silver coin of which over 36 million were minted for use in the China trade between 1873 and 1887. Subsequently, however, this practice was discontinued and Mexican silver pesos again reigned supreme in East Asia until the early twentieth century.

---

NOTES

1   Attman, *American Bullion in the European World Trade*; Atwell, "International Bullion Flows and the Chinese Economy"; Chaudhuri, *The Trading World of Asia and the English East Asia Company*; and von Glahn, *Fountain of Fortune*, are important and representative studies that focus on the silver trade in different regions of the world.

2   Flynn and Giráldez, "Born with a Silver Spoon," 201.

3   An interpretation of mercantile credit based on letters of exchange in the sixteenth century is Boyer-Xambeau et al., eds., *Monnaie privée et pouvoir des princes*.

4   Ibid., 216–17.

5   TePaske's "New World Gold Production in Hemispheric and Global Perspective" reviews the literature on estimates of silver and gold production over the centuries and comes to the conclusion that Humboldt's estimates were remarkably accurate in the light of much subsequent research. See charts in Humboldt, *Ensayo político sobre el reino de la Nueva España*, 431–33.

6   Flynn and Giráldez, "Born with a Silver Spoon," 214.

7   Nueva Granada (Colombia), Mexico, Chile, and, to a lesser degree, Guatemala were also gold producers in the eighteenth century but paradoxically they also

suffered from relative scarcity of internal circulation of this precious metal, since practically all the gold was exported to Spain. On New World gold production see the pioneering work by TePaske, "New World Gold Production." Morineau's *Incroyables gazettes et fabuleux métaux* provides much information on the Brazilian gold trade in the colonial era.

8   Bakewell, *Miners of the Red Mountain and Silver and Entrepreneurship in Seventeenth-Century Potosí*; Brading, *Mineros y comerciantes en el México borbónico*; Hoberman, *Mexico's Merchant Elite*; and Langue, *Los señores de Zacatecas*.

9   Assadourian, *El sistema de la economía colonial*.

10  Tandeter, *Coacción y mercado*.

11  Salvucci, "The Real Exchange Rate of the Mexican Peso," provides the estimates of the rising prices of silver at this time.

12  "Sus múltiplos fueron las piezas de dos, cuatro y ocho reales (éste último el peso de plata), y sus submúltiplos fueron las piezas de medio real y la de cuarto de real o cuartillo": Céspedes del Castillo, *Las cecas indianas*, 34.

13  Comment by Flandreau at the November 2002 Paris Conference of the Association d'Histoire Economique de France on my paper "The Silver Peso as Universal Money of the Ancien Regime."

14  Céspedes del Castillo, *Las cecas indianas*, 53.

15  Cortés Conde and McCandless, "Argentina," 384.

16  Morineau, *Incroyables gazettes et fabuleux métaux*, 323.

17  Céspedes del Castillo, *Las cecas indianas*, 251.

18  Humboldt, *Ensayo político sobre el reino de la Nueva España*, 457. For estimates of the total flows of silver and gold from the Americas to Europe see Morineau, *Incroyables gazettes et fabuleux métaux*.

19  These calculations, found in Marichal, *La bancarrota del virreinato*, chap. 2, are substantially higher than the relevant percentages offered by Klein, *The American Finances of the Spanish Empire*, but it should be noted that Klein did not use consolidated accounts, nor did he discount the costs of fiscal administration or take seignorage into account.

20  For a critique, see Munro, "Precious Metals and the Origins of the Price Revolution Reconsidered," 35–50.

21  Morineau, *Incroyables gazettes et fabuleux métaux*, 51.

22  Cipolla, *Conquistadores, piratas, mercaderes*, 57.

23  However, note that Boyer-Xambeu et al., *Monnaie privée et pouvoir des princes*, 134–38, argue that in the late sixteenth century most Spanish silver actually was transferred to Italy by Genoese bankers. There the silver was exchanged for gold, which was later sent to Flanders. On later silver transfers see Stein and Stein, *Silver Trade and War*, chap. 2.

24  Álvarez Nogal, *El crédito de la monarquín hispánica*, contains much statistical information.

25  Marichal, *La bancarrota del virreinato*, chap. 1.

26  Morineau, *Incroyables gazettes et fabuleux métaux*, 265.

27  Ibid., 302.

28 A fundamental study by metallurgical chemists interested in estimating the American silver content of contemporary European coins is Morrison et al., *Or du Brésil.*

29 Attman, *American Bullion in the European World Trade.*

30 Ibid. and Attman, *Dutch Enterprise in the World Bullion Trade.*

31 On the monetary history of the Ottoman Empire, see Pamuk, "Crisis and Recovery."

32 Kindleberger, *Spenders and Hoarders.*

33 However, it is wise to recall that until the eighteenth century, silver pesos were not legal tender in China. As Kann, *Currencies of China*, indicates, in China silver was a commodity as much as a currency and was constantly being cut in pieces and resmelted.

34 Atwell, "International Bullion Flows and the Chinese Economy," 79.

35 Von Glahn, *Fountain of Fortune;* Flynn and Giráldez, "Born with a Silver Spoon" and "China and the Spanish Empire."

36 Flynn and Giráldez, "China and the Spanish Empire," 316.

37 Von Glahn, *Fountain of Fortune,* chap. 4.

38 Dermigny, *La Chine et l'Occident,* 2:688, indicates that at the start of the century the English paid for 90 percent of their purchases in silver, but that by the end of the century, the figure had fallen to 65 percent.

39 The classic study is Schurz, *The Manila Galleon.*

40 For additional references, see Souto and Yuste, eds., *El comercio exterior de México,* and Alvarez and Fradera, eds., *Imperios y naciones en el Pacífico.*

41 Dermigny, *La Chine et l'Occident,* 2:754.

42 The major studies are Chaudhuri, *The English East India Company;* Chaudhury, *Trade and Commercial Organization in Bengal;* Prakash, *The Dutch East India Company and the Economy of Bengal.*

43 Quiason, *English "Country Trade" with the Philippines.*

44 Chaudhuri, *English East India Company.*

45 Chaudhury, *Trade and Commercial Organization in Bengal* and "European Trade, Influx of Silver and Prices in Bengal."

46 Prakash, "Precious Metal Flows," 1.

47 Ibid.

48 Ibid., 15.

49 In view of the fact that the ancien regime economies normally grew by no more than 1 percent of gross product per year, these fiscal extractions reduced most possibilities of growth. See Marichal, *La bancarrota del virreinato.*

50 Garner and Stefanou, *Economic Growth and Change in Bourbon Mexico,* provides a summary of price history in Bourbon Mexico.

51 Romano, *Moneda, seudomonedas,* chap. 2, emphasizes the contraband trade through Jamaica.

52 Von Grafenstein, *Nueva España en el circuncaribe,* has abundant information on this subject.

53 For details, see Kann, *Currencies of China.*

## BIBLIOGRAPHY

Alvarez, Luis Alonso, and Josep Fradera, eds. *Imperios y naciones en el Pacífico*. Vol. 1, *La formación de una colonia: Filipinas*. Madrid: CSIC and Asociación Española de Estudios del Pacífico, 2001.

Álvarez Nogal, Carlos. *El crédito de la monarquín hispánica en el reinado de Felipe IV*. Ávila: Junta de Castilla y León, 1997.

Attman, Artur. *American Bullion in the European World Trade, 1600–1800*. Humaniora 26. Göteborg: Acta, Regiaea Societatis Scientarum et Litterarum Gothoburgensis, 1986.

——. *Dutch Enterprise in the World Bullion Trade, 1550–1800*. Humaniora 23. Göteborg: Acta, Regiaea Societatis Scientarum et Litterarum Gothoburgensis, 1983.

Atwell, William S. "International Bullion Flows and the Chinese Economy, circa 1530–1650." *Past and Present* 95 (1982): 68–90.

Bakewell, Peter. *Miners of the Red Mountain: Indian Labor in Potosí, 1545–1650*. Albuquerque: University of New Mexico Press, 1984.

——. *Silver and Entrepreneurship in Seventeenth-Century Potosí: The Life and Times of Antonio López de Quiroga*. Albuquerque: University of New Mexico Press, 1988.

Bordo, Michael, and Roberto Cortés Conde, eds. *Transferring Wealth and Power from the Old World to the New: Monetary and Fiscal Institutions in the 17th through the 19th Centuries*. Cambridge: Cambridge University Press, 2001.

Boyer-Xambeau, Marie-Thérèse; Ghislain Deleplace; and Lucien Gillard, eds. *Monnaie privée et pouvoir des princes: L'Economie des relations monétaires à la Renaissance*. Paris: CNRS, 1986.

Brading, David. *Mineros y comerciantes en el México borbónico, 1763–1810*. Mexico City: Fondo de Cultura Económica, 2001.

Braudel, Fernand, and Ruggiero Romana. *Navires et marchands à l'entrée du port de Livourne, 1547–1611*. Paris, 1951.

Céspedes del Castillo, Guillermo. *Las cecas indianas, 1536–1825*. Madrid: Museo Casa de la Moneda, 1996.

Chaudhuri, K. N. *The English East India Company: The Study of an Early Joint-Stock Company, 1600–1640*. London: F. Cass, 1965.

——. *The Trading World of Asia and the English East India Company, 1660–1760*. Cambridge: Cambridge University Press, 1978.

Chaudhury, Sushil. "European Trade, Influx of Silver and Prices in Bengal, 1650–1757." In Session 15 of the XIII Congress of the International Association of Economic History, Buenos Aires, 2002.

——. *Trade and Commercial Organization in Bengal, 1650–1720*. Calcutta, 1975.

Cipolla, Carlo M. *Conquistadores, piratas, mercaderes: La saga de la plata espagnola*. Buenos Aires: Fondo de Cultura Económica, 1999.

Dermigny, Louis. *La Chine et 1'Occident: Le Commerce à Canton au XVIIIᵉ Siècle, 1719–1833*. 3 vols. París: Ecole Practique des Hautes Etudes, 1964.

Flynn, Dennis O., and Arturo Giráldez. "Born with a Silver Spoon: The Origin of World Trade in 1571." *Journal of World History* 6, no. 2 (1995): 201–20.

——. "China and the Spanish Empire." *Revista de Historia Económica* 14, no. 2 (1996): 309–38.

——, eds. *Metals and Mining in an Emerging Global Economy.* Brookfield, Vt.: Variorum, 1997.

Garner, Richard L., and Spiro E. Stefanou. *Economic Growth and Change in Bourbon Mexico.* Gainesville: University Press of Florida, 1993.

Hamilton, Earl. *American Treasure and the Price Revolution in Spain, 1501–1650.* Cambridge: Harvard University Press, 1934.

Hoberman, Louisa. *Mexico's Merchant Elite, 1590–1660: Silver, State, and Society.* Durham: Duke University Press, 1991.

Humboldt, Alejandro de. *Ensayo político sobre el reino de la Nueva España.* (Paris, 1811.) Mexico City: Universidad Nacional Autónoma de México, 1991.

Kann, Eduard. *Currencies of China: An Investigation of Silver and Gold Transactions Affecting China.* Shanghai: Kelly & Walsh, 1927.

Kindleberger, Charles P. *Spenders and Hoarders: The World Distribution of Spanish American Silver, 1550–1750.* Pasir Panjang, Singapore: Institute of Southeast Asian Studies, 1989.

Langue, Frédérique. *Los señores de Zacatecas: Una aristocracia minera del siglo XVIII en Zacatecas.* Mexico City: Fondo de Cultura Económica, 1999.

Malamud Rikles, Carlos Daniel. *Cádiz y Saint Malo en el comercio colonial peruano, 1698–1725.* Cádiz: Diputación de Cádiz, 1986.

Marichal, Carlos. *La bancarrota del virreinato: Nueva España y las finanzas del Imperio español, 1780–1810.* Mexico City: El Colegio de Mexico, Fondo de Cultura Económica (Fideicomiso Historia de Las Américas), 1999.

Morineau, Michel. *Incroyables gazettes et fabuleux métaux: Les retours des trésors américains d'après les gazettes hollandaises, XVII–XVIII^e siècles.* New York: Cambridge University Press, 1985.

Morrison, Christian; Jean-Noël Barrandon; and Cécile Morrison. *Or du Brésil: Monnaie et croissance en France au XVIII^e siècle.* Cahiers Ernest-Babelon 7. París: Centre Nationale de la Recherche Scientifique, 1999.

Moutoukias, Zacarías. *Contrabando y control colonial en el siglo XVIII.* Buenos Aires: Centro Editor de América Latina, 1988.

Munro, John H. "Precious Metals and the Origins of the Price Revolution Reconsidered." In Dennis O. Flynn, Michel Morineau, and Richard von Glahn, eds., *Monetary History in Global Perspective, 1500–1808,* 35–50. Seville: Fundación Fomento de la Historia Económica, Universidad de Sevilla, Instituto de Estudios Fiscales, 1998.

Pamuk, Sevket. "Crisis and Recovery: The Ottoman Monetary System in the Early Modern Era, 1585–1789." In Dennis O. Flynn and Arturo Giráldez, eds., *Metals and Mining in an Emerging Global Economy,* 97–108. Brookfield, Vt.: Variorum, 1997.

Prakash, Om. *The Dutch East Company and the Economy of Bengal, 1630–1720.* Princeton: Princeton University Press, 1985.

——. "Precious Metal Flows into India in the Early Modern Period." In Dennis O. Flynn, Michel Morineau, and Richard von Glahn, eds., *Monetary History in Global Perspective, 1500–1808,* 73–84. Seville: Fundación Fomento de la Historia Económica, Universidad de Sevilla, Instituto de Estudios Fiscales, 1998.

Quiason, Serafin D. *English "Country Trade" with the Philippines, 1644–1765.* Quezon City: University of the Philippines Press, 1966.

Romano, Ruggiero. *Coyunturas opuestas: La crisis del siglo XVII en Europa e Hispanoamérica.* Mexico City: El Colegio de Mexico, Fondo de Cultura Económica (Fideicomiso Historia de Las Américas), 1993.

——. *Moneda, seudomonedas y circulación monetaria en las economías de México.* Mexico City: Colegio de México, Fondo de Cultura Económica, 1998.

Salvucci, Richard. "The Real Exchange Rate of the Mexican Peso, 1762–1812." *Journal of European Economic History* 23 (1994).

Schurz, William Lytle. *The Manila Galleon.* New York: E. P. Dutton, 1959.

Sempat Assadourian, Carlos. *El sistema de la economía colonial: El mercado interior, regiones y espacio económico.* Mexico City: Nueva Imagen, 1983.

Souto, Matilde, and Camen Yuste, eds. *El comercio exterior de México, 1713–1850.* Mexico City: Instituto Mora. 2002.

Stein, Stanley J., and Barbara H. Stein. *Silver, Trade and War: Spain and America in the Making of Early Modern Europe.* Baltimore: Johns Hopkins University Press, 2000.

Tandeter, Enrique. *Coacción y mercado: La minería de plata en el Potosí colonial, 1692–1826.* Buenos Aires: Sudamericana, 1992.

TePaske, John Jay. "New World Gold Production in Hemispheric and Global Perspective, 1492–1810." In Dennis O. Flynn, Michel Morineau, and Richard von Glahn, eds., *Monetary History in Global Perspective, 1500–1808.* Seville: Fundación Fomento de la Historia Económica, Universidad de Sevilla, Instituto de Estudios Fiscales, 1998.

Von Glahn, Richard. *Fountain of Fortune: Money and Monetary Policy in China, 1000–1700.* Berkeley: University of California Press, 1996.

Von Grafenstein, Johanna. *Nueva España en el circuncaribe, 1779–1808: Revolución, competencia imperial y vínculos intercoloniales.* Mexico City: Universidad Nacional Autónoma de México, 1997.

# 2

Indigo Commodity Chains
in the Spanish and British Empires,
1560–1860

David McCreery

*Indigo . . . was the most important and universal dyestuff known to man
from prehistoric times.*—Jenny Balfour-Paul, Indigo in the Arab World

AS A SOURCE OF BLUE and as a base for other colors, indigo
has been in use for thousands of years and was known to the
ancient Egyptians and to the classical Mediterranean world.[1]
Hundreds of plants worldwide contain the basic chemical elements of
indigo but only three or four are productive enough to make commercial
exploitation, as opposed to use in home textile production, worthwhile.
Most important of these plants is *Indigofera tinctoria*. Early modern Europe
knew indigo chiefly as an import from India, via the silk routes, and its
origins and methods of production remained so shrouded in mystery that
most people imagined the dye, which arrived in small, hard cakes, to be a
mineral. Its rarity and cost limited the market for indigo, and the dye's
use in Europe also encountered strong opposition from the growers of
woad, a local blue coloring agent. But woad could not be concentrated as
indigo could to allow long-distance shipment, and the blue it rendered
was clearly inferior in color and wear to that of the eastern import. Nevertheless, price and guild opposition, backed by state policy,[2] restricted
the spread of the use of indigo until Portugal discovered an all-water
route to the East, which lowered the costs and increased the availability of
a variety of "spices," including the dye.

At the same time that Portugal's caravels were opening Asia to European seaborne commerce, the Spanish were settling the New World, and
among the first agricultural exports of these new colonies was indigo.[3]

Initially the Spanish required the indigenous populations to gather wild native indigo plants as part of their tax obligations, but soon the Europeans introduced more productive varieties and set up large-scale plantations, chiefly in southern Mexico and northern Central America. With shorter distances to travel, as well as control over the entire production chain, the Spanish were able to supply a better-quality commodity at a lower price to European markets and soon drove out Indian indigo almost entirely.[4]

But by the second quarter of the seventeenth century labor shortages, in part the result of population declines, and transport problems stemming from the general paralysis of the Spanish Empire undercut New World indigo exports.[5] These problems, together with the rise of mercantilism, promoted non-Spanish European powers to seek sources of the dye within their own empires.[6] England initially attempted to revive imports from India, chiefly from the western part of the subcontinent: local indigenous producers grew and processed the dye and sold it to English traders, who complained not only of high prices but of uneven quality.[7] At the same time planters in the West Indies began to experiment with the crop. Soon the dye exported from the French West Indies set the standard for European and, despite mercantilist concerns, English markets, again forcing out Indian producers.

## INDIGO IN THE EIGHTEENTH AND NINETEENTH CENTURIES: AN OVERVIEW OF THREE COMMODITY CHAINS

The cultivation and processing of indigo required land, labor, capital, and suitable technical knowledge, but these factors could be, and were, combined in various ways at different times and in different places to produce the commodity. Such permutations were not random but the outcomes of specific historical circumstances and choices, of what actors could think in specific circumstances as well as what they could do. Thus, to compare indigo commodity chains we must first understand the history in which they were embedded.

The planters of lowland South Carolina experimented with indigo in the late seventeenth century but found rice more profitable and largely abandoned the dye for the next half century.[8] However, in the 1740s exploding demand for indigo in England linked to the growth of the Industrial Revolution, together with a crisis in rice markets brought on by the century's almost incessant wars, prompted South Carolina landowners to revisit the dye.[9] After a period of experimentation, output surged, and from 1750 to 1775 the colony and the crop enjoyed something of a golden age. Indigo had the advantage of supplementing rather than conflicting or competing with existing rice production and so did not threaten the dominant economic or social system of the colony. Indigo also brought prosperity to impoverished areas of the backcountry, drawing small landowners into slaveholding and aligning their interests more closely with those of tidewater elites.[10] But with the independence of the thirteen colonies, South Carolina lost access to its best market, and by the 1790s the attention of local planters was shifting to cotton.

The state of Central America's economy paralleled the living death of the Spanish Habsburg monarchy. Only in the second half of the eighteenth century did conditions begin to improve.[11] Bourbon reforms that freed colonial commerce and shipping, together with, ironically, a growing contraband trade driven by Great Britain, stimulated a revival of indigo production in Central America, particularly in the *alcaldía mayor* of San Salvador, on the Pacific side of the isthmus. A new generation of immigrant merchants and new flows of capital arrived after mid-century in Guatemala City, the capital of the captaincy general.[12] From there money and mercantile talent found their way into indigo, improving both the quantity and quality of output. During the second half of the eighteenth century, and particularly after revolution devastated St-Domingue, "Guatimala" indigo became the world standard. Since the name "Guatimala" applied to a commodity derived from the San Salvador district of the captaincy general, however, it suggested the nature of a growing conflict between the producers and the capital city's export merchants, who worked to control the profits of the industry. But the revolution that crippled St-Domingue soon engulfed Spain as well, and war, tax increases, and a decline in the availability of shipping, together with a series of natural disasters, hit Central America's producing areas hard after 1800.[13] When the economy began to recover in the 1840s and 1850s, the emphasis had shifted to coffee.

Beginning in the 1770s the East India Company moved to revive indigo production, but now in eastern India around the company stronghold of Calcutta.[14] The purpose was in part to diversify the cash economy and provide cargo for company ships, but, more important, indigo production was meant also to address the problem of remittances. Although profiting from trade both within the subcontinent and with China, "John Company," and indeed all of Europe, suffered a constant specie drain to

China and consequent liquidity problems. In order to send profits to Europe, the company and the company's "servants" trading on their own account needed a vehicle that could be purchased in India and readily sold in London: "a legal conveyance of their fortunes to this country."[15] Indigo, with its high value per weight and size, served admirably, and the dye offered as well better speculative possibilities than bills of exchange.[16] Initially the company bought dye from local growers, but gradually European capital and European technology, especially in processing, spread into indigo production. The intent was to ensure a regular supply and the uniform quality standards necessary for success in Europe's markets. But production of the raw material itself remained in the hands of Indian peasants. The inability of exporters to exert full control over the entire production process generated a series of conflicts and contradictions already evident in the 1820s.

### FACTORS OF PRODUCTION: LAND

A key question for the production of indigo was access to land and who controlled the land and under what conditions. Political or cultural circumstances could make otherwise suitable land unavailable, and transport costs could render good land uneconomic for indigo. Competition could mean that production in a given area was no longer viable, or state policy or a monopoly could shield a commodity from market forces. But these conditions might, and indeed almost certainly would, change over time, and in doing so could change the utility of land.

Generally land was not a problem in eighteenth-century South Carolina, both because large areas of the colony remained unsettled and because indigo made use of a different sort of land than did rice. Within the same plantation, the lower, swampy areas served for rice and higher, sandier patches proved suitable for indigo.[17] The dye, in other words, allowed the planters to make profitable use of a resource which to that point had been of little value. Planters without indigo land "manipulated" the boundaries of their properties to engross useful areas.[18] For the smallholders away from the coast or the rivers and without rice land, indigo was the first crop that promised profitable access to the export economy, apart perhaps from naval stores or hides. Many planted indigo together with their subsistence crops, and some produced the dye, while others specialized in furnishing seed to the large growers.[19] Indigo generated unprecedented wealth in the backcountry and gave the coastal planters and the piedmont farmers for the first time common economic concerns.

Although there were large plantations in late-eighteenth-century El Salvador, most of the production, and much of what was generally acknowledged to be the best-quality indigo, came from smallholders (*poquiteros*).[20] Many of these farmers did not have legal title to their land, but in this period challenges to squatters' rights were rare. Apart from subsistence farming and cattle grazing, there were few competing uses for land, and indigo growers often encouraged the pasturing of cattle in their fields, as the animals ate weeds while generally leaving the spiny indigo leaves alone. Some of the largest landholders were the indigenous communities,[21] and commonly these communities either produced indigo themselves or rented land to outsiders for the crop. Paying rent rather than squatting might be worthwhile in specific cases that involved better-quality land or good communications. Not part of the American "near Atlantic," San Salvador and its exports suffered a disadvantage in transport costs, and ready access to what roads were available counted for a lot among indigo exporters.

From the start access to land proved difficult for European indigo producers in India. Hoping to keep down rural unrest, the East India Company initially forbade the purchase or even direct leasing of land by Europeans in Bengal, except in the immediate environs of Calcutta. Indigo producers instead generally depended on the Indian peasant (*raiyat*) working his own land to supply the plants they needed for the processing mills. But how to ensure that these peasants would in fact grow indigo rather than some other crop, without offering prices processors deemed unreasonable? The key was rent. The peasants did not own their land in fee simple but rather had rights to it based on the payment of rents to local *zamindar* or rent-collecting classes; these men, in turn, were obligated to remit rents and taxes to higher-ups. To pay his rent and ensure access to land and survival, the raiyat obtained cash advances from the indigo processors, to be repaid with indigo plants at the next harvest.[22] As a result, much of the rural population quickly became enmeshed in debt, which, through bad luck or chicanery, seemed to grow every year and might even be passed from father to son. Whatever the initial advantages of indigo, by the 1820s it was clear to the peasants that they could profit more by producing rice, but the indigo exporters used the debts, together with physical intimidation, to force them to continue with the dye. Not surprisingly, feelings ran high, and the tensions eventually exploded in the "Blue Mutiny" of the late 1850s.[23]

Blocking the expansion of Indian indigo production was the failure of capital to penetrate the countryside and restructure agriculture on the basis of capitalist rationality; the contradictions of this partial transition resulted in increasing conflict. For planters of San Salvador and South Carolina, on the other hand, land in the late eighteenth century was not a major concern. In South Carolina, though political, social, and crop shifts occurred, control of land remained little changed into the next century, but in San Salvador changes prompted by indigo laid the groundwork for much greater shifts in the next century. Once outsiders penetrated the indigenous communities as renters, they proved reluctant to leave and not uncommonly found the means to convert the land they used into private property. With independence, and especially with the rise of coffee after 1840, the struggle for land between commodity producers and indigenous subsistence farmers became the central feature of modern Salvadorian rural history.

### FACTORS OF PRODUCTION: LABOR

A traditional assumption of economic history has it that the shift to capitalism in the eighteenth and nineteenth centuries produced a similar shift toward free labor. While this assumption has considerable validity for core areas, in much of the periphery quite different conditions obtained. Here, commodity production brought the reinvigoration or implementation of labor systems dependent on coercion: chattel slavery, "vagrancy" systems, and debt peonage. The commercial production of indigo depended on several forms of coerced labor.

The large South Carolina plantations used predominantly African slaves. Indigo had several advantages for this labor system. For example, since dye production generally required workers at different times of the year than did rice, the same workers could be used for both. This system kept the slaves busy, always a priority on the plantations, and by maintaining them at profitable work more of the time, the owner more quickly amortized his costs. The skilled tasks of indigo processing also allowed masters to reward favored slaves with better conditions without freeing them. Small-scale producers typically began indigo with family labor, but if they prospered, they too bought slaves, reinforcing ties with the elites.[24]

Indigo was readily accepted into the existing system at all levels precisely because it reinforced that system and did not threaten but rather enhanced the situation of those with power.

By contrast, labor was the Achilles' heel of Salvadorian indigo production. Faced with truly catastrophic population losses in the second half of the sixteenth century, the Spanish crown banned indigenous workers from activities thought to damage their health, including cultivation of indigo. The wastes from processing the dye attracted flies that tormented men and animals and were thought to spread disease.[25] Indigo planters instead were to use either free labor, such as poor mulattos or mestizos, or African slaves, but none of these people proved satisfactory. Free labor was too undisciplined and slaves were too expensive.[26] Instead, a fine/bribe system developed in which the growers exploited indebted Indians and periodically paid fines or bribes to crown inspectors to be allowed to continue the practice.

As the economy revived and demand for indigo grew in the eighteenth century, however, growers pressed for more and cheaper workers. Thus, in 1738 the crown ended the ban on the use of free indigenous workers, and then in the 1760s allowed the implementation in San Salvador of *repartimientos*, a system of forced wage labor for Indians already in use in other areas of the colony.[27] This system served the interests of the large planters more than those of the small growers, who depended on the cooperative labor of their family or community. It was indicative, too, of general crown policies that in its last years the empire tended to promote the interests of Guatemala City merchants at the expense of the small growers, whose percentages of the harvests declined. This policy, in turn, undercut the quality of the overall output, and since San Salvador depended on a reputation for quality to offset its distance and price disadvantages, a fall in perceived quality was a serious blow to the industry.

Although there were some large European-owned indigo plantations in Bengal, especially after 1830, most production was on small plots worked by family labor. There was no immediate European involvement in the organization of this workforce, nor was this labor normally directly coerced. But the system nevertheless was shot through with coercion and actual or potential violence. The processor who held the raiyat's debt cared not how he produced the leaves but only that he deliver them when needed, and the Europeans readily resorted to all manner of force, including, if necessary, attacks by hired thugs, to make certain that the indigo was available and on time: a widow, for example, begged for protection from "the violence of the indigo gentleman."[28] Because commercial capital failed to penetrate to the first levels of production, extraction of surplus value took place not in the labor process but at the level of exchange, aided by measures such as underweighing and the downgrading of quality.

Different indigo commodity chains supported quite different forms of labor mobilization and control, forms that in some cases changed dramatically over time. South Carolina, already committed to African slavery for rice because of an absence of locally exploitable workers, simply shifted the slaves part of the year to indigo. Indeed, the new crop helped spread African slaves into the interior, where farmers now could obtain credit to buy them. Labor in El Salvador at once evolved and stayed the same: from the beginning the crop made use of coerced indigenous workers, and forms and levels of coercion increased toward the end of the colonial period. At the far opposite end of the scale of coercion would appear to be Bengal, where the raw materials were always the products of formally free peasants working land to which they had rights. But the raiyati purchased these rights at the cost of a heavy load of debt that bound them to an increasingly profitless crop.

## FACTORS OF PRODUCTION: CAPITAL

In comparison with many other tropical commodities, indigo did not require a large commitment of capital. It demanded no expensive central (centralized sugar mill) or large-scale railroad construction or extensive port facilities. Production did entail investment in labor mobilization and control and in processing equipment, but the costs of the latter were minimal, and those of the former varied widely, from expensive African slaves to relatively cheap repartimiento workers and self-exploiting peasant families. And because growers relied heavily on forced labor, the capital invested in indigo did not have to make the average rate of profit.

One of the attractions of indigo for South Carolina growers was precisely that it required little capital input above that already committed to agriculture, whether on the large plantation or the small property. With land and labor readily available, the only investment required was for simple processing equipment that could be build from locally available materials, and a planter could avoid even this expenditure by selling seed or unprocessed leaves to better-equipped neighbors. Planters seeking capital to purchase slaves or open new land typically could obtain it from Charleston merchants at very reasonable rates. By mid-century Charleston was overpopulated with merchants ready to make long-term loans at 8 percent against land or crops and at only slightly higher rates for current accounts.[29] Access to capital was not a barrier to entry into indigo for either the planter or the small grower.

It helped to be a colony of England rather than of Spain in the mid–eighteenth century, and compared to South Carolina, Central America suffered constant shortages of capital and the high cost of the little that was available. Merchants in Guatemala City, operating independently or as agents for home-country houses, funneled investment into Salvadorian indigo production through a variety of channels. Large-scale growers, for example, could obtain financing in cash or goods directly from capital city merchants, and sometimes they passed a bit of their borrowings along to their less well-off neighbors, at marked-up interest rates.[30] In the 1780s the government created a *montepío de añil* (indigo charitable fund). In theory the fund was to facilitate financing for the poquiteros, but the scheme soon collapsed in a welter of unpaid loans that had been handed out to the politically well-connected. Instead, small producers received financing on a year-to-year basis either from merchants' representatives operating at one of the several indigo fairs or from a crown officeholder such as a *corregidor* (district governor) working in cooperation with a Guatemala City merchant.[31] Because church laws forbade "usury," most agreements simply specified delivery of a certain amount of indigo or set a price for liquidation of the loan a small amount below the market price at the time of delivery. As conditions became more unstable late in the century, with war, lack of shipping, and a series of locust attacks, small growers increasingly fell behind in their payments and forfeited their properties to Guatemala City merchants. This was a key factor in the independence-era split of El Salvador from Guatemala and the ensuing hostilities between the two countries.

European-controlled indigo production in Bengal got its start with financing from the East India Company. After at first directly funding experiments with the new crop, the company turned to funneling capital through "agency houses": local trading organizations set up by Europeans and capitalized chiefly with the savings and investments of company employees.[32] The houses traded in export commodities and European imports. As demand for indigo grew, they obtained permission from the company to send Europeans upcountry to organize and supervise processing mills, and they financed these operations.

After 1802 the company effectively withdrew from financing indigo, preferring to buy the dye it needed through contracts or on the spot market. As a result, the role of the agency houses grew. Because remittances as much as market demand drove indigo, there was a tendency toward overproduction. The agency houses overextended themselves financing this production, and many collapsed during the 1830s.[33] Several newly formed banks, particularly Calcutta's "Big Union," took over the financing of the crop, but it too failed during the late 1840s in a welter of speculation.[34] As India became less and less an exotic outpost and more and more integrated in the mainstream imperial economy, factors and branches of English merchant houses settled in Bengal and took up the financing slack, as did several trading ventures funded with Indian capital.

Individual Bengal planters and the agency houses sometimes suffered financing mishaps, but as the heart of the Industrial Revolution, Great Britain had adequate capital available at low rates to finance indigo production, whether in India or South Carolina. San Salvador, by contrast, was a marginal colony of a failing empire. Starved of capital by decades of wars and payments to Europe's bankers, Spain never had available sufficient public or private funds to support indigo adequately. What financing did reach Central America too often was dissipated in corruption or simple incompetence.

### FACTORS OF PRODUCTION: TECHNICAL KNOWLEDGE

What stands out immediately in the comparative study of indigo commodity chains is the relative uniformity of the processing technology over time and between producing regions.[35] The manner of converting leaves and stems into indigo cake changed little for 400 years after 1550, and indeed, peasant production in present-day El Salvador would be entirely recognizable to the manager of a late-eighteenth-century Bengal processing plant. For this reason, what follows is a generic description of indigo preparation, with significant variations noted.

Indigofera tinctoria grows as a shrub to one to two meters in height, and depending on local conditions, it can be cut from two to four or more times a year. The stalks with the leaves attached are tied into bundles and transported to the processing plant, where they are submerged in water. The vats for this and the subsequent steps may be aboveground and constructed of wood, stone, or metal or can be simply pits dug into the ground and lined with sand and pitch. After the bundles had been twenty-four hours or so in the first vat, the workers drained the liquid off to a second vat and discarded the noxious pulped leaves and stalks. The second stage was the crucial one, for now the liquid was agitated to precipitate out indigo granules, and it was here that the process experienced some of its few innovations over the centuries. Whereas the Indians in San Salvador initially stood in the liquid and beat or stirred it by hand, subsequently aeration by wooden paddles or buckets with screens in the bottom predominated, as did the use of animal or water power to drive the machinery. Processors learned also to add lime water to the mixture to speed separation. At precisely the right moment, and this was the supervisor's skill, workers drew the water off, packed the indigo in cloth bags, and squeezed and hung them up to dry. With most of the moisture removed, workers cut the dye into small cakes for the retail market.

That this technology developed more or less uniformly across time and space was due to several factors. To a very considerable extent world markets, by defining what is acceptable as a commodity, largely determine how processing must occur. That is, the product has to meet certain standards of size, finish, and quality to become a commodity. It was possible, for example, in the late nineteenth century to produce sugar in a backyard horse-driven *trapiche* (sugar mill), but the result could not become a commodity on world markets because these markets would not accept the quality or price of trapiche-made sugar. Similarly, Costa Rica entered world markets in the 1830s exporting rough, dry-processed coffee, but competition and consumer demand forced most producers to shift to wet processing by century's end. Purchasers of indigo too came to expect a certain color, consistency, and finish and to associate these qualities with particular production areas.[36] In the absence of modern chemical tests, this was how buyers evaluated indigo, and dye that failed to meet expected standards could be sold only at a greatly reduced price, if then. A reputation good or bad, once established, resisted change and prompted new entrants into the market not to argue the special qualities of their commodity but to attempt to imitate as closely as possible those of an established popular "brand."

Processing also became standardized because of communications about and between commodity chains, despite apparently nationalist competitions. Information about indigo, together with samples of the more productive strains, made their way from India to the New World, and especially to Central America, in the sixteenth century; in the wake of the United States' independence the East India Company imported planters from the American South and the West Indies to bring the latest techniques back to India; and in the late nineteenth century growers in El Salvador could read in the newspaper detailed information on the industry in India.[37]

Overall, what may be striking is not so much the homogenization of indigo production technology across time and space but the failure of the industry to develop modern, capitalist-based systems parallel to, for example, those put in place for sugar and coffee. It is worth remembering that the major innovations in coffee and sugar processing came in the second half of the nineteenth century, when artificial dyes evidently had doomed indigo. Too, the major indigo exporter in the nineteenth century was India, where British capital never was able to fully penetrate the production process. And since existing production/processing capacity largely met demand, and because the future for natural demand looked bleak after mid-century, there was scant incentive to invest in improved or rationalized production. Add to this that the market was largely monopolized, and it is easy to see why few innovations blessed indigo processing during the nineteenth century.

## TRADE AND COMMERCE

A fundamental characteristic of the eighteenth- and nineteenth-century indigo trade was extraordinary levels of uncertainty, and the principal thrust of both merchants and the states dependent on tax receipts was to reduce uncertainty as much as possible. States fostered mercantilism and merchants favored monopsony or oligopsony, but these proved of limited effectiveness and always were under assault by contraband trade. Aggravating these problems were the additional difficulties caused by adulteration and substitutability.

Whereas the river system allowed planters in the colonial upper South to trade directly with England, eighteenth-century commerce between South Carolina and the mother country took place primarily through Charleston. Merchants bought and bulked raw products such as rice, indigo, and hides for shipment to England and imported manufactured goods.[38] Upcountry farmers dealt with crossroads merchants, usually agents for a Charleston house. Competition among these merchants, both locally based traders and London-linked factors, together with a tendency to overstock finished goods, conspired to give the planters the upper hand in most commercial exchanges; they could demand cash payments for their crops and buy manufactures on credit. Some of the larger rice and indigo producers on occasion contracted shipping space on their own or even chartered a ship and sold directly in London. It was common for planters to attempt to manipulate market expectations, predicting loudly a bumper harvest and hoping to attract large numbers of ships in order to drive down shipping costs.[39] Charleston merchants failed utterly in attempts to control South Carolina's indigo trade. In fact, though, both producers and merchants operated on the edge of a global market about which they had at best imperfect information and over which they had no control.

Guatemala City's merchants labored mightily during the second half of the eighteenth century to monopolize or, more properly, oligopolize the indigo export trade, together with the import of manufactures. The state too favored monopoly for ease of tax collection. These merchants represented both local and home-country capital, and it was competition between and among these groups and individual members that blocked more effective monopsony. The indigo traffic began at local and regional trade fairs in San Salvador and Guatemala, where producers delivered their dye to the merchants or merchants' agents who had financed their crop and from whom they borrowed the funds or merchandise necessary for the coming year. A few who had cleared their debts sold on the spot market, but this practice was not common. From the fairs indigo moved by mule to the capital to be bulked for future sale or directly to a port for overseas shipment. Because of a lack of shipping to Central America during much of the seventeenth and early eighteenth centuries, indigo in these years traveled overland all the way to Veracruz for export; after 1750 Caribbean ports such as Omoa and Santo Tomás handled increasing amounts of exports and imports, but shipping costs remained a serious consideration for the indigo industry. Competing with the legal trade was a growing contraband traffic, offering better prices for the dye and cheaper consumer goods.

At least until the mid–nineteenth century the indigo trade in Bengal functioned through a state-licensed monopoly, the East India Company. "John Company" provided much of the initial capital for the European takeover of the commodity, controlled transport to London, and even determined who could reside in the colony and what activities they might pursue. The company's precapitalist reluctance to invade the subcontinent's existing political and production systems, however, set up a series of contradictions that plagued the indigo industry. Chief among them was the question of landownership, but also for most of this period two parallel court systems operated. Europeans could not be required to appear in "native" courts, but if they wished to undertake legal action against a raiyat, they had to make use of these notoriously corrupt institutions.[40] Most preferred to rely on extralegal physical violence and coercion, revealing, once again, the partial and incomplete penetration of capitalism into the indigo industry and the problems this engendered.

Indigo in hand, the processors or the agency houses had several options. If not bound by contract to the company, they could sell on the spot market, and here they encountered not just company buyers but agents representing, for example, U.S. and European interests. In other cases they might forward the indigo directly to London, paying the company for shipping and selling the dye there on their own account. Ultimately, though, and this set the Bengal indigo system apart from others, the amount of indigo delivered to the London markets depended not entirely on actual or anticipated demand or even on price but on the need of the company and of private businesses in Bengal to remit payments and profits to Europe. It is not surprising, therefore, that the London market for indigo underwent violent and wholly unpredictable swings, stimulating speculation and leaving a waste of bankruptcies in their wake.[41]

Almost all agricultural exports during the eighteenth and nineteenth centuries suffered at one time or another from adulteration or the effects of hurried or defective preparation. Sometimes this problem was the result of actions taken by the producers themselves, but at least as often it was the work of merchants and distributors. In South Carolina, for example, observers commented repeatedly on the relatively poor "appearance" of the local indigo.[42] The problem was that growers, in their rush to get to market, commonly failed to dry the dye adequately before cutting it into cakes. The result was that instead of having the hard feel and coppery sheen of the best "Guatimala," Carolina indigo was dull and the cakes flaked and crumbled at the edges. Producers were urged to pay more attention to this problem, but by ignoring it they may have made an entirely rational decision: because merchants and buyers tried to beat down the quality, and therefore the price, of the indigo offered them, it made sense for the planters to produce as much as they could even if the product was of lower quality rather than take the chance of obtaining a higher price that would compensate for the additional care required. Similarly, merchants in Central America tried to force all the indigo they bought into the lowest *corte* quality even as they sought to export it as the more valuable *flor*, and European buyers were warned to check each package individually, as exporters sometimes mixed dirt or other foreign matter with the indigo to increase its weight.[43] Before the English took over direct control of processing, there were complaints about the uneven quality of Indian indigo batches. The local product did not match the best from Central America or the West Indies, but adulteration, though it must have occurred, was not a problem much remarked upon in the Bengal indigo trade.

Substitutability is the vulnerability of a commodity and a commodity producer to replacement by a different supplier or by another commodity. The rise and decline the three indigo commodity chains examined here demonstrate clearly the principle of replaceability. And in each case, and this was not uncommon, the reasons for the shifts in production were not so much economic as political: Bengal replaced South Carolina when the United States became independent and was no longer part of the British mercantile system, and independence similarly undermined the Guatemala City–San Salvador production axis; in each case the availability of a substitute crop, cotton in South Carolina and coffee in El Salvador, softened the blow for planters and limited efforts to preserve the existing chain. Commodities may also be substituted by new products, either because a better or cheaper version of the old commodity becomes available or because changing tastes abandon the old item for something new. After the decline of woad, no natural dye product competed with the blue of indigo, but beginning in the 1850s an entirely new source of colors, aniline dyes made from coal tar, heralded the end of natural colors. Still, indigo held on for almost fifty years more, because of initial failures to develop a synthetic substitute specifically for the blue dye.

### DO THE ELEMENTS WITHIN A CHAIN PARTICIPATE IN MORE THAN ONE COMMODITY CHAIN?

For South Carolina planters one of the attractions of indigo was that it complemented existing crops and allowed large landowners to make more efficient use of their productive resources and small upcountry farmers to integrate themselves into the export economy. Both groups were able to take operations already functioning as part of other commodity chains and fit them into a new indigo chain without having to abandon their previous export activities. Further, both the planters and the small-scale farmers also grew subsistence crops for their own use or for sale at local markets, and indigo did not threaten this aspect of their economies. Indigo instead broadened their possibilities.

In contrast, Spanish crown officials and local residents alike complained that the spread of indigo undercut the traditional subsistence agriculture of rural San Salvador, causing food shortages and increased prices.[44] Given the lack of a unified market for food products in upper Central America, however, and the often dramatic seasonal and year-to-year swings in prices brought about by natural conditions, it is impossible to show that the onset of indigo in the region withdrew resources from other commodity chains or, if it did, how those commodities were affected. There was no necessary conflict between cattle raising and indigo, cacao had long ceased to be a major commercial crop, and coffee would not become important until after 1840, so it is hard to see how during the eighteenth and early nineteenth centuries indigo could have diverted resources to the detriment of other exports. In the subsistence sector, given a relative abundance of land at this point, the only real competition could have been for labor. But indigo was not a particularly labor-intensive crop; between harvests it required little day-to-day attention. Except perhaps around the local capital, San Salvador, it is unlikely that construction of this new commodity chain seriously affected other chains or subsistence food production.

In Bengal the development of indigo made considerable use of resources that had been or might have been deployed in other commodity chains, particularly rice. Whereas in South Carolina the two crops proved complementary, in early-nineteenth-century Bengal they competed directly for land and labor. By the 1820s the raiyati discovered that they could profit more by producing rice than by producing indigo but found themselves tied to the dye by advances and debts. Thus the productive resources controlled by the peasants were actual or potential key elements in at least two commodity chains, and the tension this created fostered violence and coercion.

In each case the resources used to develop indigo were in fact or potentially part of alternative commodity chains or subsistence production, but the effects were quite different. In South Carolina indigo allowed a fuller use of available resources and the integration of the hinterland into the export economy, at the price of expanded slavery. In Bengal, by contrast, the crops of indigo and rice competed for resources, prompting exporters to employ coercion against reluctant raiyati. In San Salvador the situation was less clear. Demands for land and labor for indigo may have cut into the food supply, and they certainly laid the groundwork for the impoverishment of the peasantry that accompanied the spread of coffee a half century later.

## THE DISTRIBUTION OF PROFITS AND RISK

Growers in South Carolina, especially the large-scale planters, were able to take advantage of competition among Charleston merchants and of an abundance of available capital to drive bargains that generally favored their interests. However, they still had substantial fixed investments, such as slaves bought on credit, that threatened their survival in periods of prolonged downturn. At least during boom years large planters could appropriate most of the profit while transferring some but not all of the risk to the merchants; the small farmers that paid more for money and received less for their indigo had a more difficult situation. In San Salvador, by contrast, the merchants, with a tighter oligopsony and with strong support from the state, were able to lay off most of the risk on the planters, especially on the poquiteros, in the form of higher prices for credit or foreclosure. The system fell apart with independence, not only because of the violence and destruction of the political wars of the first half of the nineteenth century but because tariff barriers now separated the growers in El Salvador from the merchants in Guatemala City. Bengal processors and agency houses were able to some extent to offset risk through the mechanism of coercion of the direct producers. For the company and the agency houses, too, a situation where liquidity was at least as important as price skewed calculations of profit and risk.

## THE ROLE OF THE STATE IN THE
## PRODUCTION AND MARKETING OF INDIGO

The governments of Great Britain and Spain intervened vigorously in trade and markets, as did all eighteenth- and early-nineteenth-century states. The purpose was fiscal and the effects were felt and often loudly protested by producers and merchants alike. But more feared than intervention was its absence and the instability its absence threatened. Genuinely free trade, as opposed to selective manipulation of taxes and regulations, found little support among elites in these years on either side of the Atlantic.

Indigo production and sale in South Carolina operated within the framework of the British mercantilist system developed in the seventeenth and early eighteenth centuries. On balance, this system was, at least initially, an advantage for the colony's growers. Not only did it guarantee them privileged access to the most important dye market of the time, but Parliament granted a series of bounties that were crucial in the early years of the industry.[45] Of course, mercantilism came back to bite the South Carolinians after 1783, when they found themselves outside the British Empire and subject to tax penalties and imperial preferences that ruined the industry.

For Central American producers mercantilism was not so advantageous and prompted more than a few to attempt to evade the system. Because Spain lacked an important textile industry in the second half of the eighteenth century, merchants simply transshipped most of the indigo they imported to France or southern Europe, at marked-up prices that did not benefit growers. At the same time, Central American producers were required to buy expensive "Spanish" imports that commonly were simply goods transshipped in Spain from England or France and sold at monopoly prices. In other words, state regulation offered few advantages to Central American producers, and it is not surprising that substantial quantities of the dye leaked out of the official circuit: across the Pacific in the Philippines trade, down the coast to Guayaquil or Lima, or to England through ports in Campeche, the Bay Islands, or Nicaragua.

Bengal indigo was, in most ways, the limit case of state or state-substitute participation among the eighteenth- and early-nineteenth-century indigo industries. At least initially producers enjoyed privileged access to the home market as well as help with financing. After the turn of the century company paternalism gave way to partial capitalist penetration of the countryside, backed by the state: in 1829 Europeans received the right to directly lease land for export production, in 1830 a distraint law allowed creditors to impound the crops of defaulting borrowers, and from 1833 on Europeans could buy rural properties.[46] Ironically, this growing power of the state turned the situation against them, or so many protested, in the 1850s. Under the influence of both Christian missionaries and free trade advocates company courts began to intervene between the raiyati and processors to stop physical coercion and in 1859 ruled that creditors could not use debts to force peasants to grow indigo. This ruling undermined the power of the indigo mills without freeing the farmers. Rural zamindars switched from rent collecting to money lending and, with population increases in the second half of the century, the raiyati remained in debt, if to a different master.

The state as such had little role in eighteenth-century Bengal, where a private company ruled, but that company was effectively a state substitute and took a leading position in early indigo experiments: the first European-owned plantations were set up by John Prinsep with company financing.[47] Over time, however, the company withdrew first from financing, then from monopolizing the indigo crop, and finally it allowed competing shipping into the traffic, but it had created and continued to maintain the legal-political structure within which the trade operated. The Spanish state did not have funds available to finance indigo but it nevertheless attempted to enforce even stricter political and commercial restrictions, with a notable lack of success. Both merchants and crown officials systematically subverted the state for their own purposes. In South Carolina the indigo trade had no particular problem with mercantilism, or broadly with the British legal-political structures, and even benefited from bounties denied other producers. South Carolina was not among the leaders of the United States' independence.

From the comparisons presented here it is clear that definitions of commodity chains that miss the political factor, in particular the role of the state, err.[48] Land, labor, capital, appropriate technology, and the rest are necessary but not sufficient for the construction of a commodity chain. Except perhaps in an ideal free trade environment, political decisions are typically key to the constitution and the destruction of commodity chains. Chains may fail because the basic resource gives out or because of a change in taste or the availability of a substitute, but they are much more likely to collapse because of political changes. None of the chains examined here came to an end because of problems with land or labor or capital, and even when faced with the possibility of a cheaper substitute, natural indigo fought a successful delaying action for more than half a century.

By the third decade of the twentieth century, however, the natural product had effectively disappeared from large-scale international trade, replaced by synthetic indigos.[49] But natural indigo never disappeared. Parallel to the commercial circuits had always existed production for local use, and this continued, and it continues today, because of cultural conservatism or because the home weavers cannot afford commercial dyes. Synthetic indigo itself was in decline at mid-century, replaced by a variety of other blues. Ironically, it was the dye's chief commercial failing, its tendency to run and to fade more rapidly than more modern chemical dyes, that prompted a major resurgence in popular demand in the 1960s and since. Fashionable North American, European, and Japanese youths now pay hundreds of dollars for prefaded indigo-dyed clothing, while hard, bright colors characterize shirts, pants, and dresses in the urban Third World.

---

## NOTES

1   An excellent overview of the history of indigo is Balfour-Paul, *Indigo*. Also useful is Brunello, *The Art of Dyeing in the History of Mankind*. For Europeans the term "indigo" derives from the dye's origins in India. The Arabs called it *nil*, and from this term come the Spanish *añil* and the Portuguese *anil*.

2   Brunello, *Art of Dyeing*, 196.

3   On the early history of indigo exports from Central America, see MacLeod, *Spanish Central America*, 176–87.

4   Balfour-Paul, *Indigo*, 66–67. The West Indies also produced excellent indigo but this crop gave way to the more profitable sugarcane.

5   Rubio Sánchez, *Historia del añil o xiquilite en Centro América o xiquilite en Centro América*, 229.

6   Brazil, for example, produced indigo: Alden, "The Growth and Decline of Indigo Production in Colonial Brazil."

7   Balfour-Paul, *Indigo*, 46–47.

8   For an overview of indigo in South Carolina, see Jelatis, "Tangled Up in Blue."

9   On the legend of Eliza Lucas and the reintroduction of indigo to South Carolina in the 1740s, see Gray, *History of Agriculture in the Southern United States to 1860*, 290–91.

10  Lynch, "A River in Time."

11  For a survey of this period that carries past MacLeod's 1720, see Wortman, *Government and Society in Central America*. On indigo, see Smith, "Indigo Production and Trade in Colonial Guatemala."

12  Molina, "Colouring the World in Blue," chap. 1. On the rise of the new class of merchants, see Brown, *Juan Fermín de Aycinena*.

13  For the problems of the early nineteenth century, see McCreery, *Rural Guatemala*, 29–30.

14  Tuck, ed., *The East India Company*. A thorough overview of the late-eighteenth- and nineteenth-century economy of Bengal is found in Bose, *Peasant Labour and Colonial Capital*, 2.

15  Macpherson, *The History of the European Commerce with India*, 201.

16  Kling, *The Blue Mutiny*, 19–20.

17  Edelson, "Planting the Lowcountry," 231.

18  Ibid., 66.

19  Terry, "Champaign Country," 259.

20   Rubio Sánchez, Historia del añil, 105.

21   On indigo and community land, see Lauria Santiago, An Agrarian Republic, chap. 2.

22   Marshall, Bengal—The British Bridgehead, 169; Bose, Peasant Labour and Colonial Capital, 47–48; Kling, The Blue Mutiny, 127.

23   Kling, Blue Mutiny.

24   Jelatis, "Tangled Up in Blue," 32.

25   MacLeod, Spanish Central America, 185–86.

26   On problems with free labor, see Rubio Sánchez, Historia del añil, 88–94.

27   Wortman, Government and Society in Central America, 176–79; Smith, "Forced Labor in the Guatemalan Indigo Works," 319–28.

28   Sinha, The Economic History of Bengal, 210.

29   Sellers, Charleston Business on the Eve of the American Revolution, 55.

30   Molina, "Colouring the World in Blue," chap. 5; Brown, Juan Fermín de Aycinena; Floyd, "The Guatemalan Merchants, the Government, and the Provincianos."

31   On relations between merchants and crown bureaucrats, see Molina, "Colouring the World in Blue," chap. 6.

32   Singh, European Agency Houses in Bengal. On early experiments with company financing, see Marshal, "Private British Investment in Eighteenth-Century Bengal."

33   Singh, European Agency Houses in Bengal.

34   Kling, Blue Mutiny, 22–23.

35   One of the best descriptions by an eighteenth-century source is in Merrens, The Colonial South Carolina Scene, 154–58. For a contemporary painting of an indigo mill, see Balfour-Paul, Indigo, 71.

36   Molina, "Colouring the World in Blue," 48–49.

37   MacLeod, Spanish Central America, 176–78; Balfour-Paul, Indigo, 71; Rubio Sánchez, Historia del añil, 295–98.

38   Sellers, Charleston Business on the Eve of the American Revolution; Edelson, "Planting the Lowcountry," chap. 5.

39   Edelson, "Planting the Lowcountry," 409–10.

40   Sinha, Economic History of Bengal, 210.

41   Singh, European Agency Houses in Bengal, analyzes the markets for indigo year by year from the 1790s to the 1830s.

42   Merrens, ed., The Colonial South Carolina Scene, 147–48.

43   Rubio Sánchez, Historia del añil, 79–80, 383–84.

44   Ibid., 127–28.

45   Gray, History of Agriculture in the Southern United States, 292. The system was poorly administered and bounties were paid for low-quality indigo that should not have qualified.

46   Bose, Peasant Labour and Colonial Capital, chap. 4.

47   Sinha, Economic History of Bengal, 97.

48   For example, "a network of labor and production processes whose end is a finished commodity": Hopkins and Wallerstein, "Commodity Chains," 17.

49   On the rise, decline, and rise of synthetic indigo, see Balfour-Paul, Indigo, 81–87.

## BIBLIOGRAPHY

Alden, Dauril. "The Growth and Decline of Indigo Production in Colonial Brazil: A Study in Comparative Economic History." *Journal of Economic History*, March 1965.

Balfour-Paul, Jenny. *Indigo*. London: British Museum Press, 1998.

Bose, Sugata. *Peasant Labour and Colonial Capital: Rural Bengal since 1770*. Cambridge: Cambridge University Press, 1993.

Brown, Richmond F. *Juan Fermín de Aycinena: Central American Colonial Entrepreneur*. Norman: University of Oklahoma Press, 1997.

Brunello, Franco. *The Art of Dyeing in the History of Mankind*. Vicenza: N. Pozza, 1973.

Edelson, S. Max. "Planting the Lowcountry: Agriculture, Enterprise, and Economic Experience in the Lower South, 1695–1785." Ph.D. dissertation, Johns Hopkins University, 1998.

Floyd, Troy. "The Guatemalan Merchants, the Government, and the Provincianos, 1750–1800." *Hispanic American Historical Review* 41, no. 1 (February 1961): 90–110.

Gray, Lewis Cecil. *History of Agriculture in the Southern United States to 1860*. Washington: Carnegie Institute of Washington, 1933.

Hopkins, Terence K., and Immanuel Wallerstein. "Commodity Chains: Construct and Research." In Gary Gereffi and Miguel Korzeniewicz, eds., *Commodity Chains and Global Capitalism*, 17–50. Westport, Conn.: Greenwood, 1994.

Jelatis, Virginia Gail. "Tangled Up in Blue: Indigo Culture and Economy in South Carolina, 1747–1800." Ph.D. dissertation, University of Minnesota, 1999.

Kling, Blair B. *The Blue Mutiny: The Indigo Disturbances in Bengal, 1859–1862*. Philadelphia: University of Pennsylvania Press, 1966.

Lauria Santiago, Aldo A. *An Agrarian Republic: Commercial Agriculture and the Politics of Peasant Communities in El Salvador, 1823–1914*. Pittsburgh: University of Pittsburgh Press, 1999.

Lynch, Suzanne Cameron. "A River in Time: A Cultural Study of the Yadkin/Pee Dee River System to 1825 (South Carolina, North Carolina, and Virginia)." Ph.D. dissertation, University of South Carolina, 1993.

MacLeod, Murdo. *Spanish Central America*. Berkeley: University of California Press, 1973.

Macpherson, David. *The History of the European Commerce with India*. London: Longman, Hurst, Rees, Orme, & Brown, 1812.

Marshal, Peter. "Private British Investment in Eighteenth-Century Bengal." In Patrick Tuck, ed., *Trade, Finance and Power*, vol. 4 of *The East India Company, 1600–1858*. New York: Routledge, 1998.

Marshall, P. J. *Bengal—The British Bridgehead: Eastern India, 1740–1828*. New York: Cambridge University Press, 1987.

McCreery, David. *Rural Guatemala, 1760–1940*. Stanford: Stanford University Press, 1994.

Merrens, H. Roy, ed. *The Colonial South Carolina Scene*. Columbia: University of South Carolina Press, 1977.

Molina, José Antonio Fernández. "Colouring the World in Blue: The Indigo Boom and the Central American Market, 1750–1810." Ph.D. dissertation, University of Texas at Austin, 1992.

Rubio Sánchez, Manuel. *Historia del añil o xiquilite en Centro América*. San Salvador: Ministerio de Educación, Dirección de Publicaciones, 1976.

Sellers, Lelia. *Charleston Business on the Eve of the American Revolution*. Chapel Hill: University of North Carolina Press, 1934.

Singh, S. B. *European Agency Houses in Bengal (1783–1833)*. Calcutta: K. L. Mukhopadhyay, 1966.

Sinha, Narendra Krishna. *The Economic History of Bengal*. Vol. 1. Calcutta: K. L. Mukhopadhyay, 1965.

Smith, Robert J. "Forced Labor in the Guatemalan Indigo Works." *Hispanic American Historical Review* 36, no. 3 (August 1956).

———. "Indigo Production and Trade in Colonial Guatemala." *Hispanic American Historical Review* 39, no. 2 (May 1959): 181–211.

Terry, George. "Champaign Country: A Social History of an Eighteenth-Century Lowcountry Parish in South Carolina: St. Johns Berkeley County." Ph.D. dissertation, University of South Carolina, 1981.

Tuck, Patrick, ed. *The East India Company, 1600–1858*. 6 vols. New York: Routledge, 1998.

Wortman, Miles L. *Government and Society in Central America, 1680–1840*. New York: Columbia University Press, 1982.

# 3

# Mexican Cochineal and the European Demand
# for American Dyes, 1550–1850

Carlos Marichal

IN THE MID-1520S, shortly after the conquest of Mexico, Charles V wrote to Hernán Cortés urging him to send information on a new red dyestuff of high quality known as cochineal, which was cultivated and produced by Indian peasants in Mexico's *meseta central*. That the emperor should request a report of this nature is indicative of the high value placed in Europe on this quite special commodity. Cochineal (*grana cochinilla*) became, after silver, the most important Mexican export for over three hundred years, or down to approximately 1850. A still unanswered question is why this was so.

A few studies have described important aspects of the production of cochineal in Mexico but virtually none has explained the reasons why this commodity consistently had such a strong secular demand in Europe. One reason for the paucity of studies on this subject appears to be economic historians' neglect of the trade in dyes from the Americas, including indigo, brazilwood, *palo de Campeche*, and cochineal, all of which were of critical importance for Europe's textile industries from the sixteenth century down to the mid–nineteenth century. The most important of the American dyes in terms of volume was indigo, which is discussed in Chapter 2, but the most expensive was cochineal, and therefore cochineal exports rivaled those of indigo in total value. The scarcity of studies on the transatlantic dye trade is rather surprising given the critical input of natural dyes to the key sector of textiles in the European economy for over three centuries. The fortunes of these dyes from the New World followed the trajectory of the labor-intensive textile production of the ancien regime, which was later supplanted by factory production of textiles. Hence, this is a story of how proto-industrialization and early industrialization at first expanded the markets for natural dyes and later replaced them.

Since this is a vast subject, I have chosen to focus on cochineal, which was the most highly valued of the dyes exported from the Americas. It was, in many senses, the classic dye for luxury textiles. Its attractiveness lay in a combination of factors: its long-lasting and deep red color allowed silks and woolens dyed with cochineal to exude their rich hues for many decades, in some cases for over a century. The princes of church and crown inevitably fancied and valued such attractive and durable fabrics. Furthermore, cochineal was a relatively scarce commodity which had to be brought from afar, after a complex and labor-intensive system of cultivation and production. The final price was therefore so high that only the very wealthy could buy it, which also added to its prestige value in ancien regime societies.

The study of cochineal is also of interest because it can help demonstrate how, from the sixteenth century, European demand for an expensive, labor-intensive dyestuff directly affected the lives of tens of thousands of members of Mexican indigenous peasant communities. The peasants devoted a large amount of labor to cultivating the cochineal that was used to dye the finest fabrics used by popes, princes, nobles, military officers, and wealthy residents of European cities and towns. The economics of an early international commodity chain thus can also help elucidate the complex transatlantic social dynamics which it generated.

The story of cochineal and other American dyestuffs offers a splendid counterpoint to the much better known story of the silk trade that spanned much of Asia and Europe from the early medieval period. Most silks were produced by thousands of Chinese peasants, who cultivated silkworms in a process as laborious as that of the communities of peasants who cultivated cochineal insects in colonial Mexico. The silk brought across Asia by camel caravans or by sea found its main markets in the leading luxury textile manufacturing centers of Europe: Florence, Milan, Lyons, Bruges. And it was to these same markets that came the American cochineal and indigo, among other dyestuffs. Indeed, it may be argued that the cochineal commodity chain meshed with the silk commodity chain for several centuries.

This essay is organized around three themes: (1) the origins of demand in Europe for cochineal in the sixteenth century and the rise of the international trade in this commodity, with special emphasis on analysis of trends of production and prices in the period 1750–1850; (2) the specific characteristics of the production of cochineal in Mexico, principally in the Oaxaca region; (3) the role of both Spanish-American and European merchants and merchant bankers in the international commerce of cochineal and their control of the complex networks (commodity chains) which developed around this branch of transatlantic trade. I conclude with observations on the gradual decline of Mexican cochineal as an international commodity in the first half of the nineteenth century.

## EUROPEAN DEMAND FOR COCHINEAL AND
## INTERNATIONAL TRADE TRENDS, 1550–1850

It is my hypothesis that the valuable cochineal trade originating in Mexico was demand-driven from the early sixteenth century on. It was the high premium which European elites were willing to pay for this deep scarlet dye that impelled the development of an extraordinarily complex transatlantic commodity chain that prospered for over three centuries. But to understand the origins of the international trade in cochineal, it is necessary to focus attention first on the sixteenth century and particularly on the European luxury textile industries and their multiple connections to the Spanish and Spanish-American economy. It is well known that Spanish merino wool was already one of the most valued and expensive primary goods consumed by the leading cloth manufacturing centers of the period. It is less well known that the ecclesiastical and secular elites all over Europe also came to depend on dyestuffs imported from Mexico by Spanish merchants for their most luxurious and long-lasting fabrics, particularly wools and silks.

The importance of cochineal was reflected in its price: indeed, expensive dyes often represented a larger proportion of the final cost of fine cloth than the other materials essential to its manufacture, including the raw or processed fibers (wool, silk, linen). But why were high-quality dyestuffs so expensive? Scarcity, of course, played a major role, but certain colors were especially appreciated because they had symbolic importance for certain hierarchies and therefore socioeconomic significance in traditional societies. In this regard, it should be noted that from the medieval era, one of the colors most prized by crown, church, and nobility in

Europe for their finest fabrics was carmine or deep crimson. That this should be so was due in part to the symbolic importance of this hue as representative of the preeminence of the upper orders in human society.[1] Other colors—in particular deep blue, gold, and silver—had similar prestige, as may be observed in the Renaissance paintings of the princes of monarchy and church, but undoubtedly the crimsons stood out. Whether the fabrics were fashioned into cloaks, robes, uniforms, dresses, or stockings, or into cushion covers, curtains, or canopies, it is clear that silks, linens, and woolens of a deep red color were always in heavy demand by wealthy and powerful Europeans of the ancien regime.

Another reason for the high demand was the durability and depth of the color of cochineal when it was used to dye woolens and silks. Cochineal had a distinguishing asset: when mixed with a mordant (especially alum), it became fixed inextricably with wool or silk textiles. Since these textiles, like cochineal, are of animal or insect origin, the chemical interaction of proteins makes for permanent bondage. On the other hand, cochineal did not do well with cottons and textiles of vegetable origin. But it should also be recalled that silk and woolen textiles tended to be the most valued in the Europe of the medieval and early modern ages.

From the fourteenth century, if not earlier, the leading luxury textile centers of Europe, in particular Florence and Flanders, produced crimson cloth of various shades and tones by using a variety of red dyestuffs. According to John Munro, the "medieval scarlets" owed their "splendor, fame and high cost to the dyeing process,"[2] largely because such dyestuffs (particularly those derived from insects, such as the kermes from the Mediterranean) were relatively rare and because the dyeing processes were complex and required great skill.

In an extraordinarily detailed analysis of medieval scarlet textiles, Munro has demonstrated that the dyeing process was responsible for a large proportion of the final price of cloth; sometimes it was the largest single component of production costs. At the luxury textile center of Malines in the fourteenth century, the scarlet dye known as kermes accounted for 40 percent of the total cost of production of the cloth. The variety of colors or tones were obtained by the use of mordants, including alum, tin, chrome, and copper, which respectively produced hues of crimson, scarlet, purple, and claret, and furthermore allowed the dyes to fix fast to the cloth and to last for decades.[3]

The expensive scarlet or crimson fabrics could be acquired only by the wealthiest members of late medieval society. Munro cites the case of

Henry VI's wardrobe account of 1438–39, in which the cheapest scarlets cost more than £14 sterling, a huge sum at the time. He notes: "A master mason, then earning sixpence a day, would have had to spend his full wages for 565 wordays (about two years and nine months) to buy one. . . . For that same amount of money in 1440, the following goods could have been purchased at the Antwerp market: approximately 2,720 kilos of Flemish cheese, or 850 kilos of butter, or 22,000 smoked red herrings or 1,100 litres of good quality Rhine wine."[4]

Despite these high costs, from the early sixteenth century the demand for luxury crimson and scarlet cloth continued to climb all over Europe, perhaps most noticeably in England, Flanders, France, and Italy. And inevitably the demand for high-quality and long-lasting red dyestuffs also rose. From the late 1520s Mexican cochineal began to appear on European markets in small quantities but soon gained wide acceptance as the finest crimson dyestuff for textiles. According to one historical study, "Cochineal possessed from ten to twelve times the dyeing properties of kermes; it also produced colors far superior in brilliancy and fastness."[5] This dyestuff thus quickly won growing markets in the leading luxury textile manufacturing centers of Europe, including Segovia in Spain; Suffolk in England; Florence, Milan, and Venice in Italy; Rouen, Malines, and Lyons in France; and various centers in Flanders. Interdisciplinary studies provide concrete evidence of the rapid expansion of European demand for cochineal. Indeed, a laborious program of chemical research on hundreds of samples of medieval and early modern dyed textiles has provided "concrete evidence to substantiate the historical assertion that Mexican cochineal within fifty years of its introduction into Europe (c. 1520–30) fully displaced kermes in scarlet textile dyeing."[6] The expansion of this trade was constant throughout the sixteenth century and then reached a plateau in the early seventeenth century. Subsequently, demand remained relatively consistent, although additional studies are required on the trade data. The statistical information on the last great century of the cochineal trade, which lasted from 1750 to the 1850s, is considerably better, as we shall see.

The luxury textile industries of Italy were among the most important of sixteenth-century Europe and hence were among the major markets for expensive dyes. Substantial quantities of the grana cochinilla sent from Veracruz to Seville and Cadiz made their way to the port of Livorno. The Spanish economic historian Felipe Ruiz Martín has used the correspondence of contemporary Spanish merchant bankers to trace the exports to Florence, where a booming luxury textile industry consumed large quantities of dyes. But he also notes that a not unsubstantial volume of cochineal was transshipped from Livorno to Venice, where it was used to dye the cheaper textiles—*panni*—sent to Constantinople as well as for the famous Venetian fez. According to both Spanish and Genoese merchants heavily involved in this trade, this crimson dyestuff was always profitable, and in fact its price quadrupled over the sixteenth century even as the volume of trade rose rapidly.

Despite the few stimulating pages by Ruiz Martín and two pioneering articles by Raymond Lee on mercantile aspects, historians have not devoted much attention to the subject of Mexican cochineal in the European textile industry of the sixteenth century or to the consumption patterns of these crimson fabrics.[7] This seems to be a striking lacuna, since the Mexican grana cochinilla became for three centuries the most demanded and expensive luxury dyestuff in the Western world.

According to an old but classic article by Raymond Lee, it may be estimated that by 1600 average annual imports of cochineal to Spain ranged from 10,000 to 12,000 arrobas (each arroba being about 25 pounds). The dyestuff was later transshipped from Seville and Cadiz to a number of ports in northern Europe, as well as to Marseilles, Livorno, and Venice. Leading merchant banking firms handled this highly lucrative commerce from as early as the late sixteenth century, as we will have occasion to note later in this essay.

The published data and information on the cochineal trade is scarcer and much more scattered for both the seventeenth century and the early eighteenth century. Louisa Hoberman, however, has provided some important information with regard to the cochineal trade in the early seventeenth century in her excellent study on the merchants of New Spain of the period. According to her research, on average, it can be estimated that one pound of cochineal would cost anywhere between 4 and 6 silver pesos in the early seventeenth century. Hoberman adds that the high unit value of cochineal can perhaps be best judged by comparison with other commodities. In the decade of 1610–20, for instance, 25 pounds of cochineal cost 60 times more than an equivalent weight of sugar; in the 1630s, cochineal was worth 30 times the value of an equivalent weight of sugar.[8]

Hoberman also notes that prices for cultivated cochineal in the decade of 1610–20, for example, varied from a low of 110 silver pesos per arroba to a high of 150 pesos. This price range appears to have remained remarkably stable for a very long time: according to data published by Alicia Contreras Sánchez, the prices registered for cochineal at Cadiz varied from a low of 80 silver pesos per arroba to a high of 150 pesos between 1780 and 1800.[9] As is well known, the silver peso was the most widely used coin in the majority of ancien regime societies and therefore provides a good index, particularly because of its relatively stable relation with gold for over three centuries in European monetary systems.

While data on cochineal exports to Europe in the seventeenth century are scarce, there is more abundant statistical information on the Mexican cochineal trade for the second half of the eighteenth century and the first half of the nineteenth, on which I will briefly comment in order to provide an overview of the final century of the international trade in this commodity. The most complete series is based on data registered at the local treasury of Oaxaca on annual production by weight and value, as well as annual price trends. The long-term tendencies are quite clear. Overall, physical production declined, as did the total value of the harvests of cochineal. At the same time, prices moved down, but with marked fluctuations. This downward trend might suggest a decline in international demand, but historians have also pointed to domestic reasons for the decline in Mexican production, particularly in the last decade of the eighteenth century. The analysis of the data, therefore, suggests a need for a further breakdown from the century-long trend to shorter time periods.

Analysis of the years 1758–83 demonstrates that these were clearly prosperous years, as far as cochineal was concerned: annual production averaged 922,600 pounds, which, at a price of almost 20 silver *reales* (2.5 silver pesos = 10 shillings) per pound, produced over 2 million pesos per year for local producers and merchants (see Figure 1). However, production declined to slightly less than half a million pounds per year from 1784 until 1803; at the same time, prices declined slightly, hovering at an annual average of 16.4 silver *reales* per pound until the turn of the century. The reasons for the steep reduction in the production of cochineal in Oaxaca were apparently not related to the rather modest price decline, but rather have been ascribed to two factors: (1) the plagues and demographic crisis of 1784–85, when over 300,000 people died in New Spain, is believed to have deeply affected Oaxaca's peasant communities and disrupted production; (2) fiscal and administrative reforms restructured traditional forms of commercialization of cochineal locally and implied higher taxes on this commodity.[10] At any rate, it is evident that a complex

1. Prices of cochinilla registered at the Oficina del Registro y la Administración
Principal de Rentas, Oaxaca, 1758–1854 (pesos plata)

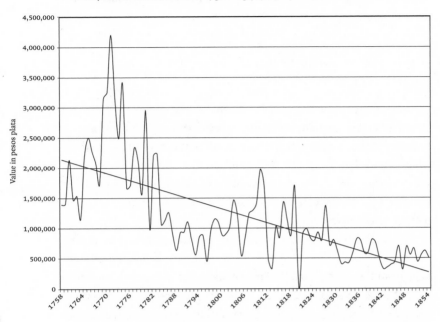

Source: Barbro Dahlgren, *La grana cochinilla*. Mexico City: Instituto de Investigaciones
Antropológicas, Universidad Nacional Autónoma de México, 1990), 331–32.

series of new conditions (demographic, fiscal, administrative, and mercantile) disrupted traditional levels of local production of cochineal in
Oaxaca and initiated a phase of relative decadence.

During the following fifteen years, 1804–19, production of Oaxaca
cochineal continued to decline (stabilizing at a plateau of 328,000 pounds
per year) but was compensated in good measure by the rise in the international price of the dyestuff, which rose to an average of 26 silver *reales*
per pound during these years of war and intermittent interruption of
navigation between Mexico and Europe. Oaxaca peasants and merchants
benefited, since international conflict pushed the prices of this relatively
scarce commodity steeply upward, but, paradoxically, local production
still continued to fall in these difficult years.

After Mexico won independence in 1821, the international price of
cochineal dropped steadily because of the end of Mexico's monopoly on
cochineal and the emergence of competing production in other regions
of the world. However, it should be noted that despite the fall in prices,
annual production of Oaxaca *grana* (as measured in pounds) increased, a

fact which suggests that peasant producers sought to maintain income levels by intensifying their labors to counter the drop in profitability, and continued to do so for decades.

## THE OAXACA INDIAN COMMUNITIES AND
## SECULAR PRODUCTION OF COCHINEAL

Up to this point, this essay has concentrated on the origins and long-term evolution of the international trade in cochineal. However, in order to understand the complete commodity chain of this dyestuff, it is worthwhile to attend to the specific locale and social conditions of production. We will begin with a few comments on the ecology of cochineal and then summarize some features of the peasant labor involved and local commercial mechanisms.

The name of the most expensive American dye of the ancien regime, *grana cochinilla*, was imported directly from Europe, being derived originally from the Latin *coccina* (in Spanish *cochinilla*), which was used from ancient times to refer to the rich red colors produced by insects, which when desiccated were described as *granas* (little seeds). The modern scientific name of the little Mexican insect that produces the famous dye is *Coccus cacti*, which refers to the fact that it thrives on the cactus known as nopal, abundant in central and southern Mexico.[11]

During the colonial era, a wild variety of cochineal, called *grana silvestre*, was found and cultivated in relatively small quantities not only in Mexico but also in Guatemala, Peru, and Tucumán, Argentina. It was harvested up to six times per year but produced a relatively low-grade dyestuff. The truly valuable and important variety of cochineal was the domesticated type known as *grana fina*, which was twice the size and produced a much richer dye. However, as Munro notes, it could yield only three harvests (May, July, and October) with production levels of about 250 kilos of these insects per hectare of planted nopals. The enormous amount of peasant labor expended is indicated by the fact that one pound of the final dye known as grana cochinilla required the desiccation of 70,000 of the tiny insects.[12]

The cochineal insects were cultivated with extraordinary care by Mexican Indian peasants on the nopal plants and later killed directly by hot water and then dried (red-brown). Alternatively, they were baked slowly in the hot sun, which gave them a silver color, or in hot pans or ovens, which made the final color of the grains black. Subsequently the grains were packed together by diverse procedures until finally the valuable "bricks" (zurrones) of dried dyestuff were ready for shipment, mainly to Europe.

Originally the insects were cultivated in Tlaxcala and several other regions of New Spain, but production came to be concentrated in Oaxaca by the late sixteenth century. The high population density of peasant communities in this mountainous territory was an important precondition for the highly labor-intensive cultivation of the cochinilla on the nopal plants. Colonial descriptions of the cultivation of cochineal recall the enormous amount of meticulous peasant labor required for the production of silkworms in China and Europe in the same era.

The Spanish colonial regime gradually put in place a complex incentive structure that made specialization in the production of cochineal attractive to Oaxaca peasants. Poor soils, limited markets, and high transport costs made agriculture a perilous livelihood. The high prices of cochineal, however, allowed Indian families to obtain modest but welcome income from the dyestuffs. In many Oaxaca towns they also obtained income from the sale of cotton produced in the valleys and from the manufacture of richly colored textiles.

For the Spanish crown, there were clear fiscal advantages to the large-scale production of cochineal. Since the Indian communities (called *repúblicas de indios*) were obliged to pay tribute to tax collectors of the colonial administration from the sixteenth century, it was soon stipulated that in Oaxaca they should do so preferentially in cochineal. The royal functionaries made substantial profits by selling the dyestuffs to merchants for silver or gold, whereas they had more difficulties in selling other commodities produced by the Indian peasant communities.

But the mechanisms of the colonial administration also included a complex dynamic of mercantile control of the cochineal production and trade, which operated on the basis of a close alliance between merchants and local bureaucrats who exploited the Indian communities as far as they could. Brian Hamnett and Carlos Sánchez Silva have underlined the coactive methods that were employed to force Oaxaca peasants to produce cochineal from the sixteenth century to the end of the colonial regime.[13]

However, coaction was not the only factor involved. Jeremy Baskes has argued that incentives provided by both merchants and the viceregal administration help explain the continued specialization of Oaxaca peas-

2. The cochineal trade: Mercantile networks in Mexico

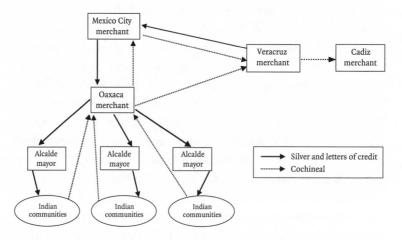

ants in the cultivation of the cochineal insects and the production of the dyestuff. Certainly, it would appear that the repartimiento system (which lasted until 1787) proved quite successful in ensuring a consistently large cochineal harvest each year. In very basic terms, repartimiento functioned as follows: leading Mexico City merchants advanced funds to Oaxaca merchants, who in turn provided funds to local bureaucrats (*alcaldes mayores*) in the cochineal-producing towns and villages (see Figure 2). The functionaries would lend the money to peasants so that they could plant nopal plants or pay for sustenance until the cochineals were harvested and sold. In exchange for the funds advanced, the peasants agreed to pay the alcaldes mayores with cochineal at a fixed price lower than the current international price.[14]

That production should have fallen so abruptly after 1784 and continued to remain depressed despite Oaxaca's continuing monopoly of cochineal would seem to suggest that it was the disruption of this complex credit-mercantile mechanism that contributed to the decline of cochineal. Baskes demonstrates the remarkable fall in production after the abolition of the repartimiento schemes and argues that peasants depended heavily on the old credit mechanisms.[15] Other authors have insisted that additional factors were involved, such as increasing taxation in the final decades of the eighteenth century,[16] but Baskes's arguments are convincing. At any rate, the subject would appear to merit future research.

While the production and trade of cochineal inside Mexico had many facets, the international commerce in this valuable dyestuff was of perhaps greater complexity. Its axis originated in Mexico because the Spanish crown made it a policy to stimulate a virtual production monopoly of grana fina in the Oaxaca region. It should also be noted, however, that New Spain was simultaneously important as intermediary for other American dyes, in particular indigo (some produced in Mexico but mostly in neighboring Guatemala) and Campeche wood (*palo de Campeche*). Indigo was in particular demand in Europe for the making of blue cloths, while Campeche wood dyes were used for deep blacks, in great demand for clerical garments in both Catholic and Protestant countries as well as for the clothing of the expanding middle classes in Europe.

Cochineal was distinguished from the other dyes because of its greater (and more specialized) demand and higher prices. This probably explains why it appears more prominently in the correspondence of international merchants from the sixteenth century down to the early nineteenth century. Moreover, the possibility of cornering the market was apparently greater in the case of cochineal than in the other dyestuffs, and hence cochineal was generally seen as offering more potential for profit by persons in a position to invest large sums in such speculations.

From the mid-sixteenth century, leading European merchants and merchant bankers became as interested in cochineal as they were in other high-value commodities with low weight, such as precious metals, pepper, and alum, which made them easily transportable and the objects of financial speculation (although they could also lead to great losses if prices did not evolve as predicted). At any rate, the relatively small volume of cochineal stocks facilitated frequent price manipulations by the oligopoly of mercantile firms that controlled the bulk of cochineal stocks in European ports.

Felipe Ruíz Martín has described clear examples from the late sixteenth century of attempts to corner the cochineal markets in Europe. According to this distinguished Spanish economic historian, the cochineal trade inside Europe was very soon dominated by groups of Spanish and Italian merchant bankers, a number of them closely linked to the finances of the Habsburg monarchy. These merchant bankers were engaged in the trade circuits linking Seville/Cadiz, Genoa, Livorno, and Florence. The cochineal arrived from Mexico at Seville and Cadiz and from there was redistributed to the rest of Europe. Most of the cochineal that went to Italy went to Livorno in the same ships that brought the famous merino wool that was also a primary commodity for the Florentine luxury textile manufacturing sector.[17] A close look at the Livorno trade, following the classic study by Fernand Braudel and Ruggiero Romano, could prove fruitful in this regard.[18]

Ruíz Martín edited a selection of the abundant correspondence of the Spanish merchant Simón Ruiz with Italian merchants, which includes 290 references to cochineal.[19] The most spectacular speculative operation related to cochineal cited was that carried out in 1585 by the Capponi merchant banking family of Florence, who, in alliance with the powerful Maluenda merchant bankers of Burgos, Spain, attempted to corner the entire shipment of cochineal from Mexico arriving at Seville in 1585. They also bought up the bulk of stocks in other European ports in order to reinforce a strategy aimed at gaining a virtual monopoly of the valuable dyestuff. The ambitious plans of the speculators were quite successful and allowed them to push prices up, although artisans in Europe's leading textile centers put up stiff resistance. Ruíz Martín notes that in some cases the decline in demand obliged the merchants to offer extended time spans for payment of the cochineal.[20]

A review of the trade in cochineal over the seventeenth and eighteenth centuries indicates that speculation continued to be an astonishingly common feature of the international trade in this dyestuff. In 1788, two centuries after the Italian merchant bankers tried to corner the cochineal market, two of the leading merchant banks of Europe, Hope and Company of Amsterdam and Baring Brothers of London, were hard at work attempting the same feat, but with rather more mixed results.

Marten Buist, the historian of the Hope merchant banking firm, has described the huge cochineal speculation of 1788 in considerable detail. The operation involved buying up most of the stock of cochineal in all the principal European ports: Cadiz, Marseilles, Rouen, Genoa, Amsterdam, London, and even St. Petersburg, with the object of obtaining a virtual monopoly (Figure 3). The transactions required particular attention to acquisition of practically all the dyestuffs received from Mexico in Cadiz. Failure there would condemn the whole vast transaction. Hope's agent at Cadiz was not entirely successful in this part of the project, and rival merchants were able to buy up substantial stocks of cochineal at other

3. The commodity chain of cochineal from Veracruz to Europe, c. 1780

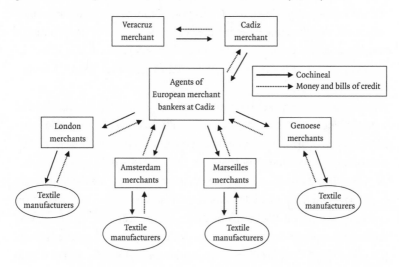

ports, probably because they had got wind of the aims of the Hope-Baring alliance. As a result, the monopoly was nowhere complete and attempts to rig prices failed, causing substantial financial losses to the main partners in the speculation.[21]

But European merchants were not alone in the international cochineal business. Some of the great eighteenth-century mercantile firms of Mexico City and Veracruz were also heavily involved in the management of this complex commodity chain on the American side and in its connections to both Europe and Asia. Studies by various historians on the operations of the wealthy Iraeta merchant family of Mexico City reveal the complexity of the control of trade inside New Spain and of the connections to Cadiz merchants, on the one hand, and to Asian markets for cochineal via the Manila Galleon, on the other. Similarly, Brian Hamnett's pioneering work describes the complex transactions of other Mexican merchant firms which were heavily involved in the cochineal trade in the late eighteenth century.[22]

## INTERNATIONAL COMPETITION AND THE DECLINE OF MEXICAN COCHINEAL, 1820–1870

Why did the cochineal trade decline in the nineteenth century? Research in this realm is relatively scarce and so all the answers are not yet in. It is well known that the Spanish crown had been remarkably successful in maintaining a virtual Mexican monopoly of cochineal production from the sixteenth century down to 1820. It is also known that in the late eighteenth century, the French botanist Nicolas-Joseph Thierry de Menonville smuggled some cochineal insects out of New Spain and took them to St-Domingue (Haiti), where he attempted to promote their cultivation, but with scant success.[23]

It is less well known that from the mid-1820s, after Mexico had gained independence, cochineal began to be cultivated successfully and on a large scale in nearby Guatemala and in the Canary Islands. Indeed, cochineal became the leading export of both Guatemala and the Canary Islands between the 1820s and the 1850s.[24] Guatemala was Mexico's greatest rival. David McCreery has demonstrated that local cochineal production began expanding in the 1830s but reached its peak only in the 1850s, when production and exports of this product reached almost 2 million pounds a year.[25] Later production in Guatemala declined but rather slowly in the 1860s, and it was not until the 1870s that coffee displaced cochineal as the premier export of that country. In any case, the increase in international cultivation and production of the dyestuff between the 1830s and 1850s caused a steady decline in price per pound. Despite this turn of events, Oaxaca peasants responded by increasing production after 1824, although profitability was falling year by year.

Then at mid-century came advances in the chemical dye industries in Germany, and synthetic dyes came to be substituted for natural ones until cochineal became something of a curiosity. This last chapter in the history of three hundred years of the cochineal trade is a subject on which further research is required, but it is essential to further understanding of the way the second industrial revolution would lead to the demise of the old dye trades and the old luxury textile industries that had been so important in the Atlantic economies.

---

**NOTES**

1   Two works are especially illuminating in this regard: Lovejoy's classic *The Great Chain of Being* and Brusatin's *Storia dei colori*.
2   Munro, "Medieval Scarlet," 39.
3   Hofenk–De Graaff, "Chemistry of Red Dyestuffs," 73.
4   Munro, "Medieval Scarlet," 66.
5   Lee, "American Cochineal in European Commerce," 206.
6   Hofenk–De Graaff, "Chemistry of Red Dyestuffs," 75.
7   Ruíz Martín, *Lettres marchands échangés entre Florence et Medina del Campo*; Lee,

"American Cochineal in European Commerce" and "Cochineal Production and Trade in New Spain."

8   Hoberman, *Mexico's Merchant Elite*, 121–22.

9   Contreras Sánchez, *Capital comercial y colorantes en la Nueva España*, 193–95.

10  Hamnett, *Politics and Trade in Southern Mexico*; Contreras Sánchez, *Capital comercial y colorantes*, and Sánchez Silva, *Indios, comerciantes*, take this view.

11  Miño Grijalva, *La manufactura colonial*, 74, notes that in the colonial era it was also known as *Nopalae coccininelifera*.

12  Munro, "Medieval Scarlet," 63.

13  Hamnett, *Politics and Trade in Southern Mexico*; Sánchez Silva, *Indios, comerciantes y burocracia*.

14  Baskes, *Indians, Merchants, and Markets*.

15  Ibid.

16  Sánchez Silva, *Indios, comerciantes y burocracia*, chap. 3; and Contreras Sánchez, *Capital comercial*, 110–23.

17  Ruíz Martín, *Lettres marchands*.

18  Braudel and Romano, *Navires et marchands à l'entrée de Livourne*.

19  Ruíz Martín, *Lettres marchands*. The mercantile correspondence of Simón Ruiz is among the richest in contemporary Europe. Over 6,000 of his letters are now on deposit at the University of Valladolid.

20  Ibid., 125–28.

21  Buist, *At spes non fracta*, chap. 15, has a fascinating description.

22  Hamnett, *Politics and Trade in Southern Mexico*.

23  Sarabia Viejo, *La grana y el añil*, 35–36.

24  See Heers, "La búsqueda de colorantes," and Rubio Sánchez, *Historia del cultivo de la grana o cochinilla en Guatemala*.

25  McCreery, *Rural Guatemala*.

## BIBLIOGRAPHY

Baskes, Jeremy. *Indians, Merchants, and Markets: A Reinterpretation of the Repartimiento and Spanish-Indian Economic Relations in Colonial Oaxaca, 1750–1821*. Stanford: Stanford University Press, 2000.

Braudel, Fernand, and Ruggiero Romano. *Navires et marchands à l'entrée du port de Livourne, 1547–1611*. Paris, 1951.

Brusatin, Manlio. *Storia dei colori*. Turin: Einaudi, 1983.

Buist, Marten. *At spes non fracta: Hope & Co., 1770–1815: Merchant Bankers and Diplomats at Work*. The Hague: Nijhoff, 1974.

Contreras Sánchez, Alicia. *Capital comercial y colorantes en la Nueva España, segunda mitad del siglo XVIII*. Zamora: Colegio de Michoacán, Universidad Autónoma de Yucatán, 1996.

Hamnett, Brian. *Politics and Trade in Southern Mexico, 1750–1821*. Cambridge: Cambridge University Press, 1971.

Heers, Jacques. "La búsqueda de colorantes." *Historia Mexicana* 11, no. 1 (1961): 1–27.

———. *Gênes au XVᵉ siècle, activité économique et problèmes sociaux.* Paris: S.E.V.P.E.N., 1961.

Hoberman, Louisa. *Mexico's Merchant Elite, 1590–1660: Silver, State, and Society.* Durham: Duke University Press, 1991.

Hofenk-De Graaff, Judith H. "The Chemistry of Red Dyestuffs in Medieval and Early Modern Europe." In N. B. Harte and K. G. Ponting, eds., *Cloth and Clothing in Medieval Europe.* London: Heinemann, 1983.

Lee, Raymond. "American Cochineal in European Commerce, 1526–1625." *Journal of Modern History* 23 (September 1951): 205–24.

———. "Cochineal Production and Trade in New Spain to 1600." *The Americas* 4 (September 1948): 458–63.

Lovejoy, Arthur. *The Great Chain of Being.* Cambridge: Harvard University Press, 1936.

McCreery, David. *Rural Guatemala, 1760–1940.* Stanford: Stanford University Press, 1994.

Miño Grijalva, Manuel. *La manufactura colonial: La constitución técnica del obraje.* Jornadas no. 123. Mexico City: Colegio de México, 1993.

Munro, John. "The Medieval Scarlet and the Economics of Sartorial Splendor." In N. B. Harte and K. G. Ponting, eds., *Cloth and Clothing in Medieval Europe.* London: Heinemann, 1983.

Rubio Sánchez, Manuel. *Historia del cultivo de la grana o cochinilla en Guatemala.* Guatemala City: Tipografía Nacional, 1994.

Ruíz Martín, Felipe. *Lettres marchands échangés entre Florence et Medina del Campo.* Paris: Ecole des Hautes Etudes, 1965.

Sánchez Silva, Carlos. *Indios, comerciantes y burocracia en la Oaxaca poscolonial, 1786–1860.* Oaxaca : Instituto Oaxaqueño de las Culturas, Fondo Estatal para la Cultura y las Artes, Universidad Autónoma Benito Juárez de Oaxaca, 1998.

Sarabia Viejo, María Justina. *La grana y el añil: Técnicas tintóreas en México y América Central.* Seville: Escuela de Estudios Hispano-Americanos de Sevilla, 1994.

# 4

# Colonial Tobacco: Key Commodity of the Spanish Empire, 1500–1800

Laura Nater

BEFORE THE ARRIVAL of the Spaniards, tobacco was known and widely used throughout the Americas. It was consumed by Native Americans in a variety of ways: it was smoked in pipes or rolled up like a cigarette, it was inhaled through the nose in powdered form, it was drunk in infusions, it was used as an ointment for the skin, and the leaves were chewed.[1] For Native Americans tobacco was linked to magic and religion, and this may also explain why tobacco was also widely adopted by African Americans, who found it had ritual applicability. For Europeans, on the other hand, the magical-religious motivation could not be openly adduced; thus, those who adopted tobacco in Europe did so, as Fernando Ortíz has suggested, "for the pleasure of its aroused sensuality and [because it] was recommended by those returning from the Americas."[2] Nevertheless, it was necessary to justify its use according to motives more in keeping with European culture, so medicinal properties were stressed.

In a short time, tobacco became known as a kind of panacea capable of alleviating all kinds of ailments.[3] Toward the close of the sixteenth century tobacco was so widely accepted that it became a negotiable commodity. According to Fernand Braudel, the success of Spanish tobacco dates at least back to 1558, although widespread commercialization took place only from the early seventeenth century in Lisbon, Seville, and especially Amsterdam. In any case, Braudel argued that tobacco would soon conquer the world, and "its success was even greater than that of tea or coffee, which is quite a lot to say for it."[4]

Tobacco was no longer a source only of pleasure but also of wealth. Its value and demand increased constantly, and as a result it came to be treasured by the merchants of the era. At the same time, tobacco soon became an economic resource of interest to governments, since it was soon made subject to taxes and began to produce substantial returns for European states. Ortíz describes the early measures as "fiscal blows of the cruelest type, which at the same time were the most approved of."[5] Despite taxes, the consumption of tobacco increased spectacularly. Braudel noted that the most popular forms were powdered tobacco and smoking tobacco. Powder, preferred in Europe, was obtained by grinding the leaves. During the sixteenth century in Spain, the leaves for making the powder were moistened in orange flower water. But this practice was abandoned in the early seventeenth century, and adulteration was prohibited for the sake of obtaining a product that would highlight tobacco's natural aroma. Therefore, the Spanish powder acquired its factory seal and enjoyed international fame and prestige. Another form of powder was snuff, which spread from France to become a predominant fashion in the eighteenth century. Snuff was thicker than the Spanish powder and was seasoned with a variety of substances. In the Americas, smoking tobacco was preferred, wrapped in either corn husks, paper, or tobacco leaves (cigars).[6]

Tobacco production soon spread worldwide. From the sixteenth century, seeds were introduced in various countries in Europe, Africa, and Asia, but American leaves continued to be preferred, and for that reason it was in the New World that the cultivation of this product increased most significantly. As a result, tobacco leaf from the Spanish and Portuguese colonies was the first to be exported to Europe. Yet as soon as other European states secured possessions in the Americas (from the early seventeenth century), they also promoted tobacco production, especially the English in Virginia and the French in St-Domingue (now Haiti).

Before the end of the sixteenth century, tobacco markets in Europe had already been established by a variety of intermediaries who meshed supply and demand, thereby contributing to tobacco's diffusion. At the same time, as the Spanish historian Guillermo Céspedes del Castillo has noted, specialization produced "a distinction in qualities, consumption preferences, and prices."[7] Rising demand, in turn, led to improvement in packaging techniques that facilitated the transportation of tobacco on mules and preserved its quality, sustaining prices. It was at this time that the benefits of aging were discovered. When practiced appropriately, aging improved tobacco's quality, smoothness, and aroma.

In summary, tobacco was the first agricultural product from the Americas to conquer the Europeans. In less than a century it became one of the foremost commodities in international trade. Eventually it became one of the most important products in the trades of the Spanish monarchy. In this essay I analyze the chain of production and marketing of Cuban tobacco, in which the Spanish imperial state played a decisive role: in short, this is a study of a commodity chain that was largely organized and controlled by a state.

## EUROPEAN DEMAND

The demand for tobacco in Europe in the early seventeenth century determined a rise in production in the colonies of the Americas. The growth in the demand must be understood within the context of profound changes that took place in European consumption patterns in the sixteenth century. The establishment of new transoceanic routes permitted the widespread adoption by Europeans of a series of commodities from the Americas and the Orient which had been unknown or were not yet widely consumed: tobacco, sugar, cacao, coffee, and tea, among others.[8]

Of all the crops native to the Americas, tobacco was the first to win its own international market. And it was the first one to be transformed from a luxury or rarity into a common and even necessary commodity: by the early seventeenth century, its consumption was normal and widespread at many levels of European societies.[9] American tobacco—be it from Spanish, English, Portuguese, or French colonies—was sent to the European metropolises and then redistributed throughout the continent.

However, tobacco production grew so fast that by the 1640s, markets became saturated and prices dropped. Nonetheless, the cheapening of this commodity even further stimulated its consumption: tobacco was increasingly accessible to a wider social spectrum, with the result that demand continued to rise. For example, shipments from British America increased from 150 tons in 1630 to 1,000 tons in 1650 to as much as 10,000 tons by the end of the seventeenth century.[10]

Tobacco from the Spanish-American colonies was sent above all to Seville. The rise of tobacco exports to that city from 15,328 pounds in 1609 to 404,564 pounds in 1613 (202 tons) serves as one early indicator of the increase in European demand. Spanish-American tobacco supplied a growing demand in the Iberian peninsula but also was increasingly trans-shipped from Seville to Marseilles, since French society shared many commercial affairs and tastes with the Spanish. Although trade with France was interrupted during the French-Spanish War of 1635–59, exports of Spanish tobacco to France through indirect trade from Genoa were broadly reported.[11]

By the 1650s the other European powers had also begun to promote the cultivation of tobacco in their own colonies in the hopes of meeting the increasing demand and obtaining commercial benefits. British imports of tobacco were significant when we consider trends in European demand. England had one of the most developed tobacco markets in Europe at the close of the seventeenth century, as well as one of the highest levels of consumption.[12] Moreover, the growth of British tobacco imports remained constant throughout the eighteenth century, indicating a clear and continuous tendency to increase.[13] While the majority of these imports came from Virginia, they also included tobaccos from Spanish and French colonies.[14]

The consistent increase in the European demand for tobacco and the expansion of this crop in the colonies called the attention of the absolutist states to the potential for commercializing tobacco leaves and the possibility of converting this product into a source of tax revenue. In 1625, Charles I of England imposed a tax on the first shipments of this plant from North America. Shortly thereafter the first tobacco monopoly and fiscal enterprise was organized in 1627 in the dukedom of Mantua. France imposed a tobacco tax in 1629, and Spanish and Austrian tobacco monopolies were established in 1636 and 1670, respectively. Throughout the seventeenth century, the policy of taxing tobacco for the benefit of the royal treasuries became a preferential source of income for these states.[15]

## THE CARIBBEAN AS SCENE OF BATTLE

At the same time as tobacco consumption, production, and trade were increasing in the seventeenth century, commercial competition intensified among the European powers. The Caribbean became a major scene of this competition and one of the privileged zones for the production of tobacco and also, inevitably, for its consumption.

The Caribbean became filled with French, British, and Dutch privateers as well as pirate ships that preyed on Spanish vessels transporting precious metals to Europe. But in the early decades of the seventeenth century, the intruders launched a new strategy. The Dutch, and then the English and the French, established permanent settlements on the islands that had not been effectively colonized by the Spaniards. While piracy continued, the merchants of Jamaica, St-Domingue, Curaçao, and other islands fostered a profitable interloper trade with the Spanish colonies, generating a flourishing contraband trade in the entire region. Thus they deflected the riches of the Americas to other European powers and undermined Spanish dominance based on trade monopolies.[16]

The situation became more complicated for Spain when these new colonies in the hands of rival powers underwent what is known as the sugar revolution from the late seventeenth century on. The non-Spanish islands of the Caribbean became huge producers of sugar, a commodity that was in great demand in Europe and thus fed an intense transatlantic trade, providing impressive profits for everyone who cultivated sugarcane or engaged in the slave trade or the sugar trade itself. The triangular traffic, so called because of the three axes on which it was sustained (the Caribbean, Africa, and Europe), furnished slaves to the nascent sugarcane plantations, supplied the European sugar market, and consequently stimulated European exports to the Americas.[17]

The Caribbean thus became one of the most dynamic regions in international trade, and consequently rivalries among the leading European powers active there frequently degenerated into naval wars during the second half of the seventeenth century and throughout the eighteenth century. Despite the fact that Spain maintained important colonies in the Caribbean and the silver-rich viceroyalties of Peru and New Spain, it was hard pressed to defend its empire, particularly between 1650 and 1750. Its commercial system of fleets and galleons declined, as can be seen from the fact that between 1669 and 1700, the fleet sailed on only fourteen occasions and the galleons only eight times.[18] Thus Spain's colonies, particularly the poorest ones in the Caribbean, were not adequately supplied with the goods necessary to sustain their populations, nor did they have a sure means of selling their products. As a result, contraband was practically their only alternative.

Smuggling enabled the Spanish colonies of the Caribbean to acquire European manufactured goods, wheat, and slaves. The colonies often paid for these purchases with the silver they received from *situados* (shipments of official monies from one colony to another) arriving from New Spain or Peru. In most cases, they did so with the approval of local officials, who even came to participate in this illegal trade. Colonies that engaged in contraband trade also paid for their purchases in kind. Tobacco, cacao, salt, ginger, and a variety of dyes and precious woods were easily shipped out to Europe in exchange for manufactured goods, while locally produced timber, leather, and meat served to meet the needs of colonies that produced only sugarcane.

Even though the Spaniards had not demonstrated much interest in stimulating colonial agro-industries, this attitude began to change with the increase in the demand for tobacco and later of cacao in the Old World and the large profits to be made from selling them. Initially, however, the Spanish monarchy did not officially promote these crops. In the case of tobacco, for example, it preferred to fight contraband, prohibiting the planting of tobacco for a period of ten years in Santo Domingo, Cuba, Margarita, Puerto Rico, Cumaná, and New Andalucía, according to a royal decree issued in 1606.[19] Thus, instead of attempting to control this trade effectively, royal functionaries preferred to eliminate production in order to avoid allowing their enemies to trade in this commodity. Nevertheless, contraband trade in tobacco continued to increase not only in the Americas but even in the Iberian Peninsula.[20]

But the Spanish monarchy faced a problem even more serious than contraband. The most important and valuable export commodities of Spanish America were precious metals. They served to pay the crown's foreign debts and also to cover the commercial deficits of the metropolis. This was the result of the relative backwardness of Spanish industry vis-à-vis the development of other European powers. Spain's production was not sufficient to supply its domestic needs and those of the colonies. As a result, there was a continuous flight of gold and silver that could not be recuperated because Spain lacked enough additional commodities to offer on the international market. Tobacco was an obvious choice.

## SUGAR VS. TOBACCO

In the seventeenth century, the two tropical products with the greatest demand in Europe were tobacco and sugar. All the powers that established colonies in the Americas experimented with both. The first settlers of the British and French colonies in the Caribbean cultivated tobacco on small plots. In fact, Fernando Ortiz felt that tobacco was "the main inspiration for initial colonization in America during the early decades of the seventeenth century by nations that were enemies of Spain."[21]

In 1614, James I of Great Britain had established taxes on foreign tobacco in order to favor tobacco from his own colonies. In response, Philip III of Spain eliminated his previous prohibition of planting tobacco in the Caribbean region and imposed capital punishment for smugglers. With this move he hoped to force the English to go to Seville and pay high prices for the most popular tobacco of the era.[22] On the other hand, a pamphlet published in 1615 proposed that tobacco be cultivated in England to avoid adding to the profits of the import trade, "almost entirely in the hands of the Spanish."[23]

The new colonies in the Caribbean and in North America, especially Virginia, began to produce tobacco, and in 1638 overproduction led to a drop in prices. But the abundance of supply was not the only factor to have a bearing on tobacco prices. These prices also depended on the quality of the product and on the care taken in preparing and packing it. The tobacco most affected by this overproduction crisis was from the non-Spanish West Indies, which never achieved acceptable levels of quality for the European market. One late-seventeenth-century observer said that the non-Spanish islands' tobacco arrived in Europe "dry, with no aroma, rusted, stuck together, eaten by worms, grainy, and almost totally spoiled."[24] Much of this product was chewing tobacco, inappropriate for smoking or for use as tobacco powder, the types most in demand in seventeenth- and eighteenth-century Europe.

As a result of this crisis, in 1639 tobacco imports to London fell dramatically, with the exception of Spanish tobacco imports, which continued to rise. Thus the Spanish product did not suffer the consequences of the crisis that took place the previous year to the same extent as tobacco of other origins. On the contrary, it may even have benefited from this situation.

The drop in tobacco sales and prices partly explains the shift from tobacco to sugar in the mid-seventeenth century in the non-Spanish West Indies. But it was not the only factor. We cannot understand the sugar revolution without considering the enormous capital investment in the product, especially from Holland. Amsterdam traders were prepared to help the colonists of any nationality with capital and technical know-how to establish sugar plantations, to grant them long-term credits for acquiring slaves, and even to buy their harvests. With each new sugar establishment in the West Indies, Dutch shippers profited. So it is no surprise that the Dutch encouraged and protected the nascent colonies of France and Great Britain.[25] In a short time, these two metropolises would consider the Dutch their rivals, but during the first half of the seventeenth century it was more important to construct a common mercantile and naval front against Spain.

While its rivals in the Caribbean abandoned poor-quality tobacco with decreasing prices, Spain decided to stimulate production of high-quality tobacco. It is true that the Spanish monarchy had been promoting sugarcane in its Caribbean colonies since the beginning of colonization, but before the close of the sixteenth century the stagnation of the sugar industry in the Spanish West Indies (already insignificant in comparison with Brazil's production) was quite evident.[26] These initial Spanish experiments in sugar promotion had actually been carried out mainly to ensure that the islands would have some means of subsistence, and not with the intention of constructing a major source of revenue. For that purpose, royal functionaries (as well as most Seville merchants) felt that the mines of Mexico and Peru would suffice. Yet as things started to change in the first half of the seventeenth century and Spain lost territories in the Greater Antilles (Jamaica and half of Hispaniola), other considerations became foremost.

The Dutch, followed by the English and the French, demonstrated that trade in tropical products could bring spectacular profits. The weakness of the Spanish economy was becoming obvious.[27] However, as the historian Jan De Vries has observed, Spain was not a society "ignorant of what was happening." A broad school of economic reformers wrote enormous volumes of tracts defending new measures, including proposals for reviving the industry by prohibiting exports of raw materials and imports of manufactured goods.[28]

But foreigners had assigned a new and vital importance to the Caribbean region by turning it into a fundamental space for international trade, and Spain could not close its eyes to this fact. It had to regain ground in the Caribbean and in Atlantic trade. Attempting to do so by revitalizing sugarcane production was not feasible: foreign sugar had attained prices that were very hard to compete with. In a document written in 1701, traders from the merchant guild in Seville affirmed that Cuban sugar had been totally displaced from the peninsular market because it was impossible to match the prices offered by foreigners. While an arroba (about 25 pounds) of Cuban sugar was sold in Spain for over 4 pesos, Portuguese sugar cost barely 14 *reales*.[29] The same complaint had been expressed by the Cubans in a town council meeting in 1690, in which they alleged that sugar from the island was not being exported because sugar from "Brazil, Jamaica, 'land usurped from Santo Domingo,' Barbados, and other places in the Americas invaded the peninsular market."[30]

## CUBAN TOBACCO AS A FACTORY TRADEMARK

Nevertheless, Spain had a product with a recognized international trademark: Cuban tobacco.[31] Tobacco consumers had already realized that Cuban tobacco was superior to any other. Its only competitor of any importance was Virginian tobacco, but even this tobacco was unable to match Cuba's. According to a witness of that period, "throughout the entire seventeenth century, Cuban tobacco gave evidence of being far superior to that of Virginia and English smokers were happy to pay the additional price."[32] The fame of Cuban tobacco "had ended up eclipsing that of its rivals, to such an extent that its price doubled and even tripled on foreign markets as compared to the price set on tobacco from other places."[33] Cuban tobacco had a rich taste and aroma and excellent combustibility, so its fame spread quickly. The classical Spanish theater alludes specifically to the Cuban product.[34] Contemporaries, then, were not talking about just tobacco as a product but about a particular kind of tobacco—Cuban, which was not affected by foreign competition to the same degree as production from other lands, and which enjoyed constant, consistent demand that guaranteed good prices because European consumers recognized it as a gourmet product. Ramón de la Sagra, an early-nineteenth-century expert on agriculture and economics, had a clear vision of the privileged status of Cuban tobacco, which he considered the island's crop par excellence. In his words: "I believe that tobacco is the exclusive product of the island of Cuba, and its cultivation should be extended and made widespread. Fortunately, it need not fear from foreign competition nor need it fear a limit imposed on its production as a result of consumption."[35]

In the early nineteenth century, when the advisability of dismantling the Havana factory was being discussed, the Spanish Contaduría (accounting office) acknowledged that the prestige of Cuban tobacco had influenced the crown's policies: "Everyone knows that the tobacco from the island of Cuba, due to its outstanding quality and exquisite taste in all of its classes, has always been considered a *privileged product, of exclusive preference in European markets*. Cognizant of its favorable circumstances, the Government decided at the beginning of the past [eighteenth] century to establish a very high tax on consumption in the Peninsula and on foreign trade."[36]

For the famous French finance minister Jean-Baptiste Colbert, the promotion of tobacco was a logical option for Spain. The French minister, who worked so zealously to consolidate his country's economy, stated: "If I had the tobaccos and wool of Spain, then France would be happy."[37]

In short, Spanish functionaries and entrepreneurs decided not to invest much capital in sugar, especially in view of the fact that their rivals had achieved a high level of productivity and offered prices with which they could hardly compete. But they had the Cuban tobacco, which enjoyed special prestige and acceptance among the Europeans.[38] England and France competed on the sugar market and were alternately preeminent. Spain chose to take advantage of the exclusive nature of Cuban tobacco to join in the fight for Atlantic trade, astutely avoiding competition in the realm of sugar, in which it was at a distinct disadvantage by the mid–seventeenth century.

### THE ROLE OF THE IBERIAN PENINSULA:
### CONTROL OF PRODUCTION AND COMMERCIALIZATION

In order to retain the benefits of international trade which were provided by the superior quality of Cuban tobacco, it was indispensable to take certain measures. In the first place, it was necessary to preserve the product's privileged position in the market, so its quality had to be maintained. The crown pursued a systematic policy of persecuting merchants who mixed Cuban tobacco with cheaper leaves of inferior quality to get higher profits, as well as those who adulterated tobacco with various types of substances, including earth, so as to increase its weight and consequently its selling price. In the second place, the crown adopted strategies to control distribution on the European market so that the state could ensure for itself the administration of profits: for this end it began to put into practice rigorous measures to combat smuggling, especially in the tobacco trade.

The royal ministers were aware of the difficulties and also of the importance that tobacco was gaining on the international market. That has been shown by an official recommendation of the Council of the Indies in 1682, summarized by Guillermo Céspedes del Castillo. At the close of the sixteenth century, according to this document, the route between Havana as export center and Seville as distribution center had been established—the first transatlantic route capable of supplying tobacco to all of Europe if free navigation had been permitted and had cultivation in the Caribbean been promoted with incentives and protection. But that course went against the policy of commercial exclusivity, among other things.[39]

It was necessary to find a solution that would harmonize new interests with old policies. The strategy to be followed was to concentrate on the Peninsula, especially on Seville, where an attempt was made to manage this nascent trade and to combat fraud and contraband. That policy was launched in 1684, with an instruction for regulating the tobacco trade. Yet the infrastructure that would allow for implementation of the policy had already been developed before then.

From the early seventeenth century, the increase in consumption and consequently in demand stimulated the establishment of tobacco factories in Spain which produced cigarettes as well as powdered tobacco, all made with imported Cuban leaf. Of these factories, the one in Seville became the most important because of both the volume of its production and the fame of its products. This factory began to function in 1620 as a private enterprise, but the considerable profits the tobacco industry reaped from early on suggested the advisability of establishing a state monopoly over its product.[40]

In 1636, the state monopoly of Castille and Aragon was established, essentially to promote and control sales. The tobacco factory in Seville remained the only production center for the various tasks involved in the manufacture of cigarettes and powder.[41] These measures may be interpreted as a reaction to the initial boom of the tobacco trade. But they were also a response to the growing financial burdens caused by the European wars unleashed in 1618. Spain needed new fiscal revenues to pay the large debts incurred by its armies. Since tobacco recently had become well established and disseminated throughout wide sectors of society, the state had confidence in its revenue potential.[42] Hence the government leased the administration of the tobacco monopoly to private parties in exchange for increasingly large sums of money. The leased properties included the state-owned factory in Seville and the regional sales monopolies (estancos) throughout the Iberian Peninsula. That mechanism was not modified until the 1680s.[43]

In 1684, the Spanish government suspended the leasing of the estancos to private parties and entrusted their administration to the factory in Seville, which was assigned to be directly under the Royal Treasury and became the center and seat for the state-run tobacco administration. The factory in Seville was granted monopoly production and all the other factories in the peninsula were successively closed down. This was a means to cut back on fraud, since the products of the other factories existing at that time were of poor quality and could be imitated. Since the high-quality tobacco produced in Seville was of such "exquisite fineness" that it "had no competitors," it was very difficult to imitate.[44]

José Manuel Rodríguez Gordillo, a specialist in the history of tobacco in Spain, aptly analyzed the *instrucción* issued on May 3, 1684, which established the estanco. Since it established firm control over all branches of the tobacco monopoly, including norms for prices, qualities, and all other aspects of the trade, and set forth an initial project for a colonial agreement, he concluded that this text was of a markedly mercantilist nature.[45]

The 1684 instrucción left no doubt about the crown's intention to protect Caribbean production in general and Cuban production in particular. Its first article stipulated that the factory in Seville could use only tobacco imported from Havana and Trinidad de la Habana, Trinidad de la Guayra, Puerto Rico, and Santo Domingo. The second article prohibited the sale of any tobacco other than those previously mentioned and stipulated that any tobacco "of any other quality, both native and foreign," would be removed from the kingdom within four months.[46] Both the first and second articles made an exception for "Brazilian leaves," which were normally used for chewing tobacco, and therefore did not compete directly with Cuban tobacco, which was consumed in the form of cigarettes and powder. It is significant that the first two articles specified the colonial origin of tobacco to be used in the monopolistic complex then being inaugurated. These provisions make it clear that regulations applied in the metropolis were closely related to the circumstances of production and commercialization in the colonies, and that such a link was the axis around which the new tobacco policy was being organized.

The only tobacco to be used was Caribbean tobacco, and any other was completely excluded.[47] In order to meet these expectations, Article 5 ordered that the governors of said colonies "encourage and promote" tobacco planting.[48] Moreover, it was expressly forbidden to cultivate this crop in Spain itself.

When the Bourbon dynasty assumed the Spanish throne after the War of the Spanish Succession (1702–13), the idea of consolidating the tobacco monopoly was repeatedly mentioned in the state's economic projects with the ostensible aim of attaining a substantial increase in the Royal Treasury's income. The economic ideology of the period, in which to-bacco revenues already were heartily embraced, was reinforced by the fact that in the early eighteenth century, fiscal income from tobacco was already quite considerable. In 1702 the tobacco monopoly brought in 14.3 percent of the net income earned by the crown of Castile, and in 1713, 24.9 percent, more than any other individual item. In 1714 it contributed more than a third of tax income.[49]

The proven fiscal benefits of the tobacco tax made it a frequently men-tioned expedient in contemporary treatises on economic policy in the first half of the eighteenth century. The author who best documents the advan-tages and potential of this revenue source was Gerónimo de Ustáriz, in his *Teoría y práctica de comercio marina*, written in 1724 and widely known after its publication in 1742. According to Ustáriz, tobacco produced "the richest revenue of the Royal Treasury," and he added that "with that tax alone . . . well managed in Havana and in Spain, His Majesty could maintain more Forces of Land and Sea than other Kings and Queens of Europe with all their Patrimony."[50]

Aside from the fact that tobacco provided one of the richest sources of fiscal resources of the period, many people were convinced that the to-bacco trade had a great potential for increase. To that end, according to Ustáriz, it was necessary to improve its administration, create new facto-ries, renovate and obtain the greatest possible profit from the factory already in operation in Seville, and, above all, guarantee the supply of this product, both for Spanish consumption and for export to the rest of Europe. In this regard, the tobacco industry on the island of Cuba was to receive special attention, for it was called upon to supply almost the entirety of tobacco leaf and powder for the peninsular market as well as for reexport from Spain to the rest of Europe. Lastly, the tobacco tax would make it possible to cut back the tax burdens on other products that directly affected the basic needs of the crown's subjects. That would lead to an increase in consumption, which in turn would stimulate Spain's productive sectors and thus the economy in general.[51]

In order to put such economic theory into practice, the Spanish state concentrated on two flanks: Havana and Seville. In the royal stipulations, these two places almost always received differential treatment; that is, the measures that were dictated for one of them were not necessarily applicable to the other. But they were never considered as being detached from one another, for the success of tobacco policies lay precisely in the fact that the two complemented each other in pursuit of a common objective: the greatest possible utilization of tobacco as a fiscal resource for the benefit of the crown. It is worth repeating that Cuba operated as a center that exported the raw material (tobacco leaf) essential to the operation of Seville as a center for manufacturing, distribution, and reexport. The differences in the treatment received by each center responded to those different roles. In Cuba, measures were aimed at guaranteeing the provision of tobacco in great quantities to meet the needs of the factories in Seville. In Seville the goal was to increase and perfect factory production and to market the product.[52]

In 1731 the "universal administration" of the tobacco monopoly was firmly established in the metropolis. From that moment on, the monarchy wielded effective control over all aspects of the tobacco business in Spain. A few years later, the imperial instructions and rules for the better administration of the tobacco tax (*Instrucciones y reglas universales para el mejor gobierno de la Renta del Tabaco*) of 1740 confirmed this situation. These rules imposed legal norms that remained in force until the nineteenth century.[53] They summed up much of the historical experience acquired on the administration and sale of tobacco, provided sage advice on the business, and ordered the most appropriate and effective methods for obtaining good results, including methods of avoiding the most frequent frauds.[54] This document, which was reprinted in 1767 and 1788, served as a model for the state tobacco administrations throughout the Spanish Empire, which were successively established in practically all the Spanish-American colonies as well as the Philippines during the remaining decades of the eighteenth century.

The Bourbon administration also paid a great deal of attention to the infrastructure of the factories in Seville, which were subject to continuous expansion and remodeling. Until at least 1758, these material reforms were aimed at enlarging the factories in Seville and improving their technology, in order to ensure that production was in keeping with the growing demand.[55]

In 1760, one year after Charles III assumed the Spanish throne, the state-run Havana tobacco factory was created. Its main mission was to buy all the tobacco harvested on the island. It was hoped that this would be a way of fighting against contraband and guaranteeing that the factories in Seville would always be well supplied.[56] With the establishment of this factory, a new monopoly was inaugurated in Cuba. The factory began to function formally on March 1, 1761. A little more than a year later, in August 1762, the English took over the island in the midst of the incidents of the Seven-Year War. As a result, the tobacco administration was interrupted before all the measures could be put into practice and tested.

The Paris Treaty, signed on February 10, 1763, ended that war and returned Cuba to Spain. Immediately thereafter, the regulations of the factory were reactivated, and in the following years it flourished and consolidated. The consistent growth of its operations during its first ten years created a climate of optimism and nurtured the conviction that finally Spain had come across the tool to guarantee proper functioning of this trade throughout the empire.

The establishment of the state tobacco administrations (estancos) in Spain (1740) and Cuba (1760) led to the growth of a complex system of monopolies throughout the empire which were intended to achieve extensive control of the tobacco trade and to achieve optimal functioning of the whole. Particular attention should be paid to the tobacco monopoly established in the viceroyalty of New Spain (Mexico). With its inauguration in 1765, the three most important establishments of the tobacco monopoly of the eighteenth-century Spanish Empire (Spain, Cuba, and New Spain) were put in place. (See Figure 1.) From then on, other monopolies were created, each with very specific objectives, but always in line with the initial logic. In Lima, where a tobacco monopoly had been set up in the first half of that century to overcome a fiscal crisis, the institution was reorganized in the light of experiences in New Spain. Monopolies were also established in Chile and Buenos Aires as mechanisms for increasing tax revenues.[57] In other cases, the new establishments were designed to be part of a system at the service of political-strategic interests. In that sense, the best example was Louisiana, a frontier territory acquired by Spain in 1763, where the monopoly helped to provide the

1. The Spanish tobacco monopoly as an imperial company

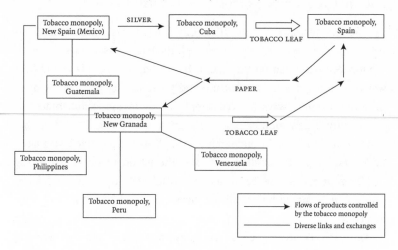

inhabitants with an important economic activity under the assumption that population is the best defense of a colonial territory.

## CRISIS OF THE TOBACCO MONOPOLIES IN THE SPANISH EMPIRE AT THE CLOSE OF THE EIGHTEENTH CENTURY

Despite numerous obstacles, the new projects for fiscal monopolies gained strength on both sides of the Atlantic, as can be observed by the continuous growth in purchases by the Havana factory and in tobacco remittances to Spain after 1760. The War of American Independence (1776–83) changed this panorama by its numerous consequences for Cuba in general and for the tobacco trade in particular. The effects of this war began to be felt even before Spain entered the conflict. In 1774, the thirteen colonies closed their ports to products from the British colonies in the Caribbean, and a year later prohibited exports to those colonies.[58] As a result, Spanish and French possessions found a good trading opportunity by filling the gap, both in North America and in the West Indies, either through permits granted by the metropolises or by smuggling. The tobacco entering the Havana factory through purchases dropped immediately, as did remittances to Spain. In 1779 Spain declared itself at war with Britain and two years later, in 1781 and 1782, the Havana factory reported the lowest levels in its history of tobacco sent to the metropolis. (See Figure 2.) Moreover, during the war a great number of soldiers arrived in Cuba from both Mexico and Spain, since Havana was the center

## 2. Pounds of tobacco leaf and snuff sent from Cuba to Spain, 1761–1812

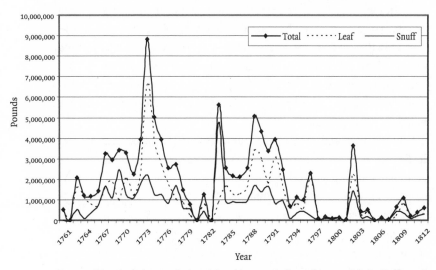

Source: "Estado de la entrada anual de tabacos en la factoría general de La Habana tanto en rama como en polvo, igualmente que sus salidas para la Isla, Europa y América desde su establecimiento en el año de 1761 hasta la fecha," in Archive of the Indies (Seville), Audiencia of Santo Domingo, file 2023.

of operations for the Spanish forces operating in the Caribbean, and from there they undertook expeditions to take control of Florida from the British. As a result, the demand for staple foods to sustain the troops increased.[59] That encouraged some farmers to abandon tobacco and devote themselves to other crops.

In the meantime, tobacco production in Britain's North American colonies diminished noticeably. The British market, which had essentially been supplied by that production, had to confront the scarcity of this product, and that further encouraged the smuggling of Cuban tobacco. So the war led to a growth in Britain's demand for Cuban tobacco in contraband trade, not only during the conflict but also in the long term. Nonetheless, this trend was counterbalanced by another new development. After the war, Spain increasingly authorized the Cubans to trade with neutral powers. This measure, however, opened up the North American market to Cuban sugar and created commercial ties which the return to peace could not reverse. Sugar production required the expansion of the land surface devoted to sugarcane cultivation, displacing tobacco from many of its traditional plots and competing for labor.

As the sugar trade became increasingly attractive, the financial mechanisms on which the Cuban tobacco monopoly depended began to fall apart. In the decades before 1778, the silver sent from Mexico to Havana for tobacco consignments had always arrived, despite occasional delays. After 1783 they seldom did. In the twenty-seven years from the end of the war in 1784 until 1811, the consigned sums were received in only nine years. This problem took on alarming proportions when for two consecutive years, 1788 and 1789, the Havana factory did not receive any monetary subsidy from New Spain.[60]

Between 1790 and 1793, the amounts of Mexican silver sent to assist the factory in its tobacco purchases rose. But the war with France (1793–95) once again interrupted silver remittances for the purchase of tobacco leaves. And there were other problems. The Haitian Revolution of 1791 eliminated sugar production in that French colony, which up until then had supplied 50 percent of the free world market. The gap left by Haiti was of great benefit to sugar producers in Cuba, who by the following year came to hold third place among the sugar producers of the world.

With the onset of the sugar boom, the Cuban economy underwent a rapid change. According to Manuel Moreno Fraginals, tobacco farmers were the first to feel the impact. The increase in sugar production increased the need for new land to fulfill four basic requirements: large extensions of land on which to plant the sugarcane, forests to supply firewood, grazing grounds for cattle used to work at the local sugar mills (trapiches) and to haul wagons, and fields for storage and buildings for slaves. The tobacco plots had many attractions: they were fertile and had natural irrigation; they conserved forests; they were well situated, with roads that linked them to shipping ports; and they were located in the only populated zones, which guaranteed a supply of wage laborers for work at the sugar mills. As a result, many of these old tobacco fields were cleared away to plant sugarcane and set up sugar mills.[61]

The factor that led to the definitive deterioration of the Havana tobacco factory operations, however, was the chronic lack of revenue that it suffered. So long as the Mexican silver remittances arrived in full, the factory functioned well and was very productive. But when this revenue became scarce, this great manufacturing establishment entered into a decline from which it never managed to recover. The Havana tobacco factory was officially closed in 1817. Yet in practice it had ceased to be operative as early as 1810. The Cuban tobacco industry failed to recover acceptable production levels until the 1840s. In Spain, on the other hand, the state

ime. In short, it may be

h the Bourbon State had

Empire during the eigh-

erica during the wars of

ated by Susan Beth Kapilian

by Carlos Marichal.

n in the pre-Hispanic world:

paste made of the leaves; c)

d) in ground powders; and

*l tabaco y el azúcar*, 115. Each

ich the Europeans ascribed

ng it. The same thing oc-

lintz provides an excellent

18–20.

20.

86–96.

olonies," 157–61.

, tobacco consumption in

per year. France, with the

that figure until the mid–

ritain fluctuated between

1738 to 1777 they were

ent of all British tobacco

percent; and in 1641–42,

inal," 2–3. By the 1610s,

American colonies; this

this product: Escoho-

bbean can be found in

el Caribe.

17   There is a large and rich bibliography on the sugar revolution and triangular trade. Two classics are Knight, "Origins of Wealth and the Sugar Revolution in Cuba," and Williams, *Capitalismo y esclavitud*.

18   Fisher, *Relaciones económicas entre España y América hasta la independencia*, 98. By an order issued in 1564, the Spanish crown stipulated that trade with the Americas would be conducted on convoys guarded by warships, whose port of entry and departure was exclusively Seville. There were two such convoys: one going to Veracruz, with stops at some ports in the West Indies, which was called "the fleet," and one transporting shipments of silver and gold from Lima via Portobelo and Cartagena, which was known as "the galleons."

19   Pérez Vidal, *España en la historia del tabaco*, 184. The *real cédula* (royal decree) of 1606 stated that "it has come to be understood that to different parts and ports of these Windward Islands there ordinarily come many ships of Dutch, English, and French rebels to get tobacco. . . . Without it being possible for my governors to remedy this situation, and aside from the damage done, they receive rights that belong to me. . . . [Therefore] it has seemed appropriate to prohibit the planting of tobacco on said islands for a period of ten years, so that with this measure the natives will attempt to work mines and other profitable activities that are more useful and beneficial for them and for my royal revenues and services." The original text is in Ortiz, *Contrapunteo cubano*, 389–90.

20   Details on tobacco contraband in Cuba during the seventeenth century are given in Rivero Muñiz, *Tabaco, su historia en Cuba*, 17–25. For the case of Spain, see Pérez Vidal, *España en la historia del tabaco*, 347–63.

21   Ortiz, *Contrapunteo cubano*, 395.

22   The new Spanish ordinance, contained in the real cédula issued on October 20, 1614, stated: "Notwithstanding the former prohibition brought about by trade with foreign enemies of our royal crown: It is our will that the residents of the Windward Islands, Terra Firma, and other parts where tobacco is planted and harvested do not lose the advantages they have in this regard, and that our royal treasury reap the benefits that come from its trade. And it is our intention to allow them to cultivate it freely, so that all the tobacco that is not consumed will be taken from each island or province to the city of Seville; and those who traded in it in other regions will suffer capital punishment and loss of their goods, such as those who work for our enemies, in which case of course we would condemn them. . . . And we send the governors to execute them without fail, warning them that the chapter of residency will be applied to them, with penalty of perpetual privation of their office, were they to do the contrary." Original text in Ortiz, *Contrapunteo cubano*, 391.

23   Cited in ibid., 435.

24   Cited in Price, *France and the Chesapeake*, 1:95.

25   Parry and Sherlock, *Historia de las Antillas*, 58, 65, 72.

26   For an explanation of that stagnation, see Mintz, *Dulzura y poder*, 66.

27   For many historians, Spain experienced a severe crisis in the seventeenth century. See Hamilton, *War and Prices in Spain*, and Elliot, "La decadencia española." In recent years, such positions have been the subject of debate. While

the analyses vary in assessment of the magnitude and consequences of this problem, it is agreed that it was a period of weakness. Ruggiero Romano, *Coyunturas opuestas*, analyzed the debate and proposed new interpretations of the European crisis and its relationship with Spanish America. David Ringrose has done a good critique of the historiography of Spain in *España, 1700–1900*.

28  De Vries, *La economía de Europa*, 40.

29  García Fuentes, *El comercio español con América*, 344–45.

30  Cited in Rivero Muñiz, *Tabaco, su historia en Cuba*, 65.

31  Fernando Ortiz has a chapter about Cuban tobacco's world prestige, titled "Del 'tabaco habano,' que es el mejor del mundo, y del 'sello de garantía' de su legitimidad" (On "Havana tobacco," which is the best in the world, and on the "seal of guarantee" of its authenticity) in *Contrapunteo cubano*, 431–38.

32  Cited in Friedlander, *Historia económica de Cuba*, 35.

33  Rivero Muñiz, *Las tres sediciones de los vegueros en el siglo XVIII*, 9.

34  Rivero Muñiz, *Tabaco, su historia en Cuba*, 14.

35  Sagra, *Historia económico-política y estadística de la isla de Cuba*, 118. Ramón de la Sagra was director of the Botanical Garden of Havana from 1822 to 1836, was full professor of natural sciences, and held a chair in agricultural botany: Puig-Samper, "Las primeras instituciones científicas en Cuba," 32.

36  "Informe sobre la abolición de la factoría de tabacos de la Habana" (Report on the abolition of the Havana tobacco factory), April 24, 1816, in AGI, Audiencia de Santo Domingo, leg. 2001.

37  Cited in "Estudio para la formación de Instrucciones para el arreglo de la Renta del Tabaco en Perú, 1773" (Study for the formation of Instructions for organizing the Tobacco Fiscal Branch in Peru, 1773), in AGNM, Rama de Tabaco, vol. 3, n.p.

38  Fernando Ortiz, severely criticizing the monopoly that the metropolis established in Cuba in the eighteenth century, stated that advantage was taken of the "*natural privilege*" of Cuban tobacco to attain "los más abusivos y absurdos privilegios fiscales y mercantiles" (the most abusive and absurd fiscal and mercantile privileges) even as early as the sixteenth century: *Contrapunteo cubano*, 431.

39  Céspedes del Castillo, *El tabaco en Nueva España*, 41–42.

40  Pérez Vidal, *España en la historia del tabaco*, 184, 227.

41  Rodríguez Gordillo, "La Real Fábrica de Tabacos," 155.

42  Rodríguez Gordillo, "El fraude en el estanco del tabaco," 63.

43  Rodríguez Gordillo, "Sobre la industria sevillana del tabaco a fines del siglo XVII," 536.

44  Pérez Vidal, *España en la historia del tabaco*, 75, 228–29.

45  Rodríguez Gordillo, "Sobre la industria sevillana del tabaco," 538.

46  The articles are partially transcribed in ibid., 540.

47  In practice, the production of tobacco did not increase as much in Santo Domingo and Puerto Rico as in Cuba, nor did it receive the same support by the state and the consumers there.

48  Rodríguez Gordillo, "Sobre la industria sevillana del tabaco," 541.

49  For data on the tax income of the crown of Castile in 1702 and 1713, see Artola,

La hacienda del antiguo régimen, 222; for data on 1714, see Ustáriz, Teoría y práctica de comercio y de marina, 151–53.

50  Ustáriz, Teoría y práctica, 366.

51  Ibid., 368.

52  Rodríguez Gordillo, "Aspectos tabaqueros en el Cádiz ilustrado," 64.

53  Ibid.

54  Pérez Vidal, España en la historia del tabaco, 337.

55  Rodríguez Gordillo, "La Real Fábrica de Tabacos" and "Aspectos tabaqueros."

56  "Ynstrucción que se forma de orden de Su Majestad para el extablecimiento de la Factoría del Tavaco en la Havana . . ." (Instruction that is established by order of His Majesty for the establishment of the Havana Tobacco Factory), AGI, Audiencia de Santo Domingo, leg. 2002.

57  On tax revenues in Peru, see Céspedes del Castillo, El tabaco en Nueva España. On the Chilean case, see Stapff, "La Renta del Tabaco."

58  Von Grafenstein Gareis, Nueva España en el circuncaribe, 127.

59  Ibid., 132.

60  "Estado que manifiesta los caudales ingresados en la tesorería de la Factoría de la Habana . . ." (Status of revenue deposited in the Havana Factory treasury), AGI, Audiencia de Santo Domingo, leg. 2023.

61  Moreno Fraginals, El ingenio, 52–55.

---

## BIBLIOGRAPHY

*Archival Sources*

AGN Archivo General de Indias (Seville)

AGNM Archivo General de la Nación (Mexico)

*Published Works*

Acuña Ortega, Víctor Hugo. "Historia económica del tabaco en Costa Rica: Época colonial." *Anuario de Estudios Centroamericanos* 4 (1979): 279–392.

Arias Divito, Juan Carlos. "Dificultades para establecer la Renta de Tabaco en Paraguay." *Anuario de Estudios Americanos* 33 (1975): 1–17.

Artola, Miguel. *La hacienda del antiguo régimen*. Madrid: Alianza/Banco de España, 1982.

Bernal, Antonio Miguel. *La financiación de la Carrera de Indias (1492–1824): Dinero y crédito en el comercio colonial español con América*. Seville: Fundación El Monte, 1992.

Bitar Letayf, Marcelo. *Los economistas españoles del siglo XVIII y sus ideas sobre el comercio con las Indias*. Mexico City: Instituto Mexicano de Comercio Exterior, 1975.

Braudel, Fernand. *Civilización material, economía y capitalismo, siglos XV–XVIII*. Mexico City: Alianza, 1984.

Céspedes del Castillo, Guillermo. *El tabaco en Nueva España*. Madrid: Real Academia de Historia, 1992.

Deans-Smith, Susan. *Bureaucrats, Planters, and Workers: The Making of the Tobacco Monopoly in Bourbon Mexico*. Austin: University of Texas Press, 1992.

De Vries, Jan. *La economía de Europa en un período de crisis, 1600–1750.* Trans. Fernando Wulff Alonso and Celia Pérez Castelló. Madrid: Cátedra, 1992.

Elliot, J. H. "La decadencia española." In Trevor Aston, ed., *Crisis en Europa, 1560–1660*, trans. Manuel Rodríguez Alonso. Madrid: Alianza, 1983.

Escohotado, Antonio. *Historia de las drogas.* Vol. 1. Madrid: Alianza, 1996.

Fisher, John R. *Relaciones económicas entre España y América hasta la independencia.* Trans. Jesús Pardo de Santayana. Madrid: Mapfre, 1992.

Friedlaender, H. E. *Historia económica de Cuba.* Havana, 1944.

García Fuentes, Lutgardo. *El comercio español con América, 1650–1700.* Seville: Excelentísima Diputación Provincial de Sevilla/Escuela de Estudios Hispanoamericanos, 1980.

González Enciso, Agustín. *Aspectos de la Renta del Tabaco en el reinado de Carlos III.* Vol. 2. Actas del Congreso Internacional sobre Carlos III y la Ilustración. Madrid, 1989.

Hamilton, Earl J. *War and Prices in Spain, 1651–1800.* Cambridge: Harvard University Press, 1947.

Harrison, John P. "The Evolution of the Colombian Tobacco Trade, to 1875." *Hispanic American Historical Review* 32, no. 2 (May 1952).

Hünefeldt, Christine. "Etapa final del monopolio en el Virreinato del Perú: El tabaco de Chachapoyas." In Nils Jacobsen and Hans Jürgen Pule, eds., *The Economies of Mexico and Peru during the Late Colonial Period, 1760–1810.* Berlin: n.p., 1986.

Knight, Franklin W. *The Caribbean: The Genesis of a Fragmented Nationalism.* New York: Oxford University Press, 1978.

———. "Origins of Wealth and the Sugar Revolution in Cuba, 1750–1850." *Hispanic American Historical Review* 57 (May 1977): 231–53.

Kuethe, Allan J. *Cuba, 1753–1815: Crown, Military, and Society.* Knoxville: University of Tennessee Press, 1986.

Le Riverend, Julio. *Historia económica de Cuba.* Havana: Ciencias Sociales, 1985.

MacLachlan, Colin M. *Spain's Empire in the New World: The Role of Ideas in Institutional and Social Change.* Berkeley: University of California Press, 1988.

Marichal, Carlos. *La bancarrota del virreinato: Nueva España y las finanzas del Imperio español, 1780–1810.* Mexico City: Colegio de México/Fondo de Cultura Económica, 1999.

Marichal, Carlos, and Matilde Souto Mantecón. "Silver and Situados: New Spain and the Financing of the Spanish Empire in the Caribbean in the Eighteenth Century." *Hispanic American Historical Review* 74, no. 4 (November 1993): 587–613.

Menard, Russell R. "The Tobacco Industry in the Chesapeake Colonies, 1617–1730: An Interpretation." *Research in Economic History* 5 (1980): 157–61.

Mintz, Sidney W. *Dulzura y poder: El lugar del azúcar en la historia moderna.* Trans. Laura Moles Fanju. Mexico City: Siglo Veintiuno, 1996.

Mitchell, Brian R. *British Historical Statistics.* Cambridge: Cambridge University Press, 1988.

Morales Carrión, Arturo. *Puerto Rico y la lucha por la hegemonía en el Caribe: Colonialismo y contrabando, siglos XVI–XVIII.* Trans. Joed Arsuaga de Tanner. San Juan: Centro de Investigaciones Históricas/Editorial de la Universidad de Puerto Rico, 1995.

Moreno Fraginals, Manuel. *El ingenio: Complejo económico social cubano del azúcar.* Havana: Ciencias Sociales, 1978.

Ortiz, Fernando. *Contrapunteo cubano del tabaco y el azúcar.* Caracas: Ayacucho, 1987.

Parry, J. H., and Philip Sherlock. *Historia de las Antillas.* Trans. Viviana S. de Ghio. Buenos Aires: Kapelusz, 1976.

Pérez Herrero, Pedro. *América Latina y el colonialismo europeo (siglos XVI–XVIII).* Madrid: Síntesis, 1992.

Pérez Vidal, José. *España en la historia del tabaco.* Madrid: Consejo Superior de Investigaciones Científicas, 1959.

Pietschmann, Horst. *Las reformas borbónicas y el sistema de intendencias en Nueva España: Un estudio político administrativo.* Trans. Rolf Roland Meyer Misteli. Mexico City: Fondo de Cultura Económica, 1996.

Price, Jacob M. *France and the Chesapeake: A History of the French Tobacco Monopoly, 1674–1791, and of Its Relationship to the British and American Tobacco Trades.* 2 vols. Ann Arbor: University of Michigan Press, 1973.

Puig-Samper, Miguel Angel. "Las primeras instituciones científicas en Cuba: El Jardín Botánico de La Habana." In Consuelo Naranjo Orovio and Tomás Mallo Gutiérrez, eds., *Cuba, la perla de las Antillas.* Madrid: Doce Calles/CSIC, 1994.

Ringrose, David R. *España, 1700–1900: El mito del fracaso.* Madrid: Alianza, 1996.

Rivero Muñiz, José. *Tabaco, su historia en Cuba.* Havana: Instituto de Historia, 1964.

——. *Las tres sediciones de los vegueros en el siglo XVIII.* Havana: Academia de la Historia de Cuba, 1951.

Rodríguez Gordillo, José Manuel. "Aspectos tabaqueros en el Cádiz ilustrado." *La burguesía de negocios en la Andalucía de la Ilustración.* Cádiz: n.p., 1990.

——. "El fraude en el estanco del tabaco (siglos XVII–XVIII)." Unpublished manuscript. Photocopy courtesy of the author.

——. "La Real Fábrica de Tabacos." Unpublished manuscript. Photocopy courtesy of the author.

——. "Sobre la industria sevillana del tabaco a fines del siglo XVII." *Cuadernos de Historia* 7 (1977): 533–52.

Romano, Ruggiero. *Coyunturas opuestas: La crisis del siglo XVII en Europa e Hispanoamérica.* Mexico City: Colegio de México/Fondo de Cultura Económica, 1993.

Sagra, Ramón de la. *Historia económico-política y estadística de la isla de Cuba o sea de sus progresos en la población, la agricultura, el comercio y las rentas.* Havana: Imprenta de las viudas de Arazoza y Soler, 1831.

Stapff, Agnes. "La renta del tabaco en el Chile de la época virreinal: Un ejemplo de la política económica mercantilista." *Anuario de Estudios Americanos* 18 (Seville, 1960): 1–63.

Tedde de Lorca, Pedro. "La empresa pública en el mercantilismo español del siglo

XVIII (de Ustáriz a Ward)." In Francisco Comín and Pablo Martín Aceña, eds., *Historia de la empresa pública en España*, 25–49. Madrid: Espasa-Calpe, 1991.

Ustáriz, Gerónimo de. *Teoría y práctica de comercio y de marina*. 1725. Madrid: Ediciones Aguilar, 1968.

Vilar, Pierre. *Oro y moneda en la historia (1450–1920)*. Barcelona: Ariel, 1969.

Von Grafenstein Gareis, Johanna. *Nueva España en el circuncaribe, 1779–1808. Revolución, competencia imperial y vínculos intercoloniales*. Mexico City: Universidad Nacional Autónima de México, 1997.

Williams, Eric. *Capitalismo y esclavitud*. Trans. Martin Gerber. Buenos Aires: Siglo Veinte, 1973.

# 5

# The Latin American Coffee Commodity Chain:
# Brazil and Costa Rica

Steven Topik and Mario Samper

FOR THE WEEKS that preceded July 14, 1789, Camille Desmoulin and other Parisian revolutionaries gathered at the Café Foy, the Procope, and other political coffeehouses to plot the storming of the Bastille and draft the Rights of Man. They championed liberty and equality in this bourgeois public space as they set in motion the overthrow of the monarchy. But they gave no thought to the contradictions embodied in the coffee they sipped as they discussed grand ideas. Few contemplated freeing the African slaves who grew the coffee in France's colony of St-Domingue or freeing the colony. A century later the factory and office workers taking their coffee breaks in the United States and Western Europe gave scant thought to the black slaves or the Mayan Indians who labored in the coffee fields of Brazil and Guatemala to provide their drinks. The leisure drink in the North demanded strenuous work in the South. This was still largely true in the twentieth century. The archive of the N. W. Ayers advertising agency has hundreds of pictures of housewives and husbands making and drinking coffee in their gleaming kitchens.[1] There is no hint that the coffee came from coffee trees in poor foreign lands. It just appeared in the cans of Hills Brothers. Only decades later did the Colombian Federación de Café introduce their "Juan Valdez" to U.S. coffee drinkers.

Of course, in Latin America people are intimately aware of the fact that coffee grows on trees and requires peasant labor. But Latin Americans have often treated the international market as remote. Coffee is grown, picked, processed, brought to port, and then transmuted into money as the freighter sets off across the ocean to supply strangers. The world market is seen as an alien, even pernicious force over which growers have little influence. In most historical studies of the world coffee economy, production and consumption not only occupy different continents and different modes of production, they reside in contrasting mental universes. The story ignores the agents of the commercial transaction— exporters, shippers, and importers. We believe that this is a partial and unsatisfactory way to understand Latin America's caffeinated link to the world.

We propose that the study of the coffee commodity chain is a helpful way to understand, historicize, and make transparent the intimate relationship between cultivation, processing, intermediation, and consumption. Coffee is a particularly important commodity for analysis not only because it has been one of the world's most valuable internationally traded goods for the past two centuries, but because Latin America has dominated production. At one time or another in the nineteenth and twentieth centuries coffee was the leading export of nearly half the countries of the Americas and an important secondary crop in a number of others. By 1930 coffee accounted for one-fifth of all Latin American exports and it is still today a major export in a dozen countries.[2] Latin American growers have been the pricemakers internationally and have led the way in technological and botanical innovations.

Coffee commodity chains serve as bidirectional links between producers and consumers worldwide, interconnecting local processes with those taking place in overseas markets. Historically, there has been an extraordinary diversity in the ways cultivation, harvesting, transport, processing, and export of coffee have been organized. Over time consumption patterns and especially consumer preferences have undergone changes that affect coffee producers throughout the tropical world in quite different ways.

Coffee commodity chains, like other agro-industrial ones, are dynamic historical constructs that change over time in respect to both the technical organization and the social organization of linkages among cultivation, harvesting, local transportation, processing, overseas transportation, and distribution abroad. Technological innovations in any phase may substantially alter the dynamics of other links, both upstream and downstream.

Participants in the various aspects of the coffee commodity chain are also involved in broader production systems, social networks, and markets. Coffee farmers have often harvested other crops and sometimes raise livestock alongside their coffee; many of them allocate their time among several economic activities, including off-farm labor; and coffee plays different roles in their livelihood strategies. Growers, processors, and traders in coffee actively negotiate their respective interests with one another and with other socioeconomic and sociopolitical actors, whether locally or on a broader scale.

Coffee farmers' responses to changing external conditions have been far from uniform, and cannot be explained merely as passive reflections of world market trends and fluctuations. Although dependency theory, one of Latin America's most original contributions to the world's social sciences, stressed that Latin American producers were victims of a foreign-controlled market, this commodity chain analysis will show that New World producers exercised considerably more power and ingenuity than has usually been recognized. This chapter will use the evolution of producers in two quite different production complexes, Brazil and Costa Rica, as a starting point for comparative discussion of interactions of local agro-ecological, economic, social, and political conditions, on the one hand, and changes in the international market for this product, on the other. They demonstrate that even within the same commodity, a range of production systems, market strategies, and power relations have coexisted since the late eighteenth century.

One of the few commodities that was already important in early modern luxury long-distance trade, coffee continues today as a key trade good. But one should not reify the coffee market. Rather than a continuous, homogeneous institution, the international mart has been marked by radical disjunctures and essential transformations as production systems have varied and changed markedly.[3] Coffee continues to enjoy great international importance because the nature of its appeal to consumers has shifted to conform to remarkable changes in the societies of the dominant buyers over the past four centuries. The social life of coffee, its meaning to producers and consumers, has changed also. The unity and continuity of the term "coffee" is quite misleading.

For most of the five centuries during which coffee has been grown in the poorer southern countries mostly for consumption in richer northern ones, control of the trade has undergone major changes. Over time, coffee consumption became increasingly segmented and increasingly a mass drink, balancing between a luxury and a necessity, a status drink and a convenience beverage. Moreover, Latin Americans have come to drink an ever larger share of the coffee they grow, so it has become progressively less an export crop.[4] The length and complexity of the chain has varied as the nationality, ethnicity, and gender of producers, intermediaries, and consumers has been transformed. As the nature of processing and the end product became more complex, the role of multinational processors and traders expanded greatly, as did their share of surplus, despite state capitalist efforts by the governments of coffee-growing countries and the establishment of international agreements.[5] Asian and African growers have enlarged their share of world coffee production, but Latin Americans still dominate.

Brazil, Latin America's largest coffee exporter, came to be a price-maker and a market shaper because it overwhelmed all other producers with low-priced beans; Costa Rica, one of the smallest continental Latin American growers, concentrated on quality rather than quantity. Both key innovators, they wielded quite different degrees of market power and occupied quite different niches in the world economy. Although both produced arabica coffee for sale in Europe and North America, their production systems, technologies, and trade partners differed and varied within each country. Yet both were successful.

## THE WORLD COFFEE ECONOMY

The nature of the international coffee market has changed dramatically over the centuries. So has control of that market, which moved away from the producer to the exporter in the eighteenth century, then in the nineteenth century to the importer, and in the twentieth century to the roaster and government institutions, and finally today to a few vertically integrated multinational firms. The world coffee market is a conceptual structure, but a malleable, human-constructed structure, and has not always been dominated by Europeans and North Americans.

Coffee began as an export commodity before 1500 in Yemen, where the trade was dominated by Arabs and Indians, not Europeans, for over two centuries. Then the Dutch were able to overtake Mocha and Mediterranean ports to transform Amsterdam into the world's leading coffee entrepôt for over a century. Although Europe was still a small luxury market, its demands outstripped Mocha's possibilities. Europeans began planting coffee in their new-won colonies. By 1750 Amsterdam's imports of

Table 1

| | Coffee exports and imports, 1851–1960 | | | |
|---|---|---|---|---|
| Years | All coffee exports (thousands of metric tons) | Brazil coffee exports (percent) | Costa Rica coffee exports (percent) | United States coffee imports (percent) |
| 1851–55 | 289.2 | 52.9 | — | 28.2 |
| 1856–60 | 319.1 | 52.8 | 1.2 | 32.2 |
| 1861–65 | 324.5 | 45.1 | 1.6 | 17.5 |
| 1866–70 | 403.6 | 45.8 | 2.2 | 24.8 |
| 1871–75 | 439.2 | 45.2 | 2.1 | 31.2 |
| 1876–80 | 472.7 | 37.8 | 2.0 | 34.6 |
| 1881–85 | 585.5 | 59.4 | 2.0 | 37.6 |
| 1886–90 | 534.4 | 57.4 | 2.0 | 38.1 |
| 1890–95 | 620.7 | 58.1 | 2.0 | 40.2 |
| 1896–1900 | 800.6 | 76.0 | 2.0 | 42.4 |
| 1901–5 | 980.8 | 76.8 | 1.6 | 50.7 |
| 1906–10 | 1,055.7 | 83.3 | 1.2 | 41.8 |
| 1911–15 | 1,101.6 | 78.7 | 1.0 | 42.3 |
| 1916–20 | 1,056.8 | 76.4 | 0.9 | 51.3 |
| 1921–25 | 1,277.2 | 70.7 | 1.2 | 47.3 |
| 1926–30 | 1,443.9 | 90.8 | 1.4 | 44.9 |
| 1931–35 | 1,549.0 | 92.0 | 1.4 | 46.9 |
| 1936–40 | 1,614.9 | 81.7 | 1.5 | 54.3 |
| 1941–45 | 1,320.0 | 57.6 | 1.7 | 86.8 |
| 1946–50 | 1,844.4 | 50.5 | 1.2 | 89.3 |
| 1951–55 | 1,946.0 | 51.1 | 1.4 | 62.5 |
| 1956–60 | 2,352.4 | 68.8 | 2.1 | 54.2 |

Sources: Calculated from Mario Samper and Radin Fernando, "Historical Statistics of Coffee Production and Trade from 1700 to 1960," in William Gervase Clarence-Smith and Steven Topik, eds., *The Global Coffee Economy in Africa, Asia, and Latin America, 1500–1989* (New York: Cambridge University Press, 2003), 418, 419, 421, 422, 432, 433, 442, 444. Figures for the United States' percentage of world imports for 1881–1915 are calculated from Edmar Bacha and Robert Greenhill, data appendix, in Marcellino Martins and E. Johnston, eds., *150 Anos de Café* (Rio de Janeiro: Marcellino Martins and E. Johnston Exportadores, 1992), 330, 331.

American production almost matched its purchases of Javanese coffee. Initially the American good was mostly colonial production from Dutch Guyana. But soon the price of French production from St-Domingue (today Haiti) made that island more attractive. Even before the French Revolution over 80 percent of the world's production originated in European colonies in the Americas.[6]

Only in the middle of the nineteenth century did European states no longer play a major role in the development of coffee production. The French lost their main coffee-growing area after the Haitian Revolution. The Dutch preferred to serve as traders and shippers in the Americas, never developing or expanding their small colonies. Great Britain, which saw the mercantilist possibilities in exploiting the Chinese and then the Indian tea trade, was the only Western European power to reduce per capita coffee consumption rather than exploit the coffee-growing potential of Jamaica, Ceylon, or India. The Spanish and Portuguese preferred cacao and tea, so their American colonies had to wait for independence to become significant coffee producers.[7] Even later, once the United States gained the coffee-producing colonies of Puerto Rico, Hawaii, the Philippines, and effectively Cuba—at a time when the United States was the world's greatest coffee consumer—it continued to import overwhelmingly from Latin America in an open market.[8] It preferred to rely on growers in independent states with comparative advantages in the world coffee market. The vast expansion of the coffee market (see Table 1) has been a postcolonial phenomenon.[9]

## BRAZIL

Coffee was treated differently than sugar and rubber in the nineteenth century because its low technological demands allowed Brazil, an independent country richly endowed with the factors of production, to begin producing it on an unprecedented scale. Fertile land was cheap, and Brazil's proximity to Africa made slave labor relatively inexpensive also. Slaves had already been used in the successful sugar industry. These advantages allowed coffee prices to plummet after 1820 and remain low until the last quarter of the century, widening the global coffee market. Brazilian production not only satisfied world demand, it stimulated and transformed it. Coffee was converted from a noble and then a bourgeois beverage to a mass proletarian drink. The slaves of Brazil slaked the thirst of the workers of the industrial countries (except England, where tea was the laboring man's fuel) and their own thirst on the *fazendas*.[10] Brazil's exports jumped seventy-five-fold between independence in 1822 and 1899, increasing world consumption more than fifteen-fold in the nineteenth century.[11]

No African or Asian colony could compete with Brazil in price or meet the large new demand in Europe and the United States, especially once disease struck East Indian coffee after the 1870s. The newly independent countries of Spanish America were embroiled in civil wars that deterred coffee cultivation. By 1850 Brazil was producing over half the world's coffee. That figure swelled in the second half of the century, since about 80 percent of the expansion of world coffee production in the nineteenth century occurred in Brazil alone.[12] By 1906 Brazil produced almost five times as much as the rest of the world combined. And this was no marginal market. At the dawn of the twentieth century, the value of internationally traded coffee trailed only grains and sugar among all global commodities.[13] In 1960 it was still the second largest agricultural export of all. Thus Brazilian production helped to redefine the nature of the consumer market by dropping prices sufficiently to create a mass market.

Although dependency theory was largely formulated by students of Brazil's history—Fernando Henrique Cardoso, Florestan Fernandes, Octavio Ianni, Andre Gunder Frank, and Stanley Stein—it failed to predict the malleable nature of coffee cultivation. The historiographic boom-and-bust tradition that traced the rise and fall of dyewood, sugar, and gold as Brazil's main exports gave scholars intellectual blinders. It is true that Brazilians did not maximize their short-run benefits from coffee. But despite the disappearance of coffee trees in many formerly prosperous areas of Brazil, on a national level the bust still has not come. Brazil has remained the world leader for 150 years while constantly transforming the nature of the coffee industry and diversifying into other crops and industrial products. No other country in the world has maintained such dominance in such a lucrative crop for so long a time.

What made Brazil singularly suitable to grow so much coffee? The conventional view is that economies of scale on slave-worked latifundia allowed Brazil to create millions of coffee addicts abroad. This is only partially true. The first problem is assuming that all of Brazil's coffee was grown on huge plantations. Although certainly some of the fazendas that developed in São Paulo after the 1880s were among the largest export agro-industrial units in the world, other regions of Brazil had medium to small units. In neither Rio de Janeiro state, Minas Gerais, Espirito Santo, nor later Paraná was the large estate the rule. Over time the size of the Brazilian coffee estate steadily declined while productivity grew. By the 1980s the average *cafezal* covered only 9 hectares (22.3 acres).

We also hesitate to attribute too much of Brazil's coffee dominance to technological improvements alone. There were no revolutions in agricultural production techniques when Brazilian *fazendeiros* burst on the world market after independence.[14] Cultivating, harvesting, and processing continued to be done manually by the same sort of slave labor that Brazilian planters had used for sugar. Slave labor was not a Brazilian or even an American innovation. Slaves had already been used for coffee cultivation on the African island of Réunion and on a much larger scale in the cane fields of St-Domingue. But the fazendas of Brazil were so much larger that the fazendeiros developed industrial-scale picking, which lowered both the cost and the quality of coffee. The explosion of coffee cultivation in the first half of the nineteenth century came from superexploitation of labor and land, not production machinery.

Technological change played a larger role in the last decades of the nineteenth century. Milling (essentially dehulling or depulping and other tasks to prepare and pack the coffee beans for export) was advanced by steam power late in the century. The advent of the railroad and the steamship in South America allowed the rate of export expansion between 1860 and 1900 to keep step with the torrid pace set in the 1830–60 period.[15] And coffee production grew rapidly despite its dependence on an increasingly aging and expensive slave labor force until slavery was abolished in 1888. Initially, at least, the expansion was due to vast, easily accessible virgin forests (meaning a sparse indigenous population with no legally recognized rights that could be violently pushed out), proper climate, an export-oriented commercial infrastructure, a large slave force, and relative political peace. Brazil had one of the most peaceful transitions to independence on the American continents, and unlike Spanish America, it was able not only to maintain its colonial unit but to expand it after independence.[16]

The railroad, if not key in initiating the export boom, was important in permitting it to continue to expand. Before the iron horse, transport had been very expensive. By one calculation, 20 percent of the male slave force were used in mule trains, and transport accounted for one-third of the final price. Moreover, the primitive form of conveyance often damaged the beans.[17] The train reduced tariffs, but not dramatically. Because of relatively little competition, bulk discounts and distance rebates were not offered. In fact, coffee rode for a considerably higher price than domestic staples. By the turn of the twentieth century, rail transport still contributed from 15 to 22 percent of production costs. But the quality of coffee was better and, more important, cheaper, more fertile lands were now accessible in the interior.[18] In other words, the railroad allowed Brazilians to take advantage of their country's natural endowments (sometimes known as "forest rent") and thereby escape the geographic trap that had prevented Yemen, Java, Martinique, Dutch Guyana, and Haiti from qualitatively transforming the world market by taking advantage of economies of scale. By 1890 Brazil had the largest rail network in Latin America, larger than all Africa and all Asia minus India. So coffee brought slavery for manual labor but also state-of-the-art transport and processing technology. The modern and the archaic were not in contradiction; they reinforced each other, just as the telephones that some prosperous slavocrats installed on their plantations to coordinate and centralize control of their huge slave crews permitted the concentration of slaveholding. In the short run, the railroad revived slavery after the prohibition of the Atlantic slave trade in 1850 seemed to doom it. Over the longer run the railroad fostered the transition to free labor by opening the interior to the predatory cultivation methods of the coastal escarpment and attracting the third largest influx of European immigrants in the Americas.[19] And the railroad did not doom Brazil to overreliance on exports; it opened markets for domestic agriculture and manufactures.

The shipping revolution contributed as much as the railroad to the coffee export boom. A great expansion of shipping enabled swelling Brazilian coffee exports to be brought to market without shipping bottlenecks.[20] This was extremely important, because although Brazil was far from its markets, they were linked by the Atlantic. A host of European steamers began regular service to Brazil, where port facilities were slowly improved. Until the end of the nineteenth century, the U.S. market was furnished mostly by European sailing ships and then steamers, although Brazilian ships dominated the coastwise trade and came to occupy an important position in transatlantic shipping. International travel was faster and cheaper than overland travel within Brazil, so Brazil's great distance from its overseas markets proved to be more an advantage than a handicap. This was true for other Latin American coffee producers as well, for whom internal travel was a much greater barrier than international freight.

Railroads and ships, by reducing transportation expenses and transit times, allowed producers to receive a greater share of the final CIF (cost-insurance-freight) wholesale price while consumers abroad enjoyed lower retail prices. Brazilian coffee helped fuel the Industrial Revolution by intensifying the labor of the industrial working class while Brazil benefited from the wider market and the cheaper finished goods the Industrial

Revolution provided. Because imports from abroad became cheaper, Brazil could enjoy steadily improving terms of trade; that is, although coffee's price in dollars did not change much, and thus encouraged mass consumption abroad, a bag of coffee paid for an increasing volume of agricultural and industrial finished imports into Brazil.[21] So the coffee boom delivered the unusual situation of supply growing quickly enough to satisfy and even stimulate continually expanding demand abroad without a jump in price. (While this situation helped to expand the world coffee market, Brazil was essentially exporting some of its natural surplus by keeping prices remarkably low and hence retarding its own industrialization. On the other hand, some of that surplus returned in the form of foreign investment and loans—some of the largest in the Third World. The fact that Spanish-American producers such as Costa Rica, Venezuela, and Colombia began to produce coffee rather than indigo, tobacco, sugar, and cacao demonstrates that the world coffee price was high enough to make it attractive for growers even while it was low enough to seduce ever more consumers.

The secret of the success of the coffee production system was partly the self-provisioning of slave and then free coffee workers. Most of their pay came in the form of permission to use small but fertile plots of land to grow provisions and graze livestock rather than in money. As a result, workers could provide for themselves and even expand their operations despite very low cash wages. This was evidenced by Brazil's surging population growth and improving life expectancy.[22] This mechanism has been missed by economic historians who count only the monetized sector and therefore conclude that coffee exports retarded economic and social development.

The low price of fertile and well-watered land also gave Brazil a competitive advantage, especially because planters and state officials ignored the current opportunity costs of their devastating techniques and the depreciation costs that future generations would bear. In a very real sense, the Brazilian coffee boom was financed by the inheritance of planters' future descendants and the destruction of other creatures' habitats.[23]

Strikingly, Brazil's coffee boom was slow to lower transaction costs. Brazilian coffee planters as well as growers in Haiti, Jamaica, and Puerto Rico were themselves market-oriented, although the slaves who worked for them were little concerned with the demands of the market. But even fazendeiros in the interior were buffered from the market by poor roads and communications until the twentieth century. A complicated web of intermediaries further shielded growers from international prices. Small growers sold to larger growers or mill owners, who sold through factors (*comissarios*), who often sold to sackers who blended the coffee and then sold to exporters, who initially were consignment merchants.[24]

There were few coffee markets in the interior and Brazil had no coffee exchange until the 1920s, so information on prices and supply was very imperfect and favored the factors. Indeed, many planters were virtually innumerate.[25] Moreover, being quite undermonetized, the world's largest coffee economy dealt in credits and notes, which relied to a great degree on personal reputation and favors, not just on impersonal market forces.[26] This meant that Brazilians and Portuguese immigrants predominated in the interior as property owners because local political influence was important to guarantee property, and labor and extended family connections were important in obtaining loans. Over time the more successful growers leveraged these personal advantages to take part in the institutionalization of the coffee economy.

Large-scale planters were agro-industrialists. In addition to acquiring and overseeing cultivation on their land, they built their own mills, where they processed their own and smaller neighbors' crops; they extended credit to dependents in their area, built roads and invested in railroads, sometimes invested in comissario houses, and occasionally participated in export houses and banks. Fazendeiros, with their economic and political control of many aspects of the coffee economy, were the axis of the Brazilian sector. Only in the 1890s did the Portuguese immigrant merchants begin intruding on the interior. Other foreign banks and traders moved upcountry after the turn of the century but successful planters, particularly in the state of São Paulo, participated ever more extensively in the urban infrastructure and the state's dramatic industrialization. Coffee did give birth to something of a national bourgeoisie in Brazil, even if planters were often not the heroic entrepreneurs of Joseph Schumpeter's dreams.

Planters were able to adjust to market conditions, despite coffee's four-to-six-year gestation period, but they were quite slow to reduce output or catch up with demand. Great price rises led to rapid expansion and geographic diversification. The Haitian Revolution at the end of the eighteenth century, for example, encouraged planting in other parts of the Caribbean, Venezuela, and Brazil's Rio de Janeiro state. The next rapid jump in prices, in the late 1880s and early 1890s, caused a fourfold jump in São Paulo's trees in fourteen years, giving it alone over half the world's production; Colombia, Mexico, as well as Costa Rica and other Central American countries also stepped up production. High prices in the 1920s again pushed Central America and Colombia to much greater output and sparked cultivation in Africa. The price rise after the Korean War encouraged Africa and the state of Paraná in Brazil. Since the collapse of the International Coffee Agreement in 1989, Vietnam has become a leading grower, while coffee in Brazil has moved to the state of Minas Gerais.

However, coffee production did not expand only while prices were on the rise. In the short run, there was of course the well-known staggered effect of several years' delay between planting and harvest, although this lag diminished with high-yielding hybrid varieties. Since coffee is a perennial crop that involves substantial investment of capital and labor, growers were also reluctant to cut down the coffee and shade trees, and some planted or replanted while prices were low in anticipation of better years to come. Furthermore, local and regional dynamics, technological innovations, the decline of other crops, and sometimes colonial or national policies could lead to growth of the area planted or of other investments in coffee, quite independently of world market prices.

While inexpensive and plentiful Brazilian production slaked the thirst for coffee of ever more North American and European consumers, its remarkable increase in cultivation did not create a monopoly. Although in 1906 Brazil produced some 80 percent of the world's coffee, the institutionalization of the market with scheduled large steamers, railroads, warehouses, standards, futures market, and—as we shall see—new convenience coffee products opened North American and European ports to other Latin American producers. Rather than a zero-sum game, this was a situation of mutual gains for coffee producers. In most years until 1929 all Latin American growers increased output. Large inexpensive Latin American production combined with plentiful sugar production allowed coffee to overshadow its competing caffeinated drinks, such as cocoa, tea, maté, and such substitutes as chicory and grains. Latin America turned much of the Western world into coffee drinkers.

## COSTA RICA

Costa Rica was one of the first Spanish-American countries to become a major coffee grower. It did not enjoy many of Brazil's apparent advantages. Costa Rica was a poor, rather backward colony of the Spanish, sometimes using cacao beans as money, with few African slaves, a comparatively small indigenous population, relatively few immigrants, mountainous terrain inland rather than near the coast, and little foreign capital. It was nonetheless able to take advantage of the growing demand for coffee that Brazil was stimulating. Costa Rica's ultimate success can be traced to early political peace, which gave the country a head start because of forward-looking municipal authorities; an unpaved road to the coast and then a railroad completed by foreign capital; peasant self-provisioning combined with small-scale commercial farming and wage labor on the larger farms; increasingly centralized wet processing; and sustained efforts to improve the quality of coffee for export.

Costa Rican coffee production expanded in the previously settled central area before the mid-nineteenth century, while international prices were relatively low. When prices began a significant and sustained rise, the ground was already prepared for coffee to spread into new mountainous areas together with settlement of outlying regions.

In Costa Rica, as in Colombia and many other countries, cultivation of coffee was not monopolized by large estates, despite their importance in certain regions and the fact that land tenure was far from egalitarian. The key to control of the coffee business and its grid of social relations was closely associated with how the wet method of processing was organized. In contrast to the cheaper dry method, which was so extensively and economically used in Brazil—and used on a much smaller scale in certain more marginal parts of Costa Rica as well—Costa Rica's wet method led to central processing plants (beneficios). They were located either on large farms or in towns and cities, with increasingly technical procedures and attention to quality. Such processing had implications for the manner of harvesting (handpicking only ripe cherries rather than Brazil's more industrial and less discerning style), the development of transportation (first oxcarts, then railroads and trucks), and relations between coffee mill owners and their suppliers of fresh coffee fruit. These "client" networks were not limited to the purchase of cherries, since private credit has played a major role in structuring the flow of funds and harvests, especially before nationalization of the banking system in 1949 but even afterward. Interactions between campesinos and beneficiadores in a given place also had other, noneconomic connotations. They crafted sociopolitical alliances or confrontations through interpersonal relations exemplified by compadrazgo (symbolic kinship), which expressed both social hierarchy and reciprocity.

Part of Costa Rica's coffee was still dry-processed in the early- to mid-twentieth century, and even in the late 1970s this was the prevailing method in certain outlying, rather marginal coffee zones where water was scarce or transportation very difficult. However, "natural" coffee beans, from sun-dried cherries, were also produced in the core coffee-producing region, often from stolen fruit and from green or defective cherries.[27] The quality of these "natural coffees" was considered very inferior, and efforts were made to sell it only in the domestic market, then called the Bolsa del Café de Consumo Nacional.

Up to the mid-twentieth century, most processing centers were located on larger farms in the Central Valley and in a few remote coffee-producing regions. Farmers or merchants might take the cherries directly to a nearby beneficio, but as competition between the buyers became more intense in the early decades of the twentieth century, the agents of certain processing firms would go to meet the oxcarts that brought coffee toward San José. Small-scale growers, coffee mills, or beneficios, not planters, were the axis of the Costa Rican coffee commodity chain. Upstream, they purchased fresh berries from several small- to medium-sized farmers, to whom they often lent money, usually requiring a commitment to deliver a specified amount of coffee, in addition to other guarantees. Downstream, several planters might supply a single exporter, whether he owned their operations or not.

The number of beneficios grew during most of the nineteenth century, then stabilized at the turn of the century at about two hundred, but in the course of the twentieth century, their numbers decreased as improved transportation and major technical improvements facilitated centralization. Smaller processing facilities nearly disappeared, and average as well as maximum amounts processed per agro-industrial plant multiplied several times, while productivity of labor in wet processing also increased dramatically. Supply networks for each coffee mill, which used to overlap locally within the Central Valley, expanded to cover much larger regions, and even brought coffee from different parts of the country. Clearly, this development altered the structural relations between farmers and processing firms, but also affected interactions among processors. Competition for clients was often keen, yet at the same time beneficiadores sought to coordinate prices offered to farmers, or at least the advances given upon receipt of the fruit, so as to improve their collective bargaining position.

Since the late nineteenth century, Costa Rican farmers were becoming better informed on prices overseas through the local newspapers, which received dispatches via submarine cable, instead of waiting for ships to arrive with news, as before. During the turn-of-the-century crisis, coffee producers began to object more vocally to joint price setting by the processing and export firms, "*quienes se han coaligado para hacer la guerra á los pobres agricultores. . . . No hay duda que es un plan preconcebido*" (who have come together to make war on poor farmers. . . . There is no doubt that it is a preconceived plan).[28] Shortly thereafter, the farmers' suspicions were confirmed as the press reported an agreement among the main processing firms in the central coffee-producing region to reduce prices. Small farmers in at least one major city reacted by rapidly mobilizing and threatening to let their coffee dry on the tree, and a week later the price paid to them had risen considerably.[29]

At least one attempt was made to eliminate price differentials in favor of coffee farmers in certain locations, where quality and recognition abroad allowed exporters to obtain exceptionally high prices. When the processing mills attempted to set a uniform price for all coffees in 1903, farmers in that area mobilized and successfully defended their advantage, while also setting a precedent by questioning the *precio corriente* (the current price paid for coffee on the local market).[30]

In the 1920s, larger farmers and owners of processing plants, grouped in the Chamber of Agriculture, set the domestic purchase price of coffee for all beneficios in Costa Rica. Perhaps more than the price level itself, this joint decision irritated small and medium producers because it effectively stopped them from negotiating better prices for their coffee at competing mills. In addition to earning those very distinguished gentlemen the sobriquet of *el Trust de la Cámara de Agricultura*, that decision served as a catalyst for the establishment of an independent association of coffee farmers, which was to play a prominent role in the struggle against unilateral price setting in the following years.[31]

In referring to the owners of beneficios as a "trust," small and medium-sized growers were identifying what an economist might call an oligopsony. The larger firms certainly did try to set prices among themselves and artificially create a buyers' market. As the leader of the Asociación Nacional de Productores de Café stated in 1932, when disputes over the local price of coffee were acute and small farmers were rallying against the processing firms, some of which had begun to take lands away from debtors unable to repay their loans in the midst of that crisis: "The owners of coffee mills have fulfilled their task like wolves."[32] However, elite solidarity was sometimes broken by a newcomer or a renegade beneficiador seeking to increase his participation in the processing and export business. One might even reinterpret the laws that subsequently regulated relations between coffee farmers and processing firms, and the very creation of the Instituto de Defensa del Café, as legal and institutional measures that not only defused confrontations between those two groups but also institutionalized price-setting mechanisms and relations among the beneficiadores. The government mediated to avoid extreme abuses that might cause renewed protests by smaller coffee farmers.

In both Brazil and Costa Rica the governments (provincial and national in Brazil, national in Costa Rica) came to play an ever larger role in the national and international markets. Because of Brazil's much stronger position in the world market, the Brazilian state came to dominate and organize the world market. But Costa Rica was not defenseless. In the Brazilian case the coffee defense plans came to defend the state's interests more than those of the planters, while in Costa Rica the state regulated relations among growers, processors, and exporters, seeking to defuse rising tensions and institutionalize mechanisms to determine distribution of the final price.

## MASS CONSUMPTION

The consumption part of the coffee commodity chain has been as crucial as the production side, if not more so (see Figure 1). During the centuries when coffee was a Muslim drink, it had had a narrow luxury market. Coffee had often been traded by pilgrimage caravans; transport, taxes, and merchant costs were high. When Europeans spread production to their colonies in Java, Réunion, St-Domingue, and Jamaica, production and transport costs fell. But mercantilist-minded colonial governments insisted on high taxes, maintaining coffee as a bourgeois beverage. Peasants and proletarians had tended to drink chicory and other substitutes.

In the nineteenth century Brazilian slaves made the beverage available to urban workers and even occasionally to rural residents. Coffee boomed not only because of Brazil's production but also because of the United States' and Western Europe's consumption. The transportation revolution and lowered transaction costs in consuming countries accelerated the relationship between Brazil and the United States. For the first time, coffee became truly a mass product in the United States. Brazil's ability to develop transport (the railroad) and marketing economies of scale combined with greatly reduced transatlantic shipping costs and the world's

## 1. The Brazilian coffee commodity chain

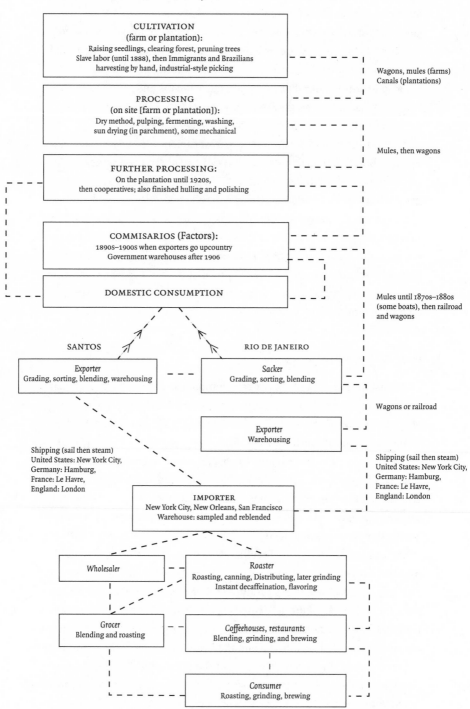

CULTIVATION
(farm or plantation):
Raising seedlings, clearing forest, pruning trees
Slave labor (until 1888), then Immigrants and Brazilians
harvesting by hand, industrial-style picking

Wagons, mules (farms)
Canals (plantations)

PROCESSING
(on site [farm or plantation]):
Dry method, pulping, fermenting, washing,
sun drying (in parchment), some mechanical

Mules, then wagons

FURTHER PROCESSING:
On the plantation until 1920s,
then cooperatives; also finished hulling and polishing

COMMISARIOS (Factors):
1890s–1900s when exporters go upcountry
Government warehouses after 1906

DOMESTIC CONSUMPTION

Mules until 1870s–1880s
(some boats), then railroad
and wagons

SANTOS            RIO DE JANEIRO

Exporter
Grading, sorting, blending, warehousing

Sacker
Grading, sorting, blending

Wagons or railroad

Exporter
Warehousing

Shipping (sail then steam)
United States: New York City,
Germany: Hamburg,
France: Le Havre,
England: London

Shipping (sail then steam)
United States: New York City,
Germany: Hamburg,
France: Le Havre,
England: London

IMPORTER
New York City, New Orleans, San Francisco
Warehouse: sampled and reblended

Wholesaler

Roaster
Roasting, canning, Distributing, later grinding
Instant decaffeination, flavoring

Grocer
Blending and roasting

Coffeehouses, restaurants
Blending, grinding, and brewing

Consumer
Roasting, grinding, brewing

most efficient internal transportation system and marketing network in the United States to stimulate a rapid rise in per capita consumption.

U.S. government policy also helped. The United States was the only major market to import coffee tax-free, which it did for all but a decade after 1832. In response, per capita consumption grew from one-eighteenth of a pound in 1783 to nine pounds a hundred years later. A fifteenfold explosion of the population of the United States in that century meant that total coffee imports grew 2,400 percent. By the end of the nineteenth century the United States was consuming thirteen pounds per capita and importing over 40 percent of the world's coffee. (Its share would grow to over 60 percent after World War II.) Half of the growth in world consumption in the nineteenth century was due to increased purchases in the United States.[33] (Almost all the rest was in Western Europe.) Coffee producers were very fortunate to find such favor in the country whose GNP was growing more quickly than any other country's.[34] U.S. per capita consumption would continue to grow, with some fits and starts, until the 1960s.[35]

Coffee's rapid expansion in the nineteenth century was due to peculiar demand conditions as well as Brazil's and then Spanish America's ability to meet that demand cheaply. Demand in the nineteenth century, in both the United States and Europe, was initially both income-elastic and price-elastic: the more income U.S. and European consumers earned and the lower the price of coffee, the more coffee they purchased. Interestingly, this was not the case in the twentieth century, despite better-quality and more accessible coffee and expanding discretionary incomes.

The reason for the change is culture. In the early nineteenth century coffee was viewed as a luxury item, a sign of bourgeois distinction, particularly to the European immigrants who arrived with a craving for coffee that had been difficult to satisfy in the old country. As coffee became available to lower-class urbanites and eventually even to rural populations at a relatively low price, they chose it over the ersatz coffees and teas they had previously drunk. They were able to do so also because the fall in the price of agricultural staples such as grains in the last decades of the nineteenth century gave wage earners greater discretionary income for luxuries such as coffee. So powerful was this appeal that the income elasticity in developed countries between 1830 and 1900 has been estimated at 1.3, meaning a disproportionately large share of income growth was spent on coffee.

Coffee was one of the few major internationally traded commodities to enjoy a real price increase in the second half of the nineteenth century and still see an increase in per capita consumption.[36] As it became an accepted part of the working class's breakfast, the amount of coffee purchased did not vary much with income or price. Once its status declined in the early twentieth century, its income elasticity did also, though it continued to be a necessity for many people.[37]

Coffee's success both generated institutionalization of the world market and resulted from that institutionalization. The coffee market began to become more globally integrated in 1874 when a submarine telegraph cable tied South America to New York and London. Information about prices and demand and supply and standards of quality became international, strengthening the hands of importers and processors in consuming countries. Merchants replaced the free-standing consignment agents in single countries who had initially formed the world coffee market. They created firms that traded in several producing and consuming lands and set the prices. Importers and roasters built warehouses that held a substantial share of the world's visible stocks, improving the market position of importers by providing both reserves and information about warehoused stocks. Exporters in Brazil ceased being consignment agents, becoming instead agents of U.S. and European importers who controlled the trade and set the prices. The creation of the Coffee Exchange in New York in 1882, followed by similar exchanges in Le Havre, Hamburg, and London, further institutionalized access to information and standardized commercial practices. This inspired the emergence of futures markets in which merchants bought the right to buy future crops as hedges against sharp price variations.

As long as all purchases had been on the spot, specific beans were judged. With the advent of futures, coffee became a more pure commodity in the sense that rights to coffee shipments were now bought and sold on the market floor without the buyer's actually seeing the lot in question. Coffees became commodities possessing a bundle of specific, graded attributes. Importers and roasters blended them together to create specific grades.

Two major problems continued to plague the trade after the establishment of exchanges in New York and Europe: it was difficult to determine the quality and origins of shipments and to get information about the size of annual crops. The former problem threatened to drive away defrauded customers and so made longer-term price calculations difficult. The quality problem was rectified not by planters and traders but by government.

In 1907 the United States' Pure Food and Drug Act decreed that imported coffee be marked according to its port of exit. Thus Santos became a specific type of coffee, as did Java and Mocha.

Social practices in the United States very much affected the nature of demand and the ability of roasters to respond to it and shape it. The fact that in the United States coffee was much more often consumed in the home, where it was roasted by the housewife, than in coffeehouses, as was the case in much of Europe, had important implications for the organization of the trade. Coffee in the United States was overwhelmingly sold in grocery stores, where consumers were more concerned with price than with quality. In response, some grocers founded roasting companies, such as Arbuckle's and the Woolson Spice Company, which created brand names for their packaged products, something slower to develop in Europe. But they could not overtake the thousands of grocers and small roasters who sold green or custom-roasted beans until they found a way to prevent ground coffee from quickly losing its flavor, a way to win consumers' confidence in the quality of packaged beans they could not see, and a stable price. The first problem was easily solved when vacuum sealing was invented in 1900, although it would require two decades for vacuum packing to gain wide acceptance. But the second required taking command of the market away from importers, who often adulterated coffee stocks. This was largely done through government intervention. In the United States, the Pure Food and Drug Act of 1907, based on a British pure food law some thirty years earlier, set standards.[38]

To protect themselves, roasters formed the National Association of Roasters. Under attack from coffee-substitute interests who decried coffee on religious grounds (Seventh-day Adventists and Mormons preached against it), on health grounds (John Kellogg claimed it was bad for digestion), and on moral grounds (caffeine was seen as an intoxicant), roasters joined government agents in enforcing the standards. Although their standards were apparently less demanding, the French, Germans, and Canadians followed suit with coffee purity laws, and international conferences were commenced to establish international standards.[39]

By gaining the confidence of consumers and providing mass-produced roasted coffee through advances in roasting technology, transport, and marketing, large industrial roasting firms began to control the market.[40] They began to integrate backward, increasingly sending their agents into the interior of Brazil and other Latin American countries to purchase coffee directly from producers.[41] Looking forward, the big mills improved roasting, grinding, and packaging technology so that processes formerly done by the grocer or the housewife were done by the roaster. By 1935, 90 percent of all coffee sold in the United States was sold roasted in packages rather than as green beans in bulk, as before.[42]

As a result, value was increasingly added by the roasting companies; that is, a larger share of the labor involved in making a cup of coffee was purchased rather than done by the end user. Thus an ever greater share of the monetary value was added in consuming countries in North America and Europe and by an ever smaller number of companies. Since roasters' profits came from using coffee as a raw material rather than as an object of speculation, as it had been previously for many merchants, roasters favored stable, predictable prices.[43] Although the European coffee trade was slower to turn to large mass roasters and retail sales of packaged coffee, brands such as the Pelican Rouge captured large markets in the early twentieth century. Later conglomerates such as Nestlé and Jacobs took hold of the market.

The gradual rise to dominance of industrial capital did not mean that the consumer market was very price-sensitive and susceptible to new coffee product lines and advertising. The expansion of large roasting companies with their superior technology, greater efficiency, more reliable and cheaper products, and greater advertising budgets and marketing sophistication did not expand coffee consumption as much as one might have expected. On the contrary, just as consolidation was beginning to occur, per capita consumption in the United States was stagnating. It would take forty years for U.S. consumers to again reach the level of 1902, when it stood at thirteen pounds per capita.[44] The jump in U.S. consumption, when it finally came, was in good part brought on by U.S. troops' introduction to instant coffee during World War II and the Korean War.

The most complete study we have found on the influences of coffee prices, done by the U.S. Federal Trade Commission (FTC) in 1954, concluded that the great price rise during the wars "cannot be explained in terms of the competitive laws of supply and demand."[45] The FTC also complained that futures speculation drove up prices out of line with supply and demand.

Speculation was encouraged by the concentration of the trade in a few hands. Ten exporting houses in Brazil sent out between 66 and 90 percent of the crops until the 1920s and continued to control over half after that. Since Brazil was exporting between 40 and 80 percent of the world's coffee and these exporting houses operated in other producing areas as well, a few houses dominated world exports. In the United States, the top ten importers (some of whom were also exporters) imported over half the total. And increasingly, a small number of roasters dominated that trade. By the 1950s the five largest roasters in the United States roasted over one-third of all coffee and held 78 percent of all stocks.

This small number of traders and roasters gave them oligopsonistic power not only over prices but over grades. Despite an apparently precise system in which all grades and sorts in New York and Europe were based on discounts or premiums on Rio number 7 and later Santos number 4 coffee, in fact, as the *Tea and Coffee Trade Journal* reported in July 1917: "The commercial classification of coffee is a matter of great complication. The factors which determine the market value of coffee are almost infinite in number" (30). Standards varied widely and were quite artisanal.[46] The companies with the largest market power could assert their standards.

### THE VALORIZATION OF COFFEE

Government intervention, which characterized the world market for coffee more than that for any other commodity for most of the twentieth century, worked to dampen the market's price mechanisms further and brought some control back to the growing countries. Beginning in 1906 some of Brazil's states held stocks off the world market to "valorize" them. This move led to a federal price-support program, the Inter-American Coffee Agreement, and finally in 1962 the International Coffee Agreement. Since the main objective of these cartels was to stabilize prices rather than corner the market, roasters in the consuming countries joined. They were willing to accept somewhat higher prices in return for guaranteed production because so much of value was added in the consuming countries. The coffee bean itself had become a low-cost raw material.

After strenuously opposing valorization at the outset, the governments of the consuming countries signed on. Their reasons were less economic than political.[47] Coffee was a pawn in the Cold War. It was no coincidence that the United States signed on to the agreement two years after the Cuban Revolution. The Kennedy administration feared that revolution might break out in coffee-growing countries. Socialist guerrilla movements in Colombia, El Salvador, Guatemala, and especially Nicaragua since the 1960s demonstrated the social tensions in several coffee-dependent economies. To allay fears of nationalist and socialist movements, coffee-producing countries were given annual quotas at prices somewhat higher than the unhindered global market would have dictated.

Political reasoning also effectively destroyed the London-based International Coffee Organization (ICO) in 1989, the year the Berlin Wall came down. The first Bush administration no longer feared Soviet aid to socialist groups and was ideologically committed to neoliberal free trade, so the United States withdrew from the ICO.

With the decline of the influence of the state on the market power of coffee-growing countries, the large roasters came to dominate the world market. They had consolidated their position gradually. Marketing played as important a role in this growth as did automation. Arbuckle's became by far the largest coffee roaster in the United States because it sold beans in one-pound paper sacks and awarded gift premiums in exchange for returned labels. The rise of chain stores such as the Great Atlantic and Pacific Tea Company, which made coffee their most profitable good, allowed wholesaling concentration, although each chain still roasted its own green coffee blends.

The situation changed in the 1950s, when the supermarket was created. Selling a vastly larger number of goods, the supermarket depended on small margins but large volume. For the first time, coffee companies competed on price rather than the quality of their blend. The rise of the supermarkets coincided with other phenomena. One was the formation of giant food conglomerates, such as General Foods, Coca-Cola, and Ralston Purina. When those conglomerates bought up smaller coffee companies, they had less interest in coffee as a family artisanal tradition than earlier coffee roasters such as Chase & Sanborn and Maxwell House. Moreover, the mechanization of coffee processing permitted the dumbing down of roasting techniques, since constant heat allowed temperature and time measurements to replace the eye of the expert roaster in determining a proper roast.

The proliferation of automobiles led to suburban living with its interest in fast foods, coffee shops, and drinking at home rather than in a café, so that convenience became the watchword rather than quality. This development facilitated the spread of a few very large companies that produced ground roasted coffee of lower quality in cans. And new coffee products that were developed after World War II, such as instant, decaffeinated, and bottled coffee, became popular. Consolidation proceeded until today four companies control 80 percent of the U.S. coffee market.

Four or five companies control half of the world's instant and roast coffee markets.

Thus although coffee was the world's second most important internationally traded commodity in many years and was produced in over a hundred countries while being consumed in virtually every country, it was surprisingly monopolized and monopsonized.

## CONCLUSIONS

Brazilian and Costa Rican producers changed the nature of the world coffee market. Far from being passive victims of an anonymous world market, they were pricemakers and intimately involved in the creation of market institutions. Brazil had a decisive influence on coffee prices and on the expansion of consumption in the world, while Costa Rica carved itself a niche where its higher-quality beans obtained better prices.

Over time, the nature of the international market shifted notably. Latin American producers played a key part in transforming coffee from an elite leisure beverage that served as a sign of distinction to a mass convenience drink. Control went from farmers to local merchants, to importers, to roasters, to multinational corporations and, for most of the twentieth century, states. Although the market's dynamism came largely from private initiatives, state intervention was necessary to institutionalize and standardize practices once the market's size outstripped merchants' ability to operate it. The ability of growers to meet demand without raising prices (initially by superexploiting natural resources and labor rather than technological improvements, later by developing new cultivars and modernizing processing and transportation), technical refinements by processors and marketers in consuming countries, and consumers' tastes and culture explain the rapid and huge expansion of the international coffee market.

Although African and Asian coffee growers have substantially increased their production, Latin America continues to be the world's leading producer and the United States the leading consumer. Still, this appearance of continuity masks a massive transformation in the actors, technology, profitability, nature of demand (what it is people are buying in a cup of coffee), and social relations in the global coffee commodity chain. A long line of people may be chained together, but their stake, control, and profit vary substantially still today as the chain has undergone major changes over time.

## NOTES

Steven Topik thanks the Humanities Center at the University of California, Irvine, and its research and travel committees for research funding for this essay. He also thanks the organizers and commentators at the Library of Congress, London School of Economics, Oxford University, and Stanford University for opportunities to present earlier versions of it.

1   Smithsonian Museum of American History, Washington.

2   At one time or another, coffee was the leading export of Brazil, Colombia, Costa Rica, El Salvador, Guatemala, Haiti, Jamaica, Martinique, Nicaragua, Puerto Rico, Surinam, and Venezuela. It has been a leading export in Cuba, the Dominican Republic, Ecuador, Honduras, and Mexico. For a brief general comparison, see Topik and Wells, *The Second Conquest of Latin America*, 37–84.

3   For an expanded discussion of the development of the world coffee market, see Topik, "The Integration of the World Coffee Market." See also Daviron, "La crisis del mercado cafetalero internacional."

4   Topik, "Coffee Consumption in Latin America."

5   Samper, "The Historical Construction of Quality and Competitiveness."

6   Crawford, *History of the Indian Archipelago*, 3:374; Steensgaard, "France, the Antilles, and Europe," 129–30. Latin America's share of world production is calculated from Ocampo, *Colombia y la economía mundial*, 303.

7   Ocampo, *Colombia y la economía mundial*, 303. In April 1909 the *Spice Mill* reported on 174 that Spanish and Portuguese coffee consumption per capita, at 0.7 and 0.5 kilos, was a fifth to a tenth of that of northern European countries and the United States.

8   Spice Mill, May 1909, 299, in an article discussing the limited amount of U.S. investment in Mexican coffee fincas (when U.S. capital was flooding into other Mexican areas), explained, "Concerning the increase in the production of coffee, Brazil continues and will continue to have no competitors in the world."

9   The French and the British made rather short-lived efforts to give preferences to coffee grown in their colonies in the twentieth century, but even in Africa and Asia, leading coffee producers such as the Ivory Coast and Vietnam waited until after independence to become major coffee exporters.

10  Stein, *Vassouras*, 164.

11  Brazil, Instituto Brasileiro de Geografía e Estatística (IBGE), *Séries estatísticas retrospectivas*, 1:85.

12  Calculated from Greenhill, "E. Johnston," 308; Ocampo, *Colombia y la economía mundial*, 303; Brazil, IBGE, *Séries estatísticas retrospectivas*, 1:84.

13  Mulhall, *The Dictionary of Statistics*, 130.

14  Wickizer noted in *Coffee, Teas, and Cocoa*, 36, that "it is sometimes said that no important changes have been made in the coffee production methods in the last 150 years."

15  Ocampo, *Colombia y la economía mundial*, 302.

16 For a discussion of the relationship between Brazil's export economy and precocious state building, see Topik, "The Hollow State."

17 Stein, *Vassouras*, 91, 94.

18 On rail costs, see Dafert, *Über die gegenwärtige Lage des Kaffeehaus in Brasilien*, 49; Centro Industrial do Brasil, *O Brasil*, 2:91. For rising land costs near Rio de Janeiro see Stein, *Vassouras*, 229, and Summerhill, *Order against Progress*, chap. 4.

19 Lewis points out in *Trade and Fluctuations*, 181, that Brazil (1.43 million) trailed only the United States (23.4 million) and Argentina (2.5 million) in receiving European immigrants between 1871 and 1915.

20 For a discussion of commercial conditions in Brazil at the end of the nineteenth century, see Topik, *Trade and Gunboats*. See also Greenhill, "Shipping"; Bairoch, "Geographical Structure and Trade Balance of European Foreign Trade," 606; North, "Ocean Freight Rates and Economic Development."

21 Leff, *Underdevelopment and Development in Brazil*, 1:80–85; Harley, "Late Nineteenth-Century Transportation, Trade and Settlement," 236; Bacha, "Política brasileira de café," 20.

22 According to Brazil, IBGE, *Séries estatísticas retrospectivas*, 1:3, Brazil's population doubled between 1854 and 1894 and then doubled again to 31.5 million by 1921.

23 For eloquent denunciations of the damage caused by coffee planters' slash-and-burn technique, see Dean, *With Broadax and Firebrand*, and Tucker, *Insatiable Appetite*.

24 For detailed studies of the Brazilian coffee market, see Laerne, *Brazil and Java*; Sweigart, *Financing and Marketing Brazilian Export Agriculture*; Greenhill, "E. Johnston."

25 Sweigart, *Financing and Marketing*.

26 Stein reports in *Vassouras*, 83, that "most planters were unwilling to use 'complicated processes of commercial accounting' and preferred to await reports occasionally forwarded by the more zealous comissários." This led to a situation noted by Laerne, *Brazil and Java*, 212, in which comissários, "from being the agents of the agriculturalists, became their bankers."

27 Jiménez, *Algunas ideas sobre comercialización de cafés naturales.*

28 "El café y sus explotadores," 1898, cited by Naranjo, *La modernización de la caficultura costarricense*, 43.

29 Naranjo, *La modernización*, 47–48.

30 Ibid., 48–50.

31 The mobilization and slogans of this movement have been discussed by Acuña Ortega, "La ideología de los pequeños." With respect to the 1921 agreement and subsequent protests, see Naranjo, *La modernización*, 233–35.

32 Marín Quirós, "Discurso ante la Asamblea de Productores de Café."

33 Calculated from Greenhill, "E. Johnston," 330–31; Abram Wakeman, "Reminiscences of Lower Wall Street," *Spice Mill*, March 1911, 193.

34 Kennedy, *The Rise and Fall of the Great Powers*, 149.

35 Actually the date of the zenith of coffee consumption in the United States is debated because the method of calculating consumption was changed. It may

be that coffee consumption in the United States has been declining ever since 1949.

36 Ocampo, *Colombia y la economía mundial*, 302–3; Bacha, "Política brasileira de café," 20.

37 Okunade, "Functional Former Habit Effects in the U.S. Demand for Coffee."

38 Anderson, *The Health of a Nation*; Friedman, *A History of American Law*, 400–405.

39 *Spice Mill*, November 1909, 702; January 1911, 30; October 1912, 857; *Tea and Coffee Trade Journal*, January 1911, 341.

40 In 1912 the Woolson Spice Company built the world's largest roasting factory in Toledo, Ohio, with 500 employees and a capacity of one million pounds of coffee a week: *Spice Mill*, January 1912, 28.

41 Goetzinger, "Arbuckle Brothers," 3; Zimmerman, *Theodor Wille*; Greenhill, "Investment Group."

42 Ukers, *All About Coffee*, 388.

43 Edward Green wrote to R. Johnston from Santos, October 12, 1903: "There is no denying the fact that all of us in Santos formerly looked upon our stock of coffee as a speculative thing to play with or a peg on which to hang larger speculations in Exchange" (Johnston Archive, University of London).

44 Jimenez, "From Plantation to Cup," 42–43.

45 U.S. Federal Trade Commission (FTC), *Investigation of Coffee Prices*, xv.

46 The *Tea and Coffee Trade Journal* reported in January 1917 that the complications were passed on to roasted coffee: "We do not believe that any two concerns use the same terms in describing their grinds and I do not believe that I have any two salesmen on the road who write up orders alike" (32). The FTC's *Investigation of Coffee Prices*, xxii, chided the industry for its "rule of thumb practices."

47 For an insightful analysis of the politics behind the rise and demise of the ICO, see Bates, *Open Economy Politics*.

## BIBLIOGRAPHY

Acuña Ortega, Víctor Hugo. "Historia económica del tabaco en Costa Rica: Epoca colonial." *Anuario de Estudios Centroamericanos* 4 (1979): 279–392.

———. "La ideología de los pequeños y medianos productores cafetaleros costarricenses." *Revista de Historia*, no. 16 (July–December 1987): 137–59.

Anderson, Oscar E. *The Health of a Nation: Harvey W. Wiley and the Fight for Pure Food.* Chicago: University of Chicago Press, 1958.

Bacha, Edmar. "Política brasileira de café." In Edmar Bacha and Robert Greenhill, *150 Anos de café*, 15–133. Rio de Janeiro: Marcellino Martins and E. Johnston, 1992.

Bairoch, Paul. "Geographical Structure and Trade Balance of European Foreign Trade from 1800 to 1970." *Journal of European Economic History* 3, no. 3 (Winter 1974): 557–608.

Bates, Robert. *Open Economy Politics: The Political Economy of the World Coffee Trade.* Princeton: Princeton University Press, 1997.

Brazil, Instituto Brasileira de Geografía e Estatística (IBGE). *Séries Estatísticas Retrospectivas*. Vol. 1. Rio de Janeiro: IBGE, 1986.

Centro Industrial do Brasil. *O Brasil: Suas riquezas naturais, sua indústrias*. Vol. 2. Rio de Janeiro: M. Orosco, 1908.

Crawford, John. *History of the Indian Archipelago*. Vol. 3. Edinburgh: Archibald Constable, 1820.

Dafert, Franz. *Über die gegenwärtige Lage des Kaffeehaus in Brasilien*. Amsterdam: J. H. de Bussy, 1898.

Daviron, Benoit. "La crisis del mercado cafetalero internacional en una perspectiva de largo plazo." In Mario Samper, ed., *Crisis y perspectivas del café latinoamericano*. Heredia, Costa Rica: Convenio ICAFE-UNA, 1994.

Dean, Warren. *With Broadax and Firebrand: The Destruction of the Brazilian Atlantic Forest*. Berkeley: University of California Press, 1995.

Friedman, Lawrence Meir. *A History of American Law*. New York: Simon and Schuster, 1973.

Goetzinger, M. E. "Arbuckle Brothers: A Sketch of Their History and Activities." *The Percolator* (February 1921).

Greenhill, Robert G. "E. Johnston: 150 Years em café." In Edmar Bacha and Robert Greenhill, *150 Anos de café*, 137–278. Rio de Janeiro: Marcellino Martins and E. Johnston, 1992.

——. "Investment Group, Free-Standing Company or Multinational? Brazilian Warrant, 1909–52." *Business History* 37, no. 1 (1995): 86–111.

——. "Shipping, 1850–1914." In D. C. M. Platt, *Business Imperialism, 1840–1930: An Inquiry Based on British Experience in Latin America*, 119–55. Oxford: Clarendon, 1977.

Harley, C. Nick. "Late Nineteenth-Century Transportation, Trade and Settlement." In Harley, ed., *The Integration of the World Economy, 1850–1914*, vol. 1. Cheltenham: Edward Elgar, 1996.

Jiménez, Alvaro. *Algunas ideas sobre comercialización de cafés naturales y el serio problema del merodeo*. San José: Oficina del Café, 1978.

Jimenez, Michael. "From Plantation to Cup: Coffee and Capitalism in the United States, 1830–1930." In William Roseberry et al., eds., *Coffee, Society, and Power in Latin America*. Baltimore: Johns Hopkins University Press, 1995.

Kennedy, Paul. *The Rise and Fall of the Great Powers*. New York: Random House, 1987.

Laerne, C. F. Van Delden. *Brazil and Java: Report on Coffee-Culture in America, Asia, and Africa to H.E. the Minister of Colonies*. London: W. H. Allen, 1885.

Leff, Nathaniel. *Underdevelopment and Development in Brazil*. Vol. 1. London: George Allen & Unwin, 1982.

Lewis, W. Arthur. *Growth and Fluctuations, 1870–1913*. London: G. Allen & Unwin, 1978.

Marín Quirós, Manuel. "Discurso ante la Asamblea de Productores de Café, celebrada en el Teatro Júpiter de Guadalupe, en la tarde del domingo 27 de marzo de 1932." *Revista de Historia* 16 (July–December 1987): 133–36.

Mulhall, Michael. *The Dictionary of Statistics*. 4th ed. London: G. Routledge, 1903.

Naranjo, Carlos. "La modernización de la caficultura costarricense, 1890–1950." Thesis, University of Costa Rica, 1997.

North, Douglass. "Ocean Freight Rates and Economic Development, 1750–1913." *Journal of Economic History* 18 (December 1958): 537–55.

Ocampo, José Antonio. *Colombia y la economía mundial, 1830–1910.* Bogota: Siglo Ventiuno, 1984.

Okunade, Albert A. "Functional Former Habit Effects in the U.S. Demand for Coffee." *Applied Economics* 24 (1991): 1203–12.

Samper, Mario. "The Historical Construction of Quality and Competitiveness: A Preliminary Discussion of Coffee Commodity Chains." In William Clarence-Smith and Steven Topik, eds., *The Global Coffee Economy in Africa, Asia and Latin America, 1500–1989,* 120–56. New York: Cambridge University Press, 2003.

Steensgaard, Niels. "France, the Antilles, and Europe in the Seventeenth and Eighteenth Centuries: Renewals of Foreign Trade." In James D. Tracy, ed., *The Rise of Merchant Empires: Long-Distance Trade in the Early Modern World, 1350–1750,* 129–30. New York: Cambridge University Press, 1990.

Stein, Stanley. *Vassouras, a Brazilian Coffee County.* 1957. Reprint, New York: Atheneum, 1970.

Summerhill, William. *Order against Progress: Government, Foreign Investment, and Railroads in Brazil, 1854–1913.* Stanford: Stanford University Press, 2001.

Sweigart, Joseph. *Financing and Marketing Brazilian Export Agriculture: The Coffee Factors of Rio de Janeiro, 1850–1888.* New York: Taylor & Francis, 1987.

Topik, Steven C. "Coffee Consumption in Latin America." In Colin Lewis and Rory Miller, eds., *The Culture of Consumption in Latin America.* London: Institute of Latin American Studies, University of London, forthcoming.

——. "The Hollow State: The Effect of the World Market on State Building in Brazil with Reference to Mexico." In James Dunkerley, ed., *Studies in the Formation of the Nation State in Latin America,* 112–32. London: Institute of Latin American Studies, University of London, 2002.

——. "The Integration of the World Coffee Market." In William Clarence-Smith and Steven Topik, eds., *The Global Coffee Economy in Africa, Asia and Latin America, 1500–1989,* 21–49. New York: Cambridge University Press, 2003.

——. *Trade and Gunboats: The United States and Brazil in the Age of Empire.* Stanford: Stanford University Press, 1997.

Topik, Steven C., and Allen Wells. *The Second Conquest of Latin America, 1850–1930: Coffee, Henequen, and Oil.* Austin: University of Texas Press, 1997.

Tucker, Richard P. *Insatiable Appetite: The United States and the Ecological Degradation of the Tropical World.* Berkeley: University of California Press, 2000.

Ukers, William. *All About Coffee.* New York: Tea and Coffee Trade Journal, 1935.

United States. Federal Trade Commission. "Economic Report of the Investigation of Coffee Prices." July 30. Washington: Government Printing Office, 1954.

Wickizer, V. D. *Coffee, Teas, and Cocoa.* Stanford: Food Research Institute, 1951.

Zimmerman, Siegfried. *Theodor Wille.* Hamburg, 1969.

# 6

Trade Regimes and the International
Sugar Market, 1850–1980:
Protectionism, Subsidies, and Regulation

Horacio Crespo

FROM THE SIXTEENTH century, the most important agricultural commodity produced and exported from Latin America
was sugar, and its importance only grew over time. The colonial history of the sugar trade has been broadly studied as well as its links
with the slave trade. Indeed, the literature on the subject is vast. The
Caribbean islands and Brazil were long the major sources of cane sugar
for Europe and, later, the United States. Jamaica was the premier producer in the first half of the eighteenth century, Haiti in the second half
of the same century, and Cuba in the nineteenth century. However, from
the mid-nineteenth century, a competitor—beet sugar—began to be produced on a large scale, first in Europe and later in the United States. This
essay documents the story of this rivalry between cane sugar and beet
sugar in international markets during a century and a half; indeed, the
competing agricultural commodity chains of advanced and less advanced
nations is a familiar story in our own age. It was the rivalry in the sugar
trade that led to the establishment of the first string of international
commodity trade accords and conventions in the 1850s. The complexity
of these constantly changing negotiations is an important chapter in the
history of modern trade regimes. As such, it points to the need to link
historical studies of commodity chains with the broader institutional
history of national and international markets.

During the second half of the nineteenth century, the international sugar market witnessed a trend toward lower prices of this most important commodity. This drop was a consequence of an increase in world production as a result of several factors, including the sustained expansion of European beet sugar, which benefited from export subsidies, and the standardization of centrifuged sugar production, made possible by technological improvements and by improvements in packing and storage processes. It was also the result of the early creation of a futures market, which enhanced the ability of bankers, speculators, and refiners to anticipate price shifts and to protect themselves from abrupt variations.[1] In the twentieth century, marked imbalances between supply and demand affected market behavior, causing successive severe crises in the form of acute shifts in prices in short-term cycles.

As regards long-term phenomena, it is important to underline two fundamental transformations. The first was the fact that during the nineteenth century sugar became a mass consumption foodstuff in Western and Central Europe as well as in the United States. This process took place in Latin America and Oceania only in the early decades of the twentieth century, and, on a much more limited scale, in the last fifty years of that century in Africa and Asia.[2] The second transformation was linked in contradictory fashion to the first: there was a sustained trend toward relative overproduction as well as growing difficulties in harmonizing the interests that came into play in the sugar business. Decisive in this process was the concern manifested by most countries to achieve self-sufficiency in foodstuffs. Of all staple foodstuff products, sugar has historically been the most sensitive to strategies for national self-sufficiency, in good measure because of the high caloric content it provides per unit of land utilized, which makes it an article especially valued by governments in their aim to attain food autarky. Yet at the same time, this valued trait can have a paradoxically negative effect, since it may neutralize national policies for controlling production and hinder the achievement of the objectives of international agreements for market stabilization.[3]

Periods of sugar scarcity throughout the world have been brief and linked closely to specific situations. World War I, for example, caused a collapse of production in European sugar beet fields. The overall tendency over the last century and a half, however, has been toward relative overproduction of sugar on an international scale. The pressure to overproduce stems from the fact that many major exporters have depended to a great extent, or almost exclusively, on sugar for their foreign exchange income. Cuba during the nineteenth century and through the period 1900–1960 is the most obvious example; from the 1960s this situation continued as a result of specific trade agreements with socialist economies. As a result, during the twentieth century Cuba, the largest sugar exporter, repeatedly increased production and sales even when prices were unfavorable.

Other countries with sugar capabilities also sought to increase their participation in international trade by promoting exports of this key commodity. Some governments supported an increase in production even if—in a strict sense—it turned out to be unprofitable, since sugar frequently operated as a dynamic force in depressed zones and provided a significant source of rural employment. In addition, political factors often played a part: under the patronage system large contingents of workers and peasants could easily be mobilized for specific politically inspired campaigns. Some governments also found themselves subject to intense pressures on the part of the major sugar producers or their representatives, who exhibited a great ability to influence political decision-making circles, especially as regards the application of subsidies and commercial protection measures.

Several analytical elements need to be underlined to explain the design of national and world sugar policies. In the first place, the main factor that has determined the volume of international demand has been the changing and growing productive capacity of the importing countries. As a result, it is clear that the effort to maintain adequate stocks and to retain and manage surpluses has fallen basically to exporting countries. Second, the particular features of sugar cultivation as an agro-industry, especially sugarcane production, makes it necessary to sustain considerable idle installed industrial capacity for a long period each year. Industrial sugar infrastructures are inelastic, particularly in the case of the sugarcane agro-industry. When prices of the final product fall, the lack of elasticity in production is notorious, although sometimes growers have partially remedied the situation by shortening the harvest period. Sugarcane cultivation requires large tracts of land and is perennial, so that even when the market situation is not good, diversification or crop variation is not feasible. The Javanese method of rotation of sugarcane with rice has represented an important innovation that has been replicated in other countries where the cane fields are irrigated.

In contrast to other commodity markets, the international sugar market cannot be characterized as one in which the commodity can circulate freely, searching for the best possible opportunity to balance supply and demand. It is a market that historically developed the first closed preferential agreements to operate on the basis of quantitative discriminatory targets (quotas), customs arrangements and compensations, or other measures that were extremely complex. The sugar conventions and international agreements began to be operative from the late nineteenth century and became progressively more extensive and detailed. For example, in 1961 only 40 percent of all the sugar produced in the world was bought and sold on the world market, and approximately half of this trade was subject to preferential agreements. Of the 54.8 million tons produced, only 11.9 were sold on a "free" market.[4]

Prices in preferential markets and in national ones are much more stable and remunerative than those to be found on the free world market, which is subject to considerable fluctuations due to the pressures exerted by an abundance of stocks rather than by the scarcity of the product. The most critical periods in the recent history of sugar have brought major changes. An excellent example is Java, which was the second most important exporter in the world but experienced the destruction of its productive capacity as a result of the Great Depression of the 1930s.[5] Hence, Indonesia was forced to reorient its sugar industry to an expanding domestic market, completely abandoning its former international presence.

Another factor that must be considered in efforts to understand the international sugar industries is the strong variation in production costs, basically between cane sugar produced extensively in lowland tropical coastal areas and sugar derived from beets or, more recently, sweeteners made from corn fructose. To these differences in production costs we have to add those that arise regionally; for example, in the United States between cane sugar producers in Hawaii and Louisiana or beet sugar producers in Texas and New Mexico as opposed to those in Minnesota or North Dakota, or among countries in the European Community, such as Italy and France. Agricultural protectionist policies help sustain marginal producers, and for that reason, both in the United States and Europe those entrepreneurs who are able to produce sugar at the lowest cost benefit from substantial profits, and are bent on keeping their privileged positions, which are politically determined.

Another feature of the world sugar business is instability of prices on international markets, with marked cycles of increases and decreases. This situation characterizes not only sugar but also other agricultural products: it tends to generate an exacerbated inelasticity in supply despite price variations with a downward trend. The typical cycle usually begins with a rise in prices caused by the lack of supply due to climate difficulties in one or another of the important supply regions. Stocks are reduced and producers react by significantly enlarging cultivated areas, either for sugarcane or for beets. The expansion of crop areas for sugarcane tends to lead to overproduction because plantations go into production for several consecutive years. Moreover, producers conduct political mobilizations to guarantee protection for their increased production. The result is a tendency for prices to drop or rise drastically. Variations can vary widely; for example, in the 1980s prices of sugarcane oscillated violently between 2.7 cents per pound and 4.1 cents.[6]

This problem of fluctuations in prices is worsened by the fact that the costs of adjustments due to a reduction in production are normally very high. Land devoted to sugarcane has few alternative uses, and movements of the labor force and of capital are particularly difficult in those areas. To this problem must be added the forcefulness with which both owners and operators of sugar mills and refineries defend their lands. Also important are speculative operations by trading firms, as well as changes in specific subsidy policies by governments.[7]

## SUGARCANE AND SUGAR BEETS: TWO ACTORS IN DISPUTE DURING THE SECOND HALF OF THE NINETEENTH CENTURY

In its origins sugar was derived from the plant *Saccharum officinarum*, and over two millennia sugarcane came to cover the world's tropical belt. In the early years of the modern age, it provided impetus to the expansion of European colonies. But on the threshold of the major expansion of the consumers' market (i.e., the beginning of widespread mass consumption of sugar), a competitor appeared. In 1747 the German chemist Andreas Marggraf demonstrated the sweetening power of beets. Later, during the French Revolution and the Napoleonic Wars, Europe's isolation from the colonies impelled an important development in the sugar industry based on sugar beets: the greatest advances took place in France in response to the English maritime blockade. Nonetheless, once "normal" relations

1. Tons of sugar produced by all countries, 1850–1985

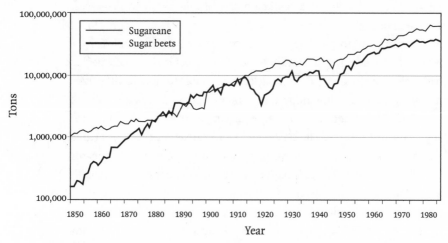

Sources: Manuel Moreno Fraginals, El ingenio: Complejo económico social cubano del azúcar (Havana: Ciencias Sociales, 1978), vol. 1, fig. 1, 35–40; and Sugar Year Book, 1960–85.

with the colonies were restored after Waterloo, this subsidized industry literally disappeared.

However, it had already been shown that large-scale cultivation and industrial processing of beet sugar was possible. Furthermore, increased rotation of crops provided a stimulus: grains and beets alternated, while beet production complemented livestock, which fed on the beets. But the essential point was that it became possible to produce sugar from beets on an industrial scale. However, experience made it quite clear that sugar made from beets was only a substitute and not yet a rival: if beet sugar was to prosper, it would be necessary to create markets protected from the competition of cane sugar produced on the colonial slave plantations.

According to Philippe Chalmin, the abolition of slavery in the French, British, and Spanish colonies in the nineteenth century encouraged the expansion of beet sugar. For Chalmin, this was a sign that slavery had made it possible for colonial sugar to be in a better competitive position. This hypothesis, if it has some truth in it, seems to be oversimplified, to say the least.[8] Other important elements that came into play included the expansion of agriculture in Russia from the 1830s, which eventually produced grain surpluses in European markets and caused wheat prices to fall. Farmers in the countries that received Russian exports compensated by partially replacing grain with beets. Moreover, in several countries, especially Great Britain, where the movement against black slavery was

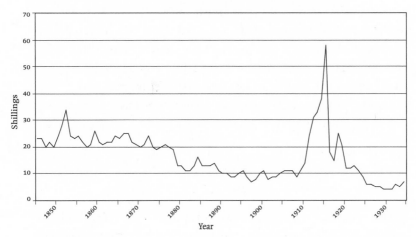

2. Price of raw sugar, London, 1850–1939 (shillings per 100 pounds)

Source: Noel Deerr, *The History of Sugar*, 2 vols. (London: Chapman & Hall, 1949–50), 2:530–31.

strongest, successive boycotts were organized against cane sugar produced in colonies or in such nations as Brazil, which continued to use slave labor. Moreover, around 1850, thanks to favorable legislation and the significant support of various states, the cultivation of beets was extended to northern France, Belgium, Holland, northern Germany, Bohemia, and Ukraine.

The overall situation of cane sugar contrasted with that of beet sugar, since the former suffered from periods of stagnation and decline due to the turbulence caused by the abolition of slavery in the plantation economies or to lack of capital for converting small manufacturing enterprises to large, centralized sugar refineries that could enjoy significant economies of scale. Without a doubt, the overall evolution of sugar production indicates that the second half of the nineteenth century was a beet period, and the resulting structural transformation of production had a great effect on the world market of this commodity.

The long-term trends of sugar production between 1850 and 1980 is shown in Figures 1 and 2. In 1840, cane sugar still represented 80 percent of world sugar production. As of the 1880s, production from cane was equal to that from beets, with a clear trend for the latter to be greater. As of 1900, the supremacy of beet sugar production was confirmed. This transformation of the relative weights of the two kinds of sugar was due fundamentally to a complex system of subsidies instituted by various

European governments beginning in the 1850s, the main beneficiaries being European and particularly British consumers. New actors, new mechanisms, and new complexities affected prices. The problems were very complicated, but all of them, without a doubt, were linked to the question of beet sugar subsidies. These subsidies began to be modified after 1902, by the establishment of the first effective multilateral international agreement on the trade of a primary commodity—sugar—signed in Brussels that year.

## THE PROTECTIONIST AND SUBSIDY SYSTEM:
## THE ORIGINS OF SUGAR DIPLOMACY

As I have pointed out, the major feature of the world sugar economy in the second half of the nineteenth century was the decrease in the growth rate of cane sugar production as opposed to the sharp increase in beet sugar production. The latter growth was sustained by the combination of an elaborate system of subsidies granted by countries that produced beet sugar and the existence of a very large free market that had Great Britain as its most important destination. This situation led to marked contradictions between the various actors in the sphere of sugar: among the colonial planters; among the planters and their European clients; among the European states; between free traders and protectionists; among industrial refiners and consumers; and more besides.[9]

At first, protectionist tariffs were established for domestic sugar, and the tax on the domestically produced commodity was set at a much lower level than the customs duties on imported products. This policy was widespread among European beet sugar producers in 1846, when Great Britain was the only country to begin to apply free trade. Another way of subsidizing sugar was to promote exports. The first mechanism was exempting sugar targeted for export from the domestic tax. An alternative method was to reimburse sugar exporters at the border or port for the domestic tax they had paid at the factory. The domestic tax was calculated on the basis of processed beet tonnage, while reimbursement was made according to the tonnage of the finished sugar product. In the end, the relationship between the two tonnages gave the exporter an additional benefit because as a rule the growing productivity of the industrial process was not taken into account and taxes were reimbursed on the basis of a greater tonnage than that actually utilized in the manufacture of the sugar that was being exported. When refined sugar was exported, the same thing occurred, as taxes were reimbursed in terms of the unrefined sugar that had been the basis of production; that is, a larger quantity was calculated than the one actually used. The end result of all these methods was that exporters could sell their sugar for a lower price abroad than in their own country. Thus they enjoyed indirect subsidies, which were frequently quite high, and when this was not sufficient, as of 1890, some European countries granted additional support by paying direct export subsidies. In addition, some governments encouraged the formation of sugar cartels to eliminate as many forms of domestic competition as possible. As a result of the various policies, in some sugar-producing countries, sugar continued to be a high-priced luxury commodity, while prices declined in countries such as Great Britain, which experienced rising mass consumption of sugar.

An examination of some of these subsidy systems can prove instructive. Germany established a domestic beet sugar tax in 1841 and gradually increased it, theoretically to the point where it equaled the customs duty for imported sugar. But the correction of this duty always lagged, with the result that a high subsidy for exporters of unrefined sugar was accumulated until 1869, and from then on for refined sugar, which grew markedly until the close of that century. German sugar exports in relation to production went from 126,000 tons (2.9 percent of production) in 1860–61 to 2 million tons (61 percent) in 1900–1901, with an accompanying 40 percent increase in productivity per ton of beets.[10] Between 1840 and 1902, the cost for the German treasury was 1.5 billion marks. Those costs led to plans in 1890 to eliminate the subsidies in five years, but bad grain harvests actually forced the German government to increase them in 1895. In 1900, a sugar cartel was formed which ensured a minimum price for refined sugar exporters but obliged them to deliver unrefined sugar only to the members of the syndicate.

The process was similar in Austria-Hungary, with even greater profits for the cartel. In Russia, each year the government decided the amount of sugar needed and established quotas among the producers, charging a differential tax: they paid twice as much for sugar destined for the domestic market as for sugar destined for export.

The system was less organized in France. Producers did not belong to a cartel. Until 1870, France had an efficient subsidy system, but afterward the system became less efficient than those in Germany and Austria-

Hungary. In 1897 France created a system of direct subsidies. Between 1884 and 1903, the French treasury spent 1.3 billion francs on sugar subsidies, but was unable to keep up with its Central European competitors.

Chalmin states that it is difficult to establish a quantitative comparison between the different subsidy systems. He feels that the French system of direct subsidies was the most advantageous for producers. In comparison with the French subsidies, Germany's ratio, like Belgium's, was 8:5, and Austria-Hungary's 8:3. Customs duties to compensate for subsidies created by the United States in 1898 also allowed France to hold first place, followed by Russia, Germany, and Austria-Hungary, but the ratio was different, since Russia was at a level equal to two-thirds of the French subsidy, and the other two producing countries were at a level of less than one-third.[11]

The effect of these policies on markets soon became evident. The collapse of prices in the late nineteenth century was spectacular.[12] But it is important to keep in mind that the international sugar markets changed quite rapidly. As of 1865, the London–Hamburg axis dominated European and, in general, international beet sugar transactions. As of 1883, the Cuba–United States and Formosa–Japan axes were formed.[13] But these markets were protected, and were either colonial or semicolonial in nature. The only market in which colonial sugar and European beet sugar competed freely was the British market because it was exempt from customs duties since 1874.[14]

At the close of the nineteenth century, Great Britain was importing 1.5 million tons of sugar, of which 80 percent was beet sugar (50 percent of it refined). Undoubtedly, British consumers benefited from continental European subsidies, especially those granted in Germany, Austria, and France, but at the same time the situation brought growing protests on the part of colonial planters and British refiners. Nonetheless, the British government insisted on its orthodox free-trade position, which failed to recognize the distorting effect of sugar subsidies until the early twentieth century, and this effect shaped all negotiation policies on the sugar subsidy followed at international meetings until 1861. These meetings were a failure, sometimes because of the position of producers favored by these policies or the position of Great Britain and its consumers, until an international agreement was reached in 1903, which, however, remained in effect only until 1908.

The negotiations regarding sugar followed an extremely complicated path. In 1861, France and Belgium signed a treaty in an attempt to limit indirect sugar subsidies granted by various means, mainly customs duties. This agreement was a failure because it was not properly enforced. The first International Sugar Conference was held in Paris in 1863, attended by representatives of France, Great Britain, Belgium, and Holland. On November 8, 1864, a multilateral treaty was signed establishing a ten-year agreement to start on August 1, 1865. The intention was to achieve a uniform subsidy system for mainly refined sugar exports. In practice, this agreement had only a minor effect on French refiners, the most powerful in Europe, since Great Britain was reluctant to apply compensatory tariffs for subsidized sugar. The effect on Central Europe and Russia was minimal. When the treaty expired, it was not renewed.

New sugar conferences were held in Paris (April 1873), London (July 1873), Brussels (May 1875), and Paris (July 1876 and February 1877). At the Paris conference, Great Britain, France, Belgium, and Holland agreed to conduct inspections of the refineries to determine the true amount of sugar refined. But this agreement was not ratified. Moreover, the nonparticipation of Germany and Austria-Hungary—two other major producers and subsidy granters—hindered its effective implementation.

On November 24, 1877, delegates of Germany, Austria-Hungary, Belgium, Brazil, Denmark, Spain, France, Great Britain, Italy, Holland, Russia, and Sweden met in London in the most significant attempt to date to achieve an effective sugar agreement. According to the chairman of the meeting, Baron Henry de Worms, this was the first time that all of the interested parties made it evident that they wished to participate in a frank general discussion. The delegates agreed to eliminate all direct or indirect subsidies and also to create a general tax on sugar targeted for consumption. But France did not ratify this agreement, and therefore it failed. Besides, Great Britain was fiercely opposed to such a policy: in 1889 the Cobden Club, which expressed the country's powerful free-trade forces, declared that the only result of the convention would be to make British refiners and colonial planters even richer than they already were.

Subsequent meetings were held in Vienna (1895) and Brussels (1896). They also failed because the British delegates affirmed that they had come only "to take note of the proposals," showing no interest at all in applying compensatory tariffs on subsidized sugar, while France and Russia were not willing to change the rules of their game. Yves Guyot, member of the Cobden Club and a convinced free trader, stated: "The entire European sugar industry is grounded on a system of subsidies. All European sugar legislation has one aspect in common: making sugar production grow, limiting domestic consumption, and encouraging foreign consumption."[15] Exasperated by this series of failures, the United States in 1897 sanctioned a unilateral duty on subsidized sugar, which came into force on December 12, 1898.

## THE BRUSSELS CONVENTION OF 1902

By the turn of the century, in Great Britain there was a fierce confrontation between free traders—defenders of consumers or of refineries that purchased foreign unrefined sugar—and imperialists, who expressed the interests of colonial producers. The pressure exerted on the British government by opponents of free trade in sugar finally forced Britain to change position, assume the defense of its domestic industry, and become antisubsidy. The convention that met in Brussels in 1902 worked efficiently, with the paradoxical but decreasing opposition of Great Britain, and the sugar treaty was signed on March 5, 1902. It established the following:

1 Elimination of all direct and indirect subsidies to sugar production, as of September 1, 1903.
2 Day and night supervision of factories and refineries by tax officials.
3 Limitation of duties: up to 6 French francs for every 100 kilograms of refined sugar or 5.5 francs for unrefined sugar.
4 A special tax for the importation of subsidized sugar, but a preferential low duty for sugar from the signatory countries.

The results of the convention marked a turning point. They led to a slight rise in prices (the first in half a century), cane sugar recovered markets, and its relative participation in world production tended to gain strength.

The sugar treaty was ratified, initially without any problem, by the House of Commons. However, during the session of the Commons held on February 27 and 28, 1905, an attempt was made to reject the Brussels Convention. Joseph Chamberlain's imperialists and Lord Balfour's conservatives managed to defeat this maneuver. The general elections held in December 1905, however, brought the Liberals to power, and as an immediate consequence in March 1906 Parliament approved Great Britain's withdrawal from the Convention, which meant, in fact, its effective annulment. Yet the process was slow: in August 1907 a new conference decided to extend the length of the convention, with the reservation that

Great Britain could fail to apply customs duties on subsidized sugar in this new period. The convention now included a system of export quotas and voluntary production limits, promoted by Russia, and this opened up new paths and methods for regulating the international sugar market that would be widely applied in the 1930s.

In February 1912, negotiations were again launched for the purpose of renewing the convention, but Great Britain declared firmly that it would not sign it, and that it would withdraw from the sugar agreement in 1913. In spite of this setback, the convention was extended until 1918. However, the outbreak of World War I devastated Europe's beet fields, destroyed the sugar trade axis between Hamburg and London, along which the main current of subsidized sugar circulated, and changed all the particulars of this issue.

To an observer in 1914 surveying the events that had occurred in the previous half century in the world sugar market, it might seem paradoxical or unexpected that the following decades of sugar diplomacy would be devoted to solving the problems of excess cane sugar production. But, in effect, that is what happened as a consequence of the rise of sugar prices during World War I and the subsequent stimulus to renewed increases in production. As I have already suggested, the main problems faced by the international sugar business lay in the extent to which colonial or formerly colonial cane sugar producers in the tropics could be competitive with the producers of subsidized beet sugar. This unequal competition discouraged the modernization of cane sugar systems and heightened problems involving competitiveness. Cuba and Java were the first to modernize their sugar industries, in the late nineteenth century, but other, traditional sugarcane producers continued to decline, in particular many in the Caribbean. The situation changed with World War I.

## THE INTERNATIONAL SUGAR MARKET IN TIMES OF CRISIS

The boom in sugar prices during World War I as well as in the immediate postwar period reached a peak in 1920. Quite soon, however, the international sugar market suffered a severe crisis of relative overproduction, causing a sharp drop in prices, which forced structural changes. The changes began to be put in place forcibly from the 1930s and became more pronounced after World War II; indeed, the effects on the world sugar industry were long-term and would be felt most notably in the 1980s. The key innovation was the regulation of the sugar market by means of quotas for participation, determined by international agreements, in the so-called world market, and by special acts passed by Congress in the U.S. market. This modification of the rules for trading sugar relegated operations of the so-called free market to a marginal space, until at least the 1980s.[16]

The historical antecedents to these dramatic changes in Latin America are important to take into account. As I have argued, in the mid-1920s it was clear that the world sugar industry had returned to a situation of relative overproduction and excess accumulation of stocks. As a result, between 1926 and 1928, the largest cane sugar producer, Cuba, was prompted to restrict its sugar harvests. But this policy proved insufficient to slow the continued drop in prices.[17] In 1930, consensus began to be generated for the creation of an international cartel in order to guarantee a reduction in sugar harvests in all producing countries as a way of confronting the world economic crisis. But before this policy was implemented, Cuba and other major producers released much of their sugar, flooding markets and causing an even greater decline in prices (see Figure 3), which reached historically low levels between 1932 and 1936, with slight variations between New York and London.

Before the crisis, Cuba had unilaterally restricted its sugar production. Then, led by Colonel José Miguel Tarafa, the Cuban authorities went about convincing the rest of the exporting countries to come to a regulatory agreement aimed at balancing sugar supply and demand in world markets. Between November 11 and 14, 1927, a meeting was held in Paris to this end, with the participation of representatives of Czechoslovakia, Cuba, Poland, and Germany.[18] The resolutions adopted were intended to strike a balance between consumption and production; hence the commitment to raise domestic consumption in order to lower exportable surpluses. For the 1928–29 harvest, they pledged to regulate sowing so long as Cuba promised not to exceed its 1927–28 harvest of 4 million English tons. A permanent committee was set up with two representatives for each sugar industry of a signatory country, plus two well-known statisticians from Europe. Cuba would pay 50 percent of the expenses during the first year. One significant concession made by the European countries was that Cuban exports to the United States would not be taken into account. The refusal to sign the agreement by the Dutch government, which represented the interests of Java, the world's second most important exporter, made it impossible for it to be an effective regulatory instrument.

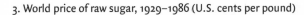

3. World price of raw sugar, 1929–1986 (U.S. cents per pound)

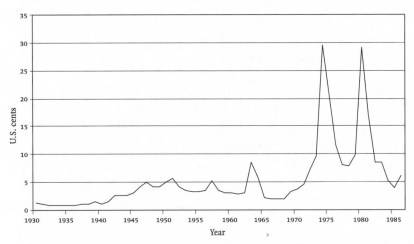

Source: Grupo Especial de Países Latinoamericanos y del Caribe Exportadores de Azúcar [Group of Latin American and Caribbean Sugar Exporting Countries], *La industria de la caña de azúcar en América Latina y el Caribe* [The Sugarcane Agricultural Industry in Latin America and the Caribbean] (Mexico City: GEPLACEA, 1986).

The predominant idea common in most contemporary economic circles in the 1920s was that Cuba was responsible for the world's relative overproduction. This was an erroneous view, as demonstrated by the fact that despite Cuba's unilateral decrease in sugar production, between 1926 and 1928 world production had risen from 20.6 million tons to 24.9 million tons. European countries returned to the levels of beet sugar production they had attained before the war, while Java reached its productive peak. Not surprisingly, after the policy of unilateral restriction had failed, Cuba increased its production once again in 1929. Inevitably, the market became saturated and prices dropped (see Figure 4).

The League of Nations took an interest in this grave economic problem, and from April 4 to 6, 1929, representatives of Germany, Cuba, Poland, Czechoslovakia, Belgium, and Hungary met to "exchange impressions." This attempt was followed by another: from June 29 to July 4, 1929, a new edition of the Brussels Convention was held, in which Germany, Belgium, Hungary, Poland, Czechoslovakia, and Cuba took part. The main idea was to include countries that both produced and imported sugar in this agreement so that they would take on purchasing commitments. The new convention reached agreement to limit exports to fixed quantities for the following four years: a quota of 200 million tons was assigned to Germany, 5 million to Cuba, 825,000 to Czechoslovakia,

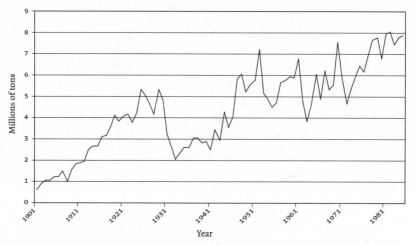

4. Tons of sugar produced in Cuba, 1901–1985

Sources: *Anuario Azucarero de Cuba: Memorias de la zafra, 1917–1933* (1934); United Nations, Food and Agriculture Organization, *La económia mundial en cifras, 1880–1959* (Rome: FAO, 1960); and *Sugar Year Book*, 1960–85.

383,000 to Poland, 100,000 to Hungary, and 60,000 to Belgium. The freezing of exports, it was thought, would force stored stocks to be consumed. But since other major export producers, such as Peru, Java, the Philippines, and the Dominican Republic, did not take part in the convention, it turned out to be another useless effort.

On other fronts, new protectionist or regulatory methods were also attempted. During the same fateful year of 1929, the U.S. Congress passed the Smoot-Hawley Act, which raised the U.S. duty to 2 cents per pound of sugar. The immediate consequence was that Cuban exports dropped by nearly 1.5 million tons between 1929 and 1930. The new Cuban strategy was to diversify and deal both with the problems of exporting to the United States and the saturation of the non-U.S. world market. A Cuban-U.S. committee was established in New York, guided by the lawyer Thomas L. Chadbourne, owner of two sugar mills in Cuba, and comprising prominent Cuban sugar producers, which developed the well-known Chadbourne Plan to regulate the international market with a system of producer quotas, the most important stipulations of which were:

1 Cuba promised to set aside a total of 1.5 million tons of sugar from its stocks and to deliver them to a new exporting company to be sold outside the United States in a period of five years.

2  Between 1931 and 1934, Cuba would limit its exports to the United States to 2.8 million tons per year, in exchange for supplying sugar for all rises in consumption in 1932 and 1933 and 50 percent of the eventual increase in 1934 and 1935.

3  Puerto Rico, the Philippines, and Hawaii pledged to restrict their sugar production until 1934 to their 1930 levels. In 1934 and 1935, they would be able to step up production in order to cover the other 50 percent of a possible increase in U.S. consumption.

One of the principal reasons for this attempt to salvage the situation by means of the Chadbourne Plan was that as a result of overproduction and the fall in prices (see again Figure 3), the United States banks that financed Cuban sugar mills found themselves obliged to absorb hefty losses in order to maintain the mills in operation. As a result, the banks had a marked interest in stabilizing markets and prices even though stabilization implied a drop in production, which inevitably would generate great social costs for the Cuban sugar producers and workers directly affected by this decrease.

As a result of the Smoot-Hawley Act, U.S.-Cuban sugar interests realized that they were running the risk of being partially displaced from the U.S. market. For that reason, they tried to ensure the quota of 2.8 million tons with the understanding that that was the level of production of U.S. sugar mills in Cuba, without concerning themselves with the fate of the sugar produced by Cubans. The plan failed because domestic producers did not comply with it; instead, they raised their production by amounts comparable to the decrease in Cuba's sugar output.[19]

The steady weakening of international markets led to more treaties and commitments: influenced by Chadbourne, on May 9, 1931, representatives of Cuba, Java, Czechoslovakia, Germany, Poland, Hungary, Belgium, and Luxembourg (later to be joined by Peru and Yugoslavia) signed an international sugar convention in Brussels that distributed fixed quotas among the signatory countries for five years, setting a price of 2 cents per pound of raw sugar. This plan failed because the countries that did not participate in it increased their production, so during the term of the accord the effective international price of sugar was less than half that considered in this agreement.

The agreement was negotiated with the aim of achieving a balance between production and consumption and eliminating surpluses so as to raise prices. To this end, the following was agreed:

1  A system of quotas would be established for participation in the market in order to limit exports.

2  An international sugar council would be created, in charge of verifying compliance with the convention, collecting statistics, suggesting measures for adjusting production and exports, and entering into agreements with countries not included in this agreement.

This was the first important agreement. The countries included represented 50 percent of production and 60 percent of world exports. However, the accord did not include the United States, Great Britain and its empire, Japan, Brazil, and the Dominican Republic. Its scope was limited, the effect on sugar prices was minimal, and the only real accomplishment was a 30 percent decrease in stocks. But regardless of what was effectively achieved by this agreement, significant progress was made both in the conceptualization and the realization of a world sugar cartel.

In the following years, efforts to negotiate and structure the world market continued. On May 6, 1937, a new international sugar agreement was signed in London by twenty countries: South Africa, Germany, Austria, Belgium, Brazil, Czechoslovakia, China, the United States, France, Haiti, India, the Netherlands, Peru, Poland, Portugal, the United Kingdom, the Dominican Republic, the Soviet Union, Yugoslavia, and Cuba. This accord included basic export quotas controlled by the International Sugar Council. The United States pledged not to decrease the quotas set by the Costigan-Jones Act. But, in fact, the agreement was suspended after the outbreak of World War II in September 1939.

## THE UNITED STATES' SUGAR TARIFF POLICY

In their important study *The World's Sugar*, Vladimir Timoshenko and Boris Swerling come to the conclusion that both in the nineteenth century and in the twentieth, the root of the sugar issue can be found more in political than in economic factors. To a great extent, the rationale for industrialized countries' sugar programs was and is based on considerations involving national policy. Between 1789 and 1934, the United States used sugar duties not only to generate customs income but also as a means of protecting the industry of its forty-eight states. Nevertheless, after a lengthy protectionist period, it became evident that the high duties were not sufficient to protect continental producers of both cane and beet sugar from competition by the sugarcane planters of Hawaii, the Philippines, and Puerto Rico; for this reason, a system of quotas to regulate the market was adopted.

After the Civil War, the United States became the main customer for Cuban sugar, and in 1871 Cuba exported at least 60 percent of its production to the United States. In 1884, the United States signed a commercial treaty with Spain, allowing for the export of raw or semirefined Cuban sugar to the United States in exchange for a notable opening up of the Cuban market to U.S. products. The treaty, however, came under attack by U.S. protectionist sectors and was not ratified by the Senate, which also feared the loss of significant customs income. In June 1891 a new treaty was signed tending toward the establishment of trade reciprocity, although it was later denounced by President Grover Cleveland's administration in 1895.[20] In 1903, once Cuba had gained its formal independence, the policy of sugar protectionism was taken up once more as regards its production, with a duty of 1.34 cents per pound. This duty was decreased during World War I. In 1921, protectionist sugar policies were put into effect again. On May 24, 1921, a duty of 1.60 cents per pound was sanctioned. The Fordney-McCumber Act of 1922 raised the duty again to 1.76 cents per pound. In any event, and despite these successive increases, Cuban sugar continued to supply over 50 percent of the U.S. market.

In 1930, the Smoot-Hawley Act raised the duty to 2 cents per pound, thus favoring cane and beet sugar producers in the continental United States and the so-called colonial island producers: those in Hawaii, Puerto Rico, and the Philippines, with open discrimination toward Cuba. Between 1930 and 1934, Cuba decreased its share of the U.S. market by 50 percent, while continental U.S. and Hawaiian producers continued with their previous shares and Puerto Rico and the Philippines increased their shares by 50 percent. Cuba paid the price for all of them. In addition, the outcome was greater concentration in production in an attempt to cut back costs and be more competitive. Yet for every effort by the Cubans to lower costs—with the corresponding adjustment in workers and colonists—an increase in the U.S. duty eliminated that decrease.

The main lobbyists in Congress in Washington were U.S. beet sugar producers, who feared that Cuba would offer unbearable competition or eliminate them from the market altogether.[21] Customs duties always served as an instrument for pressuring Cuba to limit production, either with threats or with active measures. As a result of this whole process of duty manipulation, Cuba's share of the U.S. market decreased from 52 percent to 24 percent, and the 2-million-ton difference was covered by increases of 1.8 million tons from Puerto Rico and the Philippines. Without a doubt, the final effect was the displacement of Cuba by island producers dependent on the United States. The sugar beet areas did not benefit from a widening of participation because the islanders did not pay duties and enjoyed better production conditions than they did. However, they conserved their historic levels and harmed the competitor they had originally considered to be most dangerous.

The United States reacted to the general economic crisis unleashed in 1929 with commercial protectionism and state intervention in the economy particularly as a result of the triumph of Franklin D. Roosevelt and the Democrats in 1932. On May 12, 1933, Congress passed the Agricultural Adjustment Act, which created and authorized the Agricultural Adjustment Administration to control production, set subsidies for domestic producers, and determine types of licenses and trade agreements related to seven basic agricultural and livestock products: wheat, cotton, corn, pigs, rice, tobacco, and dairy products. On May 9, 1934, sugar beets and sugarcane were included in this list of staples subject to federal regulation. On May 1, 1937, a special regime was created for sugar, with a law geared to controlling imports so as to protect the domestic sugar industry and defend consumers' interests. The essential feature of this regime was the implementation of a quota system for supplying the United States. A basic level was set for the prices of foreign sugar that made local sugar competitive with it. In general, this measure led to a situation in which sugar prices were much higher in the United States than anywhere else. The quota system operated on the basis of estimates of annual sugar consumption in the country made by the Department of Agriculture. On the basis of that estimated volume, supply was divided among domestic producers of beet and cane sugar—both continental and in Hawaii, Puerto Rico, and the Virgin Islands—with a specific quota for the Philippines, and the rest was distributed among other producers, a majority share going to Cuba. The sugar act was suspended during World War II and put into effect again in 1948, with the structure of the quota system unmodified.

Another effect of the Roosevelt administration's policies was that the duty dropped from 25 to 18.75 cents per pound of sugar, along with the 20 percent reduction for Cuba included in the 1902 treaty, which meant 15 cents per pound for imports from that island. Then came the passage of the Costigan-Jones Act for a term of three years, from 1934 to 1937. This act initiated the system of market quotas. Congressional legislation determined the quota for mainland sugar beet zones, while the quotas for the other areas were set in accordance with criteria dictated by the Department of Agriculture. Moreover, it was determined that the basis for assigning the quotas would be the most representative three-year period between 1925 and 1933. For Cuba the worst quota was selected, 29.2 percent of the market, somewhat better than its most recent share, but considerably lower than its historical average (by more than 20 percent of the market total; i.e., nearly half the volume exported at the best of times).

The 1933 crisis brought on by the Cuban Revolution and negotiations for its resolution included the signing of a new treaty that was to regulate relations between Cuba and the United States, the Reciprocity Treaty of 1934. That treaty stipulated a reduction of sugar duties to less than 10 cents per pound, a concession that was not too significant because U.S. protectionism was no longer exercised by means of customs duties, but rather through the establishment of share quotas. In 1937 the U.S. Congress passed a new sugar act that mostly repeated the former act, but with certain slight differences that were unfavorable for Cuba, such as a decrease of a bit more than 1 percent in its quota, nonparticipation in the deficit of quota supply by the Philippines, and the setting of a specific amount for refined sugar instead of 22 percent of the quota and lower. The growing need for sugar in the United States after the outbreak of World War II and the dislocation of the circuit of international supply, especially in the Pacific, led to the suspension of the system.

## THE SUGAR MARKET AFTER WORLD WAR II

The Second World War led to major changes in sugar markets. As regards the U.S. market, the principal change was the elimination of production in the Philippines and the corresponding increase of Cuban production to replace it. During this period, Cuba practically recovered the share of the market it had had before the 1930s; once again it came to supply almost 50 percent of U.S. sugar needs. The quotas set by the Costigan-Jones Act were suspended between 1942 and 1947.

Reestablished in 1948, these quotas returned the situation to its former status: the United States went back to protecting domestic production of both cane sugar (Louisiana) and beet sugar, and integrated cane sugar production in the Philippines, Puerto Rico, and Hawaii. Cuban exports declined as a result, and came to represent only 27 percent of the market (just slightly lower than its share during the 1930s) instead of the 46 percent it had achieved between 1945 and 1947. A special clause obliged Cuba to supply all the sugar required by the quota if the price of sugar on the world market were greater than the U.S. price. In 1953, in the face of threats of relative overproduction, Cuba again restricted its sugar harvests, as it had done in the late 1920s.[22] This policy was not taken up by other producers, as had been the case previously, and as a result, Cuba dropped from 20 percent of world production in 1951–52 to only 12 percent in 1954–55.[23]

Thirty-eight countries met in London on August 24, 1953, and agreed to a renewal of the International Sugar Agreement, to enter into effect on January 1, 1954. By means of this instrument, the countries also returned to the quota system for exports in operation in the period between the two world wars, but many countries were unable to comply with it. A meeting was held in New York in May 1956 and continued in October in London for the purpose of revising the agreement. Changes were granted in quotas and mechanisms were set up for cutting back or increasing quotas in keeping with price movements. If prices rose above 4 cents per pound, the quota system would be suspended so as to allow the market to operate freely. Actually, in any event, the conceptual error remained because the amount of the quotas was much higher than the market's absorption capacity. This was clearly expressed by the fact that the price of sugar never went beyond 4 cents per pound as an average annual value between 1953 and 1971, except in 1957, 1963, and 1964. This agreement was extended until 1963.

Meanwhile, the U.S. market continued to be regulated by the sugar acts passed by Congress, approved successively in 1953 and 1956. In the first one, Cuba's share was raised to 31 percent because the Philippines were unable to cover their quota, and this helped alleviate the accumulation of Cuban surpluses. In 1956, Cuba's share went down to historically low levels. The Sugar Manufacture (Amendment) Act of 1962 included significant modifications, derived to a great extent from the conflict arising from the break in relations between the United States and Cuba in 1960, after the Castro revolution. Cuba's quota was cut back to half and was also left "suspended" until such time as its government was officially recognized. Other important suppliers in other production zones were accepted, including members of other preferential agreements.

Although the U.S. sugar acts and successive international agreements were the essential instruments for structuring and regulating the sugar market, other preferential agreements also had a considerable impact on this process in the aftermath of World War II. According to an agreement reached by the British Commonwealth, instituted in 1951 and revised in 1962, the government of Great Britain promised to purchase yearly specific quantities under quotas from other member countries at "negotiated and prudently remunerative prices." Other preferential agreements benefited France's overseas departments and colonies. In addition, the European Economic Community and the socialist trade bloc (COMECON/ CAME), to which Cuba subscribed, generated regulatory agreements for the sugar trade. As a result of these successive measures, the "free" world market was considered residual and by its very nature was subject to major price fluctuations. But these prices, in turn, were very often considered a benchmark for setting other prices in exchanges within preferential markets.

The combined result of the most recent policies regarding the sugar market can be summed up as follows: Commercial protection by highly developed countries has led to a significant decline in the exports of peripheral countries, and even to an increase in subsidized exports from some of the producers of the former group, especially the European Community. The result has been a decline in prices, a loss of foreign income for traditional exporting countries, and the lack of economic feasibility of significant regions devoted to cultivating sugarcane and producing cane sugar. The growing importance of sweeteners made from corn fructose worsens this situation, in many cases to critical levels. The international sugar market is a significant historical example of the fact that in the agricultural sphere, the freedom of competitive trade has turned out to be more of a proclaimed ideology than an effective practice.

*Translated by Susan Beth Kapilian*

---

NOTES

I thank Carlos Marichal and Steven Topik for their extensive and careful revision of the translation of this essay.

1 Moreno Fraginals, El ingenio, 16–29. Piqueras, *Cuba, emporio y colonia*, chap. 6, is an excellent study on the impact of these new conditions on the world's main cane sugar producer.

2 In 1954, annual per capita consumption in Europe was 25.6 kg; in North America, 46.0 kg; in Central America, 25.6 kg; in South America, 28.5 kg; in Asia, 4.5 kg; in Africa, 9.3 kg; in Oceania, 52.1 kg. In 1985 the figures were: Europe, 41.2 kg; North America, 31.5 kg; Central America, 44.2 kg; South America, 38.5 kg; Asia, 10.9 kg; Africa, 14.7 kg; and Oceania, 41.8 kg, according to data from the *Sugar Year Book*. European consumption appears lower in

1954 because of the effects of the war, whereas consumption grew to more than 30 kg in 1959 and to 40 kg in 1972; another aspect to be stressed is the marked declining trend in North America after peaks of around 50 kg between 1966 and 1973.

3   For the general process of sugar as a staple foodstuff and the way it developed historically, see Mintz, *Sweetness and Power*.

4   *Sugar Year Book 1962*.

5   The protective measures adopted in the 1930s by the Indian government against sugar imports from Java also had a major impact.

6   Crespo and Vega Villanueva, *Estadísticas históricas del azúcar en México*, 822–24 (Table 190.8).

7   For a discussion of the major features of the international sugar market in the second half of the twentieth century and the effects on historical trends see Pan American Union, *Problemas de la comercialización del azúcar en el ámbito continental y mundial*; Grissa, *Structure of the International Sugar Market and Its Impact on Developing Countries*; Marks and Marcus, *The Economics and Politics of World Sugar Policies*; Cerro, *El mercado internacional del azúcar*. I am indebted to these works for the preparation of this essay, beyond the information provided.

8   Chalmin, "The Important Trends in Sugar Diplomacy before 1914," 9.

9   Ibid., 12–14.

10  Ibid., 12 (Table 2.4).

11  Ibid., 17.

12  On the London market, prices fell between 1883 and 1914, from a minimum ratio of 7:1 to a maximum of 15:1, according to the index in Noel Deerr, *The History of Sugar*, 2:530–31. This movement, involving a decrease in sugar prices, should be inscribed within a secular trend from the end of the Napoleonic Wars; see Deerr, *The History of Sugar*, 2:530–31.

13  Piqueras, *Cuba, emporio y colonia*, chap. 5.

14  Chalmin, "Important Trends in Sugar Diplomacy," 14.

15  Ibid., 16.

16  Cerro, *Mercado internacional del azúcar*, 11–12.

17  Prices were to remain very low until 1942, when for the first time the conditions created by the war raised prices above the 1929 level. See Le Riverend, *La República, dependencia y revolución*, 252; Pino-Santos, *El asalto a Cuba por la oligarquía financiera yanqui*, 182–85. The series of prices utilized is drawn from Grupo Especial de Países Latinoamericanos y del Caribe Exportadores de Azúca, *La industria de la caña de azúcar en América Latina y el Caribe*.

18  Silva León, *Cuba y el mercado internacional azucarero*, 28–29. When Silva León calls it "the first international conference of its kind in the world" (39), he fails to take into account all the negotiations held before the First World War.

19  Silva León, *Cuba y el mercado internacional azucarero*, 39.

20  Piqueras, *Cuba, emporio y colonia*, 161.

21  We should note that Representative Joseph W. Fordney was from a sugar beet district in Michigan, while Senator Reed Smoot was himself an important sugar producer.

22 For information on Cuba's sugar policies during the 1950s, see Winocur, *Historia social de la revolución cubana*, 37–64; Pierre-Charles, *Génesis de la revolución cubana*, chap. 3.

23 United Nations, Food and Agriculture Organization, *La economía mundial del azúcar en cifras*, 21–30; see Table 1.

## BIBLIOGRAPHY

Abbott, George C. *Sugar*. London: Routledge, 1990.

Albert, Bill. *An Essay on the Peruvian Sugar Industry, 1880–1920, and the Letters of Ronald Gordon, Administrator of the British Sugar Company in Cañete, 1914–1920*. Norwich: University of East Anglia School of Social Studies, 1976.

Albert, Bill, and Adrian Graves, eds. *Crisis and Change in the International Sugar Economy, 1860–1914*. Edinburgh: ISC Press, 1984.

———, eds. *The World Sugar Economy in War and Depression, 1914–1940*. London: Routledge, 1988.

Ballinger, R. A. *A History of Sugar Marketing*. Washington: U.S. Department of Agriculture Economic Research Service, Agricultural Economic Reports, 1971.

Bravo, María Celia. "Cañeros industriales y mecanismos de arbitraje azucareros en la década del '20." *Población y sociedad* 1 (December 1993).

———. "Cuestión regiona, azúcar y crisis cañera en Tucumán durante la primera presidencia de Yrigoyen." *Ruralia: Revista argentina de estudios agrarios* 4 (October 1993).

Campi, Daniel. "El noroeste argentino y el modelo agroexportador, 1870–1914." In *Reestructuración regional y producción azucarera*. Jujuy en la historia: Avances de investigación, no. 2. Jujuy: Universidad Nacional de Jujuy, 1995.

———. *Estudios sobre la historia de la industria azucarera argentina*. Vol. 1. Tucumán: Facultad de Ciencias Económicas, Universidad Nacional de Tucumán, 1991.

Cerro, José Antonio. *El mercado internacional del azúcar*. Mexico City: GEPLACEA, 1984.

Chalmin, Philippe. *The Making of a Sugar Giant: Tate & Lyle, 1859–1989*. Chur: Harwood, 1990.

———. "The Important Trends in Sugar Diplomacy before 1914." In Bill Albert and Adrian Graves, eds., *Crisis and Change in the International Sugar Economy, 1860–1914*. London: Routledge, 1988.

Conrad, Glen R., and Ray F. Lucas. *White Gold: A Brief History of the Louisiana Sugar Industry, 1795–1995*. Lafayette: Center for Louisiana Studies of the University of Southwestern Louisiana, 1995.

Crespo, Horacio. *Historia del azúcar en México*. 2 vols. Mexico City: Azúcar S.A./Fondo de Cultura Económica, 1988–89.

Crespo, Horacio, and Enrique Vega Villanueva. *Estadísticas históricas del azúcar en México*. Mexico City: Azúcar S.A., 1989.

Curtin, Philip D. *The Rise and Fall of the Plantation Complex: Essays in Atlantic History*. Cambridge: Cambridge University Press, 1990.

Deerr, Noel. *The History of Sugar*. Vol. 2. London: Chapman & Hall, 1950.

Eisenberg, Peter. *The Sugar Industry in Pernambuco: Modernization without Change, 1840–1910*. Berkeley: University of California Press, 1974.

Fleitas, María Silvia. "Desarrollo regional: Azúcar y política en el noroeste argentino, 1910–1930." In *Jujuy en la historia: Avances de investigación*, no. 1. Jujuy: Universidad Nacional de Jujuy, 1993.

Fourastié, Jean. *L'évolution des prix a long term*. Paris: Presses Universitaires de France, 1969.

Galloway, J[ock] H. *The Sugar Cane Industry: An Historical Geography from Its Origins to 1914*. Cambridge: Cambridge University Press, 1989.

Gonzales, Michael J. *Plantation Agriculture and Social Control in Northern Peru, 1875–1933*. Latin American Monographs, no. 62. Austin: University of Texas, Institute of Latin American Studies, 1985.

Goslinga, Cornelis Ch. *The Dutch in the Caribbean and in Surinam, 1791/5–1942*. Assen: Van Gorcum, 1990.

Grant, Alison. *Bristol and the Sugar Trade*. Harlow: Longman, 1981.

Grissa, Abdessatar. *Structure of the International Sugar Market and Its Impact on Developing Countries*. Paris: Development Centre of the Organization for Economic Cooperation and Development, 1976.

Grupo Especial de Países Latinoamericanos y del Caribe Exportadores de Azúcar [Group of Latin American and Caribbean Sugar Exporting Countries]. *La industria de la caña de azúcar en América Latina y el Caribe* [The Sugarcane Agricultural Industry in Latin America and the Caribbean]. Mexico City: GEPLACEA, 1986.

Guy, Donna. *Política azucarera argentina: Tucumán y la generación del '80*. Tucumán: Fundación Banco Comercial del Norte, 1981.

Heston, Thomas J. *Sweet Subsidy: The Economic and Diplomatic Effects of the U.S. Sugar Acts, 1934–1974*. New York: Garland, 1987.

Inter-American Economic and Social Council. *Latin America and the United States Sugar Market*. Washington: Organization of American States. 1973.

International Sugar Council. *The World Sugar Economy: Structure and Policies*. London: Brown, Wright & Truscott, 1963.

Labys, Walter C. *Primary Commodity Markets and Models: An International Bibliography*. Aldershot: Gower, 1987.

Lagos, Marcelo. "Estructuración de los ingenios azucareros jujeños en el marco regional (1870–1930)." In *Jujuy en la historia: Avances de investigación*, no. 1. Jujuy: Universidad Nacional de Jujuy, 1993.

Le Riverend, Julio. *Historia económica de Cuba*. Havana: Ciencias Sociales, 1985.

———. *La República: Dependencia y revolutión*. Havana: Editores Ciencias Sociales, 1975.

Marks, Stephen V., and Keith E. Markus. *The Economics and Politics of World Sugar Policies*. Ann Arbor: University of Michigan Press, 1993.

Mintz, Sidney W. *Sweetness and Power: The Place of Sugar in Modern History*. New York: Viking, 1985.

Moreno Fraginals, Manuel. *El ingenio: Complejo económico social cubano del azúcar*. Havana: Ciencias Sociales, 1978.

Pan American Union. *Problemas de la comercialización del azúcar en el ámbito continental y mundial*. Washington: Organization of American States, 1963.

Pierre-Charles, Gérard. *Génesis de la Revolución Cubana*. Mexico City: Siglo Veintiuno, 1976.

Pino-Santos, Oscar. *El asalto a Cuba por la oligarquía financiera yanqui*. Havana: Casa de Américas, 1973.

Piqueras, José A. *Cuba, emporio y colonia: La disputa por un mercado interferido (1878–1895)*. Madrid: Fondo de Cultura Económica, 2003.

Rothman, H.; F. Rosillo-Calle; and R. Greenshields. *The Alcohol Economy: Fuel, Ethanol and the Brazilian Experience*. London: Francis Pinter, 1982.

Santamaría García, Antonio. "La industria azucarera y la economía cubana durante los años veinte y treinta." Ph.D. dissertation, Universidad Complutense de Madrid, 1995.

Scott, C. D. *Machetes, Machines and Agrarian Reform: The Political Economy of Technical Choice in the Peruvian Sugar Industry, 1954–74*. Norwich: University of East Anglia School of Social Studies, 1979.

Silva León, Arnaldo. *Cuba y el mercado internacional azucarero*. Havana: Ciencias Sociales, 1975.

Singelmann, Peter, ed. *Mexican Sugarcane Growers: Economic Restructuring and Political Options*. San Diego: Center for U.S.-Mexican Studies, 1995.

Sombart, Werner. *Luxury and Capitalism*. Ann Arbor: University of Michigan Press, 1967.

*Sugar Year Book*. London: International Sugar Organization, annually.

Timoshenko, Vladimir P., and Boris C. Swerling. *The World's Sugar: Progress and Policy*. Stanford: Stanford University Press, 1957.

United Nations, Food and Agriculture Organization. *La economía mundial del azúcar en cifras, 1880–1959*. Rome: FAO, 1960.

Winocur, Marcos. *Historia social de la revolución cubana (1952–1959)*. Mexico City: Universidad Nacional Autónoma de México, 1989.

Zolla, Carlos. *Elogio del dulce: Ensayo sobre la dulcería mexicana*. Mexico City: Azúcar S.A., Fondo de Cultura Económica, 1988.

# 7

# The Local and the Global: Internal and External Factors in the Development of Bahia's Cacao Sector

Mary Ann Mahony

AT THE BEGINNING of the nineteenth century, landholders in southern Bahia, Brazil,[1] grew and marketed some sugar, coffee, cacao, and manioc, but they earned most of their income from timber. Over the course of the next century, however, they would devote more attention and resources to agriculture, and especially to growing cacao, the principal ingredient in chocolate. By 1890, they had made Bahia one of the world's most important producers of cacao.[2]

Cacao became so important in southern Bahia over the course of the nineteenth century because planters and farmers gradually chose to plant it rather than any other crop. This took time: only slowly did they become seriously interested in agriculture rather than timber, and when they did, for the most part they planted sugar and manioc, Bahia's traditional crops. When they finally began to experiment with other crops, like many other Brazilians at the time, they became interested in coffee. It was only gradually that they grasped the fact that cacao was best suited to their region at that particular historical juncture.

The concept of the commodity chain can help us to understand why these planters and farmers ultimately chose to grow cacao. As Steven Topik and Mario Samper indicate in chapter 5 of this volume, the commodity chain draws our attention to the linkages between producers and consumers worldwide, as well as to the connections between local and global processes. In the particular case of cacao, it forces us to pay attention to the ways in which the emergence of the cocoa and chocolate industry in the nineteenth century shaped demand for this tropical export.[3]

That said, I have concerns about the concept of the commodity chain, particularly because it focuses narrowly on one crop, even if it follows that single crop from plantation to cup, to borrow a frequently used phrase. In southern Bahia, the history of cacao cultivation is closely intertwined with that of the timber industry and of sugar, coffee, and manioc cultivation. The commodity chain alone cannot explain, however, why planters and farmers chose to grow cacao rather than the alternatives during the second half of the nineteenth century. Nevertheless, this is an important question, because planters and farmers had other choices available to them. Cacao was not the only available possibility; eventually they would decide that it was their best one, but that was long after the Portuguese government began encouraging them to plant it in the 1780s. Only over time did they become seriously interested in cacao.

If we recall Victor Bulmer-Thomas's argument that Latin American countries faced a commodity lottery in the nineteenth century, one of the major questions that the concept of the commodity chain does not fully answer is: Why this commodity at this time?[4] After all, many parts of the tropics are appropriate to the cultivation of a wide variety of crops, and Bert Barickman has shown that in the nineteenth century, Bahia in particular was home to at least four—sugar, tobacco, coffee, and manioc—all of which would grow in the southern part of the state.[5] So why was it that in some Bahian communities planters and farmers moved away from these other crops and into cacao as the years passed?

The emergence of cacao as southern Bahia's most important crop was neither automatic nor predestined. It was the result of a series of decisions about what to grow taken by southern Bahian planters and farmers during the nineteenth century on the basis of the information available to them about the environment, forest policy, the timber industry, availability of labor, and international demand. Thus exploring the commodity chain is vital in efforts to understand the history of cacao cultivation in southern Bahia, but it is not the only explanatory tool historians must use. They must also look at the ways in which those men and women analyzed the opportunities presented by the new chocolate industry in the context of the alternatives available to them.

## THE ENVIRONMENT

In southern Bahia, as in all agricultural areas, the environment played a significant role in landowners' decisions about what to grow. As the nineteenth century opened, as we have seen, planters and farmers were already growing four crops—sugar, manioc, coffee, and cacao. Although they did not have technical studies to guide them, they could observe the behavior of these plants and determine whether or not they did well in their region.

Planters' and farmers' evaluation of the crop best suited to their region began with the weather. In the beginning of the nineteenth century, there were no distinguishable rainy or dry seasons in southern Bahia. Instead, rain fell constantly throughout the year: there were months when it rained slightly more or less than in others, but it was never very dry. In fact, it rained so much that local residents caustically nicknamed the region "heaven's urinal." In 1935, scientists confirmed that early perception when they reported that rainfall averaged 133.6 millimeters or 5.25 inches per month at the Cacao Research Station in Agua Preta.[6]

To our knowledge, local residents did not have a pithy label to describe the temperature, but they knew that it was hot in the summer and cool in the winter. As a result, despite the importance that they accorded to European mores, elite men and women did not wear formal dress in southern Bahia. Rather, well-to-do men went about in shirt sleeves, and women did not use the voluminous undergarments required of respectable elite women in Brazil. Slaves, the free poor, and indigenous people wore even less. Again, in 1935 scientists confirmed this nineteenth-century day-to-day assessment of the climate: they noted that the mean temperatures at the research station in Agua Preta ranged between 66°F in the winter months of June, July, and August and 85°F in the summer months of December, January, and February. At the same time, in the town of Ilhéus, on other sections of the coast, and in the valleys of the interior, temperatures averaged as much as 2 degrees higher than at the research station. On the other hand, at elevations above 1,200 feet, temperatures regularly dropped to as low as 50°F in the winter. Given the amount of rainfall, the weather was regularly hot and sticky in the summer and cool and damp in the winter.[7]

In 1800 this combination of temperature and rainfall sustained a complex ecosystem of forest, animals, and insects that to the untrained eye looked primeval. Immense trees with trunks that were too big for two grown men to embrace rose over 100 feet in the air, and their leafy crowns created a canopy that blocked the sun. Parasitic vines climbed the tall tree trunks, and smaller trees took advantage of the shade and protection from the rain to create an understory. The ground was thick with fallen leaves and other debris, produced when age, storm damage, or loggers felled the forest giants. Animals, birds, and insects of all sorts made this space their home: people who passed through this forest probably found the mosquitos and other biting insects most annoying and the snakes most terrifying, but they also encountered sloths, golden micro-lion monkeys, panthers, frogs, and caterpillars, to name only a few. It was a space alive with energy, and although it proved to be more delicate than settlers believed at the time, it intimidated them: they saw it as dark, wild, and closed.[8]

Whatever their fears, following their counterparts in other parts of Brazil, southern Bahian planters and farmers saw the superabundance of forest growth as evidence of the soil's fertility. They would gradually learn, however, that the soil varied significantly underneath the forest cover, and that it was much more delicate than they originally thought. Near the ocean, the soil was very sandy, while a strip slightly farther inland was composed of the reddish mixture of soil and clay known as *salões*. Beginning at the harbor of Ilhéus and spreading west roughly in an inverted triangle lay the *massapé* soil, for which the Recôncavo sugar districts had become famous. All of these soils were relatively poor in potassium, lime, and nitrogen, but the differing clay contents meant that fertility could vary significantly. The sandy soil and the *salões* were both quite porous, and the heavy rains quickly drained them of nutrients es-sential to sustained crop growth; massapé contained much more clay and so it retained its value for agriculture much longer.[9]

By the beginning of the nineteenth century, massapé soils were fa-mous in Bahia for their ability to produce sugarcane, while salões were well known to be appropriate for manioc cultivation. Nevertheless, in Ilhéus planters and farmers do not appear to have made much effort to plant crops according to soil type, probably because almost anything would grow well in freshly cleared southern Bahian earth, whether the soil was salões or massapé, and also because terrain was at least as important as soil type to southern Bahian planters and farmers in their decisions about what to plant where. Although many of the region's hills were not very high, they were very steep and covered with rocks and boulders. In many districts bedrock lurked just below the surface. Since the soil was not deep enough to allow plants to establish deep roots, they were particularly vulnerable to wind and rain. By the same token, sunlight could vary dramatically on the hillsides, which might also be subject to erosion by heavy rains. Bottom land, on the other hand, might not drain well, and delicate new plants might drown. In such circumstances, choosing which crop to plant where was not as simple as identifying what kind of soil lay under the forest.[10]

By 1800 planters and farmers had already discovered that a number of tropical agricultural crops would grow quite well in this environment, although none of them could tolerate being planted on the crests of the region's hills. Food crops could be grown virtually anywhere, although manioc preferred the districts dominated by salões. Sugarcane, they saw, would grow to great heights, but over the long term it did much better when it was planted in relatively flat massapé rather than in salões or in any hilly area. Coffee ripened throughout the year, and a tree planted in massapé would produce for decades. A variety of Theobroma cacao known as forastero did particularly well.[11]

Theobroma cacao is an understory tree crop that thrives in the shade of larger trees in the tropical forest. Southern Bahia's humid climate and forest cover, therefore, would seem to have been perfect for its cultivation. The issue was not, however, quite so straightforward. There are two general varieties of Theobroma that can be used to make chocolate: criollo, the one originally domesticated by Mesoamericans, and forastero, a variety found growing wild in Venezuela by Spanish settlers in the seventeenth century.[12] Both require forest shade, warm temperatures, and extensive rainfall, but criollo is much more delicate than forastero. It is not only susceptible to disease but very vulnerable to cold; southern Bahian planters and farmers did not grow it, because they could not. It would not tolerate the low temperatures of the region's highlands. Southern Bahian planters and farmers did grow forastero cacao: it was a hardy tree that was quite tolerant of southern Bahia's cool winter temperatures. It liked the southern Bahian climate so well, in fact, that it produced two harvests per year there—one large and one small—though in most places where it grew it produced only one.

Given the suitability of forastero cacao to the local climate, one would think that southern Bahian planters and farmers would have begun to grow large amounts of it in the second half of the eighteenth century, but they did not. Instead, those who could afford to do so built sugar mills and invested in sugar and rum production into the 1840s. Those who could not tended to devote their attention to manioc and other food crops. Everyone put in a few coffee and forastero cacao trees, but they did not jump into cacao.[13]

The lack of enthusiasm for cacao early on was not necessarily the result of a failure to understand the adaptability of cacao to the local environment. On the basis of environmental factors alone, it is not clear that cacao enjoyed an extraordinary advantage over the other crops. It did grow well in southern Bahia, and as a tree crop it was more adaptable than sugar to steep hillsides, but, like coffee, it would not produce a full harvest for five or six years after it was planted. Once it did begin to bear fruit, it yielded large amounts of cacao, but everything grew well in southern Bahia: it was not until planters and farmers took other factors into account that they began to see that cacao had significant advantages over other crops.

## TIMBER POLICY

Whatever planters and farmers may have thought about the environment and its relation to agriculture, their decisions about what to plant were also conditioned by the government policy in respect to the forest and the timber it contained. In the eighteenth century, the Portuguese government had prohibited economic development in the region, in part to inhibit the smuggling of gold out of Minas Gerais, which lay directly west of southern Bahia. At the same time, however, it hoped to ban unrestricted logging in the region and reserve forest hardwoods for use by the Portuguese navy. Southern Bahia was easily accessible to the port at Salvador, home to the Portuguese naval shipyard in the colonial period; in an age when ships were constructed largely of hardwoods and timbers for beams and masts were difficult to find and therefore expensive, the region offered a supply of timber vital to the security of Portugal's empire.

Throughout the eighteenth and nineteenth centuries, Portuguese and then Brazilian governments recognized the relationship between the protection of hardwoods and national defense. As a result, although government policy varied over time, from attempts to forbid the private harvesting of timber to the exercise of few controls, it generally prohibited landowners with stands of hardwoods on their properties from freely logging their lands. As ouvidor of the Comarca de Ilhéos in the late eighteenth century, Balthazar da Silva Lisboa actually recommended that the crown abolish private property in the area in order to protect the forests.

While waiting for a royal decision about his proposal, he traveled up and down the southern Bahian coast, identifying protected timber and marking those parts of the forest that were not to be logged without explicit royal permission, whether they sat on privately owned land or not. In one case in 1799, he made as much as half or three-fourths of the land claimed by planters and farmers along the Itaípe River in the town of Ilhéus off limits to logging and therefore agriculture.[14]

Although he conscientiously implemented his royal instructions, Silva Lisboa did not succeed in completely prohibiting logging on the southern Bahian coast. José de Sá Bittencourt Camara, a sawmill owner and planter, organized a timber strike among his fellow landowners and used his personal connections to the colonial secretary to argue against government restrictions on private property. Landowners in southern Bahia did not, therefore, lose their land. But neither did they receive blanket permission to harvest timber. Despite the local opposition, the Portuguese crown legislated successfully against the free logging and sale of hardwoods commonly found in the southern Bahian forests.[15] It was, of course, impossible to completely control the access of local landowners to the trees on their property, but the sources are unanimous that significant stands of old-growth forest still covered the southern Bahian coast at the end of the colonial period in 1822, so they enjoyed some success.

At independence in 1822 control over the forest passed to the new Brazilian government. With the 1850 Land Law, the government in Rio continued to restrict the logging of hardwoods appropriate for naval applications. The private logging and sale of brazilwood was completely prohibited. Sawmill owners and others who wished to log or clear their land had to request permission to do so from the provincial government and then wait for a license. Responsibility for supervising the licenses, ensuring that the loggers cut only where and when their permits allowed, fell to municipal judges with little or no ability to enforce the law.[16]

Despite the restrictions, therefore, the harvesting and sale of timber to the Brazilian government or to clandestine buyers were big business in southern Bahia by the 1820s. Landowners with good political connections had no difficulty in obtaining authorization to harvest and sell the timber on their land. In fact, royal land grants and permissions to harvest timber had been awarded simultaneously to a series of well-connected Brazilians and foreigners in the first two decades of the nineteenth century. In subsequent years, local landowners regularly requested the right to log their land, and they just as regularly received it. By 1845, in two districts of the town of Ilhéus, more than fifty landholders were asking to be allowed to cut their timber. By 1866 there were eighteen functioning sawmills in the municipality of Ilhéus alone, with at least as many more in other parts of the county. Both the mill owners and their neighbors supplied those sawmills with timber in much the same way that the *lavradores de cana* furnished sugarcane to the sugar mills of the Recôncavo.[17]

Most of the people involved in this timber industry, either as mill owners or as suppliers, also owned plantations and farms. Nevertheless, they did not indiscriminately clearcut their land, despite complaints that the law was being violated. These were loggers and mill owners seeking out construction woods for harvest and sale either to the Brazilian government, which prosecuted people who cut marketable timber on their land without permission, or to European exporters, who were not interested in cutting timber that could not be sold.[18] Some of them falsely certified to owning land containing protected timber so that they could obtain authorization to log it, and all of them logged well beyond the limits indicated in their licenses, but they did not destroy the forest in the service of agriculture, at least during the middle of the nineteenth century.[19] Not that they understood the value of old-growth forests, but, as we will see, they may not have had the labor necessary to cut down enough trees to do much damage.

Thus, in the nineteenth century when planters and farmers in Ilhéus began to think about which crops to plant, the amount of land they would have to clear in order to grow them and the value of the timber that occupied that land were important factors for them to consider. They were reluctant to clearcut any district containing marketable hardwoods solely for the purpose of planting crops. This attitude tended to inhibit all economic growth based on agriculture. It particularly curbed sugar cultivation, since sugar required full sun and large amounts of land, so that large stretches of forest would have had to be completely cleared. On the other hand, it tended to favor the introduction of tree crops such as coffee and cacao because they could be grown under a full or partial forest canopy, or in a small clearing, and therefore did not require extensive clearing of land. They could be planted in areas from which the marketable timber had been removed, even though those spaces were not necessarily very large. Finally, with their leafy crowns, the cacao and coffee trees might also help planters and farmers hide illegal timber removal from city-bred government officials who were unable to distinguish between uncut forest and forests containing groves of coffee and cacao. It is hardly surprising, therefore, that as the loggers harvested timber in inland districts, landowners ordered cacao or coffee planted in the resulting clearings, rather than sugar.

## THE AVAILABILITY OF LABOR

Southern Bahian planters and farmers were not in a position to make decisions about what they would plant simply on appropriate environment or their feelings about timber policy and the timber industry. They also had to deal with the availability of labor, or rather its scarcity. Population density had been low throughout the colonial period, and as elsewhere the Portuguese had turned to slavery—both indigenous and African—to supply the labor on their plantations and farms and in their sawmills. They assumed that it was impossible to guarantee sufficient labor for a plantation or farm without coercion.

Acquiring labor for agriculture was not particularly easy for planters and farmers on the southern Bahian coast. According to Silva Lisboa, by 1799 local Indians were in constant demand for their ability to take down the enormous trees in southern Bahia's Atlantic forest and ride the logs down the rivers to the sawmills. In the 1820s, according to a French visitor, "the most industrious among them could be usefully employed on the farms [and] in logging," and in the 1850s local sawmill owners were competing with each other for indigenous labor. Nevertheless, there were not nearly enough of such workers to meet local labor needs, in part because of the low population density, but also because the local indigenous population attempted to avoid working for planters and farmers who did not compensate them well.[20]

Because of the difficulties in obtaining sufficient labor, from the colonial period on southern Bahian planters and farmers turned to African slavery to resolve their labor needs. Doing so also presented difficulties: few southern Bahian planters or farmers were prosperous enough to purchase many slaves, and credit for doing so was scarce. The flow of capital increased to some degree when elites such as the marques of Barbacena began to acquire property in the area, but it dried up once again in the wake of the 1821–24 slave revolts at Barbacena's Santanna Plantation.[21] Merchants were reluctant to lend money to planters and farmers to acquire slaves whom they would be unable to control. Investors did not want to see their potential profits disappear into the southern Bahian forest.

By the time that Ilhéus's slaves appeared to have been thoroughly subdued, in the 1830s, planters and farmers were facing the reality of international repression of the slave trade. It began in 1815 with an Anglo-Portuguese treaty prohibiting slaving north of the equator. Further treaties in 1826 and 1831 placed additional restrictions on the trade and finally prohibited it completely. As scholars have correctly pointed out, these treaties and laws were largely ineffectual and thousands of enslaved Africans were introduced to Bahia between independence in 1822 and the end of the trade in 1850. In Bahia, however, no one could avoid understanding that the slave trade was in danger: one of Brazil's largest slave traders, José Cerqueira Lima, was bankrupted when the British navy confiscated four of his ships, laden with slaves, on the high seas and sailed them to England. The trade continued, more or less publicly, but after 1840 it was subject to more and more repression, and by 1850 the supply of new Africans had essentially dwindled to nothing. Ilhéus was one of the few places in Brazil where Africans were successfully unloaded after 1850, but even so, the high prices charged for them made their acquisition even more difficult after 1850.[22]

In response to the obstacles to obtaining large numbers of slaves in Ilhéus, southern Bahian planters and farmers developed a labor force with a fairly natural demographic profile. It appears that in the first half of the nineteenth century, there were roughly equal numbers of enslaved men and women and large numbers of children on the plantations and farms of Ilhéus. By the time of the 1872 census, enslaved females outnumbered enslaved males by 13 percent, or 554 to 487. About 23.6 percent of these enslaved people were children between the ages of 1 and 11, while another 17 percent of slaves were men and women over 40. Adults in their twenties and thirties accounted for only 35 percent of the labor force. By the mid-1880s, perhaps as many as 250 free children of enslaved mothers had reached an age when they might be usefully employed in agriculture, and they therefore provided another source of labor to local planters and farmers.[23] By that time, however, men and women who had been in their thirties in 1872 were in their forties and fifties, and less useful as field hands.

This was hardly an ideal labor force for labor-intensive agriculture, particularly sugarcane cultivation. Cane had to be replanted every eighteen months and weeded regularly until the stalks matured. Once the crop matured, planters and slaves had to rush to get it harvested, transported to the mill, and processed. Cutting cane was difficult work that required both strength and endurance, since slaves had to bend over constantly to cut the plant near the base, and there was no shade in the fields. Once it was harvested, the cane had to be transported immediately to the mill, because its quality deteriorated rapidly if it was not processed within forty-eight hours. Many of the slaves on an Ilhéus plantation were not the most useful sugar workers: planters and farmers preferred young male slaves for cutting cane, not women, children, and the elderly.[24]

It was a labor force, however, that could handle cacao with little difficulty. Cacao grew on trees that, once matured, produced for decades. Therefore they did not have to be replanted every year, and new planting brought the expansion rather than the replication of existing production. Moreover, slaves could sow manioc, a rapidly maturing food crop, at the same time that they put out the new cacao seedlings, because the manioc would shade the delicate young cacao plants in their early years. They would have to weed the young plants, but newly cleared ground produced fewer weeds than land that had been planted for many years. The tree would not produce for five years, but in the meantime farmers or planters could sell the manioc or use it to feed the slaves on the property. Once the large green cacao pods turned yellow, signaling that they were ripe, a few men could be sent to cut them off the trees, and the children could collect them, while the women cut them open and scooped the seeds into baskets. One or two people then loaded the baskets onto mules and led them to the drying platforms, where the seeds were spread out to dry in the sun. Anyone, even a fairly young child, could then turn the beans over from time to time until they dried.[25]

Between 1789 and 1852, various observers, including Manuel Ferreira da Câmara, Miguel Calmon du Pin e Almeida, and Joaquim Rodrigues de Souza, suggested that planters and farmers supplement their sugar or manioc activities with cacao. Calmon and Rodrigues de Souza, in particular, linked cacao growing to the changing demographics of the Bahian enslaved population. In 1838 Calmon argued that only ten people, including the aged, the ill, or the very young, or six adult men were necessary to maintain and harvest a cacao grove of 6,400 trees. Fourteen years later Rodrigues de Souza suggested that twenty male slaves could handle 50,000 cacao trees, although more slaves would be required if women and children were employed. He even idealistically suggested that growing cacao might one day allow Bahian planters to give up slavery altogether.[26]

One might reasonably wonder why such observers as Ferreira da Camara and Rodrigues de Souza were not as enthusiastic about coffee in southern Bahia as they were about cacao, since coffee also grew on trees that produced for decades after they matured. As practiced in São Paulo at the time, harvesting was a simple matter of stripping the tree branches of berries when they were mature, and the processing requirements were simple. But in coastal southern Bahia, coffee was a bit more complicated than it was in São Paulo. In southern Bahia, the warm and rainy climate allowed coffee to ripen throughout the year, so that there was no distinct harvest season, as there was in São Paulo. Consequently, slaves could not just strip the branches. Ripe red berries had to be removed from branches still containing dozens or hundreds of immature green ones; all of them were small, and picking the red ones without harming the green ones was no easy task. Consequently, picking coffee was more difficult than collecting cacao. Elderly slaves whose vision was failing or children who did not understand the importance of separating the two kinds of berries made very poor coffee workers in southern Bahia. Indeed, southern Bahian coffee might not have been very suitable to plantation labor, since it is possible that only a farm owner would worry enough about the quality of the harvest to take the care necessary to carefully pick the ripe berries while leaving the immature ones undamaged.

When planters and farmers in southern Bahia realized the ramifications of the end of the African slave trade, they began to take the labor requirements of the various crops they were growing quite seriously. When they did, they quickly moved away from sugar, long understood to be a very labor-intensive crop requiring large amounts of adult male labor. They also ceased planting coffee because of the difficulties of harvesting it in southern Bahia. They equally rapidly began to increase the amount of cacao that they grew, because they perceived that in their region its labor requirements provided the best match for the available labor force.

### INDUSTRIALIZATION AND INTERNATIONAL DEMAND IN THE EMERGENCE OF CACAO CULTIVATION

The development of interest in cacao in southern Bahia was not only a response to such local factors as availability of labor, the timber industry, and the environment; it was also a reaction to major developments in the chocolate and cocoa industry that attention to the commodity chain can help us to elucidate. As Luis Amaral commented in 1941, the Bahian cacao sector was born alongside the chocolate industry. He meant that the growth in Bahian cacao cultivation was tied to the emergence of new in-dustrial cocoas and chocolates in Europe and North America in the nine-teenth century.[27] These were inexpensive cocoas and chocolates aimed at emerging working-class and middle-class markets, and connoisseurs considered them to be of poor quality. They grew out of a marriage between growing supplies of forastero cacao and the technological inno-vations of the Industrial Revolution.

Until the middle of the nineteenth century, chocolate was extraor-dinarily expensive. In eighteenth-century Spain, one pound of chocolate cost about twice the average daily wage of a worker. Thus, although it was widely reputed to have health benefits, it was a luxury, and its consump-tion was limited almost entirely to the aristocracy, the developing bour-geoisie, and perhaps their favored servants.[28]

Chocolate was expensive in part because its principal ingredient, ca-cao, was in short supply. As mentioned earlier, criollo cacao was a very delicate tree, and had proved almost impossible to introduce to regions beyond the Central American lowlands, where it had first been domesti-cated. Consequently, criollo cacao supplies did not expand much despite the growing demand for chocolate in Europe. Spanish settlers found forastero cacao growing wild in Venezuela, but it did not make chocolate acceptable to connoisseurs, the only people who could afford chocolate, and prices do not appear to have been strong enough to encourage exten-sive planting. Various colonists experimented with mixing forastero and criollo cacaos to develop a new variety, but it was a long, slow process and it had only limited success.[29] Problems with weather in Trinidad and disease in Venezuela devastated existing plantations, so overall cacao supplies did not grow much between 1700 and 1800. Then the wars for the independence of Spain's American colonies stopped economic ex-pansion in Venezuela and Ecuador almost completely.

The skill, strength, and time required to make chocolate exacerbated the problems caused by limited cacao supplies. Beans had to be carefully examined to be sure they were criollo and not forastero. They then had to be sorted to remove any sticks, dirt, bugs, stones, or sacking that might have become mixed in with the load. They were then carefully roasted over open fires, because they burned easily and the smell and taste of burned cacao would permeate any chocolate made with them. The roasted beans were ground and then reheated to remove the cocoa fat, known as cocoa butter, and make it soluble in water. The chocolate maker could then add sugar, vanilla, and boiling water to make the thick liquid that was the preferred breakfast drink of Europe's aristocracy at the time, or allow the cocoa mass to dry and harden so that it could be stored.[30] It was a time-consuming, difficult process that was carried out completely by hand until the eighteenth century. No wonder a pound of it cost an average person a day's pay.

Beginning in the eighteenth century, enterprising shopkeepers and millers in Europe and its American colonies began to try to make a chocolate that was inexpensive enough to find a market among the emerging middle and working classes of the growing cities.[31] As a first step, they turned to the cheaper, more plentiful forastero cacao to make the cocoa mass, hoping that the addition of sweeteners would mask its bitterness in the final product, or that customers unfamiliar with the criollo-based chocolate would not know the difference. Then they organized small shops in which artisans performed the complicated steps involved in making the cocoa mass, which they then sold to consumers. They had not found a way to make more than thirty pounds of chocolate a day, however, and so, if they were able to sell the cocoa mass inexpensively, it was only because they used cheaper cacao.

That situation changed toward the end of the eighteenth century when chocolate makers in Europe, the United States, and Canada began to use the tools of the Industrial Revolution to reduce production time and increase the amount of chocolate that could be made in a day. First, they introduced water-driven mechanical grinders to crush the roasted beans. By the end of the century, they began to harness the new steam technology to their factories, which allowed them to add roasting machines and to run multiple grinders at the same time. When this development took place is unclear. Some historians credit a French chocolatier with opening the first factory with steam-driven mechanical devices, while others mention a German prince, and still others believe a Spaniard was responsible. The English chocolate makers J. S. Fry and Sons were using steam to drive their machines by 1795. By 1805 at least one Parisian chocolate maker employed steam to power the grinding machine in his factory.[32] Regardless of who first introduced it, by the first years of the nineteenth century steam power was in widespread use for grinding and roasting cacao in Europe, and shortly thereafter in the United States.

These machines allowed industrialists to make extraordinary amounts of cocoa. One French chocolate maker claimed that his new machine, which was probably a grinder, could do the work of seven men, or presumably 210 pounds of chocolate mass per day. Another early industrial chocolate maker claimed to be able to make 600 or 700 pounds of cocoa and chocolate per day with the new machines. By the middle of the nineteenth century some chocolate makers were quoting figures as high as a ton per day. They probably did not make 365 tons of chocolate per year, however, because the cocoa mass would not solidify during the hottest months of the summer.[33]

While the grinding and roasting machines could speed up the process of making a cocoa mass, they did not allow the removal of the cocoa butter, the process that made cocoa soluble in water. Several techniques for removing excess cocoa butter existed in these early years, but each had problems. The so-called Weiched method required chocolate makers to stir "the beans in water until the seed membrane became removable and then [heat] the beans sharply until the husks broke off." Another procedure for removing the cocoa butter from the bean, called the water process, involved boiling the beans until the fat surfaced. Both of these processes, however, removed the chocolate flavor and aroma along with the cocoa butter, leading to a final product without the taste of chocolate.[34] Then in 1828 the Dutch chocolate maker C. J. Van Houten invented a machine to separate the cocoa butter from the cocoa chemically, but it would be many years before his method was widely adopted because chocolate made this way required more beans, and world cacao production was still quite limited in 1828. "Pure" cocoa was thus too expensive for working-class and middle-class housewives to buy.

Rather than use one of these unsatisfactory methods for removing the cocoa butter or perform the task by hand, manufacturers added substances to the roasted ground cocoa to make it soluble in water. When those additives were sweeteners, such as sugar or molasses, the result might be delicious, if rather sludgy, but many early industrialists cut costs by adding starch or less palatable items to their cocoa. In the middle of the nineteenth century, English and American government investigators charged that much of the cocoa made at that time contained everything from sticks, dirt, and pieces of sacking to molasses, bootblack, and umber. Much later, the English company Cadbury Brothers admitted that their early cocoas were four-fifths potato starch, flour, and molasses, and only one-fifth cocoa.[35]

Despite the problems, these technological developments allowed a group of grocers to introduce a new product, cocoa, in the first half of the nineteenth century. Aimed at competing with coffee and tea for the attention of the working-class and middle-class consumer, it needed very little processing: a housewife simply needed to put the cocoa powder in a cup and add boiling water. Chocolate was now no more difficult to make than coffee or tea, and middle- and working-class people could consume a version of the same breakfast beverage popular among aristocrats.

Demand for these "adulterated" cocoas was strong enough to encourage industrial chocolate makers to begin to market a "pure" industrial cocoa when world cacao production began to consistently exceed 20,000 tons for the first time. Old producing areas such as Ecuador (8,592 tons) and the Brazilian Amazon (3,280 tons) had increased their production, while such new areas as Bahia (570 tons), Fernando Póo, and São Thomé (396 tons) had begun to contribute small but significant amounts to world supplies. By 1870, world cacao production had increased by nearly 20 percent, and it continued to grow through the end of the century.[36] The vast majority of this new cacao was forastero. It was bitter, but it could be grown more widely and more easily than the delicate criollo, and so it was cheap.

The growth of cacao supplies and the technological innovations that enabled the widespread production and marketing of "pure" cocoas also enabled industrialists for the first time to make chocolate for eating. For most of its history, chocolate had been a drink, not a food. Beginning in the second half of the nineteenth century, industrial chocolate makers began to mass-produce chocolate bars and bonbons. These chocolates represented a significant development in the chocolate industry, but they were not the types of eating chocolates that would later become popular. They were harsh, granular, dark chocolates that contained no milk. They were, in other words, the solid equivalents of the adulterated cocoas so popular at the time. Nevertheless, for the first time, inexpensive chocolate could be wrapped in a box and given as an inexpensive gift, or carried to school, to work, or to the battlefield.

A Swiss chocolate maker, Daniel Peter, revolutionized the eating chocolate industry in 1876 when he added milk to the chocolate and created the world's first milk chocolate—the substance that is now the basis of the mass market for chocolate. In the next thirty years his invention was so successful that all of the other major chocolate companies and many minor ones attempted to produce their own milk chocolates. They were unable to do so at first, in part because Peter guarded the technology closely, but also because they did not know Peter's principal industrial secret: condensed milk. Milk is seven-eighths water, it spoils easily, and is quite heavy to transport. Peter had discovered by happy accident that only milk solids are needed for milk chocolate, because one of his closest neighbors was Henri Nestlé, owner of a company that produced and sold condensed milk throughout Europe. Peter's imitators had difficulty in finding the right form of milk to mix with the cocoa, and it was almost thirty years before they could produce a marketable milk chocolate.[37] When they did, manufacturers throughout Europe, the United States, and Canada began to bring out products whose names have become synonymous with chocolate: Hershey's Kisses, Cadbury's Dairy Milk bars, Mars bars.

The success of these cocoas and chocolates owed a great deal to the extraordinary changes that had taken place in European and North American diets and social practices. Whereas working-class and middle-class consumers had regularly consumed beer, ale, and wine throughout the day in the eighteenth century, by the close of the nineteenth century industrialization was doing away with the practice of imbibing spirits during the workday, and with it the workingman's unofficial holiday, "Saint Monday," to recover from the inebriation of the weekend. Drinking alcohol gradually earned a reputation as a social ill, as reformers attempted to move the new working and middle classes away from spirits and toward a group of stimulants—coffee, tea, and chocolate—that did not intoxicate. All of them were consumed with hefty amounts of sugar and milk, so they were a rapid source of calories as well. Chocolate had the added benefit of including nutrients that the other two did not, and so could be marketed as a healthful food appropriate for women and children as well as a beverage that provided an alternative to alcohol. Thus, as work and social life became increasingly distinct in the industrial societies developing in the United States and Europe, chocolate found an important niche alongside coffee and tea.[38]

As a result of all these changes, world consumption of cacao began to grow extraordinarily. In 1886 the Walter Baker Company of Dorchester, Massachusetts, estimated world imports of cacao at about 44,000 tons. By 1909 that figure had more than quadrupled, to 225,000 tons, and by 1927 it had doubled again, to 466,500 tons. No wonder analysts of the early-twentieth-century chocolate industry would comment that "chocolate will sell itself in any part of the world at the present time, provided that it is palatably sweet and that it tastes of chocolate."[39]

Not surprisingly, cacao supplies expanded to meet these demands. These new cocoas and chocolates were composed almost entirely of forastero cacao. While that cacao was widely considered of poor quality, as opposed to the criollo variety, it was perfect for the new industrial cocoas and chocolates. It also came from sources that had not been significant producers of cacao in the seventeenth and eighteenth centuries, and that did not offer the climatic conditions necessary for growing criollo cacao. By the opening decades of the twentieth century African producers were emerging as the world's most important suppliers of forastero cacao, with the Gold Cost leading world cacao producers. Bahia was not the world's largest supplier of raw cacao, but it had become the second most important one, and it would maintain that position for most of the twentieth century.

Bahian production grew slowly during the nineteenth century, and then took off after 1890. Regular exports of cacao date from the 1780s, but they were still limited to 26 tons a year in 1830, when Bahian officials began publishing statistical data on exports after the disruptions associated with the struggle for independence in Bahia. By 1860, however, exports had increased more than twenty times to 570 tons, and cacao was already the largest single source of revenue for southern Bahian farmers. Bahian exports had reached 10,000 tons by 1890, quadrupled to 40,000 tons by 1914, and nearly doubled again to 77,000 in 1927. Clearly, Bahian cacao production was closely tied to the changes in the market for industrial chocolates and cocoas.

It is reasonable to ask, however, to what degree we can assume developments in this market affected the decisions made by southern Bahian planters and farmers. In other words, how much did they know about these changes in the production and consumption of cocoa and chocolate? Surprisingly enough, some probably knew a great deal, although arguably most knew almost nothing. This information came from a variety of sources. Under the auspices of the Bahian Association for Industry and Agriculture, the essays of Manuel Ferreira da Câmara, Miguel Calmon du Pin e Almeida, and Joaquim Rodrigues de Souza were made available to a limited but well-connected public. Not only did those three men present papers to the members of that association, but Calmon's was published in the association's journal, while Rodrigues de Souza's was published in a newspaper and then as a separate booklet under the auspices of the association.[40] Certainly most farmers in Ilhéus would not have been aware of these presentations or publications, but the owners of the large estates were—several of them were members of the association.

Other planters and farmers knew about developments in the cocoa and chocolate industry through personal experience. There were numerous Swiss, German, Austrian, French, Spanish, and English immigrants to southern Bahia during the nineteenth century, and all of them arrived after chocolate makers began to target working-class and middle-class markets. The first owner of the Engenho Castello Novo named his plantation after his hometown, Neuchâtel, one of the early centers of chocolate making in Switzerland. It is perhaps not surprising, therefore, that he should have planted cacao as well as coffee and sugar on the plantation he built. We know less about the origins and habits of other European settlers in southern Bahia at that time, but it seems clear that throughout the nineteenth century new arrivals from Europe brought news of the growing popularity of chocolate and the development of new products in Europe.[41]

Both these European immigrants and the owners of the large estates continued to acquire news from Europe after they acquired property in southern Bahia. Some of them never lived on their properties, but continued to live in Salvador, where they had more access to the news about European demand than one might expect a planter living on the edge of the wilderness in southern Bahia to have. Those who actually lived in Iléus obtained their news when foreign travelers came to town. They came surprisingly frequently; southern Bahia was a common stop for French, German, and Austrian travelers in Brazil in the first half of the nineteenth century. Others obtained news from rare and precious letters received from relatives in Europe.[42] Still others visited Europe themselves and experienced at firsthand the new products being marketed, while others obtained their information through the commercial networks that linked Salvador and Ilhéus.

Finally, at least a few southern Bahian planters and farmers liked the taste of chocolate themselves, and may have chosen to plant cacao for that reason. Joaquim Simplicio Nogueira moved to Ilhéus from the Recôncavo sometime around 1870 and began to grow cacao. When he died in 1893, authorities found a chocolate pot among his possessions, in addition to several thousand cacao trees. He was not the owner of a large estate or a European immigrant; he appears to have been the son of a mid-sized farmer in the Recôncavo. Nonetheless, he appears to have known how to use cacao to make chocolate, and may have been drawn to southern Bahia to grow the beans required to make his favorite drink.[43]

In the twentieth century, planters in southern Bahia believed that cacao had been the natural choice for their parents and grandparents to make, and looked down on anyone who had not immediately seen it as the best crop to plant. Given all the factors discussed here, however, the excellence of cacao was not immediately clear to the people faced with the decision of what to plant in the nineteenth century, and for that reason, cacao cultivation in southern Bahia did not immediately take off as rapidly as coffee cultivation did in São Paulo. In the late eighteenth and early nineteenth century, planters and farmers in Ilhéus harvested timber and planted at least four crops for commercial sale. By the middle of the nineteenth century about two dozen large estates produced timber, sugar, coffee, cacao, and food crops, while about 300 farms produced timber, cacao, coffee, and food crops. Initially, planters and farmers had planted the crops that they understood to be culturally appropriate. Those with capital planted and produced sugar, Bahia's "noble business," while those without it grew manioc and other food crops for sale in the market of Salvador, even if they produced only what Ferreira da Câmara had termed a "mediocre happiness." Observers from Ferreira da Câmara to Rodrigues de Souza complained that southern Bahians were unwilling to invest in cacao, but for men and women making crucial decisions about the means to support themselves and their families, the decision to invest in a new crop was not easy when the market for it was only just emerging. Consequently, they gradually added cacao to their properties, but they also stayed with the tried and true—sugar and manioc—and experimented with another alternative, coffee. It was only when they observed cacao's behavior and analyzed all the factors discussed here, from the environment to the timber industry to labor to the cocoa and chocolate industry, that it became clear that cacao was the best crop for them.

In practical terms, planters and farmers probably saw those advantages in their pocketbooks. As early as 1789 observers were estimating that cacao gave phenomenal profits with almost no investment. In 1835 Calmon argued that two-thirds of the income earned in cacao would be profit. These estimates may have been too high, but it does appear that cacao profits were good or at least better than those from other sectors. Ilhéus sugar and *cachaça* prices were lower than those for coffee and cacao, despite extremely high production costs for the cane-based crop.

Prices for staple crops, such as manioc, inhames, and rice, were higher and production costs lower, but these were not prestigious crops. Coffee probably earned higher prices than any other crop locally. Although there are few statistics for coffee specifically from the cacao-producing communities, those few that do exist show that coffee prices were consistently higher than those for cacao in the 1860s, when southern Bahian planters and farmers were turning the land over to cacao rather than coffee. Unless southern Bahia farmers were completely unresponsive to prices—which seems unlikely—they must have been planting cacao rather than coffee because they earned more money for doing so despite the better prices for coffee. That was probably because cacao produced so well with so little labor, while coffee in southern Bahia was very labor-intensive because of the ripening schedule. When we take into consideration the amount of money and labor required to produce cacao in Bahia, in comparison with coffee or any other crop, it seems clear that the return on cacao must have been greater than that on the other crops.[44]

By the 1850s nearly all of the people with access to land in southern Bahia were growing at least some cacao, whether they were the owners of sugar mills and sawmills or farmers and loggers without the resources to build expensive processing facilities. By 1890, cacao was almost all they were growing. The sugar mill and sawmill owners planted the most cacao in the shortest amount of time: several of them had put in more than 50,000 trees between 1850 and 1890, and a couple planted as many as 200,000.[45] The farmers did not have the resources to plant so much cacao so rapidly, but there was a group that planted between 10,000 and 25,000 trees in the second half of the nineteenth century.[46] Another group, with access to less labor, was able to plant only between 1,000 and 5,000 trees. Farmers with no slaves were rarely able to plant more than 1,000 cacao trees unless they had many grown children to help.[47]

The small number of cacao trees on these plantations and farms did not necessarily reflect the growers' interest in cacao or the amount of land available to them. Many of them claimed or owned extensive amounts of forested land in one or more parts of the territory, but none of them could acquire enough labor to clear and plant all of the land that they owned. When their region began to earn a reputation as a place where one could make money, toward the end of the nineteenth century, that situation would change. Permanent and seasonal migrants would overrun the southern Bahian forests and establish their own cacao farms or go to work for established planters and farmers. By that time, landholders would have completely lost interest in preserving the forest, except as it allowed for protection of cacao groves.

I have argued that several factors contributed to the emergence of Bahia's cacao sector in the nineteenth century, including timber policy, climate, soil, the availability of labor and capital, and the creation of demand for industrialized cocoa and chocolate, but that cacao became Bahia's most important crop because of the choices that Bahian planters and farmers made, on the basis of the information available to them. Understanding the emergence of cacao in southern Bahia requires, therefore, understanding that it was a process in which international demand played an important—but not necessarily the only—role.

---

NOTES

1   This essay covers a period of transition in the political administration of the region in which cacao emerged as the dominant export. Prior to 1759, the region formed part of the Captaincy of São Jorge dos Ilhéus, a colonial administrative unit that stretched from Jaguaripe in the north to the Rio Pardo in the south. After 1759, the territory became a *comarca*, or county, known as the Comarca de Ilhéos, which was subordinated politically and administratively to the province of Bahia. After independence in 1822, the comarca was broken up, and Ilhéus was reduced by at least half. The name *Ilhéus* came to refer to a municipality bounded, more or less, by the Rio de Contas in the north and the Rio Pardo in the south. By the end of the nineteenth century, that space had been reduced further still; in the twentieth century, yet more territory was "emancipated" to form new municipalities, including what are today Itabuna, Uruçuca, Itajuípe, Boararema, and other southern Bahian towns. Throughout the entire period, there has also been a town called Ilhéus at the confluence of the Cachoeira, Engenho, and Fundão rivers. To reduce the confusion potentially incurred by the various uses of the place name *Ilhéus* or *Ilhéos*, I have used the term *southern Bahia* to refer to the cacao area in general, and comarca (or county), municipality, and town to specify exactly the way in which I use the term *Ilhéus*.

2   Nineteenth-century Bahian agriculture is only beginning to receive the attention it deserves. For a history of the interaction between people and the Atlantic forest, with some attention paid to southern Bahia, see Dean, *With Broadax and Firebrand*; on the eighteenth-century timber industry in southern Bahia see Miller, *Fruitless Trees*; the principal work on the Bahian sugar trade is Schwartz, *Sugar Plantations in the Formation of Brazilian Society*, although its treatment of the topic ends in the early nineteenth century; on the manioc trade and manioc farming in Bahia see Barickman, *A Bahian Counterpoint*, where brief discussions of nineteenth-century Bahian coffee and tobacco production can also be found. For the problems and pitfalls facing the Bahian sugar industry in the nineteenth century, see Barickman, "Persistence and Decline." On cacao, see Mahony, "The World Cacao Made"; Baiardi, *Subordinação do trabalho ao capital na*

lavoura cacaueira da Bahia; Guerreiro de Freitas, "Au Brésil"; Wright, "Market, Land and Class"; Garcez and Guerreiro de Freitas, Bahia cacaueira; and Garcez, "Mecanismos da formação socioeconomica no eixo Ilhéus-Itabuna."

3   This discussion of commodity chains benefited from the literature review undertaken by the editors of the volume and from the following articles: Gereffi, "Rethinking Development Theory"; Talbot, "The Struggle for Control of a Commodity Chain"; and Leslie and Reimer, "Spatializing Commodity Chains." For a discussion of the values of the commodity chain approach for cacao areas, see Clarence-Smith, Cocoa and Chocolate, esp. 5–6; and Mahony, "The World Cacao Made," 142.

4   Here I am extending Bulmer-Thomas's concept in The Economic History of Latin America, 15, which focuses on the differences in backward and forward linkages among commodities, and presumably on the "luck" of some producers in "winning" a commodity with more rather than fewer linkages, and recognizes that in nineteenth-century Latin America, economic actors were faced with a number of alternative investments, and thus were required to choose or "bet" the one they perceived as best for them. See also Clarence-Smith, Cocoa and Chocolate, 2.

5   Barickman, A Bahian Counterpoint, 17–43, demonstrates that Bahia was far from a monocultural state in the nineteenth century, and discusses the various crops produced in the Bahian Recôncavo at that time.

6   Ferreira da Câmara, "Ensaio de descripção fizica e econômica da Comarca de São Jorge dos Ilhéos," 310; Bondar, A cultura de cacao na Bahia, 78–86.

7   Silva Lisboa, "Officio do ouvidor da comarca dos Ilhéos," 107; Mahony, "The World Cacao Made," 112; Bondar, A Cultura de cacao na Bahia, 80–86; Erneholm, Cacao Production of South America, 147–49.

8   Weid von Neuweid, Viagem ao Brasil, 349–53; Spix and Martius, Viagem pelo Brasil, 2:159–65; Dean, With Broadax and Firebrand, 10–12.

9   On Recôncavo soils see Schwartz, Sugar Plantations in the Formation of Brazilian Society, 107; Barickman, A Bahian Counterpoint, 9. On southern Bahian soils see Bondar, A cultura de cacao, 87–125; on massapé in particular see 107. For a map indicating the quality of the soil in the region as a whole, see Comissão Executiva do Plano da Lavoura Cacaueira (CEPLAC), Diagnóstico socioeconômico da região cacaueira, map insert.

10  For descriptions of the southern Bahian forest around 1800 see particularly Weid von Neuweid, Através do Brasil, 349–53; Spix and Martius, Viagem pelo Brasil, 2:159–65.

11  Ferreira da Câmara, "Ensaio de descripção," 310, 315–16; CEPLAC, Diagnóstico socioeconomico, 12–13; Bondar categorized cacao forastero as Theobroma leicoparpum and only criollo as Theobroma cacao: A cultura de cacao, 43, 63. Biologists now refer to both of them as Theobroma cacao, although they recognize that the two are different varieties. See Cheesman, "Notes on the Nomenclature, Classification and Possible Relationships of Cacao Populations"; Young, The Chocolate Tree; Dias et al., "Variation and Its Distribution in Wild Cacao Populations from the Brazilian Amazon," 507.

12 Cacao cultivation in the colonial Americas is only beginning to receive the attention it deserves. See especially Alden, "The Significance of Cacao Production"; Jamieson, "The Essence of Commodification"; Gasco, "Cacao and Economic Inequality"; Ferry, *The Colonial Elite of Early Caracas* and "Ecomienda, African Slavery, and Agriculture in Seventeenth-Century Caracas"; MacLeod, *Spanish Central America*; and Piñero, *The Town of San Felipe and Colonial Cacao Economics*.

13 See, for example, Inventários, ABEBa: no. 02/795/1220/14, João Segismundo Cordier (1849); no. 03/783/1250/08, Maria Luiza da Santissima Trinidade (1850); no. 03/783/1250/09, Francisca de Jesus (1856); no. 03/783/1250/14, Guilherme Mor (1856); no. 03/1270/1739/10, José Francisco de Abreu (1863); Neezer, "Os pioneiros suiços no comercio," 41.

14 Silva Lisboa, "Auto de tombo feito em huma e outra margem do Rio de Itahaipe," Biblioteca Nacional, Manuscripts, 22-2-41; Morton, "Royal Timber in Late Colonial Brazil."

15 Morton, "Royal Timber."

16 Ernano Dantas dos Santos, juiz de direito of Ilhéus, to Presidente da Província, December 20, 1858, maço 2398, in Juizes, ABEBa/SH.

17 Madeiras, maços 4616, 4617, 4618, in Juízes, APEBa/SH; Bahia, Brazil, Presidência da Província, *Relatorio apresentado a Assembléa Legislativa Provincial da Bahia pelo excellentissimo Presidente da Provincia, o Comendador Manuel Pinto de Souza Dantas no dia 1 de março de 1866*, Anexo 8. On the relationship between the lavradores de cana and the sugar mill owners, see Schwartz, *Sugar Plantations*, 109–10, 305–8.

18 Dos Santos to Presidente da província, December 20, 1858, maço 2398, Juizes, ABEBa/SH; Proceso Cívil (PC): Manoel Cardozo da Silva v. Pedro Cerqueira Lima, Ilhéus (1868), FEBC/PCVC; Antonio Gomes Villaça, juiz de direito, to Presidente da provincia, November 29, 1868, maço 2401, and Joaquim Rodriguez de Souza, juiz de direito, to Presidente da provincia, February 17, 1851, maço 2397, both in Juízes, Ilhéus, APEBa/SH.

19 This argument contradicts those of both Dean and Miller about planters' attitudes toward the forest and government regulation. I agree with them that timber extraction was frequently wasteful of other species and harmful to the environment in general. Nevertheless, the evidence for nineteenth-century Ilhéus indicates the systematic removal of marketable hardwoods until well into the century rather than thoughtless eradication on behalf of agriculture (Dean, *With Broadax and Firebrand*, 117) or destruction to avoid government regulation (Miller, *Fruitless Trees*, 83).

20 Silva Lisboa, "Officio do ouvidor," 115, and "Memoria sobre a comarca dos Ilhéos," 17; *O Crepúsculo: Periódico instructivo e moral da sociedade instituto-literario* (1845–1847) (Bahia), January 25, 1846.

21 On the Santanna slave revolts of the 1820s, see Reis and Silva, *Negociação e conflito*, 126–30. On the wider political and economic impact that such revolts could have see Graden, "An Act 'Even of Public Security.'"

22 Barickman, *A Bahian Counterpoint*, 136–37; Eltis, *Economic Growth and the Ending of*

the *Transatlantic Slave Trade*, 37n; Verger, *Bahia and the West Coast Trade*; Bethell, *The Abolition of the Brazilian Slave Trade*, 117.

23 Clasificação dos escravos para serem libertados pelo fundo de Emancipação (1874–1886), bk., no. 7008, in Tesouraria, APEBa/SH; Schwartz, *Slaves, Peasants and Rebels*, 52; Livros de Notas, Ilhéus, no. 12, 12/4/1851–04/25/1854, Escrivão: Hostílio Tulo Albuquerque Melo, in APEBa/SJ; inventário no. 02/786/1253/06, Maria José Scola del Rei and Josefina Carolina Scola del Rei (1861), APEBa/SJ; Brazil, Diretoria Geral de Estatística, *Recenseamento da população do Brazil . . .* 1872, 3:277–78; "Livro de registro dos baptismos" (hereafter "Registro dos baptismos"); "Registro dos nascimentos dos filhos d'escravos" (hereafter "Registro dos nascimentos"), the last two in Arquivo, Cúria de Ilhéus.

24 On the predominance of male slaves on sugar plantations, see Schwartz, *Sugar Plantations*, 346–53; Barickman, *A Bahian Counterpoint*, 155–56.

25 For an example of young children working cacao see criminal case no. 06/182/15, prisoner: Diego the slave; victim: Thereza the slave, in APEBa/SJ.

26 Ferreiro da Câmara, "Ensaio de descripção," 304–21; Calmon du Pin e Almeida, "Memoria sobre a cultura de cacao"; Rodrigues de Souza, *Memoria sobre a lavoura de cacao*, 1, 4, 7.

27 Amaral, *História geral da agricultura brasileira*, 2:380. There are few scholarly studies of the development of chocolate consumption. The most important are Coe and Coe, *True History of Chocolate*, which is best on pre-Columbian and early modern chocolate consumption; Mahony, "The World Cacao Made," chaps. 1 and 5, and Clarence-Smith, *Cocoa and Chocolate*, both of which link chocolate consumption to industrialization; Schivelbusch, *Tastes of Paradise*, which connects it to its role as a mild stimulant that changed cultural norms during the Industrial Revolution; and Jamieson, "The Essence of Commodification," which also addresses chocolate's role as a stimulant. With the exception of Schivelbusch, to one degree or another all of these authors connect changes in chocolate consumption to developments in cultivation and cacao supplies.

28 Piñero, "The Cacao Economy of the Eighteenth-Century Province of Caracas," 83.

29 Erneholm, *Cacao Production of South America*; Hall, *Cacao*, 6–7, 45. The most complete historical statistics on world exports of cacao can be found in Clarence-Smith, *Cocoa and Chocolate*, Appendix 2, 234–39; Clarence-Smith (45) sees European import taxes as a significant reason for this high cost. While I do not disagree that taxes added to chocolate's cost, I see the combination of small supplies and labor-intensive production as the central issues involved in high costs. See Mahony, "The World Cacao Made," 39.

30 Zipperer, *The Manufacture of Chocolate*, 98; Dufour, *The Manner of Making Coffee, Tea and Chocolate*, 102–4.

31 Much more research is needed on the colonial chocolate industry and chocolate consumption as opposed to cacao cultivation in the Americas, because there was a significant market for cacao in the Americas when the Spanish first arrived. See Clarence-Smith, *Cocoa and Chocolate*, 10–32.

32 Walter Baker & Co., *Cocoa and Chocolate*, 28–29, 45; J. S. Fry & Sons, *The Industrial*

*Record*, 64a; Whymper, *Cocoa and Chocolate*, 16; Morton and Morton, *Chocolate*, 78; Pelletier and Pelletier, *Le thé et le chocolat*, 78.

33 Walter Baker & Co., *Cocoa and Chocolate*, 29; Zipperer, *Manufacture of Chocolate*, 98.

34 Zipperer, *Manufacture of Chocolate*, 102; Whymper, *Cocoa and Chocolate*, 170.

35 Morton and Morton, *Chocolate*, 75; Cadbury Brothers, *Cocoa and Chocolate from Grower to Consumer*, 178; Williams, *Firm of Cadbury*, 25.

36 Williams, *Firm of Cadbury*, 71; Erneholm, *Cacao Production*, 69, 109, 123. Cacao cultivation in the Americas during this period has not received nearly the attention it deserves. Exceptions include González Leal, "Insurgencia popular, oligarquía regional y estado"; Guerrero, *Los oligarcas del cacao*; and Gasco, "Cacao and the Economic Integration of Native Society."

37 Williams, *The Firm of Cadbury*, 92.

38 Schivelbusch, *Tastes of Paradise*; Mintz, *Sweetness and Power*.

39 Zipperer, *Manufacture of Chocolate*, 29; Walter Baker & Co., *Cocoa and Chocolate*, 2–5; Whymper, *Cocoa and Chocolate*, 18, 219; Clarence-Smith, *Cocoa and Chocolate*, 236–37.

40 Ferreira da Câmara, "Ensaio de descripção"; Calmon du Pin e Almeida, "Memoria sobre a cultura de cacao"; Rodrigues de Souza, "Memoria sobre a lavoura de cacao."

41 Mahony, "The World Cacao Made," 230–45.

42 Translations of a few examples of these letters, enough to indicate that they existed, can be found in Papers of Anthony Leeds, Anthropological Archives, American Museum of Natural History, Washington.

43 Autuação de um officio do sub commissionario de policia Capitão Pedro Scola Homem del Rei, Joaquim Simplicio Nogueira (1893), FEBC/PCVC.

44 Calmon du Pin e Almeida, "Memoria sobre a cultura de cacao." On returns in sugar investments, see Schwartz, *Sugar Plantations*, 226–29. Bahia, Brazil, Presidência da Província, *Relatorio*, 1866, Anexo 8; and Antonio Gomes Villaça, juiz de direito, to Presidente da provincia, in Juízes, maço 2400, APEBa/SH.

45 Inventários: no. 02/754/1220/11, Capitão Egydio Luis de Sá (1880); no. 02/786/1253/06, Maria José Scola del Rei and Josefina Carolina Scola del Rei (1861), both in APEBa/SJ; Livros de Notas, Ilhéus, no. 12, 12/4/1851–04/25/1854, Escrivão: Hostílio Tulo Albuquerque Melo, in APEBa/SJ; Maximilian I, "Mato Virgem," in *Recollections of My Life*, 3:360; Fernando Steiger e outros v. Albino Francisco Martins (1911), FEBC/PCVC; Livros de Notas, Ilhéus, no. 14, 27/04/1854–10/11/1859, Hostilio Tulo de Albuquerque Melo; no. 05/2177/2646/04, will of Pedro Cerqueira Lima (1881), in APEBa/SJ; Inventário of Pedro Antonio Cerqueira Lima (1894); Registro de Testamentos, FEBC/PCVC; Aguiar, *Descriçães práticas da província da Bahia*, 266.

46 Inventários: no. 02/750/1216/09, Maria Bonim Lavigne (1878); no. 03/1298/1767/08, Acrísio Januário Cardoso (1887); no. 02/760/1226/04, José Lopes da Silva (1888); no. 02/762/1228/12, João Carlos Hohlenwerger (1886); no. 02/759/1225/3, Domingos Lopes da Silva (1883); Domingos José de Lemos (1888), all preceding in APEBa/SJ; "Registro de Testamentos," in FEBC/

PCVC; "Registro dos baptismos," vol. 2, and "Registro dos nascimentos," in Arquivo, Cúria de Ilhéus.

47 Inventários: no. 03/1298/1767/08, Acrísio Januário da Silva (1887); no. 03/742/1207/02, João Pedro Bonim (1868); no. 02/761/1227/13, Joaquim Alves da Silva (1885); no. 02/759/1225/6, Felícia Maria Abreu e Castro (1883); no. 02/795/1220/14, João Segismundo Cordier (1849); no. 02/761/1227/13, Joaquim Alves da Silva (1885); no. 03/742/1207/02, João Pedro Bonim (1868); no. 03/1298/1767/08, Acrísio Januário Cardoso (1887); no. 02/759/1225/6, Felícia Maria Abreu e Castro (1883); no. 03/742/1207/03, Sofia Claudentina Batista, (1882); no. 03/762/1228/03, Maria Juliana Wense (1885); no. 03/742/1207/03, Agostino Antonio da Silva, 1868, all in APEBa/SJ; Registro de Testamentos, in FEBC/PCVC; Maximilian I, *Recollections of My Life*, 3:368.

## BIBLIOGRAPHY

*Archival Sources*

ABEBa: Arquivo Público do Estado da Bahia

ABEBa/SH: Arquivo Público do Estado da Bahia / Secção histórica

ABEBa/SJ: Arquivo Público do Estado da Bahia / Secção judiciaria

FEBC/PCVC: Fórum Epaminondas Berbert de Castro / Primeiro Cafório da Vara Cívil

*Published Works*

Aguiar, Durval Vieira de. *Descrições práticas da província da Bahia: Com declaração de todas as distâncias intermediárias das cidades, vilas e povoações*. 2nd ed. Rio de Janeiro: Cátedra/Instituto Nacional do Livro, 1979.

Alden, Dauril. "The Significance of Cacao Production in the Amazon Region during the Late Colonial Period: An Essay in Comparative Economic History." *Proceedings of the American Philosophical Society* 120, no. 2 (1976): 103–35.

Amaral, Luis. *Historia geral da agricultura brasileira no triplice aspecto politico-social-economico*. 3 vols. São Paulo: Nacional, 1939–41.

Bahia, Brazil, Presidência da Província. *Relatorio apresentado a Assembléa Legislativa Provincial da Bahia pelo excellentissimo Presidente da Provincia, o Comendador Manuel Pinto de Souza Dantas no dia 1 de março de 1866*. Anexo 8.

Baiardi, Amilcar. *Subordinação do trabalho ao capital na lavoura cacaueira da Bahia*. São Paulo and Salvador: Hucitec, 1984.

Barickman, Bert J. *A Bahian Counterpoint: Sugar, Tobacco, Cassava, and Slavery in the Recôncavo, 1780–1860*. Stanford: Stanford University Press, 1999.

——. "Persistence and Decline: Slave Labour and Sugar Production in the Bahian Recôncavo, 1850–1888." *Journal of Latin American Studies* 28, no. 3 (October 1996): 581–633.

Bethell, Leslie. *The Abolition of the Brazilian Slave Trade*. Cambridge: Cambridge University Press, 1970.

Bondar, Gregório. *A cultura de cacao na Bahia*. Instituto de Cacao da Bahia, Boletim Technico no. 1. São Paulo: Empreza Graphica da "Revista dos Tribunaes," 1938.

Bulmer-Thomas, Victor. *The Economic History of Latin America since Independence.* New York: Cambridge University Press, 1993.

Cadbury Brothers. *Cocoa and Chocolate from Grower to Consumer.* Bourneville, n.d.

Calmon du Pin e Almeida, Miguel. "Memoria sobre a cultura de cacao." *Boletim da Sociedade d'Agricultura da Bahia.* 1846. Reprinted in *Gazeta de Ilhéos,* October 16–30, 1904.

Cheesman, E. E. "Notes on the Nomenclature, Classification and Possible Relationships of Cacao Populations." *Tropical Agriculture* (Trinidad) 21 (1944): 144–59.

Clarence-Smith, William Gervase. *Cocoa and Chocolate, 1765–1914.* London: Routledge, 2000.

Coe, Sophie, and Michael Coe. *The True History of Chocolate.* London: Thames & Hudson, 1996.

Comissão Executiva do Plano da Lavoura Cacaueira (CEPLAC). *Diagnóstico socioeconomico da região cacaueira.* Vol. 7. Ilhéus, 1976.

Dean, Warren. *With Broadax and Firebrand: The Destruction of the Brazilian Atlantic Forest.* Berkeley: University of California Press, 1995.

Dias, Luiz Antônio dos Santos, et al. "Variation and Its Distribution in Wild Cacao Populations from the Brazilian Amazon." *Brazilian Archives of Biology and Technology* 46, no. 4 (December 2003): 507–14.

Dufour, Philippe Sylvestre. *The Manner of Making Coffee, Tea and Chocolate Newly Done out of the French and Spanish.* London: William Crook, 1685.

Eltis, David. *Economic Growth and the Ending of the Transatlantic Slave Trade.* New York: Oxford University Press, 1987.

Erneholm, Ivar. *Cacao Production of South America: Historical Development and Present Geographical Distribution.* Gothenburg: C. R. Holmqvist, 1948.

Ferreiro da Câmara, Manuel. "Ensaio de descripção fizica e economica da comarca de São Jorge dos Ilhéos." *Memórias Econômicas da Academia das Sciencias da Lisboa* 1 (1789): 304–50.

Ferry, Robert J. *The Colonial Elite of Early Caracas: Formation and Crisis, 1567–1767.* Berkeley: University of California Press, 1989.

——. "Encomienda, African Slavery, and Agriculture in Seventeenth-Century Caracas." *Hispanic American Historical Review* 61, no. 4 (November 1981): 609–35.

Garcez, Angelina Nobre Rolim. "Mecanismos da formação socioeconomico no eixo Ilhéus-Itabuna." Master's thesis, Universidade Federal da Bahia, 1977.

Garcez, Angelina Nobre Rolim, and Antonio Fernando Guerreiro de Freitas. *Bahia cacaueira: Um estudo da história recente.* Estudos Baianos, Universidade Federal da Bahia, no. 11. Salvador: Núcleo de Publicações do Centro Editorial e Didatico da Universidade Federal da Bahia, 1979.

Gasco, Janine. "Cacao and Economic Inequality in Colonial Soconusco, Chiapas, Mexico." *Journal of Anthropological Research* 52, no. 4 (1996): 385–410.

——. "Cacao and the Economic Integration of Native Society in Colonial Soconusco, New Spain." Ph.D. dissertation, University of California, Santa Barbara, 1987.

Gereffi, Gary. "Rethinking Development Theory: Insights from East Asia and Latin America." In A. Douglas Kincaid and Alejandro Portes, eds., *Comparative National Development*. Chapel Hill: University of North Carolina Press, 1994.

González Leal, Miguel Angel. "Insurgencia popular, oligarquía regional y estado en el Ecuador liberal (1895–1925): La huelga general de Guayaquil, 1922." *Anuario de Estudios Americanos* 54, no. 1 (1997): 159–84.

Graden, Dale. "An Act 'Even of Public Security': Slave Resistance, Social Tensions and the End of the International Slave Trade to Brazil, 1835–1856." *Hispanic American Historical Review* 76, no. 2 (1996): 249–82.

Guerreiro de Freitas, Antônio. "Au Brésil: Deux régions de Bahia (1896–1937)." Ph.D. dissertation, Université de Paris IV, 1992.

Guerrero, Andrés. *Los oligarcas del cacao*. Quito: Conejo, 1980.

Hall, C. J. J. van. *Cacao*. 2nd ed. London: Macmillan, 1932.

J. S. Fry & Sons. *The Industrial Record*. Somerdale, n.d.

Jamieson, Ross W. "The Essence of Commodification: Caffeine Dependencies in the Early Modern World." *Journal of Social History* 35, no. 2 (2001): 269–94.

Leslie, Deborah, and Suzanne Reimer. "Spatializing Commodity Chains." *Progress in Human Geography* 23, no. 3 (1999): 401–20.

MacLeod, Murdo. *Spanish Central America*. Berkeley: University of California Press, 1973.

Mahony, Mary Ann. "The World Cacao Made: Society, Politics, and History in Southern Bahia, Brazil, 1822–1919." Ph.D. dissertation, Yale University, 1996.

Maximilian I, Emperor of Mexico. *Recollections of My Life*. 3 vols. New ed. London: R. Bentley, 1868.

Miller, Shawn William. *Fruitless Trees: Portuguese Conservation and Brazil's Colonial Timber*. Stanford: Stanford University Press, 2000.

Mintz, Sidney W. *Sweetness and Power: The Place of Sugar in Modern History*. New York: Viking, 1985.

Morton, F. W. O. "Royal Timber in Late Colonial Brazil." *Hispanic American Historical Review* 58, no. 1 (1978): 41–61.

Morton, Marcia, and Frederic Morton. *Chocolate: An Illustrated History*. New York: Crown, 1986.

Neezer, Carlos Hermann. "Os pioneiros suiços no comercio." *Revista da Bahia* 16 (March–May 1990): 41.

Pelletier, Eugene, and Auguste Pelletier. *Le thé et le chocolat dans l'alimentation publique*. Paris, 1861.

Piñero, Eugenio. "The Cacao Economy of the Eighteenth-Century Province of Caracas." *Hispanic American Historical Review* 68, no. 1 (1988): 75–100.

——. *The Town of San Felipe and Colonial Cacao Economics*. Philadelphia: American Philosophical Society, 1994.

Reis, João José, and Eduardo Silva. *Negociação e conflito: A resistencia negra no Brazil escravista*. São Paulo: Letras, 1989.

Rodrigues de Souza, Joaquim. *Memoria sobre a lavoura de cacao e suas vantagens primsipalmenta na Bahia*. Bahia: Carlos Poggetti, 1852.

Schivelbusch, Wolfgang. *Tastes of Paradise: A Social History of Spices, Stimulants, and Intoxicants*. New York: Pantheon, 1992.

Schwartz, Stuart. *Slaves, Peasants, and Rebels: Reconsidering Brazilian Slavery*. Urbana: University of Illinois Press, 1992.

——. *Sugar Plantations in the Formation of Brazilian Society: Bahia, 1550–1835*. Cambridge: Cambridge University Press, 1985.

Silva Lisboa, Balthazar da. "Auto de tombo feito em huma e outra margem do Rio de Itahaipe." Biblioteca Nacional, Manuscripts, 22-2-41.

——. "Memoria sobre a comarca dos Ilhéos." *Annaes da Biblioteca Nacional* 37 (1915): 1–22.

——. "Officio do ouvidor da comarca dos Ilhéos Balthasar da Silva Lisboa para D. Rodrigo de Sousa Coutinho, no qual lhe communica uma interessante informaçó sobre a comarca dos Ilhéos, a sua origem, a sua agricultura, commercio, população e preciosas mattas, Cairú 20 de março de 1799." *Annaes da Biblioteca Nacional* 36 (1914): 102–17.

Spix [Johann Baptist von] and Martius [Carl Friedrich]. *Viagem pelo Brasil*. Vol. 2. São Paulo: Melhoramentos, 1976.

Talbot, John M. "The Struggle for Control of a Commodity Chain: Instant Coffee from Latin America." *Latin American Research Review* 32, no. 2 (1997): 117–35.

Verger, Pierre. *Bahia and the West Coast Trade, 1549–1851*. Ibadan: Ibadan University Press, 1962.

Walter Baker & Co. *Cocoa and Chocolate: A Short History of Their Production and Use*. Dorchester, Mass., 1899.

Weid von Neuweid, Maximilian. *Viagem ao Brasil*. Belo Horizonte: Editora Itatiaia, Editora da Universidade de São Paulo, 1989.

Whymper, Robert. *Cocoa and Chocolate: Their Chemistry and Manufacture*. Philadelphia: P. Blakiston, 1921.

Williams, Iolo A. *The Firm of Cadbury, 1831–1931*. London: Constable, 1931.

Wright, Angus Lindsay. "Market, Land, and Class: Southern Bahia, Brazil, 1890–1942." Ph.D. dissertation, University of Michigan, 1976.

Young, Allen M. *The Chocolate Tree: A Natural History of Cacao*. Washington: Smithsonian Institution, 1994.

Zipperer, Paul. *The Manufacture of Chocolate*. New York: Spon & Chamberlain, 1902.

# 8

Banana Boats and Baby Food:
The Banana in U.S. History

Marcelo Bucheli and Ian Read

THE PEJORATIVE TERM "banana republic" has been used to depict a backward country ruled by a despotic dictator, populated by poor peasants, and dependent on the will of foreign multinational corporations. Opinions about the United Fruit Company have helped shape this prevalent historical image of Central America. This Boston-based company, established in 1899, created a huge production and marketing network of bananas from the Caribbean to the United States that included plantations in the tropics, housing facilities, hospitals, railways, telegraph lines, ports, and the largest private steamship fleet in the world, the Great White Fleet. With this network United Fruit created the most successful vertical integration in the agrarian sector in the first two decades of the twentieth century—a time when the world witnessed other processes of industrial vertical integration in such companies as Ford and Standard Oil.[1] United Fruit controlled the international banana trade during the first six decades of the twentieth century and had an extremely high degree of control of the local economies of Honduras, Guatemala, and Panama, countries that depended on bananas for most of their foreign trade. So many aspects of the host countries' societies were affected by the company's operations that the locals nicknamed it El Pulpo (the Octopus).

The idea that this company exploited its workers or meddled in Latin American politics has gone far beyond academia and has been illustrated by important writers such as Gabriel García Márquez, Miguel Angel Asturias, and Pablo Neruda.[2] Likewise, scholarly writers interested in United Fruit have generated a body of literature focused on the political, economic, social, and ethnic features of banana production and export by the fruit company.[3] The story usually ends, however, when the stems of bananas were loaded into the holds of steamers, leaving the strikes, revolutions, and tropical intrigues behind.

What happened after the banana ships left port? By using the idea of commodity chain as a unit of analysis, we wish to follow the bananas from the port to the kitchen of the American consumer. We assume that United Fruit—for decades the world's largest producer and supplier of bananas—made its investments in Central America with one specific goal: to sell its bananas to American grocery stores. Of course, had Americans not been eager to buy and eat the fruit, the company would not have constructed the production infrastructure in Latin America; and the political, labor, and social conflicts that rose around this industry would not have occurred. To understand how the company behaved on its Latin American plantations and why, it is crucial to understand how its consumer market evolved, what factors affected the consumption of bananas, and how United Fruit was constrained and altered by media representation and U.S. politics.

A long-term analysis of the banana market in the United States shows that most of the change in consumption patterns took place during the twentieth century. Banana imports grew steadily since their inception in U.S. markets except during World War I, the Great Depression, and World War II (Figures 1 and 2). Not only did the volume of bananas imported to the United States increase throughout the twentieth century, but so did per capita consumption. In 1909, Americans ate an average of 17 pounds of bananas a year; in 1997 they were consuming about 27 pounds. The crises generated by World War I, the Great Depression, and World War II negatively affected per capita consumption but there was also a long period of stagnation and decline during the 1950s and 1960s. It ended in the 1970s, when Americans rediscovered bananas as a health food. What caused these fluctuations?

We approach this problem by asking two questions. First, what factors affected banana consumption in the United States? Second, what factors affected United Fruit's operations? Before World War II the demand for fresh fruit could not be satisfied by local production because of the seasonal availability of most fruits in the United States. The growing urban

1. Millions of stems of bananas imported by the United States, 1920–1960

Source: Adapted from Marcelo Bucheli, *Bananas and Business: The United Fruit Company in Colombia, 1899–2000* (New York: New York University Press, 2005), 25.

population and lack of substitutes steadily increased the demand for bananas, and the expanding United Fruit Company satisfied this demand by vertically integrating its operations, eliminating competitors, and aggressively marketing its product. By these means, the company helped stimulate demand and maintain an oligopoly over the production of bananas in Latin America and the distribution of the fruit in the United States. The company's dominant position arose during an era of trust-busting, but it did not face strong legal opposition from the U.S. government because of a strategic relationship between the company and the State Department and because many of the media saw the company as a "civilizer of the tropics." After World War II, the company's privileged position ended. First, the demand for bananas in the United States decreased because of the introduction of new substitutes such as frozen and canned fruit, and demand recovered only in the 1970s, when concerns about a healthy diet revived consumption of bananas. Second, the strength of the company waned because of legal action it faced from the U.S. government and new criticism in the American media. These interrelated factors, along with a more competitive market, put the company

2. Tons of bananas imported by the United States, 1920–1999

Source: Marcelo Bucheli, *Bananas and Business: The United Fruit Company in Colombia, 1899–2000* (New York: New York University Press, 2005), 26.

in financial jeopardy. In the end, it was compelled to share the market with its competitors, a process that was also influenced by labor and political problems in Latin America. Directly related to the decline in its market share, the company lost much of its influence over Latin American politics and was forced to change its relationship with its plantation laborers. The era of banana republics had ended.

This essay is divided into two parts: first we study the factors affecting the demand for bananas, the structure of the banana industry, and United Fruit's relationship with the U.S. government between 1880 and 1945. In the second half, we explore how these themes changed after World War II. Our sources include U.S. congressional and State Department records, Department of Agriculture statistics, the United Fruit Company's annual reports, the *New York Times* and popular magazines, and statistical information from various government agencies. We conclude with a brief discussion of the use of commodity chains in writing history.

## FROM LUXURY HOTEL SUITES TO LUNCHBOXES:
## THE GROWTH OF THE BANANA INDUSTRY IN
## THE UNITED STATES, 1880–1945

In the 1880s, bananas were considered an exotic and expensive fruit, but their allure did not last beyond the 1920s. The fruit became a cheap product that was increasingly a part of the basic diet of the growing American working class. Before the Second World War, bananas came to satisfy a demand for fresh fruit that could not be fulfilled by local production. Americans had long relied on their own farmers for most of their agricultural products, and the winter months eliminated many foods, including fruits, from regular diets. But bananas were shipped year round from the tropics since the mid-1880s and could capture much of the winter fruit market. Imports of bananas had an impressive growth from a level of zero in 1884 to more than $10 million in the 1900s, as detailed in United Fruit's first annual report, which described gains made from the growing demand for the fruit in the U.S. market. The numbers mentioned by the company's president, Andrew Preston, show the dramatic changes within the market:

> Through its distributing department, the Fruit Dispatch Company, your company has organized a most thorough and systematic method of disposing of its products throughout the United States, agencies for marketing of the fruit having been established in all of the principal cities of the country. While only a short time has elapsed since its organization was perfected, the results have been extremely gratifying, not only enabling the consumer to purchase bananas at less cost than ever before, but largely increasing the consumption of the fruit. During the year 1901 the Fruit Dispatch Company distributed 18,906 carloads of tropical products, against 16,197 the preceding year, an increase of 2,709 carloads, or nearly 16 percent.[4]

This substantial growth continued for the first decade of the company's existence. In 1902, the company reported an increase of 12 percent in banana sales over the previous year and a significant reduction of transportation costs. Through the company's marketing efforts and continuing growth in consumer demand, the number of branches of Fruit Dispatch increased 50 percent in 1905 and 17 percent the following year. The company reported that demand was also growing in Europe, a market it planned to target next.

In the early years of the twentieth century Americans' perceptions of bananas also changed. This fruit, at first exotic and peculiar, took on an ordinary and common quality as supply met the increases in demand and the commodity's price dropped to a generally affordable level. But invisible market forces are not the whole story, since United Fruit placed itself at the forefront of advertising strategy and marketed a new image of the fruit. Recent studies have demonstrated how the banana's cultural position changed.[5] For example, in the late nineteenth century bananas were advertised as an item served only in upscale hotels and restaurants, but by the early twentieth century, women's magazines began to publish recipes that called for bananas as an ingredient. George Gershwin and other songwriters featured bananas in their songs, and many Americans hummed the tunes of "Yes, We Have No Bananas!" and "Banana in Your Fruit Basket." John Soluri has even found a larger role for bananas in everyday language, with such terms as "top banana," "banana boat," and "go bananas" entering the common vocabulary.[6] Thus, as bananas gradually disappeared from the menus of expensive restaurants, they increasingly found a place in our common culture.

As bananas were associated to a greater degree with the diet of the poor and the immigrant, the import companies tried to influence demand by distributing books and pamphlets that highlighted the benefits of bananas for everyone. Their main target was housewives, who not only were introduced to banana recipes but also were assured of the nutritional value of the fruit and its advantages as baby food. Infants, the importers asserted, would not fuss over the fruit's texture and taste. Distribution companies worked to change the popular belief that respectable ladies should not eat bananas in public. These efforts were so successful that many people began to think of bananas as a fruit only for women and children.[7]

The changing beliefs about the banana were evident when in 1913 the Senate Finance Committee proposed a tax of 5 cents per bunch. This bill faced strong opposition from import companies, consumer groups, and the media. Many of the small import companies argued that the tax would put them out of business and reinforce the dominating power of the United Fruit Company. The members of the Tariff Reform Committee argued that this tax was regressive because bananas were widely consumed by poor people and was the only fruit available all year in grocery stores at an affordable, stable price. Furthermore, several consumer organizations testified that the tariff was going to hurt working-class families. Finally, the *New York Times* published several articles criticizing the regressive nature of the tariff. The debate continued until the end of the year, when the banana tax was quietly dropped from the tax list in the Underwood-Simmons Bill.[8]

Were the opponents of the bill right or wrong? One can speculate on the legislation's effects and the ubiquity of bananas in the United States by analyzing the per capita consumption of bananas during this period. Between 1909 and 1914 the consumption of bananas per person during the year climbed from 17 pounds to 18.1 pounds. This increase becomes even more significant when one calculates the weight of bananas among all fresh fruits. Bananas represented 20.9 percent of all fresh fruits in 1909, and climbed to 26.5 percent in 1914.[9]

Bananas were important in the diets of American consumers by the early twentieth century. Taxing this fruit would have increased the price of more than a quarter of the fresh fruit consumed by Americans. Figures are not variable by season, but in view of the scarcity of apples, oranges, and other American fruits in the winter, bananas were eaten in greater proportions. By 1910, processed fruits represented just 9.9 percent of the per capita consumption of all fruits (processed and fresh) in the United States, increasing to 15.4 percent in 1914. Since fruit-processing technology had not been fully developed, canned fruit was not a popular substitute for fresh fruit. When strained fruit in little jars for babies became available in the mid-1930s, banana advertisements increasingly targeted young mothers.

A period of rapid urbanization, industrialization, and steady population growth helped expand the banana market. But this growth was interrupted by the First World War, when the U.S. government required United Fruit and the far smaller Standard Fruit to lend their ships to the war effort. Imports of fruits on the basis of per capita consumption declined dramatically, but they recovered when the conflict ended. In fact, United Fruit's management had enough confidence that the demand would increase that its 1919 annual report announced that it would expand the amount of land under cultivation, despite several years of deflated profits.[10]

The rise in imports after World War I can be attributed to the increasing demand of an unsaturated market. The per capita consumption of bananas increased at a very fast pace during the 1920s, stimulating the import companies to bring more and more fruit to the country. United Fruit also benefited during this period and it continued to advertise new ways to eat bananas. In 1924 it distributed a recipe book that encouraged consumers to eat their bananas with corn flakes and milk for breakfast.

Five years later, the company enlarged the advertising department of its Fruit Dispatch Company, which focused on new ways to consume bananas. This agency continued to push the bananas-with-cereal idea and even struck deals with cereal companies to promote each other's products. An educational department formed in the late 1920s sent information packets to elementary schools: teachers were to encourage their pupils to eat balanced meals by including bananas.[11] In 1925 the Education Department also began to publish a bimonthly periodical called *Unifruitco*, which featured articles on the company's plantations and ships. These tactics benefited the company but could not prevent a large slump in sales when the stock market collapsed in 1929, ushering in the Great Depression. The company's growth stagnated throughout the 1930s, and shareholders would wait until the end of World War II before they saw profits rise again.

The crisis of the 1930s affected the entire banana sector. The import companies faced challenges in their efforts to keep their imports afloat. Although the per capita consumption of all fresh fruit fell during the first four years of the Depression, the proportion of bananas eaten among all fresh fruits also declined. With money scarce, consumers had to concentrate their spending on necessities. Bananas reached their lowest point of sales of the interwar period in 1933, the same year in which per capita consumption of fresh fruit was at its lowest.[12]

Banana consumption increased in the late 1930s, together with a general improvement of the national economy. Contrary to what happened in other sectors of the U.S. economy, the outbreak of World War II halted the growth of the banana industry. During the war, both per capita consumption and total imports of bananas to the United States sank again to its lowest level in history, but, as we will see, the fruit companies' profits rose. Once the war was over, the banana import companies prepared themselves to resupply the U.S. market with the fruit, but they found that the market had once again changed: Americans were consuming more processed food and less fresh fruit, a problem United Fruit had to deal with in the following decades.

## CONCENTRATION WITHIN THE BANANA INDUSTRY: THE RISE OF THE UNITED FRUIT COMPANY

Since United Fruit controlled between one-third and two-thirds of the entire banana market between 1900 and 1970, special attention needs to be given to its actions. United Fruit was incorporated in 1899 after the merger of several production and transportation companies. Then began a period in which the company was able to influence both the price of bananas in the United States and the actions of many governments in the producing Latin American countries. Some companies, such as the Cuyamel Fruit Company and the Standard Fruit and Steamship Company, tried to compete with United Fruit, but they never really challenged its dominant position. Standard Fruit was established in 1923 in New Orleans by the Vaccaro brothers, a family of banana importers. The company managed to control around 15 percent of the banana market but could begin to compete more seriously with United Fruit only after World War II, when it introduced some technological innovations that increased its plantations' productivity. Standard Fruit also got a boost when it acquired United Fruit's properties in Guatemala after the U.S. government forced United Fruit to divest its Guatemalan lands for failure to comply with antitrust legislation.[13] Cuyumel had a much different fate: it was acquired by United Fruit in 1933 after a price war failed to unseat the banana king. United Fruit's dominant position would continue until the end of the Second World War, when a variety of factors contributed to a decline in its market share and the slow deconcentration of the industry.

Between 1880 and 1900, more than a hundred companies or firms entered the banana business, affecting the growth of imports.[14] Many of these enterprises were small producers and importers that disappeared when the industry underwent quick consolidation at the end of the century. Minor C. Keith, a railroad entrepreneur who had planted banana trees alongside his tracks, approached Andrew W. Preston, president of the Boston Fruit Company, with a proposition to create the company from their holdings. Preston, a Bostonian like Keith, liked the idea and they incorporated United Fruit under New Jersey law in 1899. Their diverse assets proved to be complementary. Keith ran his railroad network and plantations in Central America and marketed his bananas to the southeastern United States. Preston grew bananas in the West Indies, ran a large number of ships, and sold to the northeastern states. By enlarging the area where they produced bananas, they could avoid being ruined by the floods and hurricanes that are common in the region.

Keith and Preston's leadership also proved lucrative for the new company. United Fruit's production infrastructure grew steadily as Keith cut narrow corridors through thick jungles to lay track. Railroad construction took an enormous toll on the mostly West Indian workers who laid the tracks. Trevor Purcell wrote in 1993 that the great-grandchildren of these workers still remarked that "under every one of those *poleen* [railroad ties] is the body of a colored man."[15] In order to lay its railroad, the company purchased long-term contracts at extremely favorable rates from Central American dictators such as General Miguel Dávila of Honduras and Jorge Ubico of Guatemala. It planted banana trees on both sides of the new tracks and erected small mud-and-grass huts for its workers. Punctuating the dark green ocean of banana leaves were the white Cape Cod houses that the company built for its American plantation managers.

The company's plantations proliferated. During its first two decades, for example, the company's land quadrupled. The growth of production reflected an increase of demand in the United States and the company benefited enormously through the Fruit Dispatch Company's success in distributing bananas throughout the Midwest. The subsidiary continued to expand rapidly. In 1899 it had sixteen agencies selling bananas; by 1914, sixty agencies handled more than 50,000 railroad cars of bananas.[16] While these tactics benefited the company enormously, when the Great Depression hit and sales slumped, no amount of advertising or propaganda would recover the company's previous levels of profits.

The quick growth of the company before the Depression had caught the attention of newspapers and magazines, and they helped transform United Fruit into a household name. Journalists capitalized on the positive image of the company, symbolized by its "Great White Fleet," the largest private fleet in the world. During the 1920s and 1930s, fashionable Americans toured the tropics on "banana boats," and thousands of young couples enjoyed romantic honeymoons between New York and Central America. In an age before affordable air travel, the cruises attracted nearly 70,000 passengers each year, allowing Americans to enjoy the winter warmth and a few exotic sites within the two weeks that employers typically allotted for a vacation.[17] Americans were fascinated by the convergence of modern technology, gourmet cuisine, and attentive service, all contained within the white steel hulls of United Fruit's ships. Newspapers supplied detailed information on minor route and fare changes along with the development and "civilization" that the company brought to the wild expanses of tropical jungles.

Media coverage of the company exemplified and reinforced these attitudes. By the 1930s, the majority of newspapers published articles on the day-to-day business affairs and other aspects of the Great White Fleet, such as ship christenings. Many articles presented positive accounts of development in Latin America, while a few reported the increasing number of strikes occurring on the company's plantations. The American press did not notice United Fruit's often bloody repression of early strikes, including the massacre of banana workers by Colombian troops that García Márquez vividly portrays in *One Hundred Years of Solitude*.[18] Only in 1934, when American marines and Army Air Corps squadrons began chasing the rebel Augusto César Sandino through the Nicaraguan jungles, did the *New York Times* describe the strikes breaking out in nearby United Fruit plantations. Mirroring the newspapers, popular magazines also depicted the company favorably. The spirit of their coverage can be captured by articles titled "Story of a Great New England Enterprise," "Green Gold of the Tropics," and "Empire Builder."[19] *Fortune* dedicated almost all of its March 1933 issue to the "amazing story" of United Fruit's rise. The author, Ernest Hamlin Baker, commended the company for supplying "hospitals, sanitation, power, lights, water, railways, docks, schools, Coca-Cola, beef, tourists, and beer," all the necessary components of civilization. *Time*, *Newsweek*, and *Today* featured similar articles.

The generally rosy picture of the company painted by the media also reflected the views of most U.S. government officials. A small but occasionally vehement group of officials, however, criticized the company. In 1908 Everett Wheeler, president of the American Banana Company, appeared before the Senate to argue that United Fruit's president was running a monopolistic business that was illegal under the Sherman Antitrust Act.[20] Even if, as Wheeler claimed, many "great combinations of capital that we hear so much talked about and discussed in public and private have had beneficial results," United Fruit nonetheless was breaking the law by controlling Latin American banana production and influencing the prices of bananas sold in the United States. Senator Joseph Johnston (D-Ala.) agreed and opined, "This government ought to take the matter in hand."[21] The senator's recommendation came to naught; the government did not sue the company. Johnston must have been frustrated a year later to hear that the Supreme Court had decided that monopolistic practices of American companies abroad did not fall within the jurisdiction of the United States.[22] Yet, as Wheeler argued, United Fruit also held a very strong grip on the distribution of bananas within the United States, an aspect of the business that, if found to be monopolistic, was punishable under the Sherman Antitrust Act.

A small number of high government officials such as Senator Johnston continued to criticize United Fruit occasionally.[23] During the Senate hearings on the company in 1956, for example, Judge Stanley Barnes, assistant attorney general of the antitrust division of the Justice Department, testified that in 1913 the department had conducted investigations that "indicate[d] in some people's opinion [that] suit should have been filed," and in fact "there has been no secret around the division for some—what is it, forty-five years—that it might be a good idea to file suit; but for various reasons, suit was not filed until 1954."[24] What were the "various reasons" that had prevented the government from ending the concentration of the banana industry? Jurisdictional issues had partly prevented action, but there is strong evidence that the Justice Department did not file suit against United Fruit because it saw the company as a necessary ally.

The State Department was particularly interested in four resources that the company controlled. First, United Fruit operated the only fleet that could carry mail to parts of Latin America, including correspondence to the marines stationed in the Canal Zone.[25] Along with mail, the Great White Fleet carried heavy provisions and construction materials for the Panama Canal, which accounted for 40 percent of its cargoes between New Orleans and Panama in 1910.[26] Second, the company began working with the Department of Agriculture to introduce abaca, a relative of the banana native to the Philippines, into Panama as a "national security measure."[27] Abaca was the principal source of fiber used for marine cordage and other types of rope. Political instability in the Philippines during the 1920s threatened to interrupt trade and jeopardize the principal supply of this important material. The United States looked toward Central American and United Fruit plantations as a possible alternative source of abaca. Third, United Fruit was a pioneer in radio telecommunications and it was one of the first companies to use radios on its ships. The State Department relied on United Fruit's radio subsidiary, Tropical Radio, and another larger company, All-American Cables, to send its messages to and from its ambassadors and consuls in Mexico and Central America. Finally, United Fruit owned more miles of railways in Central America than any other private or government enterprise. The company augmented its vast and elaborate infrastructure with numerous ocean ports that allowed it not only to dominate the banana business but also to be the chief importer of almost all other goods into Central America. As the war loomed in Europe toward the end of the 1930s, the U.S. government was fearful of German influence, particularly in Guatemala, which had a substantial German immigrant population. Despite United Fruit's apparent monopolistic practices, it seemed to be the lesser of two evils.[28] The use of these four resources, combined with jurisdictional issues, prevented the U.S. government from filing suit against the company and permitted the banana industry to remain tightly controlled by one company. But United Fruit's maverick status would change significantly after the Second World War.

## FINDING SUBSTITUTES FOR BANANAS, 1945–1970

When the Buyers' Association protested to the federal government against the tariff on banana imports in 1913, they argued it would have a negative impact on the American working class. This claim made sense at a time when American consumers depended on the fruit during the winter, but in the post-World War II period new technology permitted better preservation of all fruit and altered the entire fresh fruit market.

When the war ended, Americans had been living without one of their favorite fruits for nearly four years. When the importation of bananas resumed, their return was celebrated. The middle class had grown markedly, filling new suburbs and commuting to jobs with packed lunches. Banana sales reached record levels by the late 1950s, but this reflected a growing number of people consuming the fruit rather than an increase in consumption per person. The banana market also responded to changes on the supply side. First, per capita consumption declined in the postwar years when processed fruit became a substitute. Second, retail prices for bananas fell when higher productivity of banana plantations in Latin America boosted imports.

The per capita consumption of bananas reached its highest historical level, an average 21.8 pounds of bananas, in 1948, when imports resumed. This level was slightly higher than its previous peak in 1937, when consumption per capita was 21.3 pounds. Thus the demand for bananas at the per capita level had not changed during the war, but it could not be satisfied by the importing companies. However, per capita consumption began to gradually fall during the 1950s.[29]

The decline in per capita consumption and a boost in imports came at the same time that the retail price fell in both the U.S. and European markets. Most fresh fruit experienced a similar pattern, mostly because technology developed during the war allowed processed foods to be produced and transported cheaply. Processing decreased the perishability of food, increased its storage life, and placed nonseasonal fruits on grocery shelves at all times of the year. The advantage bananas had enjoyed during the winter had ended. In 1909, processed fruit represented about 5 percent of all the fruit consumed in the United States, but by the early 1960s more than 40 percent of fruit sold was processed. Canned foods and baby food in jars lowered the popularity of fresh bananas among families with infants. While in 1934 the total supply of canned baby food was 21 million pounds, in 1956 it was a billion pounds.[30] In other words, fresh bananas as baby food had been replaced by Mr. Gerber's baby food in glass jars.

Consumer preferences shifted in parallel with an increase of productivity by Latin American growers. During the second half of the 1950s, Standard Fruit and United Fruit experimented with a new kind of banana that had a higher yield, was more resistant to disease, and could withstand strong winds. This higher productivity helped to push down prices at the same time that demand was falling. The banana companies dealt with this situation by diversifying their operations and investing in the processed foods industry.[31]

The commodity chain of vertical integration and strong control over production in Central and South America differed from the model that developed in the Caribbean. Because of protections offered by European countries to their colonies, United Fruit and its rivals never invested heavily in Caribbean plantations. With the impetus of the British and French colonial governments, small banana growers, many with little means, formed associations and enlisted shipping companies to supply the European market.[32] Public officials of the colonizing countries encouraged this development as a way to stimulate their colonies' economies and reduce unemployment. The banana industry in the Windward Islands, for example, took its modern form in the 1950s after the United Kingdom established quotas and tariffs for bananas in Britain. The quality of life for many banana growers on these islands improved under the system and most were able to retain their plots of land and styles of life until the 1980s, despite occasional difficulties with the shipping companies.[33]

## THE OPENING OF THE BANANA INDUSTRY:
## THE FALL OF THE UNITED FRUIT COMPANY

Unquestionably, the Second World War also changed the fruit company's business environment. Like many other American corporations, United Fruit profited enormously from the war. The War Shipping Agency oversaw the requisition of nearly all of the company's 110 ships but compensated the company generously.[34] The government's cost-plus agreements paid for the production of various military goods and crops on company lands plus "a fee, or profit, equal to a fixed percentage of the cost."[35] When the Office of Price Administration set high banana prices, the company saw its revenues increase from $15.4 million in 1941 to $54.1 million in 1947.[36] As the war and these special arrangements ended, United Fruit found itself facing a stagnating domestic market, expanded competition, and increasingly turbulent labor relations. When the media stopped representing the company as a paragon of business virtue and the U.S. government ended its use of the company's resources, United Fruit could no longer act as a corporate maverick.

Before the war, the majority of newspaper and popular magazine articles centered on day-to-day business changes, Great White Fleet cruises, and company development within Latin America. By 1941, the American media focused on the war and news editors sent their journalists to investigate the numerous ways in which the company was assisting the Allied war effort. The war had halted all company cruises, effectively ending coverage of the more romantic side of the company. When cruises resumed after the war, journalists chose instead to tell of the fantastic developments of passenger airlines. As the media's attention shifted from World War II to the Cold War, their coverage focused on labor unrest and fears of the spread of communism throughout Central America. By creating unfavorable conditions for its workers, United Fruit was seen to be negligent in preventing "Central American communist beachheads." Finally, day-to-day affairs of the company stopped making the papers, an indication that the company itself was no longer so newsworthy as it once was. The changing spirit of news coverage was captured in such titles as "Guatemala: Labor and the Communists," "Nationalization Blues," and "The Banana Giant That Has to Shrink" in popular magazines.[37]

The war also ended the company's strategic position in the eyes of the government. Foremost was shipping. At the war's peak in 1943, nearly a million people were working in shipyards, many of which were producing the hundreds of Liberty ships that were used throughout the war. Airmail made shipping of mail irrelevant, and competing shipping companies bought cheap reliable ships that glutted the market after the war. The U.S. government invested heavily in infrastructural projects in Central America, such as the Pan American Highway, which gave an alternative route, while plastics replaced the abaca used in cordage. Finally, mostly through the Navy, the government developed its own radio circuits that could transmit diplomatic correspondence. All in all, by 1950 United Fruit no longer enjoyed its previous protection and it was only a matter of time before the Department of Justice, responding to increasingly bad publicity on the company, initiated a lawsuit.

Ironically, the antitrust suit was filed only months after the event that has contributed most to United Fruit's imperialistic reputation: the 1954 CIA-led overthrow of the democratically elected Guatemalan president, Jacobo Arbenz Guzmán.[38] Evidence that supports the view that United Fruit directly assisted the CIA is scarce. Nonetheless, since the company had met Arbenz's efforts at land reform with cries of "Communism!" only a year before and because the State Department had publicly come to the company's defense, many critics of the company drew the connection.[39] Secretary of State John Foster Dulles, questioned about the company's role at a news conference shortly before the coup, bluntly stated that "if [United Fruit] gave a gold piece for every banana, the problem would remain just as it is today as far as the presence of Communist infiltration in Guatemala is concerned."[40] Soon after, at a National Security Council meeting, Dulles permitted the Justice Department to file suit. He argued that such a move was necessary because "many of the Central American countries were convinced that the sole objective of the United States foreign policy was to protect the fruit company."[41]

The antitrust trial began in 1955 and focused on the allegedly monopolistic distribution practices of the company within the United States. The trial was still under way when the Senate's Select Committee on Small Business undertook its own investigation of the company. According to one testifying banana jobber, United Fruit's subsidiary Meloripe put almost every independent jobber in its area out of business by cutting off their supply of green bananas. When the company began to fear that it might lose, it chose to settle. In agreeing to a settlement, the U.S. government indirectly reduced the company's foreign influence by measures aimed at its distribution practices and sidestepped the jurisdictional issues that had impeded its previous efforts. The banana industry began to open because of the suit and competition from processed fruit. Companies such as Del Monte and Dole filled the vacuum left by United Fruit and rigorously set up new and more efficient operations in Latin America. The era of United Fruit ended in 1970 when the company merged with AMK-John Morrell, a meatpacking company, and created a new company called United Brands. This company continued with a strong marketing campaign for bananas, promoting its Chiquita Bananas, while at the same time investing heavily in a wide range of processed foods. The company changed its name to Chiquita Brands International in 1989. In 2001 Chiquita filed for bankruptcy after a costly conflict over import quotas with the European Union, but in late 2004 it began to offer its shareholders dividends, an indication that it was recovering.

## CONCLUSION

We have attempted first to demonstrate the growth and fluctuations in demand for bananas. United Fruit, a company that maintained a powerful position in Central America, satisfied most of this demand. The actions and behavior of the fruit company must be analyzed in a larger framework that includes demand as a driving variable of profitability and power and the influence of the media and the state on the company's behavior. United Fruit lost its previous advantageous and oligopolist position when demand fell, media representation soured, and the U.S. Justice Department filed suit.

We hope that this case will shed light not only on the specifics of this important commodity but on the use of commodity chains in historical studies. Commodity chains place emphasis on the complicated process that goods undergo before they reach the final consumer. Products, especially manufactured goods, may follow innumerable steps and require inputs from many places around the world. A commodity's production, transportation, distribution, and consumption are all highly interdependent and eventually determine the cost and availability of the product. As we have argued, demand must be a central factor in the formation of commodity chains because the cost of each stage depends on whether the product will meet a buyer. While bananas require few transformations or additions after the stems have been cut from the stalk, their perishability forces the path between production and consumption to be very fast and efficient. Also particular to the banana business are the frequent natural disasters that prevent geographic concentration. These factors result in a banana business that to this day is conducted mostly by a few multinationals that operate with remarkable speed on a scale that is wider than the path of a hurricane.

While commodity chain analysis can contribute enormously to studies of the relationship between plantations, multinationals, and nations, it also has a few limitations. For example, before the Second World War, United Fruit operated in a business environment that was conducive to the creation of an oligopoly. Many observers thought that the company brought "civilization" to the wilds of the tropics, and many others were enamored of its Caribbean cruises. The State Department was also reluctant to take legal action until it relied less on resources that the company controlled. When demand fell and this business environment changed, so too did the behavior of the company. A level of historical specificity in this case would be lost if only the stages of production, transportation, and consumption were considered. Finally, this case shows that commodity chains cannot be explained without attention to changes in politics and culture.

The banana export economy did not make any of the producing countries rich. The reason is not easy to find. Since the eighteenth century, historians and economists have debated whether the insertion of a country in the international economy will improve that country's standard of living. In the case of Latin America, this discussion has been developed by the *dependentistas*—followers of the dependency school—and the neoclassical economists. The dependentistas explain Latin American underdevelopment as a product of an unequal system of trade and exchange imposed on them, through political means, by the world powers. This school of belief formed largely as a reaction to the theory of comparative advantage, which argued that all benefited from an international division of trade whereby each country focused on the products or expertise with which it was naturally endowed. Some recent studies have returned to this idea while others have argued that the institutional framework of the Latin American countries was an obstacle for the development of market forces and did not allow exports to generate development. According to the economic historian Victor Bulmer-Thomas, specialization in exports is not bad for development per se. The problem lies on how the countries use the gains generated by exports. When Bulmer-Thomas compares the richer economies of Argentina and Chile with the poorer ones of Central America, he argues that while the Southern Cone economies reinvested the gains of their exports in the nonexport economy or in other kinds of exports, the Central American countries reinvested only in the same sector and did not diversify their economies. Additionally, the preexisting extreme inequality of land and income distribution did not permit a large percentage of the population to enjoy the benefits of banana exports.[42]

Are the American corporations to blame for this situation? Is there any connection between the producing countries' poverty and the American domestic market? These questions still must be asked in order to address vital Latin American issues on social justice, delayed or unequal development, and the roots of poverty.

---

## NOTES

1   The business historian Mira Wilkins considers United Fruit a "textbook case" of successful vertical integration following the general trend seen in the American corporate sector in the late nineteenth and early twentieth centuries (*The Emergence of Multinational Enterprise*, 157–60). The process of United Fruit's vertical integration has been studied by several authors; see also Read, "The Growth and Structure of Multinationals"; Kepner and Soothill, *The Banana Empire*; and May and Plaza, *United States Business Performance Abroad*.

2   Asturias, *Strong Wind*; García Márquez, *One Hundred Years of Solitude*; Neruda, *Canto General*.

3   Many works on United Fruit have been published. For comprehensive bibliographies, see Strifler and Moberg, *Banana Wars*; and Bucheli, *Bananas and Business*.

4   United Fruit Company, *Annual Report to the Stockholders* (1901), 6–7.

5   Jenkins, *Bananas*; and Soluri, "Banana Cultures."

6   Soluri, "Banana Cultures," 49, 62.

7   Jenkins, *Bananas*, 106–7.

8   Ibid., 22–24.

9   Bucheli, *Bananas and Business*, 30.

10  Ibid.

11  One such packet, sent to Ms. E. M. Shreckengost in Brookville, Pennsylvania, included five items: (1) a small book titled *About Bananas*, detailing the (heroic) history of the company; (2) *Teaching Health through the School Lunch*, a brochure written by Professor Lydia Roberts; (3) *Health and the School*, a brochure edited by Dr. J. Mace Andress; (4) an excerpt from the book *Count Luckner, the Sea Devil: An Appreciation of Bananas by a Sea-raider Who Disrupted Allied Shipping during the World War without Taking a Human Life*; and (5) an "outline poster for coloring" that depicted a half-pealed banana and a glass of milk.

12  Bucheli, *Bananas and Business*, 32–33.

13  In 1967 Castle and Cook acquired Standard Fruit, and at the present time the company operates under the name of Dole Corporation. For a detailed history of Standard Fruit, see Karnes, *Tropical Enterprise*.

14  Adams, *Conquest of the Tropics*, 72; Taylor, "Evolution of the Banana Multinationals," 2.

15  Trevor W. Purcell, *Banana Fallout: Class, Color, and Culture among West Indians in Costa Rica* (Los Angeles: Center for Afro-American Studies, University of California, 1993), quoted in Striffler and Moberg, *Banana Wars*, 4–5.

16  Adams, *The Conquest of the Tropics*, 317, 322.

17  Inglish, "The Transportation System of the United Fruit Company."

18  This strike and massacre occurred in 1928 when Colombian soldiers, acting on orders by the Colombian government and United Fruit, fired upon and killed hundreds of strikers.

19  Thompson, "Story of a Great New England Enterprise," 12–24; Fuessle, "Green Gold of the Tropics," 186–88; "Empire Builder," 5–6.

20  Wheeler owned lands in an area that was claimed by both Panama and Costa Rica. Soon before the American Banana Company was to finish a railroad to bring the first harvest of bananas to a harbor, Costa Rican officials crossed the border recognized by Panama and stopped the company's operations. The U.S. consul argued that Panama's claim was not valid and that United Fruit's title under Costa Rican law was legitimate.

21  U.S. Congress, Senate Committee, United Fruit Company, 63.

22  Gliejeses, Shattered Hope, 88.

23  In 1930 the House Committee on the Merchant Marine and Fisheries debated an amendment that would prevent companies that operated ships under foreign flags from running American postal routes. United Fruit, which was making a bid for the routes, began its testimony with an account of the company's history. After only a minute of the speech, Congressman Frank Reid (R-Ill.) interrupted and insisted that "if we are going to start [the hearings] all over again and investigate the United Fruit Company, I would be glad to sit in on that investigation and I think it would be advisable to do it, but not at the present time." United Fruit's vice president, who replied defensively, was cut short when the congressman flatly stated, "I think they control every banana we eat and all that, but it has nothing to do with this [amendment]": U.S. Congress, House Committee, To Further Develop an American Merchant Marine, 128.

24  U.S. Congress, House Select Committee, Distribution Problems, Part 4: Banana Industry, 141.

25  In other congressional testimony, Walter Brown, the postmaster general, told Congress that he knew of no other bidder besides United Fruit for the postal route between San Francisco and Panama. U.S. Congress, Senate Committee, Treasury and Post Office Departments Appropriation Bill, 1933, 1117.

26  U.S. Congress, House Committee, Transportation Coastwise of Property Owned by the U.S., 3.

27  U.S. Congress, Senate Committee, Abaca Production Act of 1950, 22.

28  Paul Dosal gives compelling evidence on this point. He describes a conflict between United Fruit and the U.S. government over preferential rates the company was giving to freight bound for Nazi Germany. Franklin D. Roosevelt even sent Sumner Welles, architect of the "good neighbor" policy, to arbitrate. The rates were not equalized until trade with Germany was halted during the war (Dosal, Doing Business with the Dictators).

29  Bucheli, Bananas and Business, 31–33.

30  Ibid., 33–39.

31  Ibid., 165–66.

32   Reynolds, "The Story of the Banana," 27–28.

33   Grossman, "The St. Vincent Banana Growers' Association," 290–91. Because of the protections and smaller economies of scale, bananas were more expensive in Europe than in the United States. By the 1990s, American companies such as Chiquita, Del Monte, and Dole charged that European protections were preventing free trade and the sale of cheaper bananas to European consumers. After a lawsuit brought by the U.S. government and Ecuadorian growers, the World Trade Organization agreed with this line of argument and allowed the United States to threaten to impose import tariffs on European luxury goods. The resulting dispute has been called the "banana wars" and it caught newspaper headlines even at the height of Bill Clinton's Senate trial. European governments eventually agreed to end their protections and the Caribbean banana industry has begun to downsize as a result. Europeans may be enjoying cheaper bananas, but Grossman argues that "the exodus of farmers from the [eastern Caribbean] industry will mean increased unemployment, poverty, illegal drug cultivation, crime and outmigration" ("St. Vincent Banana Growers' Association," 312–14). Nevertheless, the Caribbean industry remains in marked contrast to the "dollar banana" commodity chain of Central and South America, where large landholders produce and multinational corporations ship and market their bananas in a largely oligopolist international environment (Reynolds, Story of the Banana, 28–32).

34   Not only did United Fruit have one of the largest private fleets, but the company's refrigerated holds were especially helpful to the government's efforts to ship food to Allied troops.

35   Kilmarx, America's Maritime Legacy, 188.

36   United Fruit Company, Annual Report to the Stockholders (1942 and 1948).

37   Current History 24 (March 1953): 143–48; Newsweek 4 (March 30, 1953): 49; Business Week (February 15, 1958): 109–13.

38   See Schlesinger and Kinzer, Bitter Fruit, for arguments that tie United Fruit to the government's covert operation. Gleijeses, Shattered Hope, did not find United Fruit holding a "smoking gun."

39   One of the largest pieces of evidence that a "plantation town owned by United Fruit's Honduras division" was used as a launch pad for the invasion (Schlesinger and Kinzer, Bitter Fruit, 170) has been shown to be incorrect by declassified CIA documents. The largest of the five groups led by the CIA's puppet, Carlos Castillo Armas, with 198 soldiers, gathered near the village of Macuelizo in June 1954 before crossing the border to attack Bananera and Puerto Barrios (Cullather, Secret History, 87). Macuelizo is in the Honduran highlands, miles from the banana-growing lowlands. Furthermore, the targets of these attacks were a United Fruit plantation town (Bananera) and a port (Puerto Barrios) whose facilities United Fruit owned. If this rebel group had not been quickly defeated and had instead debilitated the port and railroad (which the company also owned), they would have greatly incapacitated United Fruit's Guatemalan operations.

40   Department of State Bulletin, June 21, 1954.

41  Dulles in 202nd meeting of National Security Council, June 17, 1954, *Foreign Relations of the United States, 1952–54*, 4:224–26, quoted in Rabe, *Eisenhower and Latin America*. Cullather quotes an unnamed CIA agent or government official who, before the coup, predicted that United Fruit would have to make concessions if the Guatemalan government was replaced by a new regime. The "United States does not expect American companies to enjoy abroad immunities and privileges that would make for political instability or social injustice in other countries, because such a condition of course would be harmful to the overriding American political interest" (*Secret History*, 87–88).

42  Bulmer-Thomas, *Economic History of Latin America*, 61–67, 83–84, 124–27, 149–54.

## BIBLIOGRAPHY

Adams, Frederick U. *The Conquest of the Tropics*. New York: Page, 1914.

Asturias, Miguel Angel. *Strong Wind*. New York: Delacorte, 1968.

Bucheli, Marcelo. "United Fruit Company in Colombia: Labor Conflicts, Political Relations, and Local Elite, 1899–1970." Ph.D. dissertation, Stanford University, 2001.

———. "United Fruit in Latin America." In Steve Striffler and Mark Moberg, eds., *Banana Wars: Power, Production, and History in the Americas*, 80–100. Durham: Duke University Press, 2003.

———. *Bananas and Business: The United Fruit Company in Colombia, 1899–2000*. New York: New York University Press, 2005.

Bulmer-Thomas, Victor. *The Economic History of Latin America since Independence*. New York: Cambridge University Press, 1993.

Cullather, Nick. *Secret History: The CIA's Classified Account of Its Operations in Guatemala, 1952–1954*. Stanford: Stanford University Press, 1999.

Dosal, Paul. *Doing Business with Dictators: A Political History of United Fruit in Guatemala, 1899–1944*. Wilmington: SR Books, 1993.

"Empire Builder." *The Nation* 129 (July 3, 1929).

Fuessle, N. A. "Green Gold of the Tropics." *Outlook* 132 (October 4, 1922).

García Márquez, Gabriel. *One Hundred Years of Solitude*. New York: Harper & Row, 1970.

Gleijeses, Piero. *Shattered Hope: The Guatemalan Revolution and the United States*. Princeton: Princeton University Press, 1991.

Grossman, Lawrence S. "The St. Vincent Banana Growers' Association, Contract Farming, and the Peasantry." In Steve Striffler and Mark Moberg, eds., *Banana Wars: Power, Production, and History in the Americas*, 286–315. Durham: Duke University Press, 2003.

Inglish, Leona Frances. "The Transportation System of the United Fruit Company." Thesis, University of Chicago, 1932.

Jenkins, Virginia S. *Bananas: An American History*. Washington: Smithsonian Institution, 2000.

Karnes, Stephen. *Tropical Enterprise: The Standard Fruit and Steamship Company in Latin America*. Baton Rouge: Louisiana State University Press, 1978.

Kepner, Charles D., and Jay Soothill. *The Banana Empire: A Case Study of Economic Imperialism*. New York: Vanguard, 1935.

Kilmarx, Robert A., ed. *History of the U.S. Merchant Marine and Shipbuilding Industry since Colonial Times*. Boulder: Westview, 1979.

May, Stacy, and Galo Plaza. *United States Business Performance Abroad: The Case Study of the United Fruit Company in Latin America*. Washington: National Planning Association, 1958.

Neruda, Pablo. *Canto General*. Berkeley: University of California Press, 1991.

Rabe, Stephen G. *Eisenhower and Latin America: The Foreign Policy of Anticommunism*. Chapel Hill: University of North Carolina Press, 1988.

Read, Robert. "The Growth and Structure of Multinationals in the Banana Export Trade." In Mark Casson, ed., *The Growth of International Business*. London: Allen & Unwin, 1983.

Reynolds, P. K. "Story of the Banana." *Bulletin of the Pan American Union* 53 (December 1921).

Schlesinger, Stephen C., and Stephen Kinzer. *Bitter Fruit: The Untold Story of the American Coup in Guatemala*. Garden City: Anchor/Doubleday, 1983.

Soluri, John. "Banana Cultures: Linking the Production and Consumption of Export Bananas, 1800–1980." In Steve Striffler and Mark Moberg, eds. *Banana Wars: Power, Production, and History in the Americas*. Durham: Duke University Press, 2003.

Striffler, Steve, and Mark Moberg, eds. *Banana Wars: Power, Production, and History in the Americas*. Durham: Duke University Press, 2003.

Taylor, Timothy, "Evolution of the Banana Multinationals." In Timothy E. Josling and Timothy Taylor, eds., *Banana Wars: The Anatomy of a Trade Dispute*, 67–97. Cambridge, Mass.: CABI, 2003.

Thompson, G. A. "Story of a Great New England Enterprise." *New England Magazine* 53 (May 1915).

United Fruit Company. *Annual Report to the Stockholders*. 1900–1970.

U.S. Congress. House. Committee on Interstate and Foreign Commerce. *Transportation Coastwise of Property Owned by the U.S.* 61st Cong., 2nd sess. (May 10, 1910): Hint 61-U.

———. Committee on Merchant Marine and Fisheries. *To Further Develop an American Merchant Marine*. 71st Cong., 2nd sess. (Jan. 23, 27–29, 1930): H539-5.

———. Select Committee on Small Business. *Distribution Problems, Part 4: Banana Industry*. 84th Cong., 2nd sess. (March 28, 1956): H1547-3-D.

U.S. Congress. Senate. Committee on Appropriations. *Treasury and Post Office Departments Appropriation Bill, 1933*. 72nd Cong., 2nd sess. (March 14–19, 21–25, 28–30, 1932): S386-0-A.

——. Committee on Armed Services. *Abaca Production Act of 1950*. 81st Cong., 2nd sess. (May 17, 1950): S935-3.

——. Committee on Interstate Commerce. *United Fruit Company*. 60th Cong., 2nd sess. (April 22, 1908): Sint 60-G.

Wilkins, Mira. *The Emergence of Multinational Enterprise: American Business Abroad from the Colonial Era to 1914*. Cambridge: Harvard University Press, 1970.

# 9

# The Fertilizer Commodity Chains:
# Guano and Nitrate, 1840–1930

Rory Miller and Robert Greenhill

*If ever a philosopher's stone, the elixir of life, the infallible catholicism, the universal solvent, or the perpetual motion were discovered, it is the application of guano in agriculture*—Farmer's Magazine, 1854

FERTILIZERS WERE ESSENTIAL to the development of commercial agriculture in several parts of the world in the nineteenth century: arable farming in the United Kingdom, plantation agriculture in the United States and the tropics, and crops such as sugar beets on the continent of Europe. In Britain, the cradle of the Industrial Revolution, feeding the growing populations of nineteenth-century towns and cities depended on innovations in food production. The range of new techniques that British farmers adopted included better crop rotations, new breeds of livestock, and enclosure and drainage of land, but a significant component of the increases in productivity was the more intensive use of fertilizers, initially the manure supplied by livestock, but later artificial fertilizers rich in nitrogen, potassium, and phosphate.[1] Elsewhere in the world such fertilizers began to be applied to other crops that entered international trade in large quantities, whether as foodstuffs or industrial raw materials. Plantations growing sugar, cotton, and tobacco, for example, all benefited from additional soil nutrients.

By an accident of geography the principal source for the two most important natural nitrogenous fertilizers lay on the west coast of South America, where the dryness of the Atacama Desert coupled with the wildlife dependent on the Humboldt Current created the conditions for the accumulation of vast deposits of guano (bird dung) and caliche, the mineral deposits from which nitrate of soda was manufactured. In the mid-nineteenth century three newly formed states, Chile, Peru, and Bolivia, were the only significant sources of these fertilizers. So important were these resources that the competition to control the nitrate territory stimulated a war among the three republics that lasted from 1879 until 1883, known in English and Spanish as the War of the Pacific but in German, significantly, as the *Salpeterkrieg*.[2] Before this war Peruvian guano dominated the market; afterward, Chile's newly acquired nitrate monopoly dwarfed it in significance. It was not until the 1920s that manufactured chemical substitutes really challenged Chilean nitrates in world markets.

Historical research on these fertilizers has tended to fall into three categories. First, development economists in the 1960s and 1970s examined their linkage effects and estimated the "returned value" of the trades.[3] The outcome was to show that Peru and Chile received a much higher proportion of the export revenue from guano and nitrate (approximately two-thirds) than theories of "enclave economies" had suggested.[4] Subsequent work on their economic impact has examined the mechanisms through which the proceeds of the Peruvian guano trade were transferred into private hands, and analyzed the growth of the labor and product markets that the nitrate industry stimulated in northern Chile.[5] Second, the opening of some very rich business archives in the 1960s, primarily those of Antony Gibbs and Sons in London and Dreyfus Frères in Paris, stimulated studies framed within the contemporary debates over informal or economic imperialism and dependency.[6] These studies were concerned primarily with assessing the extent to which foreign firms controlled the development of the trades and the Latin American economies as a whole. Third, a more specialized area of studies in imperialism concerned the role that foreign interests played in two crucial conflicts, the war between Peru and Chile that commenced in 1879 and the Chilean Civil War of 1891; in other words, the international political consequences of the nitrate trade.[7]

Although there are clear continuities in the way in which the international demand for guano evolved into that for nitrate, and many of the firms and entrepreneurs that participated in the trades moved almost seamlessly from one to the other, the two have normally been analyzed separately. This is the case both for studies of their economic impact and for more detailed analyses of the roles played by states, local entrepreneurs, and international firms. As a result, significant issues that might benefit from comparative insights remain neglected. Both these export bonanzas, for example, were associated with a marked increase in domestic inflation, but there have been relatively few attempts to measure it and examine the extent to which the export booms contributed to it, especially in the case of Chile.[8] The impact on the international competitiveness of these countries' other exports and the consequences for domestic agricultural and industrial production, so-called Dutch Disease effects, also remain largely unstudied. This analytical separation of the two trades reflects the nationalist tendencies of Latin American historians; very few specialists in the modern period, even those who are not themselves Latin American, cross frontiers to consider more general issues.[9]

Our objectives in this chapter are twofold. First, we argue that the evolution of the guano and nitrate trades should be viewed as a continuous process, involving many of the same participants. The decisions taken in guano affected the subsequent structuring of the nitrate industry. Much of the knowledge and experience gained in guano could be transferred to nitrate. In both cases Latin American governments and international merchants, the key participants, attempted to maximize their share of the income from the commodities, while local entrepreneurs also sought profitable niches. Yet all these actors shared a long-term interest in maintaining the viability of trades based on depleting resources. Second, while revisiting the earlier literature, we use a different conceptual framework, that of the global commodity chain, defined as "a network of labor and production processes whose end result is a finished export commodity."[10] With the exception of W. M. Mathew, whose analysis concentrated principally on the British market for guano over a twenty-year period, very few historians have considered the construction, operation, and restructuring of the entire chain of transactions that brought fertilizers from the west coast of South America to farmers and planters in the North Atlantic world and elsewhere.

A commodity chain can be visualized as a series of linked nodes through which a product is transformed and transferred along a chain from primary extraction to final consumption. Historians who use the concept analyze more than just the conduits of trade. They explore notions of power and governance, but without the constraining terminology and perspectives of the debates over economic imperialism and dependency. This approach was initially developed from world systems theory in the mid-1980s by Terence K. Hopkins and Immanuel Wallerstein, who applied it historically to shipbuilding and the grain trade in the pre-industrial era.[11] Despite these origins, however, it was specialists in international political economy and geography who appropriated it in the 1990s in order to understand contemporary manufacturing development, with the result that the questions about the historical evolution of commodity chains and trade in primary products that Hopkins and Wallerstein had pioneered tended to be left on the margins. One particular debate centered on Gary Gereffi's distinction between what he termed buyer-driven and producer-driven commodity chains.[12] Many social scientists, obsessed with the globalization of manufacturing, ignored the possibility that some chains might be driven by actors such as international trading houses.[13] Nonetheless, the literature on commodity chains as a whole raises a number of issues of interest to economic and business historians studying trade in primary products:

—The reasons for the growth of consumption in the developed world.

—The initial construction of commodity chains, and in particular the nature and location of the nodes that link production and consumption.

—The continuous restructuring process that occurs in chains over time: as Hopkins and Wallerstein conclude, "The chains are scarcely static for a moment."[14]

—The existence of "real economic alternatives at each point of the chain," and the reasons for the selection of one particular type of organization or relationship rather than another.[15]

—The governance of the chain; the importance of controlling the high-value nodes and/or coordinating the chain in order to capture the largest share of profits from it.[16]

—The importance of information and the acquisition of knowledge to permit upgrading by local entrepreneurs at the upstream end of the chain.[17]

—The role played by nonmarket forces, in particular public policy in the developed and developing world. It is not only the state's choice of policies that is important, but also its capacity to implement and manage them.[18]

These issues, central to the literature on contemporary commodity chains, provide the framework for this analysis of the guano and nitrate trades after the middle of the nineteenth century.

## THE TRADES AND THE COMMODITY CHAINS IN OUTLINE

In comparison with the complex commodity chains of many modern agricultural and mineral products, guano's commodity chain was fairly

1. The guano commodity chain, c. 1855

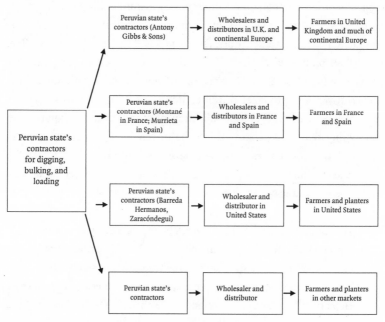

Source: Drawn from details of guano contracts in W. M. Mathew, *The House of Gibbs and the Peruvian Guano Monopoly* (London: Royal Historical Society, 1981).

simple, for three reasons. First, production was confined geographically to a few islands off the Peruvian coast; second, in 1841, shortly after the first shipment of guano to Europe, the Peruvian state asserted its rights of ownership over guano deposits; third, until the final stages of the trade in the 1870s, there was little processing required and little segmentation by quality or brand. Production was straightforward, since it merely involved digging the guano from the deposits and loading it into ships. In return for cash advances the Peruvian government awarded merchants monopoly rights to exploit individual national markets for a limited term on a consignment basis, and they chartered the ships to connect the guano islands with the markets where it was consumed. Figure 1 shows the structure of the guano commodity chain in the middle of the nineteenth century. Under this system the trade grew rapidly, as Figure 2 shows, with exports reaching their peak in the early 1870s.

After 1869 major changes occurred in the structure of the guano trade. Rather than employ merchant consignees to exploit different markets, the Peruvian government changed its policy, selling 2 million tons of

2. Metric tons of guano and nitrate exported from Peru, 1840–1880

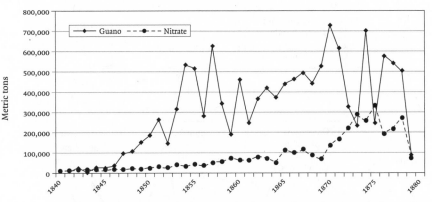

Source: Shane Hunt, "Price and Quantum Estimates of Peruvian Exports, 1830–1962" (unpublished working paper, Princeton University, 1973), 57–58.

guano to the French house of Dreyfus Frères for shipment to Europe.[19] By then much of the best-quality guano had been exhausted and nitrate production was beginning to increase markedly. During the following decade the Peruvian state tried in vain to control the competition between the two fertilizers, first through an aborted monopoly over nitrate exports and then by offering to purchase nitrate production facilities (oficinas) from their owners, in effect a partial nationalization of the trade, in order to reduce production.[20] These changes meant that by the mid-1870s the simple commodity chains of the 1850s had been replaced by a much more complex set of chains, all emanating from the west coast of South America, as shown in Figure 3.

Thanks to the weakness of the Bolivian state, which also had notional control of part of the Atacama, the upshot was the war with Chile, whose elite had already invested heavily in nitrate production in the neighboring countries. Military success permitted Chile to incorporate the Peruvian and Bolivian nitrate provinces early in 1880, providing it with a monopoly over nitrate supplies to the world market.[21]

The Chilean state used its control of these resources in a very different manner from Peru's management of guano. Shortly after capturing the Peruvian department of Tarapacá it restored the nationalized oficinas to private ownership.[22] Now the government obtained revenues from the trade by imposing an export duty, leaving private entrepreneurs to organize production, transport, and distribution. The commodity chain for nitrate in the heyday of the trade was relatively straightforward, therefore,

## 3. The guano and nitrate commodity chains in late 1876

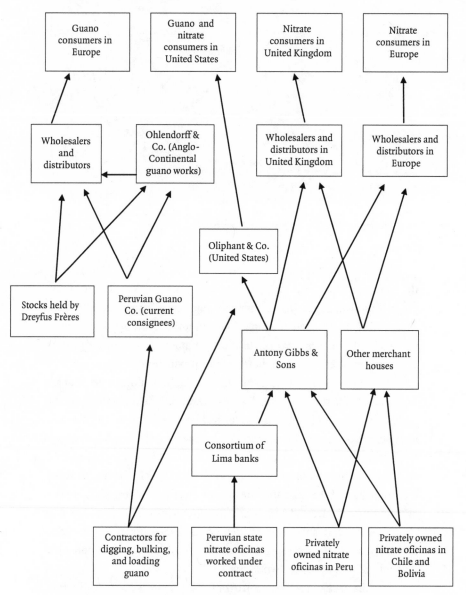

Sources: William C. Clarke, *Peru and Its Creditors* (London, 1877); A. J. Duffield, *Peru in the Guano Age* (London, 1877); Richard Roberts, *Schroders: Merchants and Bankers* (London: Macmillan, 1992); Consul-General Spencer St. John's report in Peru, *Parliamentary Papers*, vol. 72 (1878).

4. Thousands of tons of nitrates exported from Chile and U.S. dollars per ton charged, 1880–1930

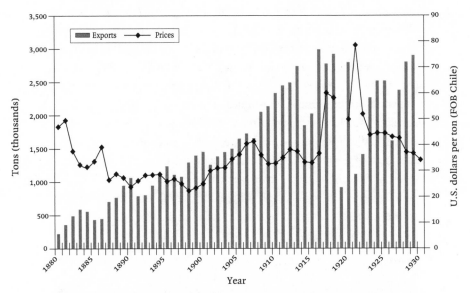

Sources: Osvaldo Sunkel, *Un siglo de historia económica de Chile, 1830–1930: Dos ensayos y una bibliografía* (Madrid: Ediciones Cultura Hispanica, 1982), 126–27; Thomas F. O'Brien, " 'Rich Beyond the Dreams of Avarice': The Guggenheims in Chile," *Business History Review* 63, no. 1 (1989): 134.

as oficinas, many of them owned or managed by foreign merchants, consigned their output to the trading houses that formed the vital link between Chile and Europe. The main problems affecting the chain in this period stemmed from the potential short-term disequilibrium between the supply of nitrate from Chile and demand overseas, which was price inelastic (Figure 4). This resulted in a succession of collusive agreements among producers, the nitrate combinations, which were at first opposed but later encouraged by the Chilean state.[23] Over the longer term, however, exports of Chilean nitrate increased steadily as the state auctioned off new grounds to the private sector.

Despite the increase in output and the development of new markets, the basic structure of the nitrate commodity chain remained largely unaltered for forty years, although the strength and strategies of individual participants varied. However, as had been the case with guano, the nitrate trade eventually ran into crisis. In the decade after the First World War, attempts by the state and private entrepreneurs to bolster their shares of the revenues from a falling market resulted in increasingly complex supply chains. From the mid-1920s part of the industry, with the reluctant support of the Chilean state, was consolidated under the control of the Guggenheims.[24] After their purchase of the largest independent nitrate company in 1929, there were in effect two parallel chains, one dominated by the Guggenheims and the other still in the hands of the European and North American firms that had managed the industry since the 1880s. Soon afterward, under the impact of the global depression, growing competition from artificial substitutes, and collapsing prices, the Guggenheims used their leverage to force the formation of the Corporación Salitrera Chilena (COSACH), a joint venture between them, the Chilean state, and the former nitrate producers, with the Guggenheims controlling both the technology and management of the new company.[25] By this point, however, there was little future for natural nitrate except as a specialty chemical, and COSACH collapsed in 1934.

## THE DEMAND FOR GUANO AND NITRATE

The growth of international demand for nitrogenous fertilizers explains why Peru and Chile were able to exploit their control of guano and nitrate resources, though not the means by which the chains were structured, which depended on governmental and business decisions and on changes in the technological and institutional environments. Global demand for these fertilizers expanded steadily for eighty years after 1840. In the case of guano, prices remained stable through the peak of the trade in the 1850s and 1860s, and the volume of sales depended on the availability of supplies and farmers' incomes. Similarly, the market for nitrate after the 1870s was income elastic but not price elastic. Without state intervention and/or business collusion it would have been subject to periodic gluts and hence price collapses, undermining corporate profits and state revenues.[26]

The initial demand for guano in the middle third of the nineteenth century was especially strong in the United Kingdom, where an expanding population with higher per capita incomes increased the demand for foodstuffs. Gradually, modern agricultural techniques spread through much of the country, increasing the need for manures and fertilizers.[27] Although the onset of free trade in the 1840s, following the repeal of the Corn Laws, exposed British farmers to competition from foreign imports, they were still protected by distance and hence shipping costs from the low-cost agricultural products of the Americas and elsewhere. Consequently rural incomes rose in this last golden age for agriculture in Britain, enabling farmers to afford to purchase imported fertilizers such as guano. Moreover, they had every incentive to do so to increase yields, output, and income.

First imported in 1841 and initially almost without competitors, guano quickly became popular. F. M. L. Thompson notes that both its smell and its taste resembled those of natural farmyard manure, and these qualities boosted consumption.[28] Guano encouraged the rapid growth of young plants and seemed as useful on heavy soils as it was on lighter land. Moreover, it could be used with a wide range of crops, though it was particularly favored for root crops such as turnips used in a four-year rotation. To add to its attractions, guano was soluble and relatively light, so it could easily be transported to remote fields. A literature emerged extolling its virtues, which the merchants who handled the trade reinforced through marketing initiatives and advertisements in specialist journals. Alongside all this, the Royal Agricultural Society encouraged scientific research into the use of fertilizers in agriculture and helped to disseminate the results.

By the 1850s the United Kingdom imported roughly half of Peru's output; at its peak in 1858 some 300,000 tons entered British ports. Guano remained the principal fertilizer purchased during the 1860s.[29] Consumption was both regional and cyclical, however. Much more was purchased in Scotland than in the southeast.[30] Demand in any particular year depended on the previous harvest (a poor one reduced farmers' incomes and hence their ability to purchase fertilizers the following spring) and on local weather conditions in March and April, the months of maximum manuring. A rainy spring reduced demand.

Continental Europe also provided a significant and growing market for guano. Although demand was small to the east of the Rhine, farmers in Western Europe purchased guano on a sizable scale. "In Belgium, especially Flanders," J. L. van Zanden argues, "there was a very long history of the use of purchased fertilizers, particularly refuse from the cities."[31] Consequently, as overall demand for fertilizer rose, Belgium imported guano to supplement local supplies of manure, as did the Netherlands, where there was a "swift and favourable reception of guano" after 1840.[32] Dutch farmers demanded new, highly effective fertilizers and were apt to experiment and innovate. In France, too, farmers frequently applied additional fertilizers to the land. W. Newell identifies manuring as one of the factors contributing to the expansion and diversification of

French agriculture in the mid-nineteenth century. As in the United Kingdom, the consumption of guano in France was regional, being concentrated in the north, where such crops as sugar beets were cultivated.[33]

While guano was employed in Europe primarily as a general-purpose fertilizer, especially for root crops, elsewhere it had other uses. It quickly developed a considerable market in the United States. Many soils in the South were low in plant nutrients or had been depleted by tobacco farming, and plantation owners became enthusiastic users of purchased inputs. "The first commercial fertilizer to be widely used in the United States," according to R. C. Sheridan, "was Peruvian guano. . . . The importation of this material began at Baltimore in 1843."[34] Shortly thereafter the Maryland state agricultural chemist appointed a guano inspector based in Baltimore to analyze all incoming shipments, and imports boomed after 1850.[35] Supporting evidence from leading farmers and publicists further encouraged guano's widespread exploitation by southern plantation owners before the onset of the Civil War. David Dickson, for example, devised an original system of "scientific" farming which emphasized intensive cultivation. "Among Dickson's greatest innovations," Chester Destler states, "was his utilization of Peruvian guano as a fertilizer."[36] Despite initial setbacks, Dickson persevered until he obtained good results. He mixed guano with other substances such as bones and salt to develop his own brand of fertilizer, Dickson Compound, suitable for a variety of crops, such as cotton and corn.[37] In the 1850s especially, guano fever swept American farms. At the beginning of the decade guano accounted for some 22 percent of commercial fertilizer sales; by 1860 this figure had risen to 43 percent.[38] So important was guano that the U.S. government first tried to question Peru's sovereignty over the Lobos Islands, which lay much farther from the coast than the main deposits on the Chinchas, and then to negotiate a preferential treaty with Peru for a cheap and stable supply of guano.

Some sugar planters also began to use guano as a means of increasing yields. Mauritius imported sizable quantities in the 1860s, although when it proved unsatisfactory in the sugar fields, animal manure came to be preferred.[39] In the following decade such sugar islands as Guadeloupe and Barbados in the Caribbean, as well as Réunion, were also importing guano.[40] From an early stage the Peruvian government issued separate contracts for the supply of guano to the Spanish sugar colonies in the Caribbean, although these sales were minor in comparison with the European trade.

After the late 1860s the market for guano in the United Kingdom began to decline as business conditions changed once again and competition from such fertilizers as superphosphates grew. The demand curve shifted decisively to the left. One problem was that the scientific approach that had increased demand for guano now began to undermine it. British farmers became increasingly skeptical about the product. Augustus Voelcker, the Royal Agricultural Society's scientific analyst, claimed in 1870 that Peruvian guano had "lost credit with the farmers of England. The supply of Peruvian guano of best quality unfortunately is diminishing year by year."[41] The facts that some crops fared better under different fertilizers, guano prices seemed fixed at high levels, and supplies of "pure" guano were becoming erratic reduced demand.[42] One consequence was an attempt by the German firm of Ohlendorff's to process guano with sulphuric acid in an effort to ensure consistent quality.[43] However, British farmers also began to lose the means to purchase imported fertilizers on the same scale. Agriculture faced far more difficult economic conditions once cheap grain from the United States made its appearance, and a succession of poor harvests in the 1870s further lowered farm incomes. According to P. J. Perry, "Not all the spectacular innovations and practices of mid-century high farming—the lavish application of artificial fertilizers, ambitious building programmes— remained economically viable during the depression. Economy became the prime objective. . . ."[44] The shift in British farming away from arable toward livestock and horticulture permanently lowered the demand for purchased inputs whose beneficial impact was much less in these sectors. Indeed, Lord Ernle notes that some landlords even stopped their tenants from using nitrate of soda on the grounds of its expense.[45]

But while the use of nitrate did not grow rapidly in the United Kingdom, it was a different story in the protected markets of Western Europe, where farmers could afford to import fertilizers. Van Zanden argues that 1870 represents a turning point for European agriculture. The farming innovations that had been introduced earlier but were still not heavily used, even in the third quarter of the nineteenth century, became much more widespread. Although much (but not all) of European farming enjoyed increasing tariff protection against cheaper imports of North American grain after 1870, which helped to maintain local prices and hence farmers' gross incomes, increases in wages and land prices also required farmers to introduce new techniques. One major land-saving innovation was the widespread employment of chemical fertilizers, which could

Table 1

Destinations of Chile's nitrate exports, 1880–1924 (thousands of metric tons)

| | United Kingdom | France | Germany | Netherlands and Belgium | United States | Other Countries | All Countries |
|------|------|------|------|------|------|------|------|
| 1880 | 56.7 | 34.2 | 54.8 | 26.0 | 30.0 | 1.3 | 203.0 |
| 1885 | 98.4 | 75.7 | 147.8 | 73.2 | 44.0 | 2.7 | 441.8 |
| 1890 | 118.8 | 201.0 | 321.3 | 140.9 | 122.0 | 17.6 | 921.6 |
| 1895 | 119.9 | 175.4 | 432.8 | 179.9 | 119.5 | 32.7 | 1,060.2 |
| 1900 | 139.6 | 284.4 | 482.1 | 266.4 | 164.9 | 53.9 | 1,390.3 |
| 1905 | 106.9 | 250.5 | 554.6 | 294.5 | 321.7 | 107.9 | 1,636.1 |
| 1910 | 126.9 | 337.4 | 785.5 | 427.4 | 524.1 | 158.3 | 2,359.6 |
| 1915 | 368.9 | 254.0 | 0 | 50.8 | 704.5 | 364.4 | 1,742.6 |
| 1920 | 71.4 | 224.5 | 64.1 | 240.5 | 1,266.8 | 526.0 | 2,393.3 |
| 1924 | 79.6 | 272.8 | 123.9 | 304.0 | 1,031.4 | 518.3 | 2,330.0 |

Source: Calculated from Sunkel, Un siglo de historia económica de Chile, 1830–1930 (Madrid: Ediciones Cultura Hispanica, 1982), 134–35.

raise crop yields substantially.[46] These changes in the geography of demand for nitrogenous fertilizers are evident in Table 1, which shows the destination of Chile's nitrate exports at five-year intervals after 1880.

The increasing importation of Chilean nitrate by the European sugar beet industry, which many governments subsidized heavily, was particularly noticeable in the final two decades of the nineteenth century. In Germany, where farmers often fertilized root crops heavily in order to force early growth, sugar beets became "the leading sector in the capitalist intensification of agriculture."[47] Local supplies of farmyard manure were insufficient, and manufactured and imported fertilizers filled the gap. The use of nitrate and superphosphates increased so rapidly in German agriculture that the country regularly imported one-third of Chile's nitrate production until the outbreak of war in 1914.[48] J. A. Perkins notes that "in the early 1880s it was not unknown for 100 kilograms per acre of Chilean nitrate . . . to be applied to sugar-beet crops on small peasant holdings."[49]

Farmers in the United States—even plantation owners in the southern states, who might have been expected to experience cash or credit shortages with the shift to free labor after the end of slavery—also turned to nitrate after the guano boom ended. Chilean nitrate entered on a large scale from the 1880s to supplement the supply of natural fertilizers, and by the beginning of the First World War the United States was taking one-fifth of Chile's nitrate exports.[50] The use of nitrogenous fertilizers in the United States doubled between 1910 and 1920, and increased a further 50 percent in the following decade.[51] By then the major importers, W. R. Grace and Company, had developed a trademarked nitrogen-potassium compound, Nitrapo, which was widely advertised as beneficial for a range of crops: tobacco, sugar beets, potatoes, and cotton.[52]

The market for nitrate at the turn of the century, as for guano fifty years earlier, thus seemed favorable from the suppliers' point of view because of the steady expansion of demand resulting from new crops and methods of farming in the North Atlantic world. However, nitrate, like guano, enjoyed no monopoly position as a fertilizer. Farmers used imports from Peru and Chile to fill the gap in domestic supplies when farmyard manure and city waste could not meet demand, and might indeed have preferred their indigenous supplies if only they had been available, since they found that not all crops or soils responded as well to nitrate as they did to ordinary manure. Furthermore, with the development of alternative fertilizers, guano and nitrate did not have the market to themselves. Peruvian guano's monopoly was fragile. Supplies of guano from southwest Africa undercut prices for a brief period in the 1840s, but, more important, the presentation of guano as an all-purpose manure attracted competition from specialist rivals. The development of scientific farming and plant and soil chemistry soon revealed that some crops, such as turnips, in fact benefited more from the addition of phosphates than from nitrogen, thus narrowing still further the market for guano. Superphosphates, which could be manufactured from bones by the addition of sulphuric acid or sourced from naturally occurring deposits in East Anglia and North Africa, created serious competition.[53] Supplies of potash were discovered in Germany in 1861; by the end of the century German farmers used 100,000 tons annually.[54] After 1900 the Haber-Bosch process to extract nitrogen from the air and combine it with hydrogen to create ammonia, which could be used to manufacture fertilizers as well as explosives, also undermined nitrate's market position.[55] After World War I, in particular, the production of synthetic nitrogen and ammonia in Europe and the United States increased rapidly.[56]

Alternative markets for guano and nitrate were strictly limited. Guano effectively possessed no use other than as a fertilizer, although nitrate could be employed in the chemicals industry, especially for production of explosives. The latter use was obviously important even before 1914, and the Great War brought a significant increase in exports and prices, despite the loss of the German market. Exports to the United States rose from 700,000 metric tons in 1915 to almost 1.7 million in 1918.[57] However, the Armistice stimulated a collapse of prices, since the Allies had stockpiled large supplies. Although nitrates could be employed to manufacture explosives for civil uses such as mining, quarrying, land clearance, and road and rail construction, the amounts required were far smaller than those consumed by farmers. Moreover, in the chemicals and explosives industries nitrate was even more susceptible to competition from artificial nitrogen, often produced by the same firms (such as Du Pont). Despite the appearance of new agricultural markets in, for example, Australia and Egypt, the trade never properly recovered from the collapse of the German market in 1914 and the replacement of Chilean nitrates by manufactured fertilizers, a process that had commenced before then but was accelerated by the blockade of Germany.

### SUPPLY AND PRODUCTION

Until the late 1860s the supply of Peruvian guano appeared relatively unlimited. Only then, as the most valuable deposits on the Chincha Islands, which had been exploited since the 1840s, approached exhaustion, did anxious observers begin to investigate the future potential of the trade.[58] Although there were alternative sources on other islands, none of them matched the quantity or quality of those on the Chinchas.[59] In the case of nitrate, supplies of the raw material, caliche, were widespread in the Atacama Desert, although the quality that was mined gradually deteriorated. But how was supply organized to meet the growing demand in Europe?

Apart from the changing technology of production, the decisions taken by governments played a crucial part. In principle, production could be organized as a state enterprise, with elements of it perhaps contracted out to the private sector, or as a completely private undertaking subject only to regulation and taxation by the state. There was also a range of intermediate possibilities: mixed state and private companies; or a separation of production, transport, marketing, and distribution between the public and private sectors. Both foreign and local businessmen might participate. All these possibilities were attempted at one time or another. Historical traditions and the changing institutional environment of international business helped to determine which model was followed and when.

The critical decision in the early stages of the guano business was the declaration by the Peruvian government in 1841, shortly after the trade commenced, that the deposits were a state monopoly. This was in accordance both with the mining laws inherited from the Spanish colonial regime, which gave the state the right to exploit mineral deposits or lease them to private entrepreneurs, and with the colonial tradition of establishing government monopolies (such as tobacco or salt) and renting them out to private contractors in return for financial advances.[60] Guano was easy to exploit: accessible to the coast and hence to shipping; demanding little in the way of labor; and requiring no advanced technology beyond picks, shovels, wheelbarrows, and occasional explosives. The Peruvian state, in the midst of civil war, did not have the human or financial resources to employ its own labor and sell the guano to merchants for export, though it was willing to help in supplying workers such as convicts to the private sector. Initially, therefore, the merchants who were awarded contracts for the export of guano organized production themselves, probably via local businessmen. With the establishment of internal peace under Ramón Castilla, however, the Peruvian state recovered some of its authority and in 1849 it awarded a single contract for extracting guano to a prominent local entrepreneur, Domingo Elías. By 1853 Elías was employing almost 1,000 workers on the Chincha Islands, including 588 Chinese indentured servants and 209 prisoners, and estimated to be grossing $750 a day from the contract. Only in the 1870s, after the exporters had recovered responsibility for production and the Chinese trade had ended, did free labor come to predominate, with 600 Bolivians and Chileans arriving on the islands in 1875.[61]

The production end of the commodity chain therefore provided opportunities for local Peruvian businessmen such as Elías and his successor, Andrés Alvarez Calderón. This was also the case with the smaller guano export contracts, which were awarded on a geographical basis. A central feature of these contracts after 1849 was the employment of merchants to transport and sell guano overseas on consignment for a limited term, in return for a commission and other payments for their services. The Peruvian government stipulated both the quantity of guano to be exported and the price at which it should be sold. In order to secure the contracts the concessionaires had to provide the government with an advance, repayable from their earnings. In the case of the six-year extension agreed with Antony Gibbs and Sons in 1853 for the European market (exclusive of France), this advance seems to have been about $1.5 million (approximately £300,000), a sum well beyond the reach of Peruvian businessmen at the time.[62] However, local merchants, prominent among them the Barreda brothers and Julián de Zaracóndegui, were awarded contracts for the United States and smaller markets such as Spain and its colonies.[63] This fits well with one central tenet of recent commodity chains analysis, the importance of local entrepreneurs' learning through experience by participating in global commodity chains and thus gaining the potential to upgrade. This process of learning, coupled with the enormous increase in financial resources available to Peruvian capitalists after the consolidation of the internal debt in the 1850s, put them in a position where in 1861 they were able to take over the contract for supplying the British market.

With guano central to the economy, the nitrate resources in Tarapacá were ignored by successive Peruvian governments until the 1870s, and supply here was dominated by small entrepreneurs without the intervention of the state. When nitrate production did take off at the end of the 1860s, it was on an entirely different basis of ownership. By then three important changes had taken place. The first was a crucial technological innovation, the introduction of steam power and mechanized processing of caliche. This innovation permitted economies of scale and substantially reduced the costs of production, though at the same time it raised the financial requirements for establishing an oficina. The second was institutional, the development of limited liability companies in Britain after the Companies Acts of 1858 and 1862 and of joint stock companies on the west coast of South America, such as the commercial banks established in Peru and Chile during the 1860s. Along with the growth of the British overseas banks and the London market for securities after the 1860s, all these developments helped to reduce the costs of capital and working finance.[64] The third was the transition from slave to free labor in Peru, alongside the growth of a landless population in Chile that provided a ready source of unskilled migrant labor to new ventures. Thus the nitrate industry, like other mining enterprises, was organized on the basis of individuals' or companies' staking out a claim and paying a fixed rent and export duties to the state. While the Peruvian part of the desert was dominated by the Tarapacá Nitrate Company, founded in 1868 and partly owned by Gibbs, many smaller enterprises were founded, especially by Chileans. The Bolivian sector was dominated by the Antofagasta Nitrate and Railways Company, a joint venture between Gibbs and Chilean capitalists incorporated in 1872.[65]

For Bolivia and Chile, where the exploitation of nitrate was just commencing when war broke out in 1879, the question of the ownership structure for nitrate was never controversial. The Bolivian state was simply too weak and the desert too remote for it to assert its authority in the way Peru had done with guano. In Chile the early stages of nitrate exploitation followed the model of private enterprise under which silver and copper exports had grown in the previous fifty years. However, for Peru the coexistence of a privately owned and rapidly expanding nitrate industry with a state-owned and declining guano industry on which it depended for revenues created serious problems, the more so since the two trades were directly competitive in international markets. It is this situation that explains the abortive attempts to limit the supply of Peruvian nitrate to world markets in the 1870s.[66] The first measure, introduced in 1873, was a direct reversion to traditions of Hispanic capitalism, a state monopoly (*estanco*) over nitrate exports that guaranteed a minimum price to producers, restricted the expansion of capacity, and permitted the state to gain from the anticipated differential between buying and selling prices. But with prices falling and producers in opposition to the scheme, implementation was delayed, although export duties were increased. As the crisis deepened as a result of the depression in Europe and increasing supplies of nitrate from Antofagasta in Bolivia, the Peruvian government introduced a different scheme in 1875 by offering to purchase oficinas, in effect undertaking a partial nationalization of the industry under which owners would be compensated with short-term bonds (nitrate certificates). However, this measure also failed because of continued competition from other producers in both Peru and Bolivia. By the time the Pacific War commenced in 1879, the guano and nitrate industries were both in crisis, the Peruvian external debt was in default, and in both Peru and Chile the domestic financial systems were in a state of collapse.[67]

As in the case of guano in the early 1840s, the crucial decision that determined the future structure of ownership and hence the supply of nitrate to the world market was taken in the context of war. For the Chilean government the failure of state intervention that the Peruvian experience had demonstrated and the benefits of private ownership were not in question; the problem was the claims of Peruvian government creditors, including the holders of the nitrate certificates, in which a secondary market had developed, and the threat of foreign intervention to support them. The solution was to return the nationalized Peruvian oficinas to private ownership, allowing those who had accumulated certificates to take control of the plants.[68] In the short term this measure resulted in a marked expansion of foreign ownership, aided by the ease with which it was possible to float nitrate companies on the London capital market in the 1880s.[69] However, over the longer term three other trends are visible. First, foreign ownership of the industry peaked in the early 1890s. Thereafter, with technology and skilled engineers freely available and the London Stock Exchange becoming markedly more skeptical toward South American company flotations after the Baring Crisis, Chilean capitalists took a greater share in the industry as they purchased new nitrate lands in state auctions. In 1910 seventy-eight companies were exporting nitrate; the top twenty included eleven that were listed in London, six that are recognizably Chilean, and three German, but Chilean firms predominated among the small and medium-sized enterprises in the industry.[70] Second, the question of periodic crises of oversupply, given the price inelasticity of nitrate, still had to be tackled: the eventual solution was for the Chilean government to encourage, rather than oppose, the operation of combinations among the producers to restrict production and to schedule auctions of new nitrate lands more carefully.[71] Third, with demand and prices both growing after the turn of the century (see again Figure 3), there was little incentive to modernize the industry.[72] The last important innovation was the introduction of steam heating, the Shanks Process, after 1878. Thereafter the technology of production remained much as it had been in the 1880s, and labor productivity fell almost continually as the quality of the deposits declined (see Figure 5).[73]

The size of the labor force in nitrate was much larger than that in guano. By 1900 the industry directly employed around 20,000; at its peak during the First World War employment had increased to over 50,000.[74] In the desert conditions of northern Chile a labor supply on this scale was not available locally. Workers were therefore recruited, through attractive offers of high wages, from the army of landless laborers that existed in central Chile and, to a lesser extent, Peru and Bolivia. In this respect the change in ownership that occurred in 1880 did not alter prewar patterns of labor recruitment, which had also relied heavily on the availability of Chileans willing to work in Tarapacá. The turnover in the labor force, which consisted predominantly of single men, was extensive; workers frequently moved between oficinas searching for higher wages or for personal reasons. The number of workers fluctuated according to the cycles of the industry (the formation of a combination to restrict output and raise prices inevitably resulted in serious unemployment) and seasonality (more workers were employed in the early months of the year in

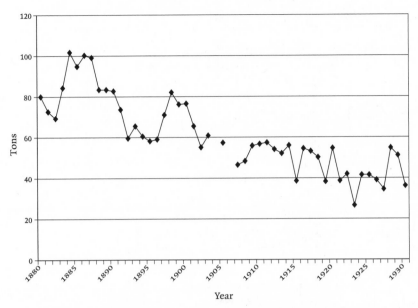

5. Tons of nitrate produced per worker, Chile, 1880–1930

Source: Calculated from Osvaldo Sunkel, *La historia económica de Chile, 1830–1930: Dos ensayos y una bibliografía* (Madrid: Ediciones Cultura Hispanica, 1982), 126–27.

order to produce fertilizer in time for the northern hemisphere's growing season).[75] In order to retain and control labor, oficinas offered credit at company stores, demanded deposits on workers' tools, or adopted collective recruiting and disciplinary procedures. The organization of labor was much more complex in the nitrate industry than in guano, where it had been divided simply into foremen and manual laborers, many of them unfree. In nitrate there was a significant division between the miners in the pampa and operatives in the oficina. Alongside those who worked for the production companies, a considerable workforce was also employed on the railways that carried the nitrate to the ports as well as on the *lanchas* that took it to ships waiting offshore. The lack of job security, exploitation through the company store, and poor health and safety conditions in the oficinas were the subjects of frequent criticisms. Not surprisingly, the nitrate provinces were among the cradles of the Chilean labor movement and the scenes of some of the most bloody massacres in Chilean history before 1973.

It was in this context that a new crisis enveloped the nitrate industry after the First World War, comparable to that which had afflicted guano in

6. The nitrate commodity chains, mid-1929

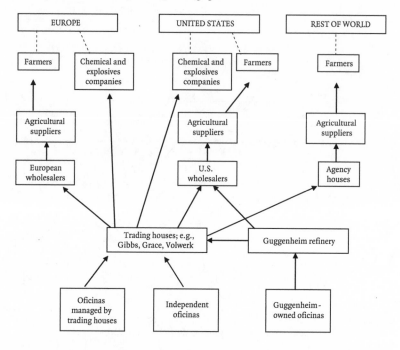

the 1870s, and as in the earlier case, a series of attempts at restructuring the supply end of the commodity chain failed. On the demand side the problem was the lack of recovery in the German market after the war because of competition from synthetic nitrogen. On the supply side the driving force was the U.S. firm of Guggenheim, whose mining engineers developed systems of large-scale extraction and refining capable of treating low-quality caliche.[76] However, although they successfully introduced the new process, aided by the ease with which new ventures could be financed in New York in the 1920s, the Guggenheims badly miscalculated, deceived by the rise in prices that followed the immediate postwar slump and failing to anticipate the expansion of synthetic nitrogen production, which doubled between 1925 and 1928. As a result, several parallel commodity chains existed alongside each other (see Figure 6). As the industry ran into increasing crisis, with serious consequences for both employment and revenues in Chile, the Chilean government was forced to intervene. The outcome was the formation of a mixed public-private company, COSACH, involving the state, the Guggenheims, and the traditional nitrate producers. However, overburdened by debt and unable to raise fresh working capital, COSACH quickly collapsed, financially weakening all those associated with it. As in the crisis of guano fifty years earlier, successive and increasingly desperate attempts to restructure supply failed in the face of financial recession, a collapse in demand, and competition that the previously monopoly supplier could not control.

## THE INTERMEDIARIES IN THE FERTILIZER COMMODITY CHAIN

Apart from linking supply with demand, commodity chain analysis also emphasizes the importance of the network of commercial transactions through which the product is transformed and transported between the initial supplier and the final consumer. The various stages of processing and shipment add value to the commodity, and each of the nodes thus yields opportunities for income and profit.[77] Hence, in the contest for control of a global commodity chain and its consequent income flows, governments seek to retain as many nodes as possible within their geographical borders; private companies aim to maximize their control over these same points while simultaneously minimizing their financial exposure to sudden changes in trading conditions.

The transfer of guano and nitrate from the west coast of South America to their final consumers in Europe and North America required several intermediary functions, and for the most part these were undertaken by foreign businessmen. International trading firms such as Antony Gibbs and Sons carried out virtually all the practical management responsibilities of the trades.[78] As already noted, the foreign merchants had little direct involvement in digging or loading guano at the Chincha Islands, tasks that were normally contracted to local entrepreneurs. But it was difficult to sell the product without them, since they provided access to a range of linked business services such as shipping, insurance, finance, warehousing, and wholesaling in Europe. Moreover, in the case of nitrate many of the merchant houses, as the example of Gibbs in the Tarapacá and the Antofagasta Nitrate Company even before 1880 shows, also sought to integrate backward into production.

The management of these business services within a network of linked nodal points was the foundation for dominance over these commodity chains. In the case of the international fertilizer trades, the possibilities for the intermediary functions to be located within the borders of Chile and Peru were slim, although a small market for nitrate did develop in Valparaíso. In addition, local banks in Peru and Chile profited from negotiating the bills of exchange arising from the trades. However, the ability of countries on the west coast of South America to supply local participation in the complementary business services was severely limited. After independence in 1821 Peru suffered decades of unstable governments and civil wars, and although there was a powerful local merchant community in Lima, it had neither the resources nor the knowledge to retain control over the growing guano trade. Thus such Peruvian entrepreneurs as Francisco Quirós were replaced by Antony Gibbs and Sons, who possessed much better access to both the financial networks and market information that management of the trade required.[79] Even when the Peruvian merchants took over the concessions for the British Isles and Europe in 1861, they still remained reliant on a British trading house, Thomson Bonar, to manage many of the intermediary activities.[80]

International trading houses were well placed to retain the intermediary functions on which the fertilizer trades depended, even if local entrepreneurs were able to obtain supply contracts or develop production facilities. Merchants could exploit economies both of scale and of scope in the provision of these functions. The scale of their operations in guano and nitrate, as well as other commodities, made it worth their while to invest independently in such services as shipping and warehousing. Links between commerce and ship owning were traditionally close. Merchants used their European connections to charter shipping on favorable terms.[81] Further, where it was cheaper to provide two or more services together using common inputs rather than separately, the trading houses enjoyed economies of scope. The same clerks in a merchant's offices on the west coast could effectively supply and exploit different but related intermediary functions. Information about one business service, say transport, is likely to be relevant to another closely related service, such as insurance.

Asymmetries in access to information and business networks also favored the expatriate firms. Such houses as Antony Gibbs and Sons could put their commercial contacts in such centers as London to further good use. Business service providers were keen to place agencies with houses on the west coast of South America where there was insufficient trade for independent branch offices. Insurers and ship owners wanted to exploit the commercial reputation of such merchants as Gibbs and Balfour Williamson, whose established local links would bring in business, both on their own account and from third parties.[82] On the merchant's part, agency work was generally straightforward, supplied a steady income, complemented existing interests, and required little marginal outlay.

The size of guano shipments in the mid-nineteenth century was such that merchants could not use their own tonnage alone. Instead they chartered sailing ships on a large scale, a business from which they normally drew a commission of 2.5 percent from the owners or brokers to the charter party.[83] Between 1850 and 1860 some 3,000 vessels (at an aggregate 1.8 million tons) were dispatched from Peru under the Gibbs contract, an average of 264 ships a year in the first five years and 300 or so annually during the second half of the decade. The average size of these ships rose over the period from 500 to 700 tons. "It would be difficult," Mathew argues, "to find another merchant house in that decade [1850–60] employing a fleet of larger dimensions."[84] While temporary booms in the demand for shipping made it difficult to hire tonnage cheaply, guano consignees such as Gibbs generally enjoyed a powerful market role because their quasi-monopolist position enabled them to bid down rates.

The process of chartering did not require great effort on Gibbs's part, since the volume of work available encouraged ship owners to approach the house seeking business. Ships could be hired locally on the west coast at such ports as Callao and Valparaíso, but increasingly tonnage was chartered in Europe. Gibbs used agents in British and continental ports under clear instructions as to price and quality, but the house was able to conduct most of the business itself, exploiting its contacts in London, Bristol, and Liverpool and avoiding the need to share its commissions. The ships very often left not in ballast but loaded to such destinations as Australia and California, where Gibbs had branches, before they sailed for South America and the guano islands, and from there back to Europe. Gibbs also arranged the insurance of the cargoes. This was particularly important when freight rates had been paid to ship owners in advance and when there was no cover if a cargo were lost. Normal practice, however, was to pay the owner of a vessel after it had docked in Europe but before the cargo was sold.

While Gibbs held the exclusive guano consignment contracts, the house enjoyed a favorable position with regard to providing the management services of shipping and insurance on a large scale. After the contracts were awarded elsewhere, Gibbs was simply one of several firms involved in ensuring the transfer of the fertilizer from the west coast to Europe, but the same system of chartering sailing tonnage and arranging insurance would have persisted. Indeed, Gibbs not only continued to charter tonnage and insure shipments on its own account but did so for clients as well. Guano shipped to the United States, which was the responsibility of such merchant houses as Oliphants and W. R. Grace and Company, would have been similarly treated.

When the international fertilizer trade switched from guano to nitrate, transport and insurance arrangements remained largely unchanged. Under the Peruvian nitrate contracts after 1875, when the state employed merchants to act as consignees to overseas markets, Gibbs managed the trade's complementary business services in bulk, rather as it had the shipment of guano. Although the depth of Gibbs's penetration into the nitrate trade was exceptional, most British houses on the west coast also took an interest in the trade. James Sawers and Sons and Graham Rowe succeeded Gibbs as the Peruvian government's consignees in 1878, while Balfour Williamson sought consignments and arranged ships' charters for independent nitrate producers.[85] Merchants based in continental Europe and in the United States pursued similar strategies. With Chile's acquisition of the nitrate fields and the reversion of the oficinas to private ownership, the transfer of fertilizer from the west coast reverted to a more atomistic pattern, until the succession of nitrate combinations at the end of the nineteenth century reinstated a combined consignment system. But the use of foreign-owned tonnage remained central to the trade from the west coast. Such ship owners as Laeisz of Hamburg and Bordes of Le Havre continued to have large sailing ships built especially for the trade until early in the twentieth century, while "Colonel" John North formed the Nitrate Producers' Steamship Company as a rival to other steamship firms.[86]

For the most part, therefore, the key intermediaries in the guano and nitrate industries were the international trading houses, which developed the knowledge and skills to organize the functions of shipping, insurance, and sales in the consuming markets, and transferred them from guano to nitrate. The fact that with the brief exception of the late 1870s, nitrate production remained in private hands offered additional opportunities for profitable business. Before the Pacific War merchants had already begun to invest upstream in nitrate deposits and oficinas, and such an integration of operations under the aegis of a trading firm that offered management and commercial services became a common feature of the trade under Chilean rule. Even after floating their oficinas as apparently independent companies on the London Stock Exchange the merchants often continued to control management and hence to retain the lucrative agencies for themselves.[87] The main exception to this pattern of merchant dominance was Colonel North, the leading promoter of nitrate enterprises at the end of the 1880s, who did not come from a trading background and so depended on a close relationship with a merchant firm, Wm. and Jno. Lockett of Liverpool. North himself preferred to invest in ancillary services such as the Tarapacá Waterworks Company, the Nitrate Railways Company, the crucial transport link between many of the oficinas and the ports, and the Bank of Tarapacá and London. In this he was an exception, and his empire was relatively short-lived.

As the U.S. market gained in importance for nitrate exports, a similar pattern emerged there. The dominant firm was W. R. Grace and Company, which had developed from an enterprise supplying the ships that loaded guano at the Chincha Islands in the 1850s. This enterprise provided the basis for a classic merchant business, headquartered in New York and with an affiliate in the Peruvian port of Callao. Grace acted as a general import-export merchant, as well as operating ships of its own and chartering others to carry guano and nitrate to the United States.[88] After the failure of Oliphants in the 1870s, Grace successfully bid for the exclusive contract to export nitrate from the Peruvian state's oficinas to the United States. Despite the collapse of this scheme in the Pacific War, Grace continued to be one of the two leading firms shipping nitrate to the United States, and indeed established its own steamship line in 1892. After the turn of the century, following the example of its British and German counterparts, it integrated backward into production with the purchase of the Jazpampa Bajo oficina, and in 1909 established Nitrate Agencies Ltd., which acted as management agents for a group of oficinas.[89] As with Gibbs, control of the intermediary management, trading, and shipping functions for several firms floated on the London Stock Exchange, aided by the appointment of senior executives to the boards of these companies, gave Grace a key role in nitrate, allowing it economies of scale at minimum risk to itself as long as the trade was growing.[90]

Warehousing, distribution, and wholesaling represented a further node in the international fertilizer commodity chains. There were strong arguments, principally on the grounds of cost, in favor of shipping cargoes direct to consuming centers. However, available statistics show that the great majority of the guano arriving in Britain docked at London, followed by Liverpool and Bristol. These destinations bore no relation to the geography of the U.K. market, since the southeast consumed little guano. One possible reason was that Gibbs could share commissions with its affiliated houses in these ports rather than splitting them with independent agents. European shipments tended to be concentrated at Le Havre, Antwerp, Rotterdam, and Hamburg. Moreover, by using a small number of ports Gibbs could more easily respond to potential demand from outlying countries and regions. Centralized in this way, guano could also be more easily secured against adulteration, a real fear, it seems, and one that required careful supervision.[91]

Once landed in bulk, the fertilizer was stored in dock warehouses before it was distributed. Gibbs appears to have had no stores of its own but to have rented space at the British and continental ports from which the guano was shipped to other markets. Indeed, Gibbs inserted a so-called continental clause into its charters enabling it to redirect vessels from their original destinations to alternative ports as demand changed between loading in Peru and arrival in Europe. If, for example, the French market appeared weak, ships would be diverted to Ostend or to Hamburg if prospects were better there. At the ports, dealers made their own arrangements for carriage from the warehouses, normally paying cash. At Leith in 1870, for example, Balfour Williamson was in negotiation with a number of local buyers to offload both guano and nitrate.[92] These buyers, in turn, sold their guano in small lots to the final consumers.

For British merchants the London end of the fertilizer business, arranging the sales, receiving the proceeds (which might be in bills of exchange sent by traders elsewhere in the United Kingdom and Europe), and remitting money to the west coast, was not arduous. For Gibbs in the 1850s it meant the employment of a few dozen clerks and a member of the firm's senior management, who reported fortnightly to the Peruvian government. Even at the end of the nineteenth century the size of the headquarters offices of the merchant houses engaged in the nitrate trade was not large. In short, the London (or Hamburg or New York) business was straightforward, under control, and largely free of risk. However, what was not available to the international trading firms was the opportunity to "industrialize" guano and nitrate at the downstream end of the chain. With consumption of these products linked largely to the agricultural market for fertilizers, the only real processing that might have taken place after shipment would have been the use of guano or nitrate as a component in recipes for mixed fertilizers. This enterprise would have required the merchants to commit capital to expenditures on research and equipment, to learn new skills, to increase their reliance on other suppliers, such as phosphate manufacturers, and to develop a new style of marketing via brand names—steps that most of them were unwilling to take.[93] In this respect guano and nitrate contrasted with other early-twentieth-century exports such as oil, meat, rubber, and tropical fruits, where a much greater degree of vertical integration took place.

The role of the international trading houses can be ascribed in part to their access to the financial resources of the City of London. Grace's entry to the nitrate trade in 1878, for example, was possible only because Grace received credit from Baring.[94] However, it was not just profits that they accumulated, but the functional and geographical knowledge and networks that made them indispensable to Latin American governments and entrepreneurs, on the one hand, and to other businessmen in the North Atlantic world, on the other. For example, when the Peruvian entrepreneurs who held the guano export contract for the United States ran into problems in 1855, they obtained financial support from Gibbs.[95] When the Peruvian government intervened directly in the nitrate trade after 1875, it was entirely dependent on the knowledge, finance, and networks supplied by foreign merchants. When the Peruvian Corporation, which was awarded exclusive rights to export guano from Peru after 1890, looked for expertise to handle the trade, the obvious partner was Gibbs.[96] Another international firm based in London, Schroders, entered the fertilizer trades after 1870 because of its association with the Paris merchant house of Dreyfus, which had obtained the guano contract in 1869 and for which it acted as London agent, and the German firm of Ohlendorff's, which was attempting to transform the poor-quality guano that now arrived from Peru into a standardized commodity. Not only did these ventures provide Schroders with substantial profits; they also allowed it to acquire important information and contacts on the west coast of South America which resulted in additional profitable business.[97] In the case of Grace and Company, even though the firm was headquartered in New York, one or more of its senior partners remained resident in London until after the First World War, such was its importance as a capital market and center for information and business networks concerning South America.

This acquisition of knowledge and networks had a number of implications. First, it enabled those trading houses that survived the financial crisis of the 1870s and the subsequent war to make the transition from guano to nitrate with surprising ease. The main newcomer in the 1880s, Colonel North, could not have gained his role in the nitrate industry without the knowledge that he had gained as an engineer in Tarapacá and the connections he had forged there with another British engineer, Robert Harvey; a banker, Robert Dawson; and a partner in the Liverpool merchant firm of Locketts.[98] Second, it enabled British entrepreneurs to finance the expansion of ancillary services such as water and railways, from which they also derived profits, taking them over from their original Peruvian and Chilean owners. In a similar way, in the early part of the twentieth century its international connections and knowledge of nitrate allowed Balfour Williamson to form a successful joint venture with Standard Oil to supply Peruvian and Californian fuel oil to the oficinas.[99] Third, the international trading houses, in particular Gibbs and Schroder, profited from the reputation that they established as a result of their participation in the fertilizer trades, becoming heavily involved in issuing shares and bonds in the investment boom of the late 1880s, not only for enterprises in Peru, Bolivia, and Chile, but for enterprises in other parts of South America as well. The role that they played in the intermediary activities of the fertilizer trades, therefore, meant not only an opportunity for profit from the trade itself, but also the development of knowledge, information, and networks that contributed to the diversification of the international firms.

The merchants involved in the fertilizer trades earned substantial profits, but, as the development economists' calculations in the 1960s and 1970s showed, both the Peruvian and Chilean states, through a monopoly and export duty respectively, also obtained significant revenues. In this regard, as Shane Hunt has put it, "the Peruvian guano sector was, as export sectors go, the very antithesis of an enclave. . . . A fiscal bonanza was presented to those in control of the Peruvian exchequer."[100] Much the same is true of Chile and nitrate. It is important to emphasize, therefore, that although the international trading houses were the dominant figures in organizing the trades, they operated within the boundaries set by public policy. Thus the surplus that the fertilizer trades generated was shared between the state and the private sector. In the case of guano the Peruvian state dictated prices and the merchants worked on commission; in nitrate the Chilean state extracted rents from the trade via export duties and the control of supply that derived from its power to auction new lands. In both trades, governments took care to keep themselves well informed. In the case of guano the Peruvian state demanded detailed reports and accounts from the concessionaires. In nitrate both the Peruvian state before the Pacific War and the Chilean government thereafter established a specialized department to monitor the industry; indeed,

Robert Harvey, North's principal partner, was employed by both before returning to London.[101] In both countries, too, members of the legislatures, many of them out of self-interest, kept a close watch on the foreigners involved in the trade. The outcome was that calculations of returned values, which measure the proportion of export revenues that make their way into the local economy, show that in the case of Peru the state obtained around 60 percent of guano earnings, while in the case of Chilean nitrate the figure was 33 percent, with at least another third going in payments to workers and Chilean suppliers of foodstuffs, equipment, and services, as well as profits to Chilean owners of nitrate oficinas.[102]

## CONCLUSIONS

The guano and nitrate industries have seldom been analyzed alongside each other, despite the continuities involved, and the development of the concept of the global commodity chain provides an appropriate framework for reappraisal. A number of conclusions flow from this study.

It is important for business historians of the developing world to understand the changing patterns of consumption and demand in the developed countries. The opportunities to develop the guano and nitrate trades arose from the growth of population and consumption of agricultural produce in the urban centers of Europe. Both trades were vitally dependent on farm incomes and on an agricultural revolution that included the dissemination of information about the benefits of fertilizers. When demand turned down or oversupply occurred, the commodity chains that had been constructed in the periods of growth came under enormous pressure, leading to restructuring, experimentation with new forms of ownership and marketing, and eventual collapse.

Even in commodity trades that have traditionally been considered as heavily dominated by foreign interests, there is some space for local capitalists at the supply end of the chain. Their participation provided opportunities for accumulation and investment elsewhere in the economy as well as for increasing participation in the chain itself. Both in guano and in nitrate local entrepreneurs were able to make some inroads into the dominance of the foreign merchants and production companies, whose access to cheaper finance had initially given them the resources to control the trades. However, this space was limited by the competitive advantage that the large trading houses possessed in international transactions, as a result of their access to finance, information, and business networks, as well as their logistical skills. Hence, the application of commodity chain analysis to international fertilizers helps to refine still further the reasons for the division of the trade's value among its various participants.

The state played a central role in altering both the structures of the chains and the nodes from which rents were extracted. While states adopt different strategies for various commodities, John Talbot argues, their decisions in the cases of specific commodities have generally not been analyzed, especially within a historical context.[103] The Peruvian and Chilean states seem to have been much more competent in organizing the guano and nitrate trades, monitoring foreign intermediaries and producers, and extracting profits than many writers, especially those in the dependency tradition, might have expected. Clearly they both benefited from being the world's main suppliers of nitrogenous fertilizers for a long time and from the scope that lack of competition allowed them. They were thus significant actors in the structuring and governance of the chains, in the Peruvian case by asserting state ownership of guano resources and contracting out the production, shipping, and marketing of the product, in the Chilean case by being able to levy export duties on nitrate in the knowledge that consumers would bear the cost. Successive governments in Peru and Chile sought to influence their relationships with expatriate firms in order to maximize their incomes, but at the same time the asymmetries of access to finance and information limited their scope to extend their influence along the chain.

Both the domestic and the international legal and financial environments were important in setting the context within which the chains were structured. At the beginning of the guano period Latin America was out of favor with foreign investors after the defaults of the 1820s. The options available to the Peruvian state were much more limited than those of Chile when it obtained its monopoly over nitrate forty years later. If guano were to be used to attract foreign investment, the state was the only channel through which such finance could flow, and merchant partnerships and government loans were the only possible sources. It was not until the 1880s that companies registered in London and with interests in Latin America began to float in large numbers, and then only in the handful of countries whose governments had maintained their credit through the crisis of the mid-1870s. Before 1914 much foreign investment took the form of free-standing companies operating in one overseas country.

Thus the individual country's credit was vital to the successful flotation of privately owned companies, in contrast to later multinationals, which could invest in less creditworthy countries without worrying unduly about Stock Exchange reactions.[104] The fact that Chile was one of the few Latin American countries that survived the 1870s crisis with its credit intact thus made it possible for the nitrate industry to expand in the 1880s on the basis of foreign investment.[105] Moreover, the flotation of nitrate companies also depended on the reputation enjoyed by key intermediaries such as Gibbs and Schroder, both of which had benefited substantially from different stages of the guano trade.[106]

A simple buyer-driven/producer-driven dichotomy is irrelevant to efforts to visualize the chains, at least in this historical example.[107] The international fertilizer chain was producer-driven insofar as the suppliers on the west coast, including successive governments in Peru and Chile, were the key agents who contracted with a network of competing suppliers of business services. However, the fertilizer chains fit much better within a formulation that allows chains to be dominated by a range of agents, including the international trading houses that drove these particular ones. The competitive advantage of such firms in the modern commodity chains for coffee, tea, and cacao, according to John Talbot, comes from two sources: "They specialize in logistics, including knowledge of where to find supplies of different commodities, and of how to ship and insure them; and in financial services, including access to large amounts of capital, and the ability to protect themselves from risk and increase profits by playing the commodity futures markets."[108] Futures markets did not develop in the fertilizer trades, but otherwise this comment is equally true of nineteenth-century firms such as Gibbs and Grace. Significantly, moreover, it was relatively straightforward for such firms to transfer their knowledge of shipping, insurance, distribution, and consumption, together with their networks of business contacts in South America, Europe, and the United States, from one fertilizer trade to another. The manner in which guano and nitrate were produced may have been quite distinct; the intermediary functions and the final markets were not.

There were two limitations to the dominance of the trading houses, however. First, the ascendancy of a single country in supply gave the host governments much more scope to extract rents from the chains than most commodity producers possess. Second, the continuation of the chain depended on international demand and the absence of substitutes, and the trading houses lost power once competitors appeared in the artificial fertilizer business. Those with resources and strategic vision, such as Gibbs and Grace, had been fortunate in being able to apply their financial, organizational, and human capital resources to benefit from the transition from guano to nitrate. They were unable to make the same transition when nitrate collapsed, although Grace, a much more diversified and entrepreneurial firm, survived rather better than Gibbs, which never fully recovered.[109]

Finally, given the emphasis of Hopkins and Wallerstein, the originators of the commodity chain concept, on the existence of "real economic alternatives," it may be worth considering the counterfactual possibilities.[110] Were these the optimal means of constructing the chains, given the circumstances of the time? Both the Peruvian and Chilean governments have come under heavy criticism for their inability to restrain foreign interests and to maximize the benefits from the export trades. Yet in the case of Peru, it is difficult to see how the alternative of allowing all comers to exploit the guano deposits would have led to anything other than a predatory economy in which neither the Peruvian state nor national and foreign businessmen would have made any long-term gains. It would have been farmers and food consumers in Western Europe and the United States who would have benefited from a free market in guano, leaving little long-term benefit to Peru.

And what if the Chilean state had attempted to monopolize nitrate exports or production in its own hands after the Pacific War? There was no technological barrier to doing so, and Chilean opinion was not totally against the principle of government intervention in business: the state operated an extensive rail network in central and southern Chile. However, to control the trade completely the state would have confronted the problem of acquiring information and financing the costs of establishing a marketing network in several consuming countries. Even if it had confined itself to the institution of an export monopoly (along the lines of the Peruvian scheme of 1873), the likelihood is that it would not have wished to take on direct responsibility for contracting shipping and organizing distribution. Thus at some point in the chain, unless it made costly and deliberate attempts to enhance its managerial capacity, especially in the logistics of international trade, the Chilean state would have been dependent on international trading firms. It would also have incurred much greater risk with regard to price volatility, which under the system that actually operated after 1880 was chiefly borne by the private sector, at least until the foundation of COSACH. State control of production might have developed the nitrate industry more slowly and succeeded in stabilizing prices at a high level, but this would have restricted employment in the industry and hence significant backward linkages into the remainder of the economy. Moreover, in economic terms, in the long run there was little point in leaving nitrate in the ground. In parallel with the experience of many other commodity cartels, limited supplies and high prices might well have accelerated the competition from synthetic nitrogen, leaving Chilean resources without value.

In conclusion, therefore, the commodity chains that were constructed in the international fertilizer trades may have been dominated by foreign intermediaries as a result of asymmetries of information and access to business networks and cheap finance, but the host economies still obtained substantial benefits and rents from the trades. When one takes into account the financial, legal, and political environments in which they were constructed, it is difficult to see that the alternatives—private ownership of the resource in the case of guano, state control of production and marketing in the case of nitrate—would have provided significantly better rewards for Peru and Chile.

---

NOTES

We are grateful to Steven C. Topik and Carlos Marichal for helpful suggestions on an earlier draft, as well as to Terry Gourvish and members of the Business History Unit seminar at the London School of Economics for their stimulating comments.

1   On British agriculture in this period, see, for example, Hueckel, "Agriculture during Industrialisation."

2   Nitrate was also frequently known in the nineteenth century as saltpeter.

3   On nitrate, see Mamalakis, "The Role of Government in the Resource Transfer and Resource Allocation Process"; on guano, Hunt, "Growth and Guano in Nineteenth-Century Peru."

4   The classic statement on enclave economies with respect to guano was Levin, *The Export Economies*.

5   The fundamental work on the conduits through which guano income was channeled into the Peruvian economy, in particular on the consolidation of the internal debt, is Quiroz Norris, *La deuda defraudada*. On the growth of product markets in northern Chile, see Sunkel, *La historia económica de Chile*, 102–14; labor is discussed in a later section of this chapter. A translation of part of this volume was published as Cariola and Sunkel, "The Growth of the Nitrate Industry and Socioeconomic Change in Chile."

6   Mathew, *The House of Gibbs and the Peruvian Guano Monopoly*; Bonilla, *Guano y burguesía en el Perú*; Greenhill, "The Nitrate and Iodine Trades"; O'Brien, *The*

*Nitrate Industry and Chile's Crucial Transition*"; Bermúdez, *Historia del salitre desde sus orígenes hasta la Guerra del Pacífico*; Monteón, *Chile in the Nitrate Era*.

7 Ramírez Necochea, *Historia del imperialismo en Chile*; Blakemore, *British Nitrates and Chilean Politics*; Mayo, "La Compañía de Salitres de Antofagasta y la Guerra del Pacífico"; O'Brien, "The Antofagasta Company"; Ortega, "Nitrates, Chilean Entrepreneurs, and the Origins of the War of the Pacific"; Sater, *Chile and the War of the Pacific*.

8 On inflation in Peru, see Gootenberg, "Carneros y chuño," 30–32, which discusses "severe guano-age inflation." On Chile, see the classic work of Fetter, *Monetary Inflation in Chile*, and Millar Carvacho, *Políticas y teorías monetarias en Chile*.

9 O'Brien, *Nitrate Industry*, which covers the transition from Peruvian to Chilean dominance of the industry, is a significant exception.

10 Hopkins and Wallerstein, "Commodity Chains in the World Economy Prior to 1800," 159.

11 Ibid., 157–70, and idem, "Commodity Chains in the Capitalist World Economy Prior to 1800." Despite the almost identical titles, these are different papers, and the second incorporates empirical studies of shipbuilding and the grain trades by associates of Hopkins and Wallerstein.

12 On the original formulation, see Gereffi, "The Organization of Buyer-Driven Global Commodity Chains," 96–100. Studies of contemporary agricultural or agro-industrial exports from Latin America that use the concept of the commodity chain include Talbot, "The Struggle for Control of a Commodity Chain"; Ponte, "The 'Latte Revolution'?"; Gwynne, "Globalisation, Commodity Chains and Fruit Exporting Regions in Chile."

13 But see Gibbon, "Upgrading Primary Production"; Talbot, "Tropical Commodity Chains, Forward Integration, and International Inequality." For a useful critique of the literature, see Raikes et al., "Global Commodity Chain Analysis and the French *Filière* Approach."

14 Hopkins and Wallerstein, "Commodity Chains in the Capitalist World Economy," 50.

15 Hopkins and Wallerstein, "Commodity Chains in the World Economy," 160.

16 Gibbon, "Upgrading Primary Production," 346; Gereffi, "Shifting Governance Structures in Global Commodity Chains, with special reference to the Internet," 1622.

17 Gereffi, "Shifting Governance Structures," 1622.

18 Talbot, "Tropical Commodity Chains," 728–29.

19 There were various reasons for the change; probably the most important was to provide security for the substantial loans that the Peruvian government wished to issue in Europe and for which Dreyfus was appointed the principal issuing house.

20 On the problems that this competition caused, see Greenhill and Miller, "The Peruvian Government and the Nitrate Trade"; O'Brien, *Nitrate Industry*, 8–41.

21 On the causes of the war, see O'Brien, "Antofagasta Company"; Mayo, "Compañía de Salitres"; Ortega, "Nitrates, Chilean Entrepreneurs."

22 O'Brien, *Nitrate Industry*, 50–55.

23 Greenhill, "The Nitrate and Iodine Trades."

24 O'Brien, " 'Rich beyond the Dreams of Avarice.' "

25 Chile's share of the world market for nitrogenous fertilizers dropped from 64 percent in 1910 to 24 percent in the late 1920s: ibid., 139, 149.

26 In this respect the nitrate trade had a strong resemblance to the coffee trade, considered in chapter 5 of this volume. In all these cases the dominance of one country in global supply—Peru in guano, Chile in nitrate, Brazil in coffee—encouraged official attempts to manage the market.

27 Thompson, "The Second Agricultural Revolution."

28 According to Thompson, "one of the recommended methods of testing a sample of guano was to taste it": ibid., 70.

29 Mathew, "Peru and the British Guano Market," 112.

30 Mathew, "Antony Gibbs & Sons, the Guano Trade and the Peruvian Government," 366.

31 Van Zanden, "The First Green Revolution," 224.

32 Mathew, "Antony Gibbs & Sons," 367; Knibbe, "Feed, Fertilizer and Agricultural Productivity in the Netherlands," 46.

33 Newell, "The Agricultural Revolution in Nineteenth-Century France"; Soubeyroux-Delefortrie, "Changes in French Agriculture between 1862 and 1962," 387–88.

34 Sheridan, "Chemical Fertilizers in Southern Agriculture," 308.

35 On the establishment of the post of guano inspector, see "State Chemist Section" of the Web site for the Maryland state archives: www.mdarchives.state.md.us/msa. On the boom in imports, see Rossiter, *The Emergence of Agricultural Science*.

36 Destler, "David Dickson's 'System of Farming' and the Agricultural Revolution in the Deep South," 32.

37 Cooper, "The Cotton Crisis in the Antebellum South," 389–90; Harris, "Crop Choices in the Piedmont before and after the Civil War."

38 Richard Cowen, "Exploiting the Earth," chap. 16 (manuscript in preparation): see www.geology.ucdavis.edu/7Ecowen.

39 Keeble, *Commercial Relations between British Overseas Territories and South America*, 75. Other evidence on direct shipments from the Chincha Islands to Mauritius also comes from ships' logs: see www.merchantnavyofficers.com/benline and www.geocities.com/mppraetorius/com-eu.

40 London to Valparaíso, May 6 and September 16, 1876, in Gibbs Archives, 11, 121, Guildhall Library, London.

41 Quoted in Greenhill and Miller, "Peruvian Government," 112.

42 Mathew, "Peru and the British Guano Market."

43 Roberts, *Schroders*, 90–91.

44 Perry, ed, *British Agriculture*, xiii.

45 Ernle, "The Great Depression and Recovery," 13.

46 Van Zanden, "First Green Revolution," 227–31.

47 Perkins, "The Agricultural Revolution in Germany," 81.

48 Greenhill, "Nitrate and Iodine Trades," 247.

49 Perkins, "Agricultural Revolution in Germany," 86–87.

50 Komlos, "Agricultural Productivity in America and Eastern Europe," 311.

51 Cochrane, The Development of American Agriculture, 109.

52 Clayton, Grace, 315.

53 Mathew, "Peru and the British Guano Market," 119–21.

54 Thompson, "Second Agricultural Revolution," 70.

55 Greenhill, "Nitrate and Iodine Trades," 249–50.

56 Cochrane, Development of American Agriculture, 229.

57 Sunkel, Un siglo de historia económica de Chile, 1830–1930, 135.

58 See, for example, Consul Hutchinson's reports in Parliamentary Papers, 1872, vol. 57, and 1873, vol. 64; "Reports Furnished to the Admiralty and Communicated to the Foreign Office Relative to the Guano Deposits of Peru," Parliamentary Papers, 1874, vol. 68; Duffield, Peru in the Guano Age.

59 It was only in the early twentieth century that thought began to be given to the possibility of conserving supplies by rotating exploitation of the various islands. On this period, see Macera, "El guano y la agricultura peruana de exportación."

60 Gootenberg, Between Silver and Guano, 119–21; Mathew, "Foreign Contractors and the Peruvian Government at the Outset of the Peruvian Guano Trade," 612–13.

61 Méndez, "La otra historia del guano"; Blanchard, " 'Transitional Man' in Nineteenth-Century Latin America," 167. Ironically, it was the income resulting from the labor of Chinese indentured servants on the guano islands that permitted the Peruvian government to compensate slave owners handsomely when slaves were emancipated in 1854: Blanchard, Slavery and Abolition in Early Republican Peru, chap. 9.

62 Mathew, House of Gibbs, 105–8.

63 The smaller contracts are detailed in ibid., 189–94.

64 On the British banks in South America, see Joslin, A Century of Banking in Latin America; Jones, British Multinational Banking. On banks in Peru, the classic is Camprubí Alcázar, Historia de los bancos en el Perú.

65 Bermúdez, Historia del salitre, chaps. 3–4.

66 For fuller discussion, see Greenhill and Miller, "Peruvian Government"; O'Brien, Nitrate Industry, chaps. 1–2.

67 Sater, "Chile and the World Depression of the 1870s," 79–84.

68 O'Brien, Nitrate Industry, 50–55.

69 Blakemore, British Nitrates and Chilean Politics, 19–22, 32–38. On Schroders' role in issuing nitrate company shares, see Roberts, Schroders, 101–4.

70 Sunkel, Un siglo de historia económica de Chile, 127–31. Shares in nitrate companies, including those listed in London, were actively traded in Valparaíso.

71 Greenhill, "Nitrate and Iodine Trades," 259–61.

72 For a good description of the way nitrate was produced, see Bergquist, Labor in Latin America, 42–45.

73 According to Mamalakis, the average nitrate content of the caliche mined fell

from 50 percent in 1880 to 18 percent in 1925: Mamalakis, "Role of Government," 198.

74 Sunkel, Un siglo de historia económica de Chile, 126–27. Much of this paragraph is based on Bergquist, Labor in Latin America, 37–47. See also Fernández, "British Nitrate Companies and the Emergence of Chile's Proletariat."

75 Monteón, "The Enganche in the Chilean Nitrate Sector," 68.

76 O'Brien, "'Rich Beyond the Dreams of Avarice,'" 141–42. The remainder of this paragraph depends on O'Brien's data, although our interpretation of the business strategy of the Guggenheims is more negative than his. Grace & Co. also applied modern metals mining techniques to nitrate: Clayton, Grace, 315–16.

77 See, for example, Talbot, "Struggle for Control of a Commodity Chain," 117.

78 On guano, see Mathew, "Antony Gibbs & Sons."

79 On the transfer of the concessions from local syndicates to foreign merchants, see Mathew, "Foreign Contractors and the Peruvian Government"; Gootenberg, Between Silver and Guano, 119–21. For the background, see Klarén, Peru: Society and Nationhood in the Andes, chaps. 5 and 6.

80 Mathew, House of Gibbs, 186, 221.

81 Greenhill, "Merchants and the Latin American Trades," 180–82.

82 Hunt, Heirs of Great Adventure.

83 Much of this and the following paragraphs is derived from Mathew, House of Gibbs, 125–35.

84 Mathew, "Antony Gibbs & Sons," 366.

85 Greenhill, "Nitrate and Iodine Trades," 236.

86 Blakemore, British Nitrates and Chilean Politics, 56–64.

87 Miller, "British Free-Standing Companies on the West Coast of South America," 227–31.

88 Clayton, Grace, 72.

89 Ibid., 200, 258–63.

90 The Stock Exchange Yearbook for 1913 shows that members of the Grace and Eyre families held directorships in nine nitrate production companies.

91 Mathew, House of Gibbs, 127–33.

92 Stephen Williamson to Allardice, June 16, 1870, in Stephen Williamson Letter Books, vol. 3, University College Library, London.

93 Grace's branded Nitrapo fertilizer depended on the availability of potassium in certain nitrate deposits, not on mixing or chemical research.

94 Clayton, Grace, 113–14.

95 Mathew, House of Gibbs, 190–191.

96 Vicary Gibbs to Herbert Gibbs, August 13 and 18, 1891, MS 11040/2, in Gibbs Archives, Guildhall Library, London; Peruvian Corporation, Annual Report of the Board, 1891, p. 13, Peruvian Corporation archive, University College Library, London.

97 Roberts, Schroders, 86–92.

98 Blakemore, British Nitrates and Chilean Politics, 22–36.

99 Miller, "Small Business in the Peruvian Oil Industry," 407–8.

100 Hunt, "Growth and Guano," 272.

101 Blakemore, *British Nitrates and Chilean Politics*, 27.

102 Hunt, "Growth and Guano," 271, 277, 297; Mamalakis, "Role of Government," 192–93.

103 Talbot, "Struggle for Control of a Commodity Chain," 118.

104 For the original formulation of the concept, see Wilkins, "The Free-Standing Company." For subsequent discussion, see Wilkins and Schröter, eds., *The Free Standing Company in the World Economy.*

105 Miller, *Britain and Latin America in the Nineteenth and Twentieth Centuries*, 124–25.

106 Schroders organized ten nitrate company flotations on the London Stock Exchange in the late 1880s, as well as other capital issues for firms operating in Chile: Roberts, *Schroders*, 101.

107 On the original formulation of the distinction between the buyer and the producer-driver, see Gereffi, "The Organization of Buyer-Driven Global Commodity Chains," 96–100.

108 Talbot, "Tropical Commodity Chains," 704.

109 On the decline of Gibbs, see Greenhill and Miller, "British Trading Companies in South America after 1914."

110 Hopkins and Wallerstein, "Commodity Chains," 160.

## BIBLIOGRAPHY

Bergquist, Charles. *Labor in Latin America: Comparative Essays on Chile, Argentina, Venezuela, and Colombia.* Stanford: Stanford University Press, 1986.

Bermúdez, Oscar J. *Historia del salitre desde sus orígenes hasta la Guerra del Pacífico.* Santiago: Universidad de Chile, 1963.

Blakemore, Harold. *British Nitrates and Chilean Politics, 1886–1896: Balmaceda and North.* London: Athlone, 1974.

Blanchard, Peter. *Slavery and Abolition in Early Republican Peru.* Wilmington: SR Books, 1992.

——. "The 'Transitional Man' in Nineteenth-Century Latin America: The Case of Domingo Elías of Peru." *Bulletin of Latin American Research* 15, no. 2 (1996): 157–76.

Bonilla, Heraclio. *Guano y burguesía en el Perú.* Lima: Instituto de Estudios Peruanos, 1974.

Camprubí Alcázar, Carlos. *Historia de los bancos en el Perú, 1860–1879.* Lima: Lumen, 1957.

Cariola, Carmen, and Osvaldo Sunkel. "The Growth of the Nitrate Industry and Socioeconomic Change in Chile, 1880–1930." In Roberto Cortés Conde and Shane J. Hunt, eds., *The Latin American Economies: Growth and the Export Sector, 1880–1930.* New York: Holmes & Meier, 1985.

Clayton, Lawrence A. *Grace: W. R. Grace & Co.: The Formative Years, 1850–1930.* Ottawa: Jameson, 1985.

Cochrane, Willard W. *The Development of American Agriculture: A Historical Analysis.* Minneapolis: University of Minnesota Press, 1993.

Cooper, William J. "The Cotton Crisis in the Antebellum South: Another Look." *Agricultural History* 49, no. 2 (1975): 381–91.

Destler, Chester McArthur. "David Dickson's 'System of Farming' and the Agricultural Revolution in the Deep South, 1850–1885." *Agricultural History* 31, no. 3 (1957): 30–39.

Duffield, A. G. *Peru in the Guano Age; Being a Short Account of a Recent Visit to the Guano Deposits . . .* London: R. Bentley, 1877.

Ernle, Lord. "The Great Depression and Recovery, 1874–1914." in P. J. Perry, ed., *British Agriculture, 1875–1914.* London: Methuen, 1973.

Fernández, Manuel A. "British Nitrate Companies and the Emergence of Chile's Proletariat, 1880–1914." In B. Munslow and H. Finch, eds., *Proletarianisation in the Third World.* London: Croom Helm, 1984.

Fetter, Frank Whitson. *Monetary Inflation in Chile.* Princeton: Princeton University Press, 1931.

Gereffi, Gary. "The Organization of Buyer-Driven Global Commodity Chains: How U.S. Retailers Shape Overseas Production Networks." In Gary Gereffi and Miguel Korzeniewicz, eds., *Commodity Chains and Global Capitalism.* Westport, Conn.: Greenwood, 1994.

——. "Shifting Governance Structures in Global Commodity Chains, with Special Reference to the Internet." *American Behavioral Scientist* 44, no. 10 (2001): 1616–37.

Gibbon, Peter. "Upgrading Primary Production: A Global Commodity Chain Approach." *World Development* 29, no. 2 (2001): 345–63.

Gootenberg, Paul. *Between Silver and Guano: Commercial Policy and the State in Post-independence Peru.* Princeton: Princeton University Press, 1989.

——. "Carneros y chuño: Price Levels in Nineteenth-Century Peru." *Hispanic American Historical Review* 70, no. 1 (1990): 1–56.

Greenhill, Robert G. "The Nitrate and Iodine Trades, 1880–1914." In D. C. M. Platt, ed., *Business Imperialism, 1840–1930: An Inquiry Based on British Experience in Latin America,* 239–46. Oxford: Clarendon, 1977.

Greenhill, Robert, and Rory Miller. "British Trading Companies in South America after 1914." In Geoffrey Jones, ed., *The Multinational Traders,* 113–22. London: Routledge, 1998.

——. "The Peruvian Government and the Nitrate Trade, 1873–1879." *Journal of Latin American Studies* 5, no. 1 (1973): 107–31.

Gwynne, Robert N. "Globalisation, Commodity Chains and Fruit Exporting Regions in Chile." *Tijdschrift voor Economische en Sociale Geografie* 90, no. 2 (1999): 211–25.

Harris, J. William. "Crop Choices in the Piedmont before and after the Civil War." *Journal of Economic History* 54, no. 3 (1994): 526–42.

Hopkins, Terence K., and Immanuel Wallerstein. "Commodity Chains in the Capitalist World Economy Prior to 1800." In Gary Gereffi and Miguel Korzeniewicz, eds., *Commodity Chains and Global Capitalism,* 17–50. Westport, Conn.: Greenwood, 1994.

——. "Commodity Chains in the World Economy Prior to 1800." *Review* 10, no. 1 (1986): 151–70.

Hueckel, G. "Agriculture during Industrialisation." In Roderick Floud and Donald McCloskey, eds., *The Economic History of Britain since 1700*, 1:182–203. Cambridge: Cambridge University Press, 1981.

Hunt, Shane J. "Growth and Guano in Nineteenth-Century Peru." In Roberto Cortés Conde and Shane J. Hunt, eds., *The Latin American Economies: Growth and the Export Sector, 1880–1930*, 255–318. New York: Holmes & Meier, 1985.

Hunt, Wallis. *Heirs of Great Adventure: The History of Balfour Williamson & Company Limited.* London: Balfour Williamson, 1960.

Jones, Geoffrey. *British Multinational Banking, 1830–1990.* Oxford: Clarendon, 1993.

Joslin, David. *A Century of Banking in Latin America: The Bank of London and South America Limited, 1862–1962.* London: Oxford University Press, 1963.

Keeble, T. W. *Commercial Relations between British Overseas Territories and South America, 1806–1914.* London: Institute of Latin American Scholars, 1970.

Klarén, Peter Flindell. *Peru: Society and Nationhood in the Andes.* New York: Oxford University Press, 2000.

Knibbe, Merijn T. "Feed, Fertiliser and Agricultural Productivity in the Netherlands, 1880–1930." *Agricultural History* 74, no. 1 (2000): 39–57.

Komlos, John. "Agricultural Productivity in America and Eastern Europe: A Comment." *Journal of Economic History* 48, no. 3 (1988): 655–64.

Levin, J. V. *The Export Economies: Their Pattern of Development in Historical Perspective.* Cambridge: Harvard University Press, 1960.

Macera, Pablo. "El guano y la agricultura peruana de exportación, 1900–1945." In his *Trabajos de Historia*, 309–499. Lima: Instituto Nacional de Cultura, 1977.

Mamalakis, Markos J. "The Role of Government in the Resource Transfer and Resource Allocation Process: The Chilean Nitrate Sector, 1880–1930." In Gustav Ranis, ed., *Government and Economic Development.* New Haven: Yale University Press, 1971.

Mathew, W. M. "Antony Gibbs & Sons, the Guano Trade and the Peruvian Government, 1842–1861." In D. C. M. Platt, ed., *Business Imperialism, 1840–1930: An Inquiry Based on British Experience in Latin America*, 337–70. Oxford: Clarendon, 1977.

——. "Foreign Contractors and the Peruvian Government at the Outset of the Peruvian Guano Trade." *Hispanic American Historical Review* 52, no. 4 (1972): 598–620.

——. *The House of Gibbs and the Peruvian Guano Monopoly.* London: Royal Historical Society, 1981.

——. "Peru and the British Guano Market, 1840–1870." *Economic History Review* 23, no. 1 (1970): 112–28.

Mayo, John. "La Compañía de Salitres de Antofagasta y la Guerra del Pacífico." *Historia* 14 (1979): 71–102.

Méndez, Cecilia. "La otra historia del guano: Perú, 1840–1879." *Revista Andina* 5, no. 1, (1987): 10–18.

Millar Carvacho, René. *Políticas y teorías monetarias en Chile, 1810–1925.* Santiago: Universidad Gabriela Mistral, 1994.

Miller, Rory. *Britain and Latin America in the Nineteenth and Twentieth Centuries.* London: Longman, 1993.

———. "British Free-Standing Companies on the West Coast of South America." In Mira Wilkins and Harm Schröter, eds., *The Free-Standing Company in the World Economy, 1830–1996.* Oxford: Oxford University Press, 1998.

———. "Small Business in the Peruvian Oil Industry: Lobitos Oilfields Limited before 1934." *Business History Review* 56, no. 3 (1982): 400–423.

Monteón, Michael J. *Chile in the Nitrate Era: The Evolution of Economic Dependence, 1880–1930.* Madison: University of Wisconsin Press, 1982.

———. "The Enganche in the Chilean Nitrate Sector." *Latin American Perspectives* 6, no. 3 (1979): 66–79.

Newell, W. "The Agricultural Revolution in Nineteenth-Century France." *Journal of Economic History* 33, no. 4 (1973): 697–731.

O'Brien, Thomas F. "The Antofagasta Company: A Case Study of Peripheral Capitalism." *Hispanic American Historical Review* 60, no. 1 (1980): 1–31.

———. *The Nitrate Industry and Chile's Crucial Transition, 1870–1891.* New York: New York University Press, 1982.

———. " 'Rich beyond the Dreams of Avarice': The Guggenheims in Chile." *Business History Review* 63, no. 1 (1989): 122–59.

Ortega, Luis. "Nitrates, Chilean Entrepreneurs, and the Origins of the War of the Pacific." *Journal of Latin American Studies* 16, no. 2 (1984): 337–80.

Perkins, J. A. "The Agricultural Revolution in Germany, 1850–1914." *Journal of European Economic History* 10, no. 1 (1981): 71–118.

Perry, P. J., ed. *British Agriculture, 1875–1914.* London: Methuen, 1973.

Peruvian Corporation. *Annual Report of the Board.* 1891. Peruvian Corporation archive, University College Library, London.

Ponte, Stefano. "The 'Latte Revolution'? Regulation, Markets and Consumption in the Global Coffee Chain." *World Development* 30, no. 7 (2002): 1099–1122.

Quiróz Norris, Alfonso. *La deuda defraudada: Consolidación de 1850 y dominio económico en el Perú.* Lima: Instituto Nacional de Cultura, 1987.

Raikes, Philip, et al. "Global Commodity Chain Analysis and the French Filière Approach: Comparison and Critique." *Economy and Society* 29, no. 3 (2000): 390–417.

Ramírez Necochea, Hernán. *Historia del imperialismo en Chile.* Santiago: Austral, 1960.

"Reports Furnished to the Admiralty and Communicated to the Foreign Office Relative to the Guano Deposits of Peru." *Parliamentary Papers,* vol. 68 (1874).

Roberts, Richard. *Schroders: Merchants and Bankers.* London: Macmillan, 1992.

Rossiter, Margaret W. *The Emergence of Agricultural Science: Justus Liebig and the Americans, 1840–1880.* New Haven: Yale University Press, 1975.

Sater, William F. *Chile and the War of the Pacific*. Lincoln: University of Nebraska Press, 1986.

———. "Chile and the World Depression of the 1870s." *Journal of Latin American Studies* 11, no. 1 (1979): 67–99.

Sheridan, R. C. "Chemical Fertilisers in Southern Agriculture." *Agricultural History* 53 (1979).

Soubeyroux-Delefortrie, N. "Changes in French Agriculture between 1862 and 1962." *Journal of European Economic History* 9, no. 2 (1980): 351–400.

Sunkel, Osvaldo. *Un siglo de historia económica de Chile, 1830–1930: Dos ensayos y una bibliografía*. Madrid: Ediciones Cultura Hispanica, 1982.

Talbot, John M. "The Struggle for Control of a Commodity Chain: Instant Coffee from Latin America." *Latin American Research Review* 32, no. 2 (1997): 117–35.

———. "Tropical Commodity Chains, Forward Integration, and International Inequality: Coffee, Cocoa, and Tea." *Review of International Political Economy* 9, no. 4 (2002): 701–34.

Thompson, F. M. L. "The Second Agricultural Revolution, 1815–1880." *Economic History Review* 21, no. 1 (1968): 62–77.

Van Zanden, J. L. "The First Green Revolution: The Growth of Production and Productivity in European Agriculture, 1870–1914." *Economic History Review* 44, no. 2 (1991): 215–39.

Wilkins, Mira. "The Free-Standing Company, 1870–1914: An Important Type of British Foreign Direct Investment." *Economic History Review* 41, no. 2 (1988): 259–82.

Wilkins, Mira, and Harm Schröter, eds. *The Free-Standing Company in the World Economy, 1830–1996*. Oxford: Oxford University Press, 1998.

# 10

# Brazil in the International Rubber Trade, 1870–1930

Zephyr Frank and Aldo Musacchio

IN THE HISTORY of commodity booms and busts, Brazil's rubber boom stands out for its meteoric rise and fall. From humble beginnings in the 1840s and 1850s, the wild rubber industry expanded to account for over 25 percent of Brazil's exports at its peak in 1910. This tale of success was all the more remarkable because rubber had to gain a share in an economy that was experiencing a substantial coffee boom at roughly the same time. By 1912, when production peaked in volume, the wild rubber industry employed tens of thousands of rubber gatherers (*seringueiros*) dispersed throughout Brazil's Amazon region. Hundreds of rubber companies were formed, some with foreign backing, and thousands of merchants (*aviadores*) made their living provisioning the tappers in the field. Similar but smaller booms took place in neighboring countries such as Bolivia and Peru. Then, in the course of a decade, Brazil's wild rubber industry collapsed in the face of brutal price competition from Southeast Asian plantation rubber. By 1922, Brazil's rubber output had fallen by 50 percent in volume and 90 percent in value from earlier peaks. The ornate opera house in Manaus, built during the heady days of the boom, became a symbol of decline and misplaced optimism; rubber became associated with shallow, unsustainable growth based on commodity trade.

Not surprisingly, the rise and fall of Brazil's wild rubber industry has been taken as an example of what is wrong with commodity trade in Latin

America. The indictment, articulated by a wide range of scholars, blames both internal and external actors for the failure of the industry to generate sustained economic development. Internally, it is held that tappers resisted regimentation of their labor and plantation development while local elites danced on the deck of a sinking ship, spending their profits on conspicuous consumption and grand public works projects. Externally, profiteering foreign investors supposedly drained away the surplus. Eventually, other foreigners set up plantations in their colonies, which undercut the price of rubber to the benefit of industrialists and consumers in the rich core.

Although there is at least a grain of truth in every item of the indictment of the wild rubber industry in Brazil, our aim here is to address an issue that has not been satisfactorily treated in the literature: the role of uncertainty and competition in the development of the natural rubber industry at every stage of the commodity chain. We note similarities with many other commodities discussed in this volume. It seems that price volatility and uncertainty were common in indigo, henequen, cacao, sugar, and perhaps other important Latin American commodities. Our analysis of the rubber commodity chain allows us also to observe volatility in prices and demand further along the chain, in the tire and automobile industries.

Rather than import the assumption that the industry was doomed in Brazil, we begin with the assumption that the actors in the rubber industry were rational but operated under the constraints of limited information and uncertainty. The concept of commodity chains is useful for such an analysis inasmuch as it highlights the connections between the supply of industrial inputs and demand for finished industrial products, which, taken together, help to explain the degree of uncertainty in the rubber market over time. You cannot make tires without rubber; you will not make tires without automobiles to mount them on. Moreover, rubber, tires, and automobiles are all produced in different locations, by different companies, using different labor systems. Transformations in the supply of and demand for rubber generated uncertainty and constrained the actors at each point along the metaphoric commodity chain.

Earlier studies have focused on Brazilian rubber, plantation rubber, the tire industry, or the automobile industry; no study systematically treats these various processes and locations of production and consumption as part of an interconnected whole. Our point of departure is not, however, commodity chain theory, even though we draw inspiration from it as a concept. Instead, we adhere to standard trade theory: factor shares and geographical conditions largely determine the location of production; risks and rewards tend to be distributed in competitive markets. We add, in keeping with the findings in many of the essays in this volume, that states and pressure groups also play important roles in deciding the location and relations of production (and consumption, for that matter).

Our discussion is divided into four parts. First, we provide a descriptive account of the rubber industry told with time series data on production, consumption, and prices; we add a discussion of previous interpretations of the rise and fall of rubber in South America and the concomitant rise of plantation production in Southeast Asia. This overview leads to the second section, in which we examine the causes and effects of uncertainty in supply, demand, and prices. In this section we argue that Brazilian rubber producers acted rationally, given the strategies available to them and the degree of uncertainty they faced in the crucial years from about 1900 to 1913. We then investigate the degree of competitiveness along the rubber commodity chain and the effect competition had on profits and investment decisions, looking beyond natural rubber production to include processing and marketing of rubber goods. Finally, we examine the role of colonialism and interest groups in determining the location and cost structure of rubber production.

## BACKGROUND: FROM NATURAL RESOURCE BOOM TO LOW-WAGE COMMODITY PRODUCTION

Natural rubber was first used by the indigenous peoples of the Amazon basin for a variety of purposes. By the middle of the eighteenth century, Europeans had begun to experiment with rubber as a waterproofing agent. In the early nineteenth century, rubber was used to make waterproof shoes. The best source of latex, the milky fluid from which natural rubber products were made, was *Hevea brasiliensis*, which grew predominantly in the Brazilian Amazon (but also in the Amazonian regions of Bolivia and Peru). Thus, by geographical accident, the first period of rubber's commercial history, from the late eighteenth century through 1900, was centered in Brazil; the second period, from roughly 1910 on, was increasingly centered in Southeast Asia (Malaysia and Indonesia in particular) as the result of plantation development. The first century of rubber was typified by relatively low levels of production, high wages, and very high prices; the period after 1910 was one of rapidly increasing production, low wages, and falling prices.

The early uses of the material were quite limited. Initially the problem of natural rubber was its sensitivity to temperature changes, which altered its shape and consistency. In 1839 Charles Goodyear improved the process called vulcanization, which modified rubber so that it would support extreme temperatures.[1] It was then that natural rubber became suitable for producing hoses, tires, industrial bands, sheets, shoes, shoe soles, and other products. What initially caused the beginning of the rubber boom, however, was the popularization of the bicycle. The boom would then be accentuated after 1900 by the development of the automobile industry and the expansion of the tire industry to produce car tires.

Until the turn of the twentieth century Brazil and the countries that share the Amazon basin (Bolivia, Venezuela, and Peru) were the only exporters of natural rubber. Brazil sold almost 90 percent of the total rubber commercialized in the world. The fundamental fact that explains Brazil's entry into and domination of natural rubber production during the period 1870 through roughly 1910 is that most of the world's rubber trees grew naturally in the Amazon region of Brazil. The Brazilian rubber industry developed a high-wage cost structure as the result of labor scarcity and lack of competition in the early years of rubber production. Since there were limited credit markets to finance the trips of the workers of other parts of Brazil to the Amazon, workers paid for their travel with loans from their future employers. Much as in the practice of indentured servitude during colonial times in the United States, these loans were paid back to the employers with work once the laborers were established in the Amazon basin. Another factor that increased the costs of producing rubber was that most provisions for tappers in the field had to be brought in from outside the region at great expense.[2] This made Brazilian production very expensive in comparison with the future plantations in Asia (see Figure 1). Nevertheless, Brazil's system of production worked well as long as two conditions were met: first, that the demand for rubber did not grow too quickly, for wild rubber production could not expand rapidly owing to labor and environmental constraints; second, that competition based on some more efficient arrangement of factors of production did not exist.

Between 1900 and 1913, these conditions ceased to hold. First, new commodity chains were created with the advent of mass-produced auto-

1. Rubber produced in Brazil and in Malaysia and Indonesia and price per ton in London, 1900–1935

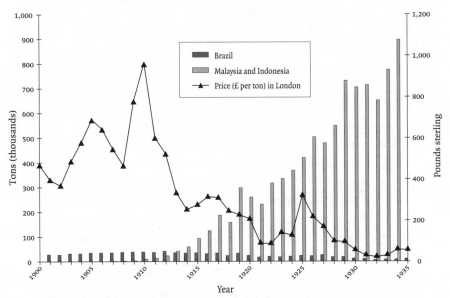

Source: International Rubber Study Group, *World Rubber Statistics Historic Handbook* (London: IRSG, 2000), 2–5, 71–76.

mobiles. Visible demand skyrocketed, especially in the United States, providing a huge incentive for other producers to enter the market. Prices had been high before, but Brazilian supply had been quite capable of meeting demand; now, prices were high and demand appeared insatiable. Plantations, which had been possible since the mid-1870s, now became a reality. Yet, because Brazil was committed to a high-wage, labor-scarce production regime, it was in Southeast Asia that plantations developed. In Asia, the British and Dutch drew upon their superior stocks of capital and vast pools of cheap colonial labor to transform rubber collection into a low-cost, labor-intensive industry. Malaysian rubber plantations, for instance, were manned by tens of thousands of Tamil and Chinese laborers. Investment per tapper in Brazil was reportedly £337 sterling around 1910; in the lower-cost Asian plantations, investment was estimated at just £210 per worker. Not only were Southeast Asian tappers cheaper, they were potentially 80 percent more productive.[3]

Ironically, the new plantation system proved equally susceptible to uncertainty and competition. On the demand side, unexpected sources of uncertainty arose in the technological development of automobile tires, which made it hard to predict the curve of future demand for natural rubber. On the supply side, competition between the British and Dutch led to overinvestment, overproduction, and plummeting prices after 1910. In addition, smallholders in both Malaysia and Indonesia proved more efficient than big plantation concerns, further undermining prices and vitiating the ability of powerful planter interests in the metropole to control production.[4] When the British did attempt to restrict production in the 1920s, in the so-called Stevenson restriction scheme, the United States attempted to set up plantations in Brazil and the Dutch were happy to take market share.[5] By 1910 or so, it was too late for Brazil: the cost structure of Southeast Asian plantations (and later smallholdings) could not be matched. In a sense, then, the game was no longer worth the candle: in order to compete in rubber production, Brazil would have had to have significantly lower wages—which would have been possible only with a vastly expanded transport network and domestic agriculture sector in the hinterland of the Amazon basin. Such an expensive solution made no economic sense in the 1910s and 1920s, when coffee and nascent industrialization in São Paulo offered much more promising prospects.

### Previous Explanations of the Rubber Boom and Bust

The collapse of the wild rubber industry in Brazil in the face of rapidly expanding world demand has been explained largely as the result of three factors. First, the system of production is claimed to have been inefficient and exploitative, hence incapable of competing with efficient plantation rubber production.[6] Second, the autonomy of wild rubber tappers is held to have prevented a transition to plantation rubber production, so rationalization of production was also impossible.[7] Third, leaf blight is claimed to have made plantation production untenable regardless of other considerations—even had inefficiency been overcome and tapper autonomy restricted, the environment would have condemned the industry to failure.[8]

Any one of these claims may be true and the second and third claims appear, in hindsight, to be largely correct. Bradford Barham and Oliver Coomes have argued, however, that the rubber industry in Latin America (Brazil in particular) was remarkably successful and that this success may have hindered the wild rubber industry's ability to respond to increasing demand and falling prices after 1912; that is, the wild rubber industry is held to have succumbed to "Dutch Disease," its very success undermining its future.[9] We agree with Barham and Coomes that the wild rubber industry was largely successful and efficient in its allocation of factors and risk. We do not agree that its success undermined its future: given the development of automobiles and vastly increased demand for rubber, given the cost advantages of the Asian plantations, and given the alternatives for investment in Brazil, there was no future for industrialization and endogenous growth in the Amazon region based on some optimal allocation of rubber-related resources—the future was already happening elsewhere, in southeastern Brazil. The Amazon, as enormous as it was, was just one relatively minor regional economy within the larger context of Brazil.

The concept of Dutch Disease, applied to regional economies, would tend to inject the kind of post hoc reasoning that we associate with dependency theory: regions "overspecialize" and become vulnerable to shocks to their narrow economic base; conversely, mixed economies are supposedly better because, although they may not grow as quickly, they are less susceptible to adverse shocks. Autonomy and stability over unbalanced growth—this is a familiar story, but it is problematic, particularly at the regional level, where gains to specialization are especially likely to occur.[10]

To these explanations of the demise of Amazonian rubber production we seek to add a firm sense of the uncertain and competitive nature of the rubber industry as it developed. We do not deny the importance of social relations of production or ecology; rather, we suggest that the commodity chain approach helps us think beyond local and regional situations to see how broader patterns emerge and how uncertainty and competition in one link in the chain can ramify into others. Our purpose is to explain why these omitted factors are useful for understanding the rubber industry and Brazil's changing place within it. Before we launch into this analysis, however, it is worth outlining the methods of extraction and commercialization used in the natural rubber industries of Brazil and Asia.

### Rubber Tapping in the Amazon Rain Forest

One disadvantage Brazilian rubber producers suffered was that the organization of production depended on the distribution of Hevea brasiliensis trees in the forest. The owner (or often lease concessionaire) of a land plot or river zone would hire tappers to gather rubber by gouging the tree trunk with an ax. In Brazil, the usual practice was to make a big dent in the tree and put a small bowl to collect the latex that would come out of the trunk. Typically, tappers had two "rows" of trees they worked on, alternating the rows day by day. The rows contained several circular roads that went through the forest with more than a hundred trees each.[11] Rubber could be collected only during the tapping season (August to January), and the living conditions of tappers were hard. As the need for rubber expanded, tappers had to be sent deep into the Amazon rain forest to look for unexplored land with more productive trees. Tappers established their shacks close to the river because rubber, once smoked, was sent by boat to Manaus (capital of the state of Amazonas) or to Belém (capital of the state of Pará), both entrepôts for the export of rubber to Europe and the United States.[12]

After collecting the rubber, tappers would go back to their shacks and smoke the resin in order to make balls of partially filtered and purified rough rubber that could be sold at the ports. There is much discussion about the commercialization of the product. Barbara Weinstein argues that the *seringalista*—the employer of the rubber tapper—controlled the transportation of rubber to the ports, where he sold the rubber, many times in exchange for goods that could be sold (with a large gain) back to the tapper. In this economy money was scarce and the "wages" of tappers or seringueiros were determined by the price of rubber. Wages depended on the current price of rubber and the usual agreement for tappers was to split the gross profits with their patrons. These wages were most commonly paid in goods, such as cigarettes, food, and tools. According to Weinstein, the seringalistas overpriced the goods to extract larger profits from the seringueiros' work. Barham and Coomes, on the other hand, argue that the structure of the market in the Amazon was less closed and that independent traders would travel around the basin in small boats, willing to exchange goods for rubber. Poor monitoring by employers and an absent state facilitated these under-the-counter transactions, which allowed tappers to get better pay for their work.[13]

From the ports, rubber was in the hands of mainly Brazilian, British, and American exporters. Brazilian producers or local merchants from the interior could choose, at least in some instances, whether to send the rubber on consignment to a New York commission house rather than sell it to an exporter in the Amazon.[14] Rubber was taken, like other commodities, to ports in Europe and the United States to be distributed to the industries that bought large amounts of the product in the London or New York commodities exchanges. A large part of rubber produced was traded at these exchanges, but tire manufacturers and other large consumers also made direct purchases from the distributors in the country of origin.[15]

### Seeds Smuggled from Brazil to Britain

The *Hevea brasiliensis*, the most important type of rubber tree, was an Amazonian species. This is why the countries of the Amazon basin were the main producers of rubber at the beginning of the international rubber trade. How, then, did British and Dutch colonies in Southeast Asia end up dominating the market? Brazil tried to prevent *Hevea brasiliensis* seeds from being exported, as the Brazilian government knew that if Brazil were the main producer of rubber, profits from rubber trading were ensured. Protecting property rights in seeds proved a futile exercise. In 1876, the Englishman and aspiring author and rubber expert Henry Wickham smuggled 70,000 seeds to London, a feat for which he earned Brazil's eternal opprobrium and a British knighthood. After botanists experimented with the seeds, some 2,700 plants were raised at the Royal Botanical Gardens in London (Kew Gardens) and then shipped to Perideniya Gardens in Ceylon. In 1877 twenty-two plants reached Singapore and were planted at the Singapore Botanical Garden.[16] In the same year the first plant arrived in the Malay States. Since rubber trees needed between six and eight years to be mature enough to yield good rubber, limited tapping began in the 1880s.

In order to develop rubber extraction in the British colonial possessions of Southeast Asia (known after 1896 as the Federated Malay States), more scientific intervention was needed. In 1888, H. N. Ridley was appointed director of the Singapore Botanical Garden and began experimenting with tapping methods.[17] The final result of his work was the discovery of how to extract rubber in such a way that the tree would maintain a high yield for a long time. Rather than making a deep gouge with an ax on the rubber tree, as in Brazil, Southeast Asian tappers scraped the trunk of the tree by making a series of overlapped Y-shaped cuts with an ax so that at the bottom there would be a canal ending in a collecting receptacle. According to C. E. Akers, the tapping techniques in Asia ensured the exploitation of the trees for longer periods, because the Brazilian technique scarred the tree's bark and lowered yields over time.[18]

### Rapid Commercial Development and the Automobile Boom

Commercial planting in Malaysia began in 1895. The development of large-scale plantations was slow because of the lack of capital and unsettled property rights. Investors did not become interested in plantations on a large scale until the prospects for rubber improved radically with the spectacular development of the automobile industry. Around the same time, land laws were modified in the Malay States, making investment more secure and encouraging the formation of companies on the London exchange to exploit this promising confluence.[19] By 1905, European capitalists were sufficiently interested in investing in large plantations in Southeast Asia to plant some 38,000 acres of trees. Between 1905 and 1911 the annual increase was over 70,000 acres a year, and by the end of 1911, the acreage in the Malay States reached 542,877.[20] The very rapid expansion of plantations was possible because of the sophistication in the organization of such enterprises. Joint stock companies were created to exploit land grants and capital was raised through stock issues on the London Stock Exchange. The high returns during the first years (1906–10) made investors ever more optimistic and capital flowed in large amounts. Plantations depended on a very disciplined system of labor and an intensive use of land—essentially the opposite of the Brazilian system.

In addition to the intensive use of land, the production system in Malaysia had several economic advantages over that of Brazil and other Amazonian producers. First, in Malaysia there was an extended tapping season, whereas in South America the rain did not allow tappers to collect rubber during six months of the year because the trails were impassable and the rain tended to fill the tappers' cups, spilling the precious latex. Second, health conditions were better on the plantations, where rubber companies typically built infirmaries and provided basic medical care.[21] In Brazil, by contrast, yellow fever and malaria made survival hard for rubber tappers, who were dispersed in the forest and without even rudimentary medical attention.[22] Finally, better living conditions and the support of the British and Dutch colonial authorities helped to attract Indian labor to the rubber plantations. Chinese labor also immigrated to the plantations in Southeast Asia in response to relatively high wages.[23] As the industry matured, local labor was also attracted to work on the growing number of smallholdings, where wages and work conditions were even better than on the plantations.

## UNCERTAINTY: PRICES, COST STRUCTURE, SCALE, AND TECHNOLOGY

Initially, demand for rubber was associated with specialized industrial components (belts and gaskets, etc.), consumer goods (golf balls, shoe soles, galoshes, etc.), and bicycle tires.[24] Before the development of the automobile as a mass-marketed phenomenon, the Brazilian wild rubber

2. Tons of rubber imported by the United Kingdom, 1880–1899, and tons forecast in early 1880s

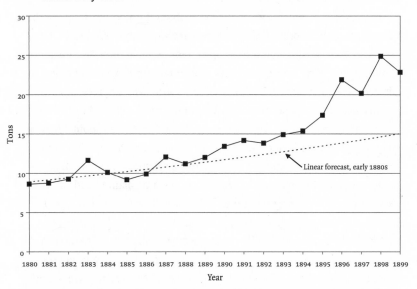

Source: International Rubber Study Group, *World Rubber Statistics Historic Handbook* (London: IRSG, 2000), 10–15.

industry was capable of meeting world demand, and furthermore, it was impossible for rubber producers to predict the scope and growth of the automobile industry before the twentieth century.[25] Thus, as Figure 2 indicates, growth in demand, as measured by imports in Britain, was not particularly rapid in the period 1880–99. There was no reason to believe, in the early 1880s, that demand for rubber would explode as it did in the 1890s. Even as demand rose in the 1890s with the bicycle craze, the rate of increase was not beyond the capacity of wild rubber producers in Brazil and elsewhere. High rubber prices *did not* induce rapid increases in production or plantation development in the nineteenth century. In this context, Brazil developed a reasonably efficient industry based on its natural resource endowment and limited labor and capital sources.

In the first three decades of the twentieth century, major changes in both supply and demand created unprecedented uncertainty in rubber markets. On the supply side, Southeast Asian rubber plantations transformed the cost structure and capacity of the industry. On the demand side, and directly inducing plantation development, automobile production and associated demand for rubber exploded. Then, in the 1920s, competition and technological advances in tire production led to another shift in the market with profound consequences for rubber producers and tire manufacturers alike.

That rubber producers were uncertain about the size and scope of the market for their product in the late nineteenth century should come as little surprise. No one could have predicted the revolution that the automobile wrought in world economic (not to mention social and cultural) history. Yet prices for rubber became extraordinarily unpredictable precisely when the size and rate of growth in the market for rubber seemed well established. That is, the peak years of price uncertainty coincide with the takeoff of the automobile industry. The explanation for this bout of uncertainty is that it coincides with the rise of plantation rubber in Asia— in the early years of plantation production the area planted and the yield expected were changing rapidly or unknown. It follows, therefore, that during the critical years from 1900 through 1913, Brazilian rubber producers faced an extreme challenge in attempting to respond to the rise of demand for rubber for automobile tires and the rise in production of Southeast Asian plantations. In the remainder of this section, we provide narrative and quantitative evidence to buttress our contention that the creation of the rubber-tire-automobile commodity chain was rife with uncertainty generated from a range of market, scale, and technological considerations.

Cars had originally been adapted from horse-drawn carriages. Some ran on wooden wheels, some ran on metal, some were shod as it were in solid rubber. In any case, the ride at the speeds cars were soon capable of was impossible to bear.[26] The pneumatic tire was quickly adopted from the bicycle, and the automobile tire industry was born—soon to account for well over half of rubber companies' sales in the United States, where the vast majority of automobiles were manufactured in the early years of the industry.[27] The amount of rubber required to satisfy demand for automobile tires led first to a spike in rubber prices; second, it contributed to the rapid development of rubber plantations in Asia.[28]

The connection between automobiles, plantations, and the rubber tire industry was explicit and obvious to observers at the time. Harvey Firestone, son of the founder of the company, put it this way: "It was not until 1898 that any serious attention was paid to plantation development. Then came the automobile, and with it the awakening on the part of everybody that without rubber there could be no tires, and without tires there could be no automobiles."[29]

The years 1905 and 1906 marked historic highs for rubber prices, only to be surpassed briefly in 1909 and 1910. The area planted in rubber in Southeast Asia grew from 15,000 acres in 1901 to 433,000 acres in 1907; these plantings matured around 1913, and cultivated rubber surpassed Brazilian wild rubber in volume exported.[30] The growth of the Asian rubber industry soon swamped Brazil's market share and drove prices well below the levels reached before the boom. By 1921, the bottom had dropped out of the market, and Malaysian rubber producers were induced by the British colonial authorities, at the behest of vocal shareholder interests in London, to enter into a scheme to restrict production.[31]

With the benefit of hindsight, it seems obvious that wild rubber production was destined to be superseded once automobile production and the attendant demand for tires took off. This was far from obvious, however, when decisions were being made in South America and in Asia as to how to arrange production relations and how much rubber to produce. Moreover, the passage of time between Henry Wickham's pilfering of the seeds of Hevea brasiliensis in 1876 and the first successful plantations in Malaysia around 1900 is generally neglected in the literature on the boom.[32] Prices alone were insufficient to induce plantation development on a large scale; the emergence of a new commodity chain linked to the automobile was necessary. For instance, the average price of rubber from 1880 to 1884 was £401; from 1900 to 1904, when the first plantations were beginning to be set up, the average price was £459 sterling. Thus Asian plantations were developed in response both to high rubber prices and to what everyone could see was an exponentially growing source of demand in automobiles. Previous commodity chains involving rubber did not show the kind of dynamism needed to spur entry by plantations into the natural rubber market on a large scale, even though prices were very high throughout most of the second half of the nineteenth century.[33]

Even with the advent of the automobile, the decision to plant was fraught with uncertainty. Consider, for example, the year 1906, in which the plantation rubber industry began to take off in Malaysia, and in which the planted area doubled—implying a doubling of production in 1912, when the trees would mature.[34] World rubber exports in 1906 amounted to 62,711 tons, 39,293 of which were wild rubber from South America. Malaysian production, on the other hand, amounted to 385 tons from the original experimental plantings before 1900. By 1912, when the acreage planted through 1906 was in production, Malaysia produced 20,300 tons of rubber. Thus, in 1906, Malaysian plantations implicitly accounted for an increase of about 30 percent in the world rubber supply—six or seven years hence. How certain could the planters have been that their additional production would find a market? Such exercises can be repeated for each succeeding year if we assume a six-year lag before planted areas enter production and another several years before they hit maximum productivity. As long as the area planted grew, it indicated economic choices based on future expectations. But were these expectations based on the assumption of exponential growth in demand over the long run? Or were they short-run decisions made to capture market share and windfall profits while prices were high? Why did Brazil fail to expand its production to meet part of this demand?

Part of the answer, we argue, is that rubber producers made decisions about production and planting during the period 1900–1913 with the aim of reaping windfall profits. High prices were an incentive for all to increase production. Yet current prices could not yield profits when investment decisions had to be made six or more years in advance, as was the case in plantation production: in order to invest in plantations, capitalists had to be able to predict future interactions in supply and demand. Demand, although high and apparently relatively price inelastic, was not entirely predictable. It was predictable enough, however, for planters to expand acreage in rubber in Southeast Asia at a dramatic rate. Planters did not predict prices; they predicted growth in demand and acted accordingly, with the assumption that prices would take care of themselves. Moreover, planters were often uncertain as to the aggregate level of supply: new plantations were constantly coming into production; others were entering into decline or bankruptcy.

One way to look at the problem of forecasting demand for rubber is to plot different forecasts for growth in the automobile industry. More cars equal more demand for tires, which implies more demand for rubber. A comparison of the real curve of automobile production with one based on an exponential forecast derived from the years 1900 to 1905 illuminates the problem. In the early years of the industry, when the initial Asian plantations were taking shape, an exponential forecast fits real automobile sales almost perfectly through 1917.[35] Therefore, if we assume that producers intuited an exponential curve to automobile production during the period 1900–1905, their decision to plant accordingly made sense through at least 1911, when plantings represented implicit production in 1917. The first years of exploding acreage in Asian rubber plantations were well timed to profit from exponential growth in the automobile industry.

Plantings between 1912 and 1916, however, were destined to come into production during a period in which growth in the automobile industry leveled off significantly owing to recession in 1920–21. Making matters worse for rubber producers, major advances in tire technology further controlled demand. The shift from corded to balloon tires decreased demand for natural rubber even as the automobile industry recovered from recession in the early 1920s.[36] In addition, better design of tire casings about 1920 led to the growth of the retreading industry, which resulted in further saving on rubber.[37] Finally, better techniques in cotton weaving lowered friction and heat and further extended tire life.[38] As rubber supplies increased and demand shifted to a flatter curve, prices plummeted: neither demand nor price proved predictable over the long run and suppliers paid a stiff price for overextending themselves during the boom years. Rubber tire manufacturers suffered the same fate. Competition and technology (which they themselves introduced) shifted prices downward and at the same time flattened demand:

> The primary reason for the long difficulties of the industry was that tires were giving continually greater mileage, so that car owners needed fewer of them. The technicians had done too good a job—tires were too good. In 1916 the industry could figure that every car running on the highway meant a business of eight tires per year. Ten years later car owners on the average bought only one and two-tenths new tires a year.[39]

Now, if one looks at the price of rubber and the rate of growth in demand as measured by imports in the 1920s, it is clear that the industry was overinvested in capacity. As we will argue later, the consequences of technological change were dramatic for tire manufacturers' profits as well as for rubber producers.

Why did Brazil opt to accommodate rather than fight the rise of East Asian plantation rubber around 1906?[40] We believe Barham and Coomes are correct to argue that the opportunity cost of shifting to plantation production was an impediment; we are convinced by Weinstein's argument that rubber tappers would have resisted such a shift; and the environmental constraints to plantation rubber in Brazil discussed by Warren Dean certainly account for the failure of plantation development to take hold over the long run. Each of these factors is sufficient to explain Brazil's failure to keep pace with Asian production.[41]

In our view, Barham and Coomes provide a thoroughly convincing explanation of why plantations did not appear at the time of the boom: it would have been expensive to change production schemes, and present profits (at the peak of the boom) would have been forgone in the hope of uncertain future gains.[42] We believe the logic of Brazilian entrepreneurs in deciding to accommodate rather than fight Asian rubber plantation development can be further explored in the descriptive form of a set of strategic interactions.

Today we know that rubber production, as developed in Southeast Asia by the British (and to a lesser extent the Dutch), allowed a tremendous expansion of production at a low cost. Brazilian wild rubber production did not offer enough flexibility to compete with the British. Thus Brazilian rubber producers saw rubber prices fall from an all-time high of $1.91 per pound in 1910 to 18 cents per pound in 1920–21—and in the process they saw their once-profitable industry collapse over the course of a few short years. The implicit question we have to answer is whether there was anything Brazilian rubber producers or the government could have done to develop new techniques or a new structure of production for rubber in order to deter the entry of the British and Dutch into the industry.

As we have noted in our discussion of alternative explanations of failed plantation development, critics have tended to ignore strategic reasons for forgoing plantation development in favor of explanations based on the environment, tapper autonomy, or state failure. In contrast, we argue that national, state, and local parties acted optimally according to the conditions of the international market. That is, we argue that to understand investment decisions in Brazil, it is important not only to understand the structure of production and the political economy of rubber production in Amazonia, but also to analyze the strategic interaction between international players and the domestic producers.

Initially, rubber was a quasi-monopoly for Brazil because of natural endowment. Although the use of rubber for industrial purposes was associated with experimentation in Europe and the United States, Brazil possessed most of the world's *Hevea brasiliensis*—the best source of natural rubber. Brazil could have kept the monopoly of rubber if it had controlled rubber as a protected species, but it is hard to imagine that such a scheme would be sustainable for a long time. In fact, several neighboring countries also possessed the same type of tree.

A second option for Brazil was to make a huge investment in capacity so as to deter competition: what in industrial organization is called "commitment." By this logic, Brazil should have committed itself to remaining the biggest producer in the market. Brazilian rubber producers should have invested to increase productivity in natural rubber, lower import and labor costs, and develop plantations. If the market price of the good is too high, then there is an open invitation for other producers to enter the market and reap some of the benefits. But if you build some capacity and commit to it (there is no reversibility in the investment), then the competitors are going to think twice about competing.

Unfortunately, this strategy was not feasible: Brazil did not have the capacity to mobilize the capital and the labor necessary to invest in large plantations, or at least large enough to deter the entry of such competitors as Great Britain. In the first place, the model assumes a stable market and not a booming market. As we have demonstrated, the expansion of the demand for rubber was unpredictable and growing. This situation created an open invitation for plantations in other countries to arise; indeed, similar conditions have obtained in other volatile and growing commodity markets discussed in this volume. In addition, labor was scarce in the Amazon region and it was expensive to bring in workers from other regions of the country. To run plantations as large as those of Malaysia, Brazil needed much more capital than was available. Capital would have been difficult to mobilize for this type of venture for several reasons. First, as Barham and Coomes argue, the opportunity cost of investing in rubber plantations in Brazil was high.[43] The profitability of wild rubber extraction was so high during the critical period 1900–1913 that to put capital to work on a plantation implied large losses, mainly because the trees required approximately six years to mature (and, in hindsight, we know that leaf blight would have wiped out the investment). Therefore, once the Southeast Asian plantations entered the market, it was better to accommodate than to commit.

The Malaysian plantations entered the market on a huge scale, with unpredictable results—although everyone at the time took note of the major growth in plantings after about 1904. *India Rubber World*, the leading industry journal, included many articles describing what the British were doing to develop a plantation system to extract rubber.[44] The rubber producers of the rest of the world knew that there were many new producers with a low cost structure; but nobody knew precisely how productive these plantations were going to be. In light of local constraints and worldwide uncertainty, Brazilian rubber producers did their best under the circumstances.

Natural rubber producers in Brazil did not miss an opportunity to achieve prosperity's promise: rather, they hedged their bets and got out without losing everything in a quixotic attempt to fend off competition from East Asian plantations. The Brazilian state, for its part, limited its exposure to the rubber debacle by ultimately refusing to bail out or subsidize the industry.[45] Capital markets, likewise, were efficient in allocating resources to coffee and the dynamic southeastern region of Brazil rather than to wild rubber in the Amazon valley. In southeastern Brazil, labor, capital, transport networks, and market power in the world coffee trade augured much better returns for investors.

## COMMODITY CHAINS AND COMPETITION: RISKS AND REWARDS

With the exception of Brazil before about 1900 (when the rubber market was still relatively small), no country or firm was in a position to reap sustained rewards from market power. Brazil attempted to do so in 1910 and was rewarded with a brief bonanza and a rapid slide to irrelevance in the rubber market; the British tried a restriction scheme in their Malaysian plantations in the 1920s but found their efforts at price stabilization undermined by competition and technological change that dampened demand for rubber at precisely the time the restriction scheme was in effect. Herfindahl index values (sum of squares of market share) of various players in the rubber commodity chain indicate a persistent degree of competition in production.

Not only was there competition at each link in the chain, the profit levels of firms along the whole chain were strongly correlated. Contrary to the exploitation model implicit in world systems theory, top-of-the-chain producers did not profit when input prices plunged. Profits for tire companies had a positive relationship with rubber prices. This counterintuitive result was driven by at least two factors. First, companies sometimes purchased rubber at high prices before one of the natural rubber industry's volatile swings, and found themselves carrying expensive stocks of rubber. Second, we believe that high profits are likely to be found in immature but rapidly growing industries rather than in mature, moderately growing industries. In other words, the long-run tendency was for profits in the tire business to fall in line with profit levels in the economy as a whole, and therefore some of the coincidence of profits and rubber prices is conjunctural, as both had a tendency to decline.[46] Equally

3. Firestone's return on equity, 1901–1940 (percent)

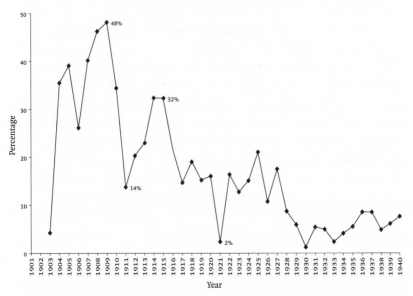

Source: Alfred Lief, *The Firestone Story: A History of the Firestone Tire and Rubber Company* (New York: McGraw-Hill, 1951), 416–17.

suggestive, however, of the consonance of tire industry profits and rubber prices is Figure 3, which plots Firestone's return on equity over the same period. The period of highest profits corresponded roughly with the period of highest prices for rubber. This analysis counters the common hypothesis among critics of international trade, who tend to assume that low prices for commodities are generally a boon to profits in the industrial core economies.[47]

There are three reasons the hypothesis generally does not hold: (1) competition, not monopoly, is common at all levels of most commodity chains; (2) very low prices (i.e., well below historic trends) are associated with economic crises affecting raw materials producers and manufacturers alike; (3) manufacturers often must purchase raw material well in advance of production, thus exposing themselves to the risk of major losses if prices fall—precisely what happened to tire manufacturers.[48] Conversely, high commodity prices usually correspond to good economic times: demand for the raw material reflects demand for finished goods; both primary producers and manufacturers stand to gain in such an environment. In short, commodity trade is not a zero-sum game played between primary producers and industry.

One more aspect of the development of the natural rubber industry is well worth exploring in light of the considerations of commodity chain theory. Because the theory is an elaboration of the world systems approach pioneered by Immanuel Wallerstein, it tends to emphasize the peripherality of raw material production and the centrality of manufacture. Some commodity chain theorists have challenged this assumption on the grounds that certain agricultural or industrial raw materials are actually produced more in the core or "semiperiphery" than in the periphery itself.[49] These theorists can be differentiated from the original Wallersteinian position in the following way: in the new formulation, the periphery, semiperiphery, and core are roughly stable zones that then determine the location of production and consumption of commodities in a dynamic matrix of interactions; in the old formulation, the periphery was what it was precisely because of the location of production of commodities. Most commodity chain analysis based on the new formulation has tended to focus on contemporary economic development. Thus it has yet to explore another set of interactions that the rubber industry throws into sharp relief: the production of raw materials in the colonies of one core economy for manufacture and consumption in another core economy.[50]

The traditional formulation of world systems theory suggests that production of raw inputs will be determined largely by developments in the industrial sector of the core economies and that the peripheral nature of much production of raw commodities implies that profits from such production should either (1) be held down so as to maximize the profits of the manufactured links in the chain in the center; or (2) be high so as to profit core investors in the production of the raw material.[51] Cheap cloth from India was exported as finished cloth to Britain; cheap bananas exported from Honduras were sold dear in New York, the profits accruing to the United Fruit Company. The newer commodity chain theory casts doubt on this pair of assumptions; it is agnostic with regard to the distribution of profits.

The structure of the rubber industry from the 1870s through the 1920s highlights the complexity of global commodity chains and reinforces our contention that there is no "systemic" formula that can be discerned regarding the distribution of profits or the location of production, manufacture, and consumption. In the beginning, a semiperipheral economy, Brazil, dominated supply. Then one core economy, Great Britain, took a leading position in the production of rubber (with significant Dutch competition, which prevented the British from reaping monopoly profits), whereas another core economy, the United States, consumed the bulk of natural rubber and transformed it into tires and other manufactured products.[52] Given what we know about the distribution of returns along the commodity chain, competition prevented any single link in the chain from obtaining long-term extra profits from market power.

In effect, Brazil lost its share of the market for natural rubber and missed out on the profits accruing to the production of tires; the British won a large but not controlling share of the market for natural rubber, yet, although they produced tires for the home market, they failed to leverage their control of the rubber supply in such a way as to dominate the tire manufacturing industry.[53] Colonialism mattered, in this sense, because it provided the British and Dutch with the necessary factors of production (cheap labor and land propitious for planting) at the same time that Brazil and the United States were cut off from one or another of these possibilities. For Brazil, it was the high cost of labor and scarcity of capital that crippled rubber production after the entry of the Asian plantations into the market. The United States came to the colonial game late and halfheartedly. The Philippines would have been a possible site of rubber plantation development, and some plantations were set up, but this possibility arose late and by then the United States was in no position to contend with the already dominant British and Dutch plantations.[54] Moreover, the British and Dutch colonial regimes had a great advantage over Brazil and the United States, inasmuch as they could mobilize vast numbers of cheap laborers from their far-flung colonies to work on the rubber estates. Tamil labor (whose recruitment and transport were subsidized) made up about two-thirds of the plantation workforce in Malaysia during the key formative years of the industry; these workers were plentiful (148,800 in 1917) and inexpensive, earning less than 50 cents per day.[55] Low-cost labor was the critical factor that allowed the British and Dutch to enter the rubber production game and crowd out the formerly dominant Brazilians and deter entry on the part of the Americans.[56]

As the chain developed, demand was centered in the United States and supply was dominated by the British and Dutch. The rubber commodity chain was not seamlessly integrated. Ironically, when the British, egged on by shareholder interests in London, attempted to use their growing market power to restrict rubber shipments and raise prices in the 1920s, the United States turned to Brazil as a potential source of plantation rubber. The Ford Motor Company invested large sums in setting up plantations in Amazonia, but the experiment was for naught: the same constraints of environment, scarce labor, and low-cost competition from Asia kept the experiment from taking root.[57] Moreover, while the Stevenson restriction was in effect in Malaysia, Dutch rubber producers in Indonesia opted for a free ride and continued their production unabated, benefiting from a brief period of higher prices owing to their competitor's restriction scheme.

It should be noted that the Stevenson scheme favored plantations over smallholders in Malaysia. Thus, the effect of colonialism on the natural rubber industry was somewhat mixed. It was colonialism that brought together the factors of production in Southeast Asia, dooming the Brazilian wild rubber industry; however, once the planter lobby saw its profits threatened by overproduction and falling prices attributable to unexpected shifts in demand driven by technology, it lobbied successfully for restriction. The problem for the planter lobby was not unlike that of Brazil: rubber was a rapidly growing commodity market marked by relatively low barriers to entry (as evidenced by the many smallholders) and competition. Restriction only encouraged more production by the Dutch and the scheme collapsed. In this regard, commodity markets in the era of globalization and "free trade" were different from those of the restrictive colonial era. Whereas in the past it may have been possible to create chains that were sealed off into metropole–colony circuits (for example, Cuban tobacco), the natural rubber industry was global and competitive and monopoly rents were not possible.

## CONCLUSIONS

The results of our research indicate the importance of competition and uncertainty in the structure of the rubber industry, particularly as the commodity chain grew larger and more complex. Commodity chain theory led us to consider Brazilian rubber production in the broadest context, from trees to tires. Along the way, this approach suggested that Brazil was not a victim of a global economy that tilted against peripheral producers of primary products or a victim of its own success, which prevented it from rising to the challenge of plantation rubber. Instead, we found that competition was present at every link in the chain, and that rates of profit in the industrial core tended to move in sync with those in the periphery. Moreover, we found that Brazilian producers adapted to the circumstances and acted optimally given their limited access to labor and capital. Given that Brazil could not develop a low-wage, large-scale production system, the door was open for other countries that did not face the same limitations to mobilize labor and capital and develop an industry based on cultivated rubber.

Another conclusion is that in complex commodity chains marked by competition and multiple producers and consumers, price and production outcomes are uncertain. The effect of uncertainty on both producers of raw material and final products is equally profound. This finding casts doubt on the traditional concept of commodity chains in the world system, in which actors in the core economies tend to concentrate profits while actors on the periphery are left to face the fickle winds of the market. Our analysis of profit data for tire manufacturers reveals that they were subject to the same forces of uncertainty as those that hit rubber producers.

Our study of the rubber commodity chain shows that researchers need to pay close attention to the position and relative power of each participant in the chain. Given the fact that the United States had emerged by the late nineteenth century as a major industrial power, and given that automobile production was concentrated there in the first decades of the twentieth century, it may appear puzzling that the United States did not come to dominate rubber production as well. Yet, just as was the case with Brazil, the United States lacked the crucial elements necessary for successful plantation development—that is, land and labor in the appropriate climate and at the appropriate wage rate. Great Britain, although a much less important automobile producer, possessed colonial territories ripe for plantation development and a vast pool of cheap and readily mobilized labor in its colonies. Once Britain had developed plantations and signaled to the rest of the world the advent of a low-wage, large-scale production system, the United States was every bit as constrained from entering the rubber plantation game as was Brazil. In this sense, the categories of core and periphery tell us little about the final shape a commodity chain will take. The Netherlands, neither a major financial power nor an automobile producer of note, provided the only significant competition to the British at the production end of the chain. Like the British, the Dutch had the right mix of land, labor, and capital to proceed with production when entrepreneurs in Brazil and the United States could not.

## NOTES

1  O'Reilly, *The Goodyear Story*, 11.
2  Barham and Coomes, "Wild Rubber," 47–49.
3  Dean, *Brazil and the Struggle for Rubber*, 40.
4  Barlow, *The Natural Rubber Industry*, 70–71.
5  Ibid., 58–62.
6  The exploitation of rubber tappers was, to be sure, real enough. Coercion and violence are emphasized, for example, in Stanfield, *Red Rubber, Bleeding Trees*. Bunker, *Underdeveloping the Amazon*, similarly attributes coercion to labor relations in the rubber zone. Taussig, "Culture of Terror, Space of Death," finds nothing less than a Conradian heart of darkness in one corner of the Amazon rubber zone. Roberto Santos's classic economic history of rubber, *História econômica da Amazônia, 1800–1920*, also places significant weight on the role of coercion in the wild rubber industry.
7  Weinstein, *The Amazon Rubber Boom*.
8  Dean, *Brazil and the Struggle for Rubber*.
9  Barham and Coomes, "The Amazon Rubber Boom."
10  By this logic, Detroit would have been better off had it developed an economy more like Chicago's. Granted, this seems obvious in the twenty-first century; but what would one have said in 1920 or 1950? Barham and Coomes, *Prosperity's Promise*, 26, admit that the Dutch Disease model would really fit their case only in the last years of the rubber boom; in other words, the conditions necessary for the critique are entirely dependent on what is being critiqued—in effect, there is no counterfactual. For an excellent overview and theoretical discussion of the geographical location of industry and sources of regional specialization, see Krugman, *Geography and Trade*, especially chap. 3.
11  Weinstein, *Amazon Rubber Boom*, 16–18.
12  Rubber tapping in the Amazon basin is described ibid.; in Barham and Coomes, *Prosperity's Promise*; and in several articles published in *India Rubber World*, the main journal on rubber trading. See, for example, the explanation of tapping in the issue of October 1, 1910, or "The Present and Future of the Native Havea Rubber Industry," January 1, 1913. For a detailed analysis of the rubber industry by region in Brazil by contemporary observers, see Schurz et al., *Rubber Production in the Amazon Valley*.
13  See Weinstein, *Amazon Rubber Boom*, 21–22; Barham and Coomes, *Prosperity's Promise*, 66.
14  Shelley, "Financing Rubber in Brazil."
15  Newspapers such as *The Economist* or the London *Times* included sections on rubber trading, such as weekly or monthly reports of market conditions, prices, and other information. For the dealings between tire manufacturers and distributors in Brazil and Malaysia, see Firestone, *The Romance and Drama of the Rubber Industry*.
16  Barlow, *Natural Rubber Industry*, 19–20.

17  Ibid., 21–22.

18  Akers, *Report on the Amazon Valley*, 78.

19  Barlow, *Natural Rubber Industry*, 28.

20  Baxendale, "The Plantation Rubber Industry."

21  For a description of the health conditions on the plantations, see Barlow, *Natural Rubber Industry*, 52.

22  Indeed, one of the chief recommendations made by Brazilian authorities in their belated attempt to resuscitate the wild rubber industry centered on the sanitation of the Amazon valley. See De Souza, *A crise da borracha*, 4.

23  See Baxendale, "Plantation Rubber Industry." Also see Bauer's classic 1948 study, *The Rubber Industry*.

24  For prosaic but revealing information on the early years of the rubber industry, see issues of *India Rubber World*. One learns, for instance, that Brazilian rubber was added to golf balls only around 1900, when the gutta-percha shell and core were sandwiched around a layer of Pará rubber, giving it its modern bounce and loft.

25  As late as 1897, in a long-winded editorial concerning bicycles and tires, *India Rubber World* reported briefly on "auto-cars" without providing any hint of how big the "auto-car" industry would soon become and how it would transform the rubber industry. Instead, the article focused on the question of steam versus petroleum power. *India Rubber World*, February 10, 1897, 133.

26  Interestingly, the automobile tire industry was retarded in Great Britain owing to speed restrictions that limited the early growth of the automobile industry. *Report on the Supply and Export of Pneumatic Tyres*, 5.

27  Pneumatic tires were first adapted to automobiles in 1896; Dunlop's pneumatic bicycle tire was introduced in 1888. The great advantage of these tires over solid rubber was that they generated far less friction and so extended tread life and, of course, cushioned the ride and allowed for higher speeds. Eight out of ten motor vehicles were located in the United States around 1920 and nine of every ten cars were manufactured there: *Facts and Figures of the Automobile Industry*, 40–42.

28  Early histories of the rubber industry tended to blame Brazilian "monopolists" for holding up supply and reaping windfall profits; see, e.g., Allen, *The House of Goodyear*, 116–17. In fact, as we will show, rubber production in Brazil was far from monopolistic; other factors account for supply inelasticity.

29  Firestone, *Romance and Drama of the Rubber Industry*, 41.

30  Drabble, *Rubber in Malaya*, 213, 220. The expansion in acreage was accompanied by a boom in company formation.

31  Drabble, *Rubber in Malaya*, 192–99. This was the so-called Stevenson Committee restriction, which lasted from 1922 to 1926.

32  Wickham was actually not the first to transplant *Hevea* seeds to Britain and its colonies. In 1873, a shipment of 2,000 seeds resulted in twelve plants, six of which were sent to Calcutta. These plantings failed; it is to Wickham, then, that the honor (or shame) accrues, although another seed pilferer, Robert Cross, may have actually been responsible. The idea of developing rubber plantations in Asia may have arisen in the early 1870s in the India Office in

London. For a discussion of these early attempts to transplant wild rubber to Asia, see Drabble, *Rubber in Malaya*, 2–3.

33  For example, the bicycle craze created a new commodity chain in the 1890s. In 1898, $26 million worth of bicycle tires were sold in the United States alone: Blackford and Kerr, *B. F. Goodrich*, 31.

34  Barlow, *Natural Rubber Industry*, 48.

35  Underlying data available upon request from the authors.

36  The change from corded to balloon tires increased average tire tread mileage from 8,000 to 15,000 miles: Blackford and Kerr, *B. F. Goodrich*, 88. By 1929, 75 percent of tires sold in the United States were of the balloon type.

37  *Report on the Supply and Export of Pneumatic Tyres*, 10–11.

38  The so-called supertwist weave allowed for the manufacture of larger, more durable tires, especially for trucks: Allen, *House of Goodyear*, 215–16.

39  Ibid., 320.

40  We focus our attention on Brazil because it was the only wild rubber producer of the size required to imagine a strategic response to plantation development. Other wild rubber producing countries were far too small.

41  Schurz et al., *Rubber Production in the Amazon Valley*, 89–90.

42  Barham and Coomes, *Prosperity's Promise*, 82–83. To be fair, Weinstein makes the same argument about the opportunity costs associated with shifting labor and capital out of rubber production: *Amazon Rubber Boom*, 95. In fact, the same idea was suggested by Eloy de Souza in his 1915 report, *A crise da borracha*, 13.

43  Barham and Coomes, *Prosperity's Promise*, 82–83.

44  Almost every week between 1905 and 1910 one of the main articles in *India Rubber World* was about the plantation system in Southeast Asia.

45  Small sums were spent on the "defense of rubber," but large subsidies and investments in infrastructure did not materialize, in spite of recommendations on the part of some Brazilian authorities. One such scheme was suggested by Eloy de Souza in *A crise da borracha*, 31–32: he proposed a huge investment of 250,000 contos for public works and labor subsidies.

46  We regressed B. F. Goodrich's profits on rubber prices, for example, and obtained the following result: $y = 0.1037x + 0.0503$, $R^2 = 0.32$, significant at the 1 percent level, with a positive and significant coefficient for profits regressed on prices. The relatively low $R^2$ value leads us to conclude that rubber input prices were a significant but not an overwhelming factor in determining profitability in the tire industry.

47  The notion that low prices for raw commodities are necessarily good for manufacturers' profits is nearly omnipresent in world systems and dependency theory. Even sophisticated observers fall into this trap. See Taplin, "U.S. Apparel Firms," 209.

48  See, e.g., Allen, *House of Goodyear*, 44–45, for why tire manufacturers purchased rubber in advance and the consequences of rapid price declines.

49  Korzeniewicz and Martin, "The Global Distribution of Commodity Chains," 83. It should be noted that the classic H-O theory of trade is also vexed by the problem of why industrial countries trade manufactured goods between them-

selves at a much greater rate than they trade with primary producers—classic comparative advantage seems not to operate well in explaining the trading patterns of large, modern industrial countries.

50 For a good overview of this school of thought, see Gereffi and Korzeniewicz, eds., *Commodity Chains and Global Capitalism*. In this collection of essays, only Wallerstein's contribution focuses on commodity chains before the 1940s. Revealingly, his is also the only essay that openly argues for a continued focus on "unequal exchange."

51 See Gereffi and Korzeniewicz, eds., *Commodity Chains.*

52 The United States accounted for an average of 62 percent of rubber imports over the period 1910–30: International Rubber Study Group, *World Rubber Statistics Historic Handbook*, 10–14; British-controlled colonial rubber plantations produced an average of 53 percent of all rubber exports during the same period (60 percent from 1913 to 1930).

53 For instance, in 1927 the value of rubber goods produced in the United States was $1.26 billion. That same year rubber consumption totaled 379,000 tons. In current prices, rubber averaged $831.60 per ton, which translates into total raw material consumption worth $315 million. Better to earn 10 percent on $1.26 billion than 25 percent on $315 million.

54 Specifically, the anti-imperialist lobby in the United States and Filipino nationalists were successful in limiting plantation development in the Philippines. The total land allowed to any individual or company was limited to 2,500 acres, and immigration restrictions kept labor prices high; as a result, the Philippines did not have significant rubber plantations until the 1940s: Allen, *House of Goodyear*, 122; International Rubber Study Group, *World Rubber Statistics*, 27–28. Outside of the Philippines, U.S. companies (primarily Firestone) also planted rubber in Liberia: Barlow, *Natural Rubber Industry*, 105.

55 Barlow, *Natural Rubber Industry*, 43–45.

56 Ibid., 41, 73.

57 Indeed, companies such as Goodyear dabbled in their own plantations in Asia but generally came to the conclusion that rubber prices were too low to compensate for the effort; instead, they elected to buy most of their rubber on the open market: Allen, *House of Goodyear*, 53.

## BIBLIOGRAPHY

Akers, C. E. *Report on the Amazon Valley: Its Rubber Industry and Other Resources.* London: Waterlow, 1912.

Allen, Hugo. *The House of Goodyear.* Akron: Superior Printing, 1936.

Babcock, Glenn D. *History of the United States Rubber Company. A Case Study in Corporation Management.* Bloomington: Bureau of Business Research, Graduate School of Business, Indiana University, 1966.

Barham, Bradford, and Oliver Coomes. "The Amazon Rubber Boom: Labor Control, Resistance, and Failed Plantation Development Revisited." *Hispanic American Historical Review* 74, no. 2 (1994): 231–57.

——. *Prosperity's Promise. The Amazon Rubber Boom and Distorted Economic Development.* Boulder: Westview, 1996.

——. "Wild Rubber: Industrial Organization and the Microeconomics of Extraction during the Amazon Rubber Boom (1860–1920)." *Journal of Latin American Studies* 26, no. 1 (1994): 37–72.

Barlow, Colin. *The Natural Rubber Industry: Its Development, Technology, and Economy in Malaysia.* Kuala Lumpur: Oxford University Press, 1978.

Bauer, Peter T. *The Rubber Industry: A Study in Competition and Monopoly.* Cambridge: Harvard University Press, 1948.

Baxendale, Cyril. "The Plantation Rubber Industry." *India Rubber World*, January 1, 1913.

Blackford, Mansel, and K. Austin Kerr. *B. F. Goodrich: Tradition and Transformation.* Columbus: Ohio State University Press, 1996.

Bunker, Stephen. *Underdeveloping the Amazon: Extraction, Unequal Exchange, and the Failure of the Modern State.* Urbana: University of Illinois Press, 1985.

Dean, Warren. *Brazil and the Struggle for Rubber: A Study in Environmental History.* Cambridge: Cambridge University Press, 1987.

De Souza, Eloy. *A crise da borracha.* Rio de Janeiro: Imprensa Nacional, 1915.

Drabble, J. H. *Rubber in Malaya, 1876–1922.* Oxford: Oxford University Press, 1973.

*Facts and Figures of the Automobile Industry.* New York: National Automobile Chamber of Commerce, 1921.

Firestone, Harvey S., Jr. *The Romance and Drama of the Rubber Industry.* Akron: Firestone Tire and Rubber Co., 1932.

Gereffi, Gary, and Miguel Korzeniewicz, eds. *Commodity Chains and Global Capitalism.* Westport, Conn.: Greenwood, 1994.

International Rubber Study Group. *World Rubber Statistics Historic Handbook.* London: International Rubber Study Group, 2000.

Korzeniewicz, Roberto, and William Martin. "The Global Distribution of Commodity Chains." In Gary Gereffi and Miguel Korzeniewicz, eds., *Commodity Chains and Global Capitalism.* Westport, Conn.: Greenwood,1994.

Krugman, Paul. *Geography and Trade.* Cambridge: MIT Press, 1991.

Lief, Alfred. *The Firestone Story: A History of the Firestone Tire and Rubber Company.* New York: McGraw-Hill, 1951.

O'Reilly, Maurice. *The Goodyear Story.* New York: Benjamin, 1983.

*Report on the Supply and Export of Pneumatic Tyres.* London: Her Majesty's Stationary Office, 1955.

Santos, Roberto. *História econômica da Amazônia, 1800–1920.* São Paulo: Queiróz, 1980.

Schurz, William Lytle, O. D. Hargis, Curtis Fletcher Marbut, and C. B. Manifold. *Rubber Production in the Amazon Valley.* U.S. Bureau of Foreign and Domestic Commerce, Department of Commerce, Crude Rubber Survey. Trade Promotion Series 4, no. 28. Washington: Government Printing Office, 1925.

Shelley, Miguel. "Financing Rubber in Brazil." *India Rubber World*, July 1, 1918.

Stanfield, Michael Edward. *Red Rubber, Bleeding Trees: Violence, Slavery, and Empire in Northwest Amazonia, 1850–1933.* Albuquerque: University of New Mexico Press, 1998.

Taplin, Ian. "U.S. Apparel Firms." In Gary Gereffi and Miguel Korzeniewicz, eds., *Commodity Chains and Global Capitalism.* Westport, Conn.: Greenwood, 1994.

Taussig, Michael. "Culture of Terror, Space of Death: Roger Casement's Putumayo Report and the Explanation of Terror." *Comparative Studies in Society and History* 26, no. 3 (1984): 467–97.

Weinstein, Barbara. *The Amazon Rubber Boom, 1850–1920.* Stanford: Stanford University Press, 1983.

# 11

Reports of Its Demise Are Not Exaggerated:
The Life and Times of Yucatecan Henequen

Allen Wells

*Discover luxury in Yucatán exotic jungle paradise. . . . Imagine a XVII century*
*Spanish Colonial Hacienda, splendidly refurbished as a deluxe hotel on 740*
*secluded acres of pristine tropical jungle replete with exotic wildlife and flora. . . .*
*The lofty restaurant retains its original name: Casa de máquinas (machine*
*house), . . . The tienda de raya (the name for the traditional on-premise*
*general store and wage payment center) has become a spacious lounge, library,*
*office and boutique featuring Maya crafts.* Advertisement for Hacienda Katanchel

PERHAPS THE HOTEL'S promotional blurb should be for-
given its excesses. Yes, Katanchel is 26 kilometers east of the
state capital, Mérida, just off the Cancún highway, but the hacienda's location, within the old *zona henequenera*, probably should not
be mistaken for an exotic tropical paradise. Interestingly, a travel Web
site auspiciously named "The Real Mexico" has related that when the
estate's current owners purchased the property, they uncovered "33 separate structures that once housed henequen workers." It seems Aníbal and
Mónica González set out to transform these "primitive worker dwellings"
into luxurious guest suites. The hotel, which opened for business in 1996,
is not for the bargain hunters among us: suites range from U.S.$300 to
$400 a day. These prices assure affluent tourists that these updated, bur-
nished red "pavilions," as they are euphemistically called, bear little to
no resemblance to the wattle-and-daub huts that Maya *campesinos* lived in
a century before. Garden plots, which late-nineteenth-century resident
peons (*peones acasillados*) cultivated to supplement their diets, have been
transformed into "enclosed Maya-style garden[s] of ornamental, medicinal and fruit-bearing plants and trees." Present-day descendants of

peones from "the time of slavery" must be pleased to learn that each pavilion has "private plunge pools . . . [with] invigorating mineral water pumped by turn-of-the-century windmills from 16 old wells."[1]

Another travel Web site informs us that guests can hitch a ride on a horse-drawn carriage alongside the estate's worn tram tracks, which formerly transported bundles of henequen leaves to the casa de máquinas and 350-pound bales of raw fiber to the nearest railhead. The casa de máquinas betrays few hints of its former industrial persona; the clunky, noisy steam-driven defibering machine (desfibradora) has given way to an "antique- and art-filled grand salon, where guests congregate for pre-dinner drinks and after-dinner conversation."[2] The new eco-conscious owners have demonstrated a marked concern with restoring the property's natural ambience, knowing all too well the high price that henequen monoculture exacted on the region's ecology.

The Hacienda Katanchel's makeover is not an isolated phenomenon. In response to incentives offered by the state government during the 1990s, more than a dozen estates have been refurbished as hotels, vacation homes, restaurants, or museums. Roberto Hernández, formerly the chairman of BANAMEX (and brother of Katanchel's co-owner Mónica González de Hernández), heads a separate company called Grupo Plan that has restored four haciendas in the henequen zone.[3]

In truth, a drive today through northwestern Yucatán's rural countryside invites a sobering reflection on the ephemeral character of export booms. A considerable portion of the northwest quadrant of the peninsula bears the mark of abandonment. After decades of boom-and-bust cycles, mismanaged agrarian reform, corruption, and massive government subsidies, the region's now privatized henequen industry is, by any measure, a shadow of its former self. Fiber production is about a tenth of what it was during the halcyon days before World War I, and despite the introduction of new technologies, yields are a third of what they were. Henequen employs only about a quarter of the workforce that it harnessed a century ago. In what must have been a staggering development to local residents, raw fiber has been imported from Brazil to meet the diminished needs of regional cordage manufacturers. In fact, the state, which routinely shipped more than 600,000 bales (a bale equals 350 pounds) a year, no longer exports raw fiber because of declining world demand; only manufactured goods made from henequen, especially rugs and wall hangings, have garnered sufficient interest abroad. CORCEMEX, the (former parastatal) cordage manufacturer, employs

500 workers today, downsized from 5,000 just two decades before. As a result, rural Yucatecans have deserted the countryside in increasing numbers over the last few decades, either seeking gainful employment in the expanding tourist industry on the Caribbean coast and in Progreso, finding work in the growing industrial-belt maquiladoras rimming the capital's outskirts, which employ more than 25,000 yucatecos, or joining the ubiquitous migrant stream to el norte.[4]

✳ Less than a century before, Yucatán had been one of the economic jewels of Mexico; its henequen plantations enjoyed a dominant position in the hard fibers market, supplying upwards of 85 to 90 percent of the fiber used to make binder twine in the cordage and twine factories of the United States and Canada. This inexpensive twine, sometimes blended with henequen's archrival, Philippine-grown manila fiber, was sold to American and Canadian farmers, who used it to tie their sheaves of wheat. Over the last four decades of the nineteenth century, the peninsula's colonial-style haciendas had been transformed into bustling modern plantations; contemporaries chronicled how cornfields and pasture had been replaced by rectilinear rows of bluish-gray spines of the agave plant. Fortunes were realized by enterprising landowners, fiber merchants, and cordage and binder twine manufacturers, who secured bountiful profits from the turn-of-the-century fiber boom. Locally, a "divine caste" of thirty families and a smaller subset of prosperous landowner-merchants dominated the henequen economy, transforming the state's capital city of Mérida into a beautiful showcase, while constructing opulent homes for themselves there and on their haciendas. State and national governments came to rely on tax revenues generated from this profitable export.

¿Qué pasó? While boom-and-bust cycles are common features of commodity exports, henequen's demise is a textbook example of what can and will go wrong when exogenous and endogenous forces combine to undermine a staple's viability in a competitive market. To understand the peculiar conjuncture of factors that led to the fiber's decline over time, I employ a commodity chain approach that is mindful of production, processing, manufacturing, financing, distribution, and consumption. In henequen's gradual but inexorable slide from lucrative monocrop to regional afterthought, particular attention must be paid to the inherent idiosyncrasies that have limited the fiber's applications; the segmented and highly competitive character of the hard fibers market, which has pigeonholed fibers into certain niche markets; and the Mexican state's misguided handling of the henequen sector.

It might be helpful first to place henequen's decline in a broader context. Commodities are distinctive in respect to their capital, labor, and technology requirements, and these factors have had significant implications for an export sector's vulnerability to price fluctuations; for its ownership, whether foreign or domestic, whether highly concentrated or diffuse; and for the product's cultivation and processing, whether labor intensive or not. As a closer examination of the hard fibers industry will make evident, each commodity charts a distinctive path in different settings.

Yet despite all these contingencies, henequen's rise and fall do not set it apart from its erstwhile rivals in the hard fibers market. Virtually all of its competitors underwent or are undergoing similar trajectories. At first glance, some observers may question how free fiber producers (henequeneros) were (and are) to chart their own imperfect destinies. As the cultural anthropologist Arjun Appadurai notes, commodities such as henequen and its rivals appear to be integral components of a "vast impersonal machine governed by the large-scale movements of prices, complex institutional interests, and a totally demystified bureaucratic and self-regulating character." But, he quickly adds, this impersonal machine belies "complex interactions between local, politically mediated systems of demand."[5] Only by examining the constraints on the hard fibers trade and the particular way commodity-producing regions responded to those limitations can we piece together why a profitable commodity market has ineluctably met its match.

Unlike some tropical commodities, such as bananas, where change—in some cases radical change—has been the rule at each stage of the commodity chain over the last century, more often than not, stasis has been the order of the day in the hard fibers trade. Workers, landowners, and exporters did not or could not adapt and respond to new competitors or unanticipated changes in this market. In contrast to the banana industry, for instance, where a constantly shifting, dialectical relationship evolved over the last century, where producers and marketers responded aggressively to serious challenges, such as plant disease, labor unrest, technological innovation, state intervention, consumers' preferences, and jobbers' expectations, Yucatán's henequen sector remained inured to external stimuli and domestic unrest. The kind of reinvention that took place within the banana industry, where well-heeled multinational corporations aggressively responded to new challenges at each phase of the commodity chain, simply was not possible in the cash-strapped, tradition-bound hard fibers trade.

To be sure, henequen and its rivals were spared the ruinous fungal infections that have beset other tropical staples, such as bananas, cacao, and rubber. As additional lands were cleared for plantation monoculture in many tropical regions, Mother Nature often would strike back with a vengeance, forcing these industries to repudiate earlier strategies and fundamentally alter the way they conducted business. Generally, monoculture meant gains in productivity, but at the same time, as plant pathogens spread throughout Latin America and the Caribbean, it often came at the cost of ecological vulnerability. Henequeneros were spared Mother Nature's wrath. Henequen probably evaded this fate because the region was so arid and the thin topsoil retained so little moisture. But if henequen was spared a fungal epidemic and the concomitant wholesale application of chemical fungicides and fertilizers during the Green Revolution's heyday, its ecological impact on Yucatán's landscape was just as catastrophic as everywhere else monoculture reared its head. Forests were vanquished, water systems poisoned, and avian habitats reduced.[6]

Like many staples, henequen was hamstrung by cutthroat competition and a fickle marketplace that constantly sought out more cost-effective supplies of hard fibers. But hard fibers did enjoy some notable advantages over other tropical commodities. Fibers were not perishable, so production, transportation, and distribution did not have to be systematically coordinated the way they did for other tropical goods. Moreover, unlike some staples, henequen was not tied to the seasons; the absence of a prescribed harvest season had important ramifications for marketing, distribution, and the labor regimen.

An overview of the hard fibers trade will make apparent henequen's relatively weak position in that volatile market. After that, I will turn to the endogenous forces that helped undermine its long-term viability.

## HARD FIBER POSTMORTEMS

A competitive trade in hard fibers developed during the nineteenth and twentieth centuries as new fibers were introduced to manufacturers— each with its own strengths, weaknesses, and particular applications.

Each new fiber jockeyed with more established rivals, and eventually the market became more segmented. Some versatile fibers had multiple applications and benefited from the growing complexity of the global market; others were confined essentially to a specific submarket. Each new fiber was first subjected to intense chemical scrutiny, followed by controlled cultivation at agricultural experiment stations, before a lengthy apprenticeship in the market. In general, each hard fiber gained ascendancy in the market for the better part of a century, as each enjoyed a brief Ricardian comparative advantage. Although in some cases new uses were found or new cultivation or processing techniques were employed to postpone the inevitable denouement, bona fide development for the regions that produced these crops proved illusory. These export economies simply did not generate sufficient forward or backward linkages to prompt sustained economic growth. Hard fiber sectors in Africa, Asia, or Latin America never acted as a growth multiplier, nor did they prompt economic integration for the host countries.[7]

Any history of the hard fibers trade must begin with hemp (*Cannabis sativa*). Cultivated as early as 4000 BCE in northern China, it had been used for multiple purposes—among them recreational—since antiquity. It was not until the late sixteenth century that Britain's navy and its merchant marine industry began to use large quantities to outfit ships. For the next three centuries, the shipping industry grew with the demands of commercial and industrial revolutions. Whalers, clippers, and eventually steamships required a seemingly endless supply of rope for rigging, cable, and towlines. The smallest schooner carried a ton of cordage; a frigate used one hundred tons. Even the advent of steamships did not curtail demand as they still required large amounts of cordage for towlines, warps, and auxiliary sails.

Cordage concerns first turned to Russian-grown hemp to satisfy the world's merchant marines and navies. Using a fermentation process called water-retting, peasants steeped the stalks in a nearby stream or pond. But the process was so arduous that much of the water-retted hemp did not reach Russian ports for export until two years after the hemp was sown. Still by 1800 the United States was importing 3,400 tons a year; and that figure would climb to 5,000 tons annually in the 1820s and 1830s. Russian hemp had disadvantages; it needed to be saturated with tar to protect it from saltwater, a procedure that not only left the rope heavier and dirtier but diminished its flexibility in colder temperatures. Another problem was uncertainty of supply; first the Napoleonic Wars and then the Crimean War left North American and Western European cordage manufacturers scrambling for substitutes.

Kentucky hemp farmers tried to crack the lucrative cordage market after 1830. Using slave labor on small and medium-sized farms in the Bluegrass region, they supplied ropewalks (cordage factories in Louisiana, New England, and Kentucky) with bales of dark gray fiber. Cordage concerns, however, preferred to pay more for water-retted hemp; even import duties on Russian hemp did not persuade manufacturers to purchase the American fiber. Kentucky farmers, for their part, refused to adopt the painstaking, labor-intensive harvesting techniques used in tsarist Russia. Instead, they dew-retted their hemp as stalks were spread on the ground and left there for three or four weeks undisturbed. Dew-retting weakened the fibers and made for a darker, rougher (and cheaper) product. Although Kentucky hemp never won the confidence of the maritime trade, it helped the burgeoning southern cotton industry by providing inexpensive baling rope and bagging. The hemp industry expanded into Missouri and Illinois, but declined after the Civil War. Some scholars contend that the hemp industry's development was arrested by farmers' reluctance to modernize; growers appeared unwilling to mechanize the crushing and breaking of stalks. The relatively small size of most hemp farms and the availability of a dependent labor force may better explain why hand brakes continued to be used on Kentucky and Missouri estates. In any case, the Civil War hurt the industry as the federal blockade of southern ports, the embargo on cotton, the Union's prohibition on the shipment of rope and bagging into the South, and the collapse of the postwar labor market all combined to weaken the industry.

Hemp's place was taken by Indian jute (*Corchurus capsularis* and *Corchurus olitorius*). Although not so strong, durable, and elastic as hemp, jute was more plentiful, cheaper to produce, and easier to manufacture. It soon conquered the bagging market. Handwoven jute bags produced on looms in the Bengal Delta region (present-day Bangladesh) had been an important cottage industry as early as the sixteenth century. Inexpensive labor costs contributed to jute's popularity with fiber buyers. By the mid–nineteenth century, power-driven jute mills in Dundee, Scotland, had overtaken the Indian handloom industry. Later, Calcutta bagging manufacturers would offer serious competition to Scottish mills. By 1910, raw jute production in East Bengal had soared to 900,000 tons a year. Although too rough for apparel, jute found a niche as a preeminent packaging material. The Dutch were the first to use the coarse fiber for coffee bags, and when the Crimean War cut supplies of Russian hemp and the U.S. Civil War caused a shortage of cotton bags, the jute industry responded. Three-quarters of manufactured jute was used as burlap to package everything from sand to sugar, from fertilizer to animal feeds.

As jute and Kentucky hemp vied for control of the bagging market, Philippine-grown manila (*Musa textilis*) proved to be a more than worthy adversary for hemp in the cordage trade. A member of the banana family, manila is extracted from the plant's bark and is naturally resistant to saltwater so that it does not have to be tarred. This clean fiber, introduced and tested by North American cordage manufacturers in 1818, is more durable and 25 percent stronger than tarred hemp, has greater flexibility and elasticity, weighs a third less, and carries a lower price tag. By 1860, manila, which was grown in the Kabikolan peninsula on southeastern Luzon, was firmly entrenched in the U.S. maritime trade, and consumption by British and other European manufacturers steadily increased. Production doubled between 1870 and 1880 alone.

The cordage industry's infatuation with manila overshadowed the introduction of a new tropical fiber. Although henequen (*Agave fourcroydes*) had been cultivated in Mexico's Yucatán peninsula since pre-Columbian times, only in the late colonial period did Spanish entrepreneurs begin to recognize its commercial potential. Commonly but incorrectly known as sisal—the name of a Gulf of Mexico port from which the fiber was shipped—henequen was earmarked for low-end cordage and rigging purposes since the fiber's low tensile strength failed to sustain heavy-duty usage. Twice as strong, more rot-resistant, and smoother than the Yucatecan fiber, manila merited its higher price and remained the fiber of choice in the maritime market. Henequen justifiably gained a reputation as an inferior but inexpensive substitute for manila. Blends of manila and henequen were marketed as such and priced midway between the "pure" twines. Hence, the prices of these commodities were inextricably bound. An abundance or a shortage of one commodity invariably affected the rival's price.

Demand was assured as technological advancements continued to find new industrial applications for the erstwhile rivals. Tests determined that rope offered the most economical means of conveying power. With new factories springing up throughout North America and Western Europe, manila proved ideally suited for power transmission cables and the expanding oil drilling industry. The new application of greatest consequence for henequen (and, to a lesser extent, manila) was binder twine. Labor-intensive hand-binding had been supplanted in the early 1870s by mechanical wire binders attached to reapers. When bits of wire clogged the machinery and found their way into flour mills and animal feed, inventors built a mechanical twine knotter in the late 1870s that substituted biodegradable twine for wire, thus revolutionizing the farm-implement industry. Now a harvesting machine with two men to pick and shock the sheaf could reap twelve to fourteen acres of wheat a day, effectively doubling previous output with substantial savings of labor. The Deering and McCormick Harvesting Machine companies quickly built their own twine binder harvesters in 1879 and 1881, respectively. Sales of mechanical grain binders soared, and by the turn of the century henequen and manila production grew exponentially to meet the insatiable demand.

When fiber prices were high, growers and merchants made bountiful profits. Local business leaders in the Philippines and Yucatán served as conduits for British and North American brokers and manufacturers, realizing sizable profits usually in the form of commissions and kickbacks but also from the usurious loan practice that access to foreign capital allowed them. Ideally, just as foreign investors sought to carve out a durable monopoly or "corner" on the trade, local collaborators wished to enjoy the benefits of a monopoly over communication with foreign interests controlling the market. With these limitations, it was difficult for local producers to adjust productivity and to predict prices; so local landholders were vulnerable to the repeated boom-and-bust cycles that afflicted the trade. Chronic price instability, coupled with the producers' inability to diversify, meant these regional economies experienced severe dislocations amid sustained growth.

By 1902, the International Harvester Company, a combination of five of the largest harvesting machine companies (including McCormick and Deering), had become the world's principal buyer of raw fiber. Binder twine, manufactured in Harvester's Chicago twine plant, was an important secondary line for Harvester, as farmers needed a regular supply of  twine to operate their binders. Since the company made its profits by selling binding machines rather than from twine sales, Harvester and its agents sought to keep twine prices low to make its farm implements more attractive. |Historians debate the leverage that Harvester enjoyed over the market, but local agents such as Olegario Molina y Compañía in Yucatán benefited greatly from access to foreign capital. Molina was able to acquire mortgages, purchase credits outright, and consolidate its hold on regional communications, infrastructure, and banking—all of which guaranteed control of local fiber production and generally worked to depress the price. In the short term, the boom enriched a small group of foreign investors, merchants, and local elites in Mexico and the Philippines while the great majority of producers and tens of thousands of laborers found themselves tied to the whims of an unforgiving market.

After World War I, henequen and manila found their comfortable niche challenged by a new fiber. Yucatecans were well acquainted with sisal (*Agave sisalana*), which was indigenous to the peninsula and had long been used by artisans to make hammocks and bagging. This true sisal reached German East Africa in the 1890s, and by the 1920s, sisal plantations flourished in Tanganyika and Kenya. Later, Java, northwest of Australia, would commit to sisal. A formidable competitor, sisal was stronger than henequen and, unlike manila, lent itself well to defibering machines. Labor costs in these areas were even lower than in Yucatán and the Philippines. By 1927, Asian and African nations accounted for nearly half the world's hard fiber production.

The Great Depression and the invention of the combine, which did not use twine, also hurt the henequen and manila trade. Production fell precipitously; henequen exports reached a low in 1940, when they were less than one-fourth the 600,000 bales exported during World War I. Although henequen would recover somewhat with the introduction of automatic baling machines, the introduction of low-cost synthetic fibers in the 1960s and 1970s would devastate all hard fiber economies. Polypropylene harvest twine gradually replaced sisal- and henequen-based baler twine as the industry standard. By 2000, the two fibers' consumption in the United States, its principal market, had fallen to less than 50,000 tons. Vivian Landon of the United Nations' Food and Agriculture Organization has offered this pessimistic assessment about sisal and henequen's future prospects: "It now seems clear that barring the introduction of completely unexpected elements or new technological developments, the world market for sisal and henequen agricultural twines has no potential for recovery on anything but a local basis. Indeed it looks set for further diminution."[8]

To add insult to injury, the economic multiplier effects of these primary commodities were limited. The local economies were too small to transfer earnings to other productive enterprises. Hard fiber exports, despite the great wealth generated for some in the short run, were unable to lead to self-sustaining economic development in Mexico, the Philippines, Africa, Bengal, or Java.

Declining demand was a critical factor in the collapse of the hard fibers market. But it was not the only culprit. We turn now to the role that the region's ecology, infrastructure, and key local actors—the state, hene-queneros, merchants, and Maya campesinos—played in this failure.

## ENDOGENOUS AUTOPSY

It is fair to say that until the export boom tethered Yucatán to the international economy, the region was a backwater. The lack of mineral resources explains why the Spanish crown never considered the peninsula economically valuable enough to be linked to major trade routes. Given the protectionist character of the Spanish Empire, commercial opportunities were limited, to say the least. Even though local elites and colonial administrators experimented with a variety of crops and products, native Mayas remained largely oriented toward subsistence agriculture.[9]

After independence, Yucatán's elites aggressively embraced a modernizing vision for their region by blending technology, human ingenuity, political muscle, and fortuitous timing to overcome their region's ecological limitations. And this was no small feat. Yucatán's physical geography has always strongly limited the location and nature of agricultural production. It is a wonder that, given its ecological impediments, the region has developed at all. The northern and north-central part of the peninsula—what is today largely the state of Yucatán—is a massive limestone rock covered with a thin layer of soil and a dry, rugged scrub forest. This tierra caliente, firmly ensconced in the tropics, has no mountains and few hills to deflect the intense heat. Large rocks strewn about this thick limestone slab inhibit the use of the plow for cultivation. Porous surface conditions make irrigation ditches impossible, as the soil loses its moisture and dries out quickly. Not surprisingly, the thin topsoil quickly becomes exhausted—and in some parts of the northwest, fields must lie fallow for up to twenty years to regenerate.

As if these conditions were not debilitating enough, this wretched land and its hardworking inhabitants suffer from a scarcity of water. Surface water is almost entirely lacking. There is little rainfall outside the rainy season; the parched vegetation has to persevere through many scorching months in succession. The scant rainwater filters quickly through the soil and rock to the water table. The summer rains, which fall in torrential downpours during late afternoons, leach the earth, diminishing the few nutrients there are.

The poor soil, the absence of accessible surface water for agriculture, the unpredictability of rainfall throughout the peninsula, and the blistering tropical heat at low elevations all limited the ability to produce surpluses. It was not until the mid–nineteenth century that local elites promoted an export staple that made the most of the environment's limitations. Indigenous henequen fits the ecosystem beautifully, because it grows on soils of partly decomposed limestone; that is, in soils that are too dry and stony for the production of most crops. The northwest quadrant affords excellent natural drainage and aeration for the plant's roots. In richer soils (where more rainfall was the norm), the agave's leaves contained too much pulp, and the extracted fiber was inferior in quality and quantity. The northwest received just enough rains for the hardy plant to prosper. Moreover, the absence of anything but a thin layer of topsoil and loam discourages to this day the cultivation of and hence competition from maize or beans.

A henequen zone grew up around the state capital, Mérida (roughly within a radius of seventy kilometers), as hacendados increasingly rationalized their land and labor and turned their cattle and corn haciendas into modern fiber estates. Henequeneros purchased increasingly greater quantities of basic foodstuffs from abroad to feed their indebted Maya workforce.

Factors such as land-tenure patterns, labor relations, technological improvements, and marketing and credit practices were either overhauled or fine-tuned in the wake of the boom. Henequen was highly inelastic to price changes in the market. Since landowners had to wait seven years to begin harvesting their crops, they invariably based their decision to expand or contract their holdings on their ability to acquire capital. Faced with such a lag between planting and first harvest, landowners could predict neither future prices nor world market demand. As a result, supply in the short run was usually out of phase with demand.

While the henequen estate may have physically resembled a commercial plantation, with modern machinery, narrow-gauge tramways, and land-intensive cultivation of the staple crop, family ownership, management, and *mentalité* continued to imbue the institution with characteristics of the prehenequen cattle and maize hacienda. Emblematic of a rural society in the midst of a complex transition, the henequen estate is best viewed as a hybrid that demonstrates some of the traits of its predecessor but reflects inevitable adjustments in land, technology, labor, and infrastructure. Moreover, the emergence of a full-fledged plantation society was inhibited by lingering vestiges of the earlier institution, particularly the way in which hacendados confronted their labor problems.

Just as the syncretic henequen estate combined characteristics of both the traditional hacienda and the commercial plantation, so, too, did its labor relations represent an amalgam of different modes of coercion. Underwritten by the assistance of the state political apparatus, three complementary mechanisms of social control—isolation, coercion, and security—allowed henequeneros to maintain the disciplined work rhythms of monocrop production. These three strategies worked in unison to cement the structural relationship that not only suited the production requirements of management but also served the subsistence needs of workers, at least until the eve of the Mexican Revolution.

Designed by henequeneros to limit the workers' mobility and autonomy, the three mechanisms were often so mutually reinforcing that it is sometimes difficult to delineate where one began and the other left off. Such institutions as the hacienda store, for example, served many functions. On one level, the store gave henequeneros a surefire mechanism for raising workers' debts (coercion). On another level, by providing basic foodstuffs and household needs, it diminished the need for resident peons to leave the property to purchase goods, thereby minimizing the chances of potentially disruptive contacts between resident peons and neighboring villagers and agitators (isolation). Finally, through the sale of corn, beans, and other staples, it ensured subsistence for resident peons (security). In sum, the hacienda store was a perfect vehicle for appropriating labor in a scarce market, since it facilitated dependency and immobility while conveying a measure of convenience and security for landless peons. Henequen monoculture's fundamental security of subsistence throughout the boom coupled with the economic demise of nearby village communities enlisted workers for and harnessed them to the disciplined work rhythms of fiber production.

Gender relations on henequen estates only reinforced these complementary mechanisms. In fact, masters and peons found common ground in their perceptions of the role Maya women should play on the estates. First and foremost, they agreed on a rigid division of labor. Debt peons toiled in the fields, performing all tasks related to planting, harvesting, and processing the fiber on the estates. If their daughters or wives occasionally worked in the fields to remove the spines from the henequen leaves after cutting (just as they had helped in the past with harvesting corn), they were accompanied by their fathers or husbands and were never paid in scrip for their labors.

Not surprisingly, women on henequen estates were relegated to the domestic sphere. Their tasks centered on rearing the family, cooking, cleaning, retrieving water from the well and firewood from the forest, bringing lunch to their husbands and sons in the fields, and tending the family garden. Ledger books occasionally listed women as domestics who worked in the landlord's "big house" or as makers of hammocks and sacks and as grinders of corn, but they were not identified as henequen workers. Indeed, it appears that the fiber boom brought little change to the campesinas' regimen, for this strictly observed division of labor on the estates was consistent with preboom patterns. Even at the height of the fiber boom, when planters were desperate for workers, Maya women were not employed in the fields.

Why didn't planters, who regularly complained about the scarcity of labor in the henequen zone and who did not shrink from employing coercive strategies when it suited their purposes, employ campesinas in the fields? By permitting the male peon to earn "wages" to provide for his family through access to corn plots and hunting and to exercise power over women in his household, the hacendado was securing the "loyalty" and limiting the mobility of his worker. As a consequence, families were rarely separated in the henequen zone, nor does it appear that hacendados used the threat of separation to ensure loyalty.

This thin veneer of reciprocity formalized gender relations on the estates. When a Maya couple married, the henequenero provided the groom with a loan—the couple's first debt—to pay for the religious and civil ceremonies and a fiesta. The result was a complicit arrangement among males on the estate in which the master permitted the peon to preside over his own household as a subordinate patriarch. If this arrangement led to cases of domestic violence, more often than not they were handled circumspectly on the estate; rarely did grievances find their way to the local courtroom. Typically, hacendados and overseers put gross offenders in the hacienda jail.

Such campesino patriarchy, however, had limits. Often enough, the henequenero or his overseer, exercising the humiliating "privilege" of the "right of first night," invaded the peon's hut and violated his spouse or daughter. While such affront undermined the reciprocal nature of the shared sense of patriarchy, it did provide the peon with one more object lesson in where power ultimately resided on the estate. The servant would seldom take revenge on his boss; more often, we learn of unfortunate cases of misdirected rage, as peons abused their wives to reassert their dominion in the home.

Planters were reluctant to tamper with the peons' patriarchal control of their families because, in the long run, it suited their economic interests. As far as the hacendado was concerned, the principal task of Maya women was to procreate and rear the next generation of henequen workers. To permit women to work in the fields would undermine that role and upset social relations on the estate—relations that reflected the acculturated Maya's evolving cultural identity as well as the requirements of fiber production.

Nonetheless, Maya peons possessed certain intrinsic advantages that contract workers imported from other parts of Mexico (such as small numbers of Yaqui and Huastecan Indians) lacked. The lingua franca, even in the acculturated northwest, was Maya, not Spanish. This enabled workers to join with neighboring villagers during the tumultuous first years of the Mexican Revolution and exact revenge against cruel masters or overseers. Peons had a familiarity with the neighboring countryside and under certain circumstances could vote with their feet, as long as they could escape the clutches of the bounty hunters and local authorities.

If the hybrid version of plantation monoculture that evolved in the zona henequenera was unquestionably detrimental to the Maya peons, in the short term the henequen boom did enrich a small group of foreign investors, merchants, and local elites.

Since henequen was only of regional importance and never amounted to more than 15 percent of Mexico's total exports, the role that it played in the national economy was much more limited than that of bananas, coffee, or sugar. State power certainly grew during the boom. The state government's relation to henequen was certainly close, because there was no contesting base of economic power in the region. Hacienda ownership, commerce, and political power became intertwined. Landlords used state power to break the power of communal villages and coerce Mayas to work on haciendas. Although henequeneros professed liberal ideals, they were anything but liberals. They confused state and personal power and aims. By 1910, Molina was the largest merchant landlord and was elected governor. Until the Revolution fought its way into the peninsula, this truly was a henequen republic. Before 1910 the Yucatecan state worked to concentrate wealth, facilitate exports, and break workers' resistance. As a result, plantation workers had little hope of improving their working conditions by petitioning state authorities. Recognizing that a frontal assault on the planters and the state would have proved futile, workers opted instead for everyday forms of resistance, joining revolts only when other groups in Yucatecan society had made collective resistance possible.

The political consequences engendered by the henequen boom were severe. Disgruntled hacendados sought to break the dominant Molina faction's stranglehold over the statehouse and the fiber trade, and when the Mexican Revolution broke out in 1911, opponents of the molinistas would even arm some of their henequen workers in a desperate attempt to seize a share of the monocrop economy.[10]

Henequen became a political football again in 1915, when the revolutionary government of Venustiano Carranza formed a cartel to push henequen prices higher. Because henequeneros had been unwilling to bend during the ancien regime, the Revolution forced some to break. Revolutionaries outside Yucatán insisted that the state reorder the relations of production, initially valorized production, and later, during Lázaro Cárdenas's presidency, created ejidos (agrarian collectives) and a state bank to finance them. An ambitious top-down agrarian reform during the late 1930s sought to mobilize Maya campesinos to form collectives and to challenge Yucatán's patriarchal social structure. A determined President Cárdenas came to Mérida in 1937, and after two hectic weeks of expropriation and surveying, 276 ejidos (comprising 61 percent of all the land under henequen cultivation) were created.[11] The peasantry that had clamored for the return of lands usurped before the Revolution now would become partners with the federal government in a sweeping revitalization of the country. Outside of La Laguna's cotton belt in northern Mexico, Yucatán's henequen zone was the agrarian showcase of the Cárdenas administration.

These well-intended reforms, however, could not overcome the intransigence of hacendados, the recalcitrance of state politicians, the divisions among the peasantry, the ineffectiveness of bureaucrats, and insufficiency of federal resources made available to the new peasant ejidos. Irregularities and inconsistencies were the order of the day during the hastily mandated breakup of henequen haciendas. Even though henequeneros were promised that they would keep their cascos—the hacienda's principal buildings and its machine houses—in a number of cases they were expropriated and distributed to ejidos. Some hacendados actually lost their entire estates. At the other extreme, many crafty hacendados preserved much more than the stipulated 300 hectares. As the historian Gilbert Joseph writes: "Typically, several members of a single family would establish legal identity and succeed in retaining a much larger block of land. By the end of 1938 it was clear that a crazy quilt of tenure arrangements had emerged as a result of Cárdenas' reform . . . most plantations were carved up in a manner that suggested the absence of rational criteria in the planning and execution of the reform."[12]

Moreover, after an initial public display of federal intervention, Cárdenas abandoned agrarian reform to state politicos who had little interest in the peasantry's welfare. The reform became both a political minefield and an economic failure. Efforts to mobilize peasants were ineffectual, key popular elements actually opposed the reform, and the state's intransigent political culture all combined to mitigate meaningful change.[13] Although in theory campesinos were now collective owners of the land they cultivated, in practice they had exchanged one *patrón* for the impersonal federal government's ejidal bank. Notwithstanding the heated rhetoric, disaffected campesinos were given a fixed wage and remained marginalized from all production and marketing decisions. Furthermore, in most cases, former landowners retained control of the desfibradoras, sanctioning a continuation of prereform modes of coercion.[14]

The agrarian reform, warts and all, did represent a sharp break from past practice in the countryside. But the politicos in Mérida never tried to reduce the region's dependence on the international economy; they felt that Yucatán simply had no alternatives. Given the region's ecological limitations, their determination to hitch their futures to the *oro verde* may not have been misplaced. State authorities were given a short reprieve when fiber prices rose during the Second World War, but by the mid-1950s, the state-managed Henequeneros de Yucatán was so rife with corruption that President Adolfo Ruíz Cortines intervened, eliminated the state agency, and assumed federal control of the henequen sector. But the federal ejidal bank bureaucracy proved itself just as inept as its predecessor. The "gross mismanagement of the henequen bureaucracy," the economist Jeffrey Brannon notes, ". . . more often than not took actions in its own interests or those of Mexico City."[15] By the mid-1960s, the zona henequenera was dependent on federal subsidies to overcome low fiber prices, and henequen cultivators effectively had become wards of the national government.

State oversight extended into the manufacturing sector as well. In the early 1960s, the federal government purchased forty private cordage mills in the hopes of modernizing and streamlining the production of finished goods and making Yucatán more competitive in the world market. A parastatal company, CORCEMEX, exercised a monopoly over the purchase of raw fiber and the production and sale of all manner of cordage products. Unfortunately, CORCEMEX came into existence just as synthetic fibers were flooding the hard fibers market. Henequen could not compete with these new synthetics, and to make matters worse, Yucatán's share of the natural fiber market declined because of increased competition from sisal fiber produced in Brazil and Tanzania, where labor costs were considerably lower than in the zona henequenera. Political machinations compounded problems for the increasingly unprofitable henequen sector. Facing growing opposition from the conservative PAN (Partido Acción Nacional) in Mérida and other urban areas statewide, the PRI (Partido Revolucionario Institucional), which had dominated national politics since the 1920s, simply threw good money after bad, plying the rural sector and CORCEMEX with kickbacks, bribes, and largesse to ensure political control in the countryside.

By 1980, Yucatán's henequen sector was a federal fiefdom. CORCE-MEX and its rural counterpart, BANRURAL, "budgeted expenditures in excess of a billion pesos for the state. This was more than five times the budget of the state government. Further, almost 80 percent of the state budget consisted of revenue-sharing funds from Mexico City."[16] The federal government had effectively replaced private initiative in the peninsula. Thirty years of national stewardship of the henequen industry had only worsened conditions for henequen workers. The 1980s debt crisis forced Mexico City to come to terms with the costs and benefits of the floundering henequen sector.

As early as 1978 President José López Portillo had admitted that the federally managed henequen sector was in disarray. Less than a decade later, López Portillo's successor, Miguel de la Madrid, took the first steps toward privatizing the industry. In 1992, with NAFTA in the works, federal and state authorities brought together international and national scientists, social scientists, and government officials to study the uncertain future of both henequen and the zona henequenera in Yucatán. "La Conferencia Nacional sobre el Henequén y la Zona Henequenera de Yucatán" featured a dazzling array of papers on the henequen industry, the demographic and economic characteristics of the henequen zone, the chronic difficulties besetting henequeneros, the region's unforgiving topography and ecology, and the idiosyncratic nature of henequen. Suggestions were offered up to improve cultivation of the agave, to study its potential biotechnological applications, as policy wonks and academics debated how to wean the peninsula's northwest quadrant from its dependence on henequen by introducing new crops there.[17] Efforts to produce citrus proved unsuccessful, and many planters lost their investments; more recent cultivation of papaya has generated some positive returns, but recent blights do not auger well for the future.

The resultant privatization of the industry, its scaling down, and the search for substitutes is very much a work in progress today. Reports of henequen's demise are sadly not exaggerated. The combination of a weak world market and an ineffectual interventionist state has written a gloomy epitaph for this once thriving commodity. If the forces of supply and demand and efforts to corner those markets shaped the industry's response during the henequen boom, political mismanagement, corruption, and inefficiencies better explain henequen's undoing after the Revolution. It is hard to imagine a scenario in which the fiber could be resurrected to its former position in the state's economic firmament.

There is irony in efforts to appropriate the hacienda's big house, the processing buildings, and the former peasant huts for upscale accommodations for vacationing tourists. Despite efforts to distance themselves from their past, it seems Yucatecans cannot escape it. Local businessmen are following a well-trod path forged by other locales yoked to extractive commodities.[18] In the meantime, old henequen haciendas will continue to be reinvented as tourist destinations, as entrepreneurs recycle old estates and tread on the region's mythic past.

---

## NOTES

I am grateful for comments and suggestions from Matthew Klingle.

1  See www.besthotelsresorts.com/haciendakatanchel.
2  See www.locogringo.com.
3  Property values have increased from $20,000 for a fixer-upper to $140,000 or more: www.sunshineparadise.com.
4  Eastmond and Robert, "Henequen and the Challenge of Sustainable Development in Yucatán, Mexico," 11–15; Mike Nelson, "Modern Henequen Production," www.mexicomike.com; Gus Gordon, "Mérida—One Year Later," www.mexconnect.com.
5  Appadurai, "Introduction," *The Social Life of Things*, 48.
6  Striffler and Moberg, *Banana Wars*; Marquardt, " 'Green Havoc' "; McCook, *States of Nature*.

7   This overview of the fiber trade draws on Wells, "Henequen." On the hemp industry, see Crosby, *America, Russia, Hemp, and Napoleon*. On the jute industry, see Ahmed, *The Progress of the Jute Industry and Trade*. On Kentucky hemp, see Hopkins, *A History of the Hemp Industry in Kentucky*. On manila hemp, see Owen, *Prosperity without Progress*. On African sisal, see Iliffe, *A Modern History of Tanganyika*.

8   Landon, "A Review of the Market in Traditional Sisal and Henequen Products (Especially Agricultural Twines and General Cordage) and an Assessment of Future Potential," www.fao.org/documents. Salum Shamte gives a more optimistic assessment in "Overview of the Sisal and Henequen Industry," ibid.

9   This section draws on Wells, "Henequen."

10  Wells and Joseph, *Summer of Discontent, Seasons of Upheaval*.

11  Brannon, "Conclusion: Yucatecan Political Economy in Broader Perspective," 245–46.

12  Joseph, *Rediscovering the Past at Mexico's Periphery*, 125.

13  Fallaw, *Cárdenas Compromised*.

14  On the flawed reform, also see Raymond, "The Impact of Land Reform in the Monocrop Region of Yucatán, Mexico"; Kirk, "San Antonio, Yucatán."

15  Brannon, "Conclusion," 247.

16  Ibid., 248.

17  Peniche Rivero and Santamaría Basulto, *Memorias de la Conferencia Nacional sobre el Henequén y la Zona Henequenera de Yucatán*.

18  For a similar reinvention of mining economies into swanky tourist destinations, see Rothman, *Devil's Bargains*.

---

## BIBLIOGRAPHY

Ahmed, Rakibuddin. *The Progress of the Jute Industry and Trade (1865–1966)*. Dacca: Pakistan Central Jute Committee, 1966.

Appadurai, Arjun. "Introduction: Commodities and the Politics of Value." In his *The Social Life of Things: Commodities in Cultural Perspective*. New York: Cambridge University Press, 1986.

Brannon, Jeffrey T. "Conclusion: Yucatecan Political Economy in Broader Perspective." In his *Land, Labor, and Capital in Modern Yucatán: Essays in Regional History and Political Economy*. Tuscaloosa: University of Alabama Press, 1991.

Crosby, Alfred W. *America, Russia, Hemp, and Napoleon: American Trade with Russia and the Baltic, 1783–1812*. Columbus: Ohio State University Press, 1965.

Eastmond, Amarella, and Manuel L. Robert. "Henequen and the Challenge of Sustainable Development in Yucatán, Mexico." *Biotechnology and Development Monitor* 41 (March 2000): 11–15.

Fallaw, Ben. *Cárdenas Compromised: The Failure of Reform in Postrevolutionary Yucatán*. Durham: Duke University Press, 2001.

Hopkins, James F. *A History of the Hemp Industry in Kentucky*. Lexington: University of Kentucky Press, 1951.

Iliffe, John. *A Modern History of Tanganyika.* Cambridge: Cambridge University Press, 1979.

Joseph, Gilbert. *Rediscovering the Past at Mexico's Periphery: Essays on the History of Modern Yucatán.* Tuscaloosa: University of Alabama Press, 1986.

Kirk, Rodney C. "San Antonio, Yucatán: From Henequen Hacienda to Plantation Ejido." Ph.D. dissertation, Michigan State University, 1975.

Marquardt, Steve. " 'Green Havoc': Panama Disease, Environmental Change and Labor Process in the Central American Banana Industry." *American Historical Review* 106, no. 1 (February 2001): 49–80.

McCook, Stuart. *States of Nature: Science, Agriculture, and the Environment in the Spanish Caribbean.* Austin: University of Texas Press, 2002.

Owen, Norman G. *Prosperity without Progress: Manila Hemp and Material Life in the Colonial Philippines.* Berkeley: University of California Press, 1984.

Peniche Rivero, Piedad, and Felipe Santamaría Basulto, eds. *Memorias de la Conferencia Nacional sobre el Henequén y la Zona Henequenera de Yucatán.* Mérida: Universidad Autónoma de Yucatán, 1993.

Raymond, Nathaniel C. "The Impact of Land Reform in the Monocrop Region of Yucatán, Mexico." Ph.D. dissertation, Brandeis University, 1971.

Rothman, Hal. *Devil's Bargains: Tourism in the Twentieth-Century American West.* Lawrence: University Press of Kansas, 1998.

Striffler, Steve, and Mark Moberg. *Banana Wars: Power, Production, and History in the Americas.* Durham: Duke University Press, 2003.

Wells, Allen. "Henequen." In Steven C. Topik and Allen Wells, eds., *The Second Conquest of Latin America.* Austin, University of Texas Press, 1997.

Wells, Allen, and Gilbert M. Joseph. *Summer of Discontent, Seasons of Upheaval: Elite Politics and Rural Insurgency in Yucatán, 1876–1915.*

# 12

# Cocaine in Chains: The Rise and Demise of a Global Commodity, 1860–1950

Paul Gootenberg

*The rising cultivation, consumption, and export of this so precious article of our agricultural production [coca]—once widely known and used for health purposes —will replace tea and coffee themselves.* La Crónica Médica (Lima), 1889

THIS CHAPTER TREATS coca and cocaine as essentially world export commodities rather than as menacing drugs. Commodity perspectives make good sense for the period at hand, 1860–1950, from the years Andean coca leaf first hit world markets to the birth of today's vast circuits of illicit cocaine. During this formative century both goods were still considered legitimate or even progressive articles of world commerce, as the epigraph suggests. Taking coca and cocaine as typical goods rather than uniquely spiritual or pariah substances may also temper some of the passionate politics that entangle these Andean products today.[1] Even the words used to describe current drug trades assume a fantastic quality. Discourse on drugs, rather than using terms appropriate to a capitalist market, reverts to images of a "feudal" crusade between evil "drug lords" and knightly "drug czars," drug "cartels" or "plagues" and haplessly "enslaved" consumers.

Andean coca leaf and cocaine make an especially strong case study on commodity chains in Latin American history. Neither existed as a significant commodity until the late nineteenth century, so their complex social transformations into marketable and exportable goods can be historically tracked. Coca and cocaine, rather than entering undifferentiated world markets, became organized into distinctive transnational commodity networks, and these networks have analytical significance, or so I argue here. Placing coca into spatially embedded relationship chains may also help to demystify drugs, usually perceived in loaded binaries of "supply" and "demand."

Conceptually, I see tension between sociological commodity chain approaches and much of neoclassical or institutional economics, though it is a good thing to try to bridge them. After all, the concept of global commodity chains, in which world markets are socially structured and power-segmented, originated in Immanuel Wallerstein's world systems theory and moreover has the constructivist spirit of the anthropological "social life of things." For historians, the commodity chain can work as both a descriptive and an analytical tool.[2] It helps grasp power differentials between actors in the "core" and "periphery" of chains, though not in the deterministic spirit of yesterday's dependency theory. By focusing on flows rather than objects or sites, a commodity chain approach challenges distinctions between *national* economies and polities still dear to neoclassical and institutional economists. In short, this holistic view helps us to overcome traditional divides between internal and external factors and between economic and noneconomic factors in Latin American history, binaries shared by neoclassical and dependency perspectives.

In this chapter I try to demonstrate the utility of thinking about coca and cocaine in discrete global commodity chains over extended time. The quantitative data derive from motley sources that do not lend themselves to reliable aggregates or comparisons.[3] Nor do I dwell on illicit tastes and trades in cocaine, which in any case (save for a brief eruption around 1905–20) were modest before the 1970s. The chapter spans two broad periods. The first, 1860–1910, saw the creation of world commodity networks around coca and cocaine. Two commercial chains linked nascent Andean coca to overseas markets, the Germany-Europe-Andes circuit and the United States–Andes circuit. The second period, 1910–1950, saw mounting political and market constraints on coca and cocaine, in part related to international narcotics control. Three new commodity chains arose which worked to displace existing Andean coca and cocaine: a hemispheric network managed by the United States, a Dutch-European colonial network, and an imperial pan-Asian Japanese network. These chains, which crumbled during World War II, were prelude to the illicit circuits of cocaine which tied the eastern Andes back into the outside world by the 1970s.

With deep roots in Andean culture, coca did not become an exportable commodity until the late nineteenth century. Coca leaf is produced by a shrub that is among the oldest domesticated plants of the Andean region, grown in mid-range subtropical Amazonian regions and closely associated with Andean cultural life and identities. The dried leaf is carried upland for mastication (so-called chewing) by highland peoples, *coqueros* who have prized coca for thousands of years for its stimulant properties (as part of ritualized high-altitude work routines), for purposes of health and nutrition (benefits it probably provides), and for spiritual and community sustenance. During the Inca era (1420–1532 A.D.), coca was declared a prestige item, off-limits to the toiling peasant masses, with no explicit exchange value, though much use likely escaped state regulation. After the Conquest of the 1530s, the Spanish partially commercialized coca, after heated religious debates about its devilish nature, establishing plantations in the Andean *montaña* for supplying mine workers in silver mining complexes such as Potosí across the high Andes. Coca use expanded. By the close of the colonial era, coca chewing constituted both a substantial business (helping monetize exchanges between lowlands and highlands) as well as a widespread marker of (degraded) Indian caste. Coastal populations and white elites did not generally indulge in coca, which they regarded as a suspiciously "Indian" habit.

Scholars often ponder why coca, unlike tobacco or coffee, proved unassimilable into the new pantheon of Europe's colonial stimulants in the early modern era, and remained a limited regional commodity in the colonized territory of today's Peru and Bolivia.[4] The negative aesthetics of chewing or its early ethnic connotations are cited as well as the fragility of coca leaves in shipment to Europe. However, perhaps it is better to see coca as indirectly a strategic commodity, as a local input into the seventeenth-century Peruvian forced-labor silver regime vital to expanding world commerce. Perhaps coca's recognition and embrace by the West ought to be seen as merely delayed for three centuries, to the mid-nineteenth century; later, as industrialized cocaine, coca accelerated into one of history's most profitable world commodities in the illicit drug trades of the 1970s.

The nineteenth-century world revolutions of commerce and science sparked renewed appreciation for coca and for its alkaloid, cocaine, first isolated in 1860. Interest emanated from Europe but sparked active responses in the Andes. Much had to change for coca to become a bona fide world commodity: its scientific, medical, and ethnic prestige had to rise in Europe and North America as well as in republican Peru and Bolivia; it needed "modern" uses and outlets, public spokesmen and colonizing planters, not to mention working networks of laborers, investors, processors, shippers, and consumers. To make a complex story short, these factors came together quickly after 1850 as European botany and medicine settled coca's (previously disputed) stimulant power, as industrializing societies embraced novel mass health stimulants (famously in this case with Vin Mariani and Coca-Cola) and touted modern medical marvels (cocaine as local anesthesia after 1885), and as the Andean nations of Peru and Bolivia desperately sought new export goods in the wake of the devastating War of the Pacific in 1879–83.

*The German Connection*

Broadly speaking, the first impulse to Andean coca and cocaine production came from "Greater" Germany and to a lesser extent France and Britain in the mid-nineteenth century; by 1900 Germany took the lead in scientific interest in cocaine and in its production. These influences were felt deeply in Peru (the largest exporter) and by the Peruvians who organized the initial coca trades.

Interest in coca as a modern stimulant was awakened by the development of German alkaloid science. Reports of such German-speaking nineteenth-century travelers as Alexander von Humboldt, Johan Jakob von Tschudi, and Eduard Poeppig sparked a veritable race to discover coca's active principle. Leading German chemists such as Friedrich Wöhler requested bulk samples of fresh coca—a great rarity in Europe—from the Austrian *Novara* scientific mission in the late 1850s, which the chemistry student Albert Niemann used in his isolation of *Kokain* in 1860. Viennese medical men, most famously the young Sigmund Freud, played a major early role in research and promotion of cocaine's medical uses. Particularly galvanizing was Karl Koller's discovery in 1884 of cocaine's local anesthetic properties, which revolutionized Western surgery.[5] All of them used scarce medicinal cocaine hydrochloride, which E. Merck manufactured in Darmstadt from modest but now regularized imports of dried Bolivian and Peruvian leaf. European interest in coca had steadily awakened since the 1850s; after 1885, a decade-long coca boom began.

Along with "scientific" alkaloid cocaine, medical, commercial, and popular fascination with herbal coca leaf grew as well. New stimulants became coveted, especially by "brain workers," living amid the exertions and neurotic disorders of modern societies. Global "coca mania" was particularly pronounced in France and Britain (and later reached its height in the United States) and had distinctive cultural roots and associations, some with imported Andean accents. In 1863 a Corsican entrepreneur, Angelo Mariani, launched his remarkably successful Vin Mariani, a mixture of coca and Bordeaux wine, which captivated the world with its arty and sophisticated marketing campaigns. Cyclists and opera singers typified the epoch's coca drinkers. Between 1863 and 1885, Mariani became the single largest user of Andean coca, and French medical interest filtered to Peru. British medical men, some obscure and some famous, also focused on coca as a health stimulant (rather than on German cocaine) and would long defend coca tonics and medicine on their own therapeutic terms. With the mid-1880s boom, the royal Kew Gardens (and later the Imperial Institute), which had worked similar wonders with Amazonian cinchona and rubber, began a crash program of coca research and botanical experiments in their colonies in India, Ceylon, and beyond (as did the Dutch, French, and even Germans in Cameroon).[6]

German interests, however, through the port of Hamburg, dominated the field (see Table 1). Merck enjoyed the experience, Andean connections, and product prestige, though the quantities it made were modest—less than one kilo a year—before 1884. After cocaine was adopted for use during surgery, production rose quickly to over 500 kilos annually in 1890, 1,500 in 1898, and more than 2,400 kilos by 1902. Merck produced about a quarter of the world's cocaine, and for a decade it was the firm's most profitable single product line. Merck transformed cocaine from an experimental medical novelty into a marketable commodity, as international prices dropped from about $1 per grain in 1884 to about 2 cents a grain by 1887. Other German firms also jumped into cocaine, among them Gehe & Co., Knoll, Riedel, and C. H. Boehringer & Sohn, some with American branch houses.

The turning point for Merck came in 1884–86, when prices and output jumped five and twenty times respectively with the use of cocaine as an anesthetic and for other medical purposes. The spike sparked a much-debated and alarming "crisis" in international coca supply. Merck's strategy was to encourage Peruvian suppliers of "crude cocaine," a semiprocessed (80–90 percent pure) jungle cocaine sulfate cake, and to this end it and other German firms sent agents to Lima. Crude cocaine shipped far

Table 1

## Kilograms of cocaine produced and of coca and cocaine imported by Merck, 1879–1918

| Year | Merck production | Coca imported from Peru | Coca imported from Java | Crude cocaine imported from Java |
|---|---|---|---|---|
| 1879–80 | 0.05 | 25 | | |
| 1880–81 | 0.05 | 25 | | |
| 1881–82 | 0.09 | 58 | | |
| 1882–83 | 0.30 | 138 | | |
| 1883–84 | 1.41 | 655 | | |
| 1884–85 | 30 | 8,655 | | |
| 1885–86 | 70 | 18,396 | | |
| 1886–87 | 257 | 3,629 | | |
| 1887–88 | 300 | | | |
| 1888–89 | 303 | | | |
| 1889–90 | 511 | | | |
| 1890–91 | 557 | | | |
| 1891–92 | 436 | | | |
| 1892–93 | 505 | | | |
| 1893–94 | 626 | | | |
| 1894–95 | 645 | | | |
| 1895–96 | 791 | | | |
| 1896–97 | 831 | | | |
| 1897–98 | 1,509 | | | |
| 1898–99 | 1,553 | | | |
| 1899–1900 | 1,564 | | | |
| 1900–1901 | 1,418 | | | |
| 1901–1902 | 1,886 | | | |
| 1902–1903 | 2,454 | | | |
| 1903–1904 | 2,157 | | | |
| 1904–1905 | 2,246 | | | |
| 1905–1906 | 2,146 | | 58,967 | 919 |
| 1907 | 1,881 | | 94,018 | 1,647 |
| 1908 | 3,642 | | 220,429 | 3,721 |
| 1909 | 4,183 | | 238,066 | 3,721 |
| 1910 | 5,241 | | 186,127 | 3,183 |
| 1911 | 4,681 | | 261,254 | 4,080 |
| 1912 | 6,049 | | 422,776 | 6,552 |
| 1913 | 8,683 | | 724,189 | 10,683 |
| 1914 | 6,212 | | 487,245 | 7,295 |
| 1915 | 265 | | 203,972 | 2,966 |
| 1916 | 44 | | 68,380 | 829 |
| 1917 | 1,246 | | | |
| 1918 | 1,738 | | 6,744 | 72 |

Source: H. R. Friman, "Germany and the Transformation of Cocaine," in Paul Gooten-berg, ed., *Cocaine: Global Histories* (New York: Routledge, 1999), Tables 4.1 and 4.2.

more easily and cheaply than bulk leaf and lasted longer. Merck processed it into medicinal-grade cocaine in Germany for its global distribution networks. This product also fitted a marked German cultural and medical preference for "pure" scientific cocaine. By 1900, almost all German imports—more than 6,000 kilos yearly at the peak in 1903–5, worth nearly £100,000—arrived in the form of crude cocaine, so that shipments of coca leaf became obsolete. The Germans' success in promoting crude cocaine was also a prime reason that rival colonial coca projects (British, Dutch, and the American Rusby mission for Parke-Davis) were largely abandoned by the 1890s.[7] Crude cocaine was in fact too successful: with world production surpassing 15 metric tons by the early twentieth century, medicinal markets were saturated. (England, France, Italy, Switzerland, and Russia also engaged in cocaine processing in a modest way for national markets.) Merck quickly diversified into other drug lines. As profits and prospects fell, German firms soon formed a cocaine "syndicate" (1905) with monopsonistic buying, cartel pricing agreements, and strong organizational ties to the German state. By 1910, the European cocaine network was no longer primarily market-driven.

A decisive factor in the emergence of coca and cocaine as a discrete commodity chain is the way European (largely German) interests infiltrated and shaped the Peruvian end of things. In the 1860s and 1870s, such Peruvian medical and cultural spokesmen as Manuel A. Fuentes and the physicians Tomás Moreno y Maíz, José Casimiro Ulloa, and José de los Ríos overcame traditional elite prejudices and began to seriously reevaluate native coca as a good and now marketable resource. French medicine held sway, and indeed, the major Peruvian worker in the field after the War of the Pacific, the remarkable Alfredo Bignon, was a naturalized French pharmacist working in Lima. But commercial developments, which made Peru the monopoly supplier of world coca and cocaine by 1900, followed German cues and connections (plus some American coca trends). In a little-known burst of pharmaceutical experiments in Lima in 1884–87—a local version of Freud's famed *Coca Papers* of the same years—Bignon perfected an original and simplified method for distilling crude cocaine, which was soon promoted by Lima medical circles and by two official Peruvian coca commissions. By 1886, German pharmacists and businessmen like Meyer and Hafemann in Lima established themselves as the main cocaine processors, sending their product on via German merchant houses (Pruis, Dammert, and others) to Hamburg.[8] Mannheim's C. F. Boehringer also sent its sole chemist to Lima as early as 1885.

But it was the dedicated Arnaldo Kitz, an immigrant German merchant in the capital and commercial agent for Merck, who went farthest to the source of supply: the eastern Andes, ancestral homeland of coca. By 1890, Kitz had marched off to isolated Amazonian Pozuzo, home of a legendary "lost" Austrian peasant colony of the 1850s, to establish the region's first working cocaine factory. Bignon's process became known as the Kitz formula in producing zones. By 1892, Peru's earnings from crude cocaine surpassed its revenues from coca leaf. In the mid-1890s, Kitz shifted operations to nearby Huánuco, with its rich montaña (Chinchao-Derrepente zone) haciendas. For the next sixty years, this district would remain the capital of Andean cocaine-grade coca, delivering most of its output to Germany until World War II. Committed Peruvian hacendados, drawing thousands of migrating peasant workers and sharecroppers, colonized or "industrialized" these coca lands from 1885 to 1910, with the help of a few Croatian immigrants. By 1900, Huánuco province was home to about a dozen cocaine manufactories (of about twenty scattered throughout the country), with a regional elite based on coca and cocaine estates. The industry became concentrated and dominated by the flamboyant regional and national political boss, Augusto Durand. These complex local structures of production—particularly of the central Huánuco region—were oriented and connected over thousands of miles to a handful of German pharmaceutical concerns.

Around 1901 (according to German consuls), Peru's legal cocaine zenith, total production peaked at 10,700 kilos of crude cocaine, which required the use of some 1,600 metric tons of raw coca leaf. Peru still also exported 610 tons of coca leaf (more than half of that northern Trujillo coca to the United States) out of an estimated national production of 2,100 tons. As usual, those numbers don't quite add up, but the export boom likely left some three-quarters of Peruvian coca in traditional indigenous circuits, much of that grown in the far Cuzqueño south.[9] Together, and fleetingly, coca and cocaine constituted Peru's fifth-highest export earner and continued to excite the developmental imagination of liberal national elites. Peru's success here, guided by German cues, was likely at the expense of neighboring Bolivia, the only other commercial coca producer. By 1900, Bolivia had failed to industrialize any of its productive Yungas coca zones (which previously exported to France and the United States) and Bolivian sales to modern commercial users in the northern hemisphere faded away. But to grasp these Andean circuits roundly we need to explore another coca commodity chain: the one between the United States and Peru.

### The North American Connection

North America's interest in coca and cocaine grew after 1860 (explosively after 1884), but in contrast to Germany, which focused on scientific cocaine, the United States had a pronounced medical, cultural, and political-economic bias toward coca leaf. By 1900, Americans were the world's largest and most avid consumers and boosters of both substances, by then seemingly domesticated all-American goods. By 1910, however, American thinking and policies dramatically shifted against both coca and cocaine, and the United States began its long global campaign to banish both products. Over the long term, Americans' attitudes toward coca must be seen in the context of expanding informal influence in the Andean region.

North America's fascination with coca leaf, sparked by exported European curiosity, took on distinctively American tones. By the 1870s American medical men, pharmacists, entrepreneurs, and hucksters were actively discovering coca. It was soon among the most widespread additives in popular patent remedies and tonics, prescribed for a vast range of conditions and ills, real and imagined. Most were related to "neurasthenia," the American condition of nerve exhaustion linked to the fast pace of modern urban life. Thus although coca had begun as a brain worker's salve, by the 1890s its use was spreading across (or down) the social (and racial) spectrum, sometimes by way of concoctions spiked instead with pure cocaine.[10] Pioneering American drug firms, such as Detroit's Parke-Davis Company, specialized in coca medicines. Dozens of leading U.S. physicians experimented with, wrote on, and debated the benefits of coca (and later cocaine), though its appeal derived mainly from the herbalist or eclectic healer tradition, still a vibrant alternative to European-style allopathic medicine. The American romance with coca resonates in Dr. W. Golden Mortimer's classic 1901 tome *History of Coca: "The Divine Plant" of the Incas* (still a wonderful source on coca) and of course lives on in our coca-laced national soft drink, Coca-Cola, launched in 1886 as a dry southern imitation of Mariani's popular health beverage and one of modernity's pioneering consumer commodities. By the early 1900s, the United States imported 600–1,000 metric tons of coca annually, mainly for this popular market.

The United States actively promoted the trade in Andean coca. In 1877, besides modest Bolivian sales, Peru exported only 8,000 kilograms of coca. When coca grew scarce from 1884 to 1887, debates on its supply raged in American pharmacy journals and domestic growing schemes were suggested. Parke-Davis sent its pioneer ethnobotanist, Henry Hurd Rusby—a towering figure in American pharmacy—on a legendary mission to scout out supplies, processing methods, and native coca therapies in Bolivia. The U.S. Navy and consuls in La Paz and Lima worked to identify and secure coca supply routes. In the 1890s, U.S. commercial attachés in Lima honed contacts with local cocaine makers (even the German Kitz) and helped Peruvians to upgrade their shipping and leaf-drying techniques. Peruvian coca producers responded well to these signs and to market signals, more than doubling their coca exports during the 1890s. Bolivia, saddled with tortuous transport costs, gradually dropped out of overseas sales, and by 1910 was focusing on regional commerce to migrant coqueros in Bolivia, northern Argentina, Chile, and even southern Peru.

American pharmaceutical companies and physicians reacted enthusiastically to the discovery of cocaine's anesthetic powers in 1884 and tested its gamut of modern medical uses (though soon enough they realized cocaine's dangers and illicit lures). By the mid-1890s, major firms—among them Parke-Davis, Schlieffelin, Mallinkrodt, and the New Jersey branch of Merck—competed vigorously with German suppliers.[11] By 1900, they refined a total of five to six metric tons of cocaine, about a third of the world supply; total U.S. consumption (including imports from Europe) peaked at around nine tons in 1903, or some two-thirds of all global usage of some fifteen tons. Even tariff politics played their part: high effective tariffs on cocaine, with herbal coca entering free, decidedly favored home production of cocaine from imported leaf. Peruvian cocaine processors themselves perceived this bias. American consumers' taste for coca, expanding with the spectacular success of Coca-Cola and countless imitators after 1900, and cheaper and faster shipments from the Andes deterred the United States from following the Germans in switching to large-scale imports of Peruvian crude cocaine.

Indeed, after 1900 U.S. buyers focused increasingly on a distinctive northern coca-leaf circuit in western La Libertad, instead of Huánuco's Amazonian cocaine lands or the Cuzco's Indian-leaf zone. Grown under drier conditions, Trujillo-branded leaf was deemed more flavorful, less alkaloid, and best for tonics, such as the secret "Merchandise No. 5" used in Coca-Cola. In fact, it was a German national, Louis Schaefer (a Boehringer chemist sent to Lima in 1885), jumping across chains, who established this business in the United States, which was soon transformed into Maywood Chemical Works, Coca-Cola's chief syrup intermediary with Peru. La Libertad's Sacamanca and Otuzco districts evolved into the long-term supply shed of its leaf, prepared specially for Coca-Cola, organized and managed by the regional merchant clans of Goicochea and Pinillos.[12] In short, the German and North American chains developed around different cultural, medical, business, and political principles and were even articulated to distinguishable zones and networks within the Andes.

Finally, one need note the initial impact of Americans' fervor against cocaine. Americans' growing fear and loathing of cocaine (and less rationally of coca) was the flip side to their early enthusiasm. Cocaine was symptomatic of the love-hate "American disease" of drugs as cure-all and scourge, to paraphrase the medical historian David F. Musto. By 1900, dominant medical, reformer, and governmental opinion began to turn against licit coca and cocaine, along with alcohol and true narcotics, and especially against spreading illicit use by the "dope fiends" of the racialized underclass.[13] By 1915, the United States had become a lonely crusader against cocaine, portraying Germany as an evil drug empire. U.S. controls of coca and cocaine, legally erected between 1906 and 1922, had many paradoxical effects, many still with us today, such as the prohibition of harmless coca leaf. As cocaine demand became regulated and reduced, using an intricate system of coca controls, the outcome was a high degree of cooperation between the state and pharmaceutical companies in defining the trade. Indeed, by the 1920s only two New Jersey firms—now fully nationalized Merck and the Maywood Chemical Works, Coca-Cola's partner—dealt with coca and cocaine, and the business assumed a monopoly character. In effect, for control purposes U.S. legislation systematized the long-standing American penchant for leaf imports.[14] The result was a cartel-like state-governed coca chain—in that sense, not so different from the formally cartelized European chain of cocaine. By 1910, global coca—in two distinctive chains tied to differing product zones in the Andes—came under conflicting pressures.

## DIVVYING UP GLOBAL COCA, 1910–1950

The period from 1910 to 1950 represents cocaine's declining middle age, between the drug's licit peak and its full global prohibition. From production of fifteen tons or more in 1905, total use was probably halved by 1930; by 1950 the U.N. set legal world medicinal needs at under four metric tons. Three factors drove this steady fall: a decline in medical usage (anesthesia) by substitutes and in medical opinion; anticocaine laws and campaigns by states and international organizations (whose efforts were focused mainly on narcotics); and withdrawal from the market and diversification of vulnerable producers and coca planters. As yet, illicit cocaine barely compensated for market blockage, after its fleeting emergence from surplus pharmaceutical stocks from the 1910s to the early 1920s. The United States, the largest consumer market, initiated national restrictions with the 1906 FDA Act, which was followed by a federal ban in the 1914 Harrison Act and a full-fledged import control system by 1922.[15] Less successfully, the United States also pushed global cocaine controls at the Hague conventions of 1912–14 and at successive Geneva antinarcotics conventions sponsored by the League of Nations starting in 1924–25.

Rather than go away, cocaine divided into a new trio of politically structured and geographically defined global commodity chains. The first was a Dutch colonial mercantilist Java-Europe chain, which by 1915 swiftly displaced Peruvian producers. The second was Japan's state-sponsored pan-Asian circuit, launched in the 1920s in reaction to League and industrial imperatives. The third chain was the residual United States–Andes nexus: increasingly linked to corporate privilege (mainly Coca-Cola) and drug control (under Harry Anslinger's Federal Bureau of Narcotics) and on the Peruvian end dividing into coca and cocaine circuits and contending national projects. This market encrustation is hardly unexpected for such a declining and politicized commodity. Global markets of coca and cocaine, built in the prior period, ceased to exist.

### The Dutch Colonial Coca Boom, 1905–1930

The rapid rise of the Dutch to prominence in the world coca and cocaine trades took interested parties by surprise, especially the Peruvians, who until 1900 felt they enjoyed a natural birthright to the world coca market. In 1904 the Dutch island of Java (now a part of Indonesia) exported only 26 tons of coca leaf; this figure soared to 800 tons in 1912 and to 1,700 tons in 1920, glutting the world market. The Dutch built an especially productive and integrated industrial cocaine regime, but it was dismantled by decree almost as quickly as it arose.

Dutch scientific and commercial interest in coca dates to the 1850s, and plantings began in the mid-1880s, when such botanical experiments spread among the European colonial powers. One advantage was accidental: the abnormally high-alkaloid coca bush Javanese planters received from the colonial botanical gardens at Buitenzorg descended from one special strand of *Erythroxylon novogranatense*, obtained from Kew. It contained twice the cocaine content of quality Huánuco leaf (up to 1.5 percent), but in a form so difficult to refine that it was practically useless for herbal coca products. Given Peru's swift entry into crude cocaine in the 1885–1900 era, not much interest was evinced in Javanese coca, though small lots reached European buyers.

After 1900, several factors refocused Dutch interest in coca, spurred on by national botanical specialists like A. W. K. de Jong and Emma Reens. One was the establishment in 1900 of Amsterdam's large Nederlandsch Cocainefabrieck, subsidized by the state bank, which took advantage of patented German technology to extract cocaine from coca leaves imported from Java. The second factor was steady investment in the productivity of plantations and the quality of their yields. Cheaper Asian field labor, four annual harvests, economies of scale and technical rationalization, and intercropping with colonial rubber and tea projects, all made the efficient Javanese plantations outpace the haphazard peasant-style coca culture of the Andes. By 1911 they captured a quarter of the world market, filtered through Amsterdam into a high-margin fully integrated cocaine industry (see Table 2).[16] The disruptions of World War I spurred Europeans to rely more heavily on this coca corridor. Dutch industrial-grade coca also made it to Japan, Belgium, France, and even the United States. In the 1920s, impressed by its reliable quality, New Jersey Merck acquired its own plantation in Java, which performed well into the 1930s. Three world cores of industrial cocaine now existed: Darmstadt, northern New Jersey, and Amsterdam, with an enlarged Nederlandsch Cocainefabrieck (NCF), the biggest single producer. Together they dramatically reduced prospects for Peruvian coca (wiped off European markets from 1908 to 1915) and crude cocaine, now confined to depressed German processors. The values of Peruvian coca and cocaine exports dropped by some 95 percent by the 1920s. Peruvians watched these developments haplessly, having neither the time, the capital, nor the expertise to respond.[17]

Paradoxically, almost as quickly as it arose the Dutch cocaine network receded. By 1920, Javanese coca basically satisfied the full world demand (twelve tons) for cocaine; prices plummeted and revenues zigzagged

Table 2

| | | | | | |
|---|---|---|---|---|---|
| | | Coca Exports from Java, 1904–1935 (kilograms) | | | |
| Year | Coca | Year | Coca | Year | Coca |
| 1904 | 25,836 | 1915 | 1,089,076 | 1926 | 1,043,000 |
| 1905 | 67,000 | 1916 | 407,984 | 1927 | 709,000 |
| 1906 | 122,000 | 1917 | 271,911 | 1928 | 385,000 |
| 1907 | 200,000 | 1918 | 661,968 | 1929 | 585,000 |
| 1908 | 417,000 | 1919 | 994,203 | 1930 | 354,000 |
| 1909 | 373,000 | 1920 | 1,676,621 | 1931 | 304,000 |
| 1910 | 430,000 | 1921 | 1,137,373 | 1932 | 209,000 |
| 1911 | 750,000 | 1922 | 1,283,503 | 1933 | 161,000 |
| 1912 | 1,075,000 | 1923 | 907,335 | 1934 | 105,000 |
| 1913 | 1,332,000 | 1924 | 1,118,000 | 1935 | 125,000 |
| 1914 | 1,353,270 | 1925 | 1,008,000 | | |

Note: 1,000 kilograms = 1 metric ton.
Source: D. F. Musto, "International Traffics in Coca through the Early Twentieth Century," *Drug and Alcohol Dependence* 49 (1998): Table 5.

throughout the 1920s. To diversify, the NCF even began to make novocaine, cocaine's closest and fully synthetic substitute. Price controls emerged to manage the surplus. Assisted by the League of Nations (interested mainly in drug-control formulas), a new formal European cocaine syndicate, the European Convention of Cocaine Producers, was formed in 1924, with eight members. It included the Nederlandsch Cocainefabrieck and the three largest German makers, with only small domestic French, British, German, and Russian firms still apart. At first this development signified more planned purchases from Java but also steadily declining cocaine quotas. A Dutch national Association of Coca Producers also formed, which soon worked to downsize itself and diversify into alternative crops. In the late 1920s, Dutch production systematically fell. From 1929 to 1931, in contradictory political moves, the Netherlands opted to comply with the export controls of the League's Geneva Manufacturing Limitation Accord, despite unhappiness with the United States' drug crusade, in part to protect its colonial opium monopolists. With a tiny home market, the annual output of the NCF withered to 250–300 kilos.[18] Japan's invasion of Java in World War II snapped the chain, and the subsequent U.S. occupation led to the mandated destruction of remaining coca plants in Java. It had been a brief but spectacular political marriage of state, industry, and colonial planter. (And a reminder today that coca could easily escape the Andes for other tropical realms if pressures mount.)

### Japanese Imperial Cocaine

Even less is known about Japan's cocaine network of the 1920s and 1930s than about the Netherlands'. It may have been spurred by the Dutch example, as well as by intriguing chain crossings. By the 1930s, Japan was one of the largest producers and purveyors of cocaine to Southeast Asia, although the size (and legality) of this state-sanctioned trade remain clouded in controversy.

The first Japanese involvements with coca and cocaine were responses to Western initiatives. Jokichi Takamine, a brilliant Japanese chemist (still known for synthesizing adrenaline), had worked for Parke-Davis in the 1890s, at the height of the firm's cocaine age, and brought his expertise back to Japan's expanding Sankyo Pharmaceuticals; he became its vice president in the late 1910s. Colonial sugar interests in Formosa (Taiwan) began to invest in coca around the same time; processors purchased Javanese and Peruvian coca and crude cocaine until they achieved self-sufficiency in the 1930s. In 1917, Hoshi Pharmaceuticals actually acquired a major coca tract smack in the middle of Peru's Huallaga valley, the Tulumayo property; it was a source not only of quality coca but probably also of know-how about the larger business. Other firms developed plantations in Java.[19] Another influence was a group of German pharmaceutical firms that used Japanese companies for shadow transshipments (banned to China) from 1912, when export controls on opiates and cocaine were imposed, through the 1920s. Given the surplus of cocaine in Europe, these transfers became substantial: some years saw more than 4,000 pounds of cocaine pass through Japan in this semilicit trade.

Japan's role in narcotics in general has been read in two contrary ways. International warnings were sounded from the start. In one sense, drug trafficking fitted Japan's Asian-oriented industrialization process and expansive trade sphere. Japan sought self-sufficiency after the trade disruptions of World War I, and close relationships of the state and large firms were a basic feature of Japanese business culture. Pharmaceuticals represented an important element of scientific modernization. To the Japanese, drug exports were a normal business. Japan—which never experienced a domestic drug scare—did not share in the Western ideal of demarcating illicit and legal substances (and later, of course, left the

League of Nations). A second view—rooted in concerns of the United States and the League during the 1920s and in testimony at the Tokyo war crimes trials—sees Japan's involvement as extraordinary or nefarious. It was based on deliberate deception (to Western drug-control bodies) and on militarist or imperialist profiteering in illicit sales across Asia.[20] Without falling into conspiratorial Japan bashing, we can at least think of the Japanese chain as emerging from the shadows of growing League jurisdictions over drugs. An increasingly autonomous Asian coca and cocaine network appeared from 1920 to 1945.

By 1920, Japan itself produced more than 4,000 pounds of cocaine, which then doubled to 8,000 by 1922. Official figures for the 1930s shrank to just under 2,000 pounds, though League officials and some historians believe that figure was doctored for external consumption. (This is a hard charge to prove, though Steven Karch has tried to prove it.) Exports across Asia officially dropped to negligible levels, though complaints were registered about Japanese firms and reporting practices, as well as reports of smuggling, such as the vials branded "Fujitsuru" and "Taiwan Governor" in India. Some specialists have noted diplomatic cooperation between Japan and international drug officials, at least until the invasions of Manchuria and China, where opiate sales became a contentious issue. The firms that made cocaine and morphine were among Japan's largest: Hoshi, Sankyo, Koto, and Shiongo Pharmaceuticals, which enjoyed growing links to major trading trusts (such as Mitsui and Mitsubishi) and to interlocking governmental, colonial, and military officials. We know that in 1934, Taiwan's Kagi district kept 694 acres under intensive coca cultivation as earlier plots on Iwo Jima and Okinawa were abandoned. Formosa harvested some 300,000 pounds of leaf annually in the late 1930s, mainly for the Taiwan Drug Manufacturing Co. Ltd. Imports of Peruvian leaf were officially discontinued in 1938 (in fact, Peru nationalized Tulumayo, which had a colorful subsequent history of its own).[21]

By World War II, the whole pharmaceutical industry, self-sufficient in imperial Japan, came under the government's jurisdiction. In that sense, if cocaine was indeed marketed for nonmedical purposes across occupied Asia—and the evidence mainly concerns opiates—the state bore responsibility. In any case, the Taiwanese coca industry was demolished by war and the Japanese pharmaceutical sector was reorganized, without cocaine, under the American occupation in 1945 (its previous practices an explicit charge of U.S. war tribunals). A two-decade autonomous coca sphere abruptly ended.

*The United States–Andes Chain, 1910–1950*

The United States–Peru chain, despite these competitors and its relative quantitative decline, proved to be the most resilient and significant in the long term. Modern trade in coca and cocaine germinated in Peru in the 1890s, with North America the defining consumer market; the United States' anticocaine policies of the early twentieth century incubated in this peculiar relationship. And in the 1960s and 1970s, when illicit cocaine took off, the new chain began in eastern Peru and worked its way famously to Miami and Hollywood. This is the historically central cocaine chain, even if it was marked by the shrinking of legal exchange during most of the century.

Aggregate statistics—the decline seen from Peru—show that coca trades, mainly to the United States, fell from an average 584,000 kilos (over a million pounds) in 1909–13 to 242,000 in 1919–23 to 128,000 in 1929–33, before climbing to the 300,000–400,000-pound range during World War II (for emergency war uses). Crude cocaine exports, mainly from greater Huánuco, fell from over 10 metric tons in their peak (1903–4, mainly to Germany) to one ton (i.e., 1,000 kilos) in 1927 and to an unstable 200–900 kilos throughout the 1930s (see Table 3). By the 1920s, no crude cocaine entered the United States (its import was strictly prohibited by law), but Peruvians had new buyers in Japan and France (and in about ten other countries that kept small national alkaloid lines). But by the mid-1930s, a politically risky Germany, with six firms still making cocaine, was effectively Peru's sole remaining cocaine customer. Combined export revenues slumped below 200,000 soles throughout the 1930s. Because of falling prices, the total drop in the values of coca and cocaine exports was more than nine-tenths of their early twentieth-century peak. It was a shattering collapse, especially given the initial national hopes for cocaine. Economically, coca and cocaine became marginal for Peru, except in a few regions.

Peru's coca and cocaine circuits became reconfigured, as can be seen by a survey of coca regions. (Bolivia's production was now confined entirely to traditional or borderlands users.) The notable fact is that as the Peruvian cocaine industry came under market and legal constraints, it neither modernized itself into an integrated or technologically upgraded industry, as some people called for it to do, nor switched to illicit trade (which appeared nowhere until the 1950s).

A major shift was the move of coca leaf back to the home market of traditional users. During the boom of the late 1890s, as much as a quarter

Table 3

| | | | | | | |
|---|---|---|---|---|---|---|
| | | Peruvian exports of coca and crude cocaine, 1877–1933 (kilograms) | | | | |

| Year | Coca | Cocaine | | Year | Coca | Cocaine |
|---|---|---|---|---|---|---|
| 1877 | 8,000 | | | 1914 | 477,648 | 979 |
| 1888 | 29,000 | 1,730 | | 1915 | 393,404 | 1,353 |
| 1890 | 6,677 | 930 | | 1916 | 265,834 | 1,576 |
| 1891 | 128,543 | 3,215 | | 1917 | 306,535 | 1,896 |
| 1892 | 377,762 | 4,550 | | 1918 | 167,449 | 2,967 |
| 1897 | 494,000 | 4,200 | | 1919 | 385,583 | 596 |
| 1898 | 406,718 | 4,346 | | 1920 | 453,067 | 1,637 |
| 1899 | 312,112 | 4,500 | | 1921 | 87,849 | 157 |
| 1900 | 565,730 | 7,745 | | 1922 | 124,357 | 778 |
| 1901 | 610,100 | 10,688 | | 1923 | 190,000 | 192 |
| 1902 | 933,284 | 8,268 | | 1924 | 169,850 | 967 |
| 1903 | 1,026,000 | 10,000 | | 1925 | 216,714 | 621 |
| 1904 | 911,000 | 9,500 | | 1926 | 204,209 | 1,048 |
| 1905 | 1,489,598 | 6,788 | | 1927 | 142,797 | 980 |
| 1906 | 1,210,652 | 5,914 | | 1928 | 150,092 | 625 |
| 1907 | 654,103 | 6,057 | | 1929 | 101,273 | 236 |
| 1909 | 496,328 | 5,266 | | 1930 | 191,609 | — |
| 1910 | 495,729 | 5,524 | | 1931 | 169,524 | 246 |
| 1911 | 768,017 | 5,434 | | 1932 | 96,647 | 420 |
| 1912 | 769,751 | 2,944 | | 1933 | 85,721 | 918 |
| 1913 | 392,918 | 3,267 | | | | |

Source: D. F. Musto, "International Traffic in Coca through the Early Twentieth Century," *Drug and Alcohol Dependence* 49 (1998): Table 6, p. 153.

of Peru's coca was reported in export channels (though that figure is questionable); by the 1930s and 1940s the tradable share was far smaller, around 3 percent by most estimates. In part, this market involution reflected the steady multiplication of Peru's rural folk and their intensified migratory labor during the twentieth century. Coca for traditional uses went from under 4.8 million kilos in the mid-1920s to 5.4 million by 1930 to over 6 million by 1940, and to 8–11 million kilos by the 1950s. Regionally, this surge translated into an advancing coca frontier, heralded by national agronomists, mainly to the newer southern tropical regions (especially Cuzco's La Convención valley), close to the indigenous "Mancha India." In the early 1940s, in a crude guess, one expert estimated Peru's entire leaf crop at 6.8 million pounds, with 6 million used by the nation's 2 million male chewers (women, who certainly did use coca, didn't count). Peru's triad of internal coca circuits were defined as northern (La Libertad, largely for export for cola flavorings), at 1.6 million pounds, or 19 percent of the total crop; central (greater Huánuco, for crude cocaine and central regional leaf trades), at 2.24 million pounds, or 34.5 percent; and southern (mostly Cuzco) at 3 million, or 46.5 percent. Even the coca specialists evidently jumbled the numbers; for example, confusing here pounds and kilos.[22] Seen as regional networks, northern leaf growers (in the Otuzco and Sacamanca districts) remained tied to the powerful Pinillos export clan, who exported two-thirds of local coca crops to Maywood Chemical, Coca-Cola's agent in the trade. Spotty experiments in crude cocaine making also registered in the north. In the center, Huánuco's economic hub remained crude cocaine, however depressed and technologically backward, as its traditional elite lost hold. Now local Chinese merchants plied provincial coca trades to the upland mining town of Junín, and new peasant-driven coca frontiers were opening up in Monzón and downstream Tingo María. About six to ten crude cocaine workshops, still using Kitz's techniques from the 1890s, carried on the industry, basically part-time, mainly on demand; that is, for special orders from abroad. They were led by a new regional magnet, Andrés Avelino Soberón, a merchant with close ties to German consigners but always struggling to diversify (even into the closed United States cocaine market). The third zone around southern Cuzco was less strategic with low-alkaloid home-market leaf and was the sole area that saw campaigns to upgrade coca agricultural practices among colonizing hacendados.

Peruvian politics of coca and cocaine after 1910 were also related to developments at the other end of the chain. In a great turnabout between 1905 and 1925, foreign campaigns against cocaine filtered to Peru via science, politics, and markets. In medical science, the new idea of cocaine as a poisonous or addictive narcotic paradoxically mutated in Peru into growing sentiments against coca as backward or harmful to national development. Combined with racism against the country's Indian majority, this view fueled a novel hygienics movement against coca by the 1930s, since toxic coca "degenerated" Peru's "Indian race." Cocaine, ironically, was still considered a modern or model Western good, with no local abuse. Peruvian officials actively ignored pressures from the United States and the League of Nations to restrict cocaine and coca after 1920.[23] In part defending Huánuco interests, officials sincerely felt that global antidrug campaigns discriminated against a Peruvian product. By the mid-1920s, Peruvian health officials embraced a few modern narcotics controls, but only in the mid-1940s did such regulation become transformed into police functions, in a prelude to the actual criminalizing of legal cocaine making in 1947–49. Meanwhile, during the 1930s a vociferous countermovement arose, led by Dr. Carlos Enrique Paz Soldán, to nationalize and modernize the entire coca and cocaine industry in a large state monopoly, in outright resistance to encroaching global constraints on cocaine. One of Peru's most respected and outspoken medical figures, Paz Soldán was appalled by cocaine's falling fortunes as well as spreading coca use by the Indian peasants. The idea, which had deep local appeal, was for Peru to face the world as the sole sanctioned exporter of medicinal cocaine hydrochloride. Although the United States opposed this statist scheme, during World War II Merck's cocaine specialist, Emile Pilli, also lobbied for modernization of the industry, including home production of "pure salts" of cocaine. Thus external market and political pressures led to schizophrenic and increasingly statist discourses on coca and cocaine. Commodity segmentation worked in strange ways.

The United States still managed the far end of this hemispheric chain (save for the shrinking Hamburg entrepôt until the eve of World War II) with increasingly defined drug controls around coca and cocaine. The chief characteristics of the United States' cocaine network were specialization in coca chains (and "de-cocainized" coca syrup); state-assisted monopolies in cocaine processing; a total (and largely effective) prohibition in the domestic market; and the intensification of global campaigns against still-licit coca and cocaine elsewhere. However, global prohibitions bore fruit only after World War II with the destruction of the three extant chains, Dutch, Japanese, and German, and Peru's entry into the Allied political sphere. The United States had been the undisputed world capital of coca and cocaine use and a pioneer in the popular abuse of cocaine, and after 1910 it worked passionately to reverse that equation. There is little doubt that illicit (as well as medicinal) use of cocaine largely dried up in the United States after 1920, though the reasons remain unclear. Popular coca products were successfully eliminated, with the notable exception of booming and now cocaine-free Coca-Cola (the company voluntarily de-cocainized its coca leaf after 1903). One factor was a political economy of control that emerged out of the prior North American penchant for coca leaf and (by 1920) the concentration of coca handling in two firms, New Jersey Merck and nearby Maywood Chemical, Coca-Cola's ally.[24] Rather than regulate thousands of pharmacists, dentists, and physicians at the retail level, the United States pinched cocaine at the top. By 1920, these two firms had become close intermediaries of the emerging federal antidrug bureaucracy (the Federal Bureau of Narcotics, or FBN), trading in intelligence and favors and ensuring that only bulky supervised coca leaf entered the port of New York. Every detail of the distillation process—of Merchandise No. 5, Coca-Cola's secret extract, made by Maywood from Trujillo leaf, and of Merck's high-grade medicinal cocaine—was tightly regulated by the FBN. For a long time this system functioned well, hastening the disappearance of illicit cocaine in the 1920s as well as helping to ensure the monopoly successes of Coca-Cola against competitors (and its monopsony with Peruvian coca dealers). Coke and Maywood focused exclusively on northern Peru, forging a closed corporate-family commodity chain with the Pinillos clan; they even won their imports their own congressional judicial status, as "special-leaf imports." As legal and illegal cocaine dwindled and addiction to Coca-Cola rose, these special nonmedicinal imports grew to an ever larger portion of Peruvian coca shipments. By World War II, the United States consumed twice as much coca in beverages (more than 200,000 kilos annually) than was used in making residual medicinal cocaine (see Table 4). By the mid-1920s, a diversified Merck, the monopoly U.S. cocaine maker, turned to imported leaf from its own plantations in Tjitembong, Java, in effect building its own in-house state-governed coca-cocaine commodity chain. Merck looked to Peru only during the war; by the mid-1950s, seeing little use, it gave up making cocaine altogether and simply bought and distributed Maywood's legal Coca-Cola cocaine residue. In effect, all American cocaine became a byproduct of the Coca-Cola empire.

American cocaine politics abroad was partly a sideshow of a more general antinarcotics diplomacy, by which the United States, with few colonial interests, became the main force behind the erection and extension of an idealistic world system of cocaine prohibitions, via ongoing Geneva conventions of the League of Nations. The first targets were the Germans, then the Japanese, and finally after 1945 the errant Peru and Bolivia. To some extent this campaign slowly worked by defining and shrinking legitimate cocaine spheres after 1920; it also backfired, by spurring the expansive Japanese shadow chain. Overall, the interwar period represents the greatest paradox in drug control: while a multiplicity of legal global cocaine chains existed, the United States experienced an idyllic era in respect to cocaine as an active domestic social problem. Moreover, the United States still exerted little or no limiting control at the

Table 4

## U.S. coca imports: medicinal (cocaine) and nonmedicinal (cola), 1925–1959 (kilograms)

| Year | Total imports | Coca leaves Medicinal | Nonmedicinal |
|------|---------------|-----------------------|--------------|
| 1925 | 72,254.578 | 72,254.578 | |
| 1926 | 133,347.054 | 133,347.054 | |
| 1927 | 114,594.886 | 114,594.886 | |
| 1928 | 110,667.347 | 110,667.347 | |
| 1929 | 61,617.962 | 61,617.962 | |
| 1930 | 89,699.155 | 89,699.153 | |
| 1931 | 221,235.522 | 122,748.931 | 98,486.591 |
| 1932 | 101,624.340 | 101,624.340 | |
| 1933 | 81,699.046 | 81,699.046 | |
| 1934 | 85,551.171 | 81,070.364 | 4,480.807 |
| 1935 | 110,330.782 | 94,468.901 | 15,861.881 |
| 1936 | 171,389.634 | 101,855.814 | 69,533.820 |
| 1937 | 189,598.231 | 101,384.362 | 88,213.869 |
| 1938 | 208,581.675 | 101,041.220 | 107,540.455 |
| 1939 | 263,814.726 | 123,138.430 | 140,676.296 |
| 1940 | 352,200.544 | 146,189.403 | 206,011.141 |
| 1941 | 420,388.955 | 127,484.210 | 292,904.745 |
| 1942 | 360,655.921 | 80,849.520 | 270,806.401 |
| 1943 | 447,395.986 | 207,408.941 | 239,987.045 |
| 1944 | 202,057.238 | 67,555.253 | 134,501.985 |
| 1945 | 316,224.374 | 45,359.188 | 270,865.186 |
| 1946 | 228,782.927 | 90,718.971 | 138,063.956 |
| 1947 | 315,237.057 | 180,183.930 | 135,053.127 |
| 1948 | 289,375.064 | 289,375.064 | |
| 1949 | 142,078.358 | 142,078.358 | |
| 1950 | 112,742.530 | 112,742.530 | |
| 1951 | 130,849.918 | 130,849.918 | |
| 1952 | 112,354.213 | 112,354.213 | |
| 1953 | 150,183.138 | 150,183.138 | |
| 1954 | 125,392.754 | 125,392.754 | |
| 1955 | 141,290.354 | 141,290.354 | |
| 1956 | 184,095.849 | 184,095.849 | |
| 1957 | 90,482.508 | 90,482.508 | |
| 1958 | 112,501.219 | 112,501.219 | |
| 1959 | 135,222.544 | 135,222.544 | |

Note: Cola leaf not clearly separated before 1930; separate reporting (but not imports) ceases after 1947.

Source: U.S. Department of Treasury, Federal Bureau of Narcotics, *Traffic in Opium and Other Dangerous Drugs in the Year 1960* (Washington: GPO, 1960), Table 10.

periphery—in coca-growing areas—the stated goal of American diplomats since 1915. In the 1920s and 1930s, partly to pressure Peru and partly to support Coca-Cola, U.S. officials began taking a deep interest in Peruvian coca and cocaine. The main achievement was cultivating an FBN–State Department drug-intelligence web in Peru, facilitated by the contacts of Maywood and Coca-Cola Company executives. Slowly, more and more North American notions of modern drug control filtered to Peru, despite the Peruvians' (and Bolivians') resistance to imported anticoca ideals.[25] FBN records reveal scant direct American meddling in Andean drug policies before World War II, though a good deal thereafter. However, in a larger sense the United States structured the options available for Peru in this realm by its ban on cocaine imports, by curtailing world markets, and by obstructing national schemes of drug control.

World War II was the turning point. During the war itself—significant for commodity chains of all kinds—the United States severed Peru's participation in the Japanese and German markets, and Japanese-occupied Java fell off the Western map. The United States' focus fell on Peru just as Good Neighbor ties multiplied during the course of the conflict, and afterward intensified with the advent of the Cold War. Cocaine became defined strategically within the wartime meanings of "licit" and "contraband" trades. Collaborating agents from the United States and Peru began watching all facets of the network.[26] By 1945, even many Peruvian officials saw the need for restrictions on coca and cocaine and recognized the commercial dead end of Huánuco's limping industry under the United States' postwar hegemony. An anticoca consensus gathered at the new American-inspired United Nations drug agencies, exemplified by the U.N.'s touring Commission of Enquiry into the Problem of Coca Leaf in 1947. Peru, under the anticommunist military regime of Manuel Odría, rushed dramatically in 1947–49 to outlaw the making of cocaine and began, at least on paper, to regulate the Indian coca bush under the auspices of a newly declared national coca monopoly. Thus in 1950 ended—at least in its licit market phase—a commodity chain born almost a century before.

Such were the commodity chains developed by licit coca and cocaine during their rise and demise as modern global drugs between 1860 and 1950. These were not simply interconnected markets of supply and demand, but institutionalized channels for the flow of science and medicine, political ideas, information and influences and varied attempts at monopoly and drug control. They were segmented by changing cultural tastes and by shifting colonial and neocolonial spheres. They reflected varied levels and forms of international power as well, between motley unequal actors and relationships involved in the growing, processing, marketing, regulation, and use and misuse of these substances. They were even discursive links, as cocaine shifted from a heroic modernizing commodity to a marginal one of rival spheres, until its postwar construction as menacing illicit substance, powered by a feudal rhetoric of criminality and violence.[27] In many ways over the long run, these commodity chains and the tensions along and between them helped create the initial legitimacy of coca and cocaine in the nineteenth-century market, and helped structure their progressive illicitness over the twentieth century.

## ILLICIT COCAINE CHAINS, 1950–2000

Since 1950, in some sense, commodity chains of coca and cocaine have become both more and less market-driven phenomena, and this illicit boom may indeed reflect, as some cynics suggest, the revenge of the coca periphery. This era is the transnational stuff of covert police records and drug-culture legends, portrayed in Hollywood's *Traffic* and *Blow*. After 1950, Andean cocaine, outlawed everywhere, escaped all state regulation and carved out its own underground niches and chains, invoking a cast of new criminalized actors. Clearly, except to politically blinded officials of the Drug Enforcement Administration (DEA), it was government and international prohibitions that pushed cocaine so radically into illicit free markets. One intriguing plot line of the story is that once cocaine was proscribed, Cold War circuits of illicit cocaine basically reverted to their original geographic spaces in the eastern Amazon and to historic links with the United States. The jungle export *pasta básica* of cocaine of the 1970s was essentially Bignon's and Kitz's old 1890s crude cocaine sulfates, now forwarded to outside criminal refiners in Colombia rather than to Merck chemists in Darmstadt. A few seasoned specialists of the Huánuco industry reinvented themselves as pioneers of illicit cocaine, which hardly existed before, though land-hungry peasants rather than regional elites became the true driving force behind this new kind of coca expansion. With the declassification of DEA archives, one can trace such developments back to 1950, to precisely the point where the trail of legal cocaine peters out.[28] Underground cocaine blazed a sinuous path across Peru and Bolivia in the 1950s and 1960s, marked by intensifying struggles between U.S. drug agents and aspiring Andean entrepreneurs, experimenting with smuggling routes through Chile, Cuba, Brazil, Panama, Mexico, and taste-testing incipient coke markets in Havana and New York City. A culture and a chain of illicit cocaine were constructed between 1950 and 1973, their paths set by politics and risk profits rather than by efficiency or factors of production. They were pushed to the fore by American pressures well before the deluge of the 1970s, as glimpsed in mounting quantities of Andean "coke" seized at U.S. borders from the late 1950s on.

After 1970, cocaine flooded into the United States to fill in the market niches carved out by speed, heroin, and marihuana, popular products of the 1960s drug culture, under siege in Richard Nixon's declared crackdown on drugs. Coke surfaced among the elite of Hollywood and the rock scene, who liberally publicized their new gourmet "soft" drug. Colombians of Medellín, well-located entrepreneurs under a weak state, soon consolidated as the core middlemen in this trade, refining and passing on with spectacular markups Peruvian and Bolivian peasant product to a diaspora of far-flung Colombian sellers in Miami and New York. As the United States invigorated its suppression of cocaine after 1980, huge segmented retail markets were discovered (middle America, ghetto crack, Dominican gangs) and coca frontiers for illicit export spread massively into the deep jungle recesses of the Huallaga Valley and Bolivia's Chaparé. Further steps against cocaine—wholesale eradication campaigns since the drug wars during the administrations of Ronald Reagan and George H. W. Bush—have led to spirals of illicit production and violence and steep drops in prices, precisely the opposite of the United States' stated objectives. Chains shifted, too: the rerouting of smuggling in the 1980s, at one time from Medellín to Miami, then from Cali to northern Mexico, obeyed the basic laws of drug suppression and commodity chains.

By the early 1990s, illicit cocaine commanded an estimated productive capacity in the range of 1,000 metric tons in a chain involving hundreds of thousands of employees (farmers, processors, guards, money launderers, corrupted officials, smugglers, street dealers, and rehab councilors) along the route, with millions of avid consumers throughout the world and revenues ranging from $50 billion to $100 billion annually. This volume was a hundred times greater than Peru's peak legal cocaine output in 1900, and with the premium in price guaranteed by its prohibition, cocaine has taken its place among the most valuable single commodity chains in world history.[29] Since the late 1970s, the coca crop sown for illicit export has dwarfed domestic-use low-potency leaf for the first time in coca's long history. It is the most dramatic commodity network ever pioneered by Latin American peasants and businessmen. In some ways coca culture is comparable to coffee culture, but it raises serious issues as to why such a lucrative export success story, inequities and all, is found only in Latin America's illicit commerce. Half of the world's 14 million regular cocaine users are North Americans, white and black, rich and poor, who snort some 250–300 tons yearly. In their use of the product they surpass surviving indigenous coqueros of the Andes, who now probably number fewer than five million, despite a recent revalorization of ritual use. Coca is used in a few minor commercial Peruvian and Bolivian concoctions (teas, toothpaste, and the like). Save for Coca-Cola's, there are no legal international exports.

The current stage, starting in the mid-1990s, has largely pushed illicit coca out of eastern Peru and Bolivia into southern Colombia, and transshippers are fleeing Mexico for more dispersed Caribbean sites. This chain is just unfolding, given the pressure exerted by the United States on Colombia to stop the flow of cocaine and now heroin. Reports suggest that overall capacity peaked around 2001 and that coca is again being planted in Peru and Bolivia. New links are being forged through Brazil (a huge emerging consumer capital) and southern Africa and on to the third-ranked markets in Europe and fragments of the former Soviet empire. Illicit cocaine, goaded on by foolhardy drug policies, could end up replicating the geography of early-twentieth-century commodity coca, globalized to such exotic venues as Indonesia, Taiwan, and West Africa— indeed, anywhere helicopters and herbicides don't yet reach.

## NOTES

Laura Sainz, my spouse, helped this essay happen by caring for Dany; Domenica Tafuro worked on the tables. Thanks to participants at the two symposiums on Latin America and global commodity chains (Stanford, 2001; Buenos Aires, 2002), particularly David McCreery and Steve Topik, for incisive comments, and to Steve for taking cocaine as the serious commodity it is.

1   See Gootenberg, ed., *Cocaine*, 12–14, for economic vs. poststructural views of drugs; the volume is organized by global commodity chains. For global drugs, see Stares, *Global Habit*; Pomeranz and Topik, *The World That Trade Created*, chap. 3. A new working group of the Social Science Research Council, Beyond Borders, studies illicit economies as commodity flows.

2   Gereffi and Korzeniewicz, eds., *Commodity Chains and Global Capitalism*; Bellone,

"The Cocaine Commodity Chain and Development Paths in Peru and Bolivia." Appadurai, ed., *The Social Life of Things*, discusses "commodity ecumene"; Mintz, *Sweetness and Power*, discusses the cultural life of commodities.

3 A work on aggregates is Musto, "International Traffic in Coca through the Early Twentieth Century"—a team effort to collate global statistics on historical coca trades. A commodity chain approach can correct flaws in such aggregates by stressing differences in providence and flows rather than artificially standardized quantities. Example: using a poorly defined "cocaine equivalent" (based on reduction of all coca commerce to a standard cocaine alkaloid content), Musto ignores robust regional trade in coca leaf for traditional use (chewing in Bolivia) or coca preparations (such as beverage syrups from northern Peru for the United States and Europe). He overestimates world cocaine consumption in the early twentieth century and underestimates the social significance of alternative coca trades.

4 Goodman, *Tobacco in History*, 49–51; Schivelbusch, *Tastes of Paradise*; Kennedy, *Coca Exotica*, chaps. 5–7. For a "commodity" look at drugs, see Courtwright, *Forces of Habit*.

5 Freud, *Cocaine Papers*. See Kennedy, *Coca Exotica*, 57–58, for an account of the *Novara* mission.

6 Martindale, *Coca, Cocaine and Its Salts*, 388–92. French coca culture needs research, though there are popular essays on Mariani and his famed advertising.

7 Friman, "Germany and the Transformation of Cocaine"; Rusby, *Jungle Memories*, chaps. 1, 8; "Production and Use of Coca Leaves" and "Exports of Crude Cocaine from Peru," *Bulletin of the Imperial Institute* (London) 8 (1910): 388–92; "Mr. Clements R. Markham on 'Coca-Cultivation,'" *Chemist and Druggist* (March 17, 1894): 387–89.

8 Gootenberg, "From Imagining Coca to Making Cocaine"; Spillane, *Cocaine*, 51.

9 On Kitz, see Gootenberg, "Rise and Shine of a National Commodity," and Tamayo, *Informe sobre las colonias de Oaxapampa y Pozuzo*, 111–12. Statistics are from "Cocaine-Manufacture in Peru," *Chemist and Druggist* (April 9, 1904). Also see Garland, *El Perú en 1906*, 180–82, 213. Thanks to Juri Soininen, a Finnish graduate student, for correcting these numbers.

10 Searle, *A New Form of Nervous Disease Together with an Essay on Erythroxylon Coca*; Mortimer, *History of Coca*; Gootenberg, "Between Coca and Cocaine."

11 Spillane, *Cocaine*, chap. 3, and "Making a Modern Drug."

12 For the syrup circuit, see Gootenberg, "Secret Ingredients"; Pilli, *Coca Industry*.

13 Musto, *The American Disease*; Spillane, *Cocaine*, chaps. 5–8.

14 Gootenberg, "Secret Ingredients."

15 Gootenberg, "Reluctance or Resistance?"

16 De Kort, "Doctors, Diplomats, and Businessmen"; Karch, *A Brief History of Cocaine*, chaps. 2, 6; Reens, "La coca de Java."

17 Derteano, "Informe que presenta el consul sobre la coca de la isla de Java"; Paz Soldán, *La coca peruana*.

18 De Kort, "Doctors, Diplomats, and Businessmen"; coca eradication was a U.S. condition for the (brief) Dutch reoccupation of Indonesia after 1945.

19 Friman, *Narcodiplomacy*, chap. 3; Meyer, "Japan and the World Narcotics Traffic"; Karch, "Japan and the Cocaine Industry of Southeast Asia."

20 Friman, *Narcodiplomacy*, is a balanced account of the Japanese and German drug trade.

21 Karch, *Brief History of Cocaine*, chap. 10, guesses Japan's production at seven metric tons (above world licit supply) on the basis of his own acreage-alkaloid ratios. Tulumayo had a remarkable history: originally owned by Kitz, then Durand, nationalized (despite protests by Japanese managers) in 1937, it became the U.S. Tropical Agricultural Station at Tingo María and then the epicenter of illicit cocaine in the 1960s.

22 Pilli, *Coca Industry*, 4–5, 8. Pilli also has an estimate—by bulk?—of 70 percent chewing, 15 percent exports, 15 percent cocaine manufacturing. Paz Soldán, *La Coca Peruana*, xvi, has Cuzco 50 percent, Huánuco 21 percent, La Libertad 7 percent, Ayacucho 17 percent, others 5 percent. Also Gerbi, *El Perú en marcha*, 183–87 (Table 18).

23 Gootenberg, "Reluctance or Resistance?" 56–63; Paz Soldán, "El problema médico-social de la coca en el Perú"; Gagliano, *Coca Prohibition in Peru*, chaps. 6–7.

24 Gootenberg, "Secret Ingredients"; Pilli, *Coca Industry*; U.S. Department of the Treasury, *Traffic in Opium and Other Dangerous Drugs*, Table 10.

25 Gootenberg, "Reluctance or Resistance?"; McAllister, *Drug Diplomacy in the Twentieth Century*.

26 Gootenberg, "Reluctance or Resistance?" 63–70.

27 Commodity chains (which can go beyond economics) are akin to two spatial conceptions of power: Bourdieu's "fields" of contested/capitalized power and Mann's four territorial bundles of power. See Wacquant and Bourdieu, *An Invitation to Reflexive Sociology*; Mann, *The Sources of Social Power*. The global commodity chain approach assumes the continuum and complicity of state market, and society and of licit and illicit spheres.

28 Gootenberg, "Birth of the Narcs"; U.S. Department of the Treasury, *Traffic in Opium and Other Dangerous Drugs*.

29 For today's networks, see Clawson and Lee, *The Andean Coca Industry*, Table 1.1, Fig. 1.4; Painter, *Bolivia and Coca*, Table 3.10; U.S. Bureau of International Narcotics and Law Enforcement Affairs, *International Narcotics Control Strategy Report*, "Policy and Program Overview," 35–45; Forero, "Hide and Seek among the Coca Leaves."

**BIBLIOGRAPHY**

Appadurai, Arjun, ed. *The Social Life of Things: Commodities in Cultural Perspective.* Cambridge: Cambridge University Press, 1986.

Bellone, Amy. "The Cocaine Commodity Chain and Development Paths in Peru and Bolivia." In Roberto Patricio Korzeniewicz and William C. Smith, eds., *Latin America in the World-Economy.* Westport, Conn.: Greenwood, 1996.

Clawson, Patrick L., and Rensselaer Lee III. *The Andean Coca Industry.* New York: St. Martin's Press, 1996.

Courtwright, David T. *Forces of Habit: Drugs and the Making of the Modern World.* Cambridge: Harvard University Press, 2001.

De Kort, Marcel. "Doctors, Diplomats, and Businessmen: Conflicting Interests in the Netherlands and Dutch East Indies." In Paul Gootenberg, ed., *Cocaine: Global Histories,* 126–43. London: Routledge, 1999.

Derteano, M. A. "Informe que presenta el consul sobre la coca de la isla de Java." *Boletín del Ministerio de Relaciones Exteriores del Perú* 15 (1918): 347–48.

Forero, Juan. "Hide and Seek among the Coca Leaves." *New York Times,* June 9, 2004.

Freud, Sigmund. *Cocaine Papers.* Ed. Robert Byck. New York: Stonehill, 1974.

Friman, H. Richard. "Germany and the Transformation of Cocaine." In Paul Gootenberg, ed., *Cocaine: Global Histories,* 83–104. London: Routledge, 1999.

———. *Narcodiplomacy: Exporting the U.S. War on Drugs.* Ithaca: Cornell University Press, 1996.

Gagliano, Joseph. *Coca Prohibition in Peru: The Historical Debates.* Tucson: University of Arizona Press, 1994.

Garland, Alejandro. *El Perú en 1906.* Lima: Imprenta del Estado, 1907.

Gerbi, Antonello. *El Perú en marcha: Ensayo degeografíaeconómica.* Lima: Banco de Crédito, 1943.

Gereffi, Gary, and Miguel Korzeniewicz, eds., *Commodity Chains and Global Capitalism.* Westport. Conn.: Greenwood, 1994.

Goodman, Jordan. *Tobacco in History: The Cultures of Dependence.* London: Routledge, 1993.

Gootenberg, Paul. "Between Coca and Cocaine: A Century or More of U.S.-Peruvian Drug Paradoxes, 1860–1980." *Hispanic American Historical Review* 83, no. 1 (2003): 119–50.

———. "Birth of the Narcs: The First Illicit Cocaine Flows in the Americas, 1947–1973." Unpublished manuscript, 2004.

———. "From Imagining Coca to Making Cocaine: Inventing a National Commodity in Peru, 1850–1890." Unpublished manuscript, 2000.

———. "Reluctance or Resistance? Constructing Cocaine (Prohibitions) in Peru, 1910–50." In Paul Gootenberg, ed., *Cocaine: Global Histories,* 46–82. London: Routledge, 1999.

———. "Rise and Shine of a National Commodity: Peruvian Cocaine, 1885–1910." Unpublished manuscript, 2000.

———. "Secret Ingredients: The Politics of Coca in U.S.-Peruvian Relations, 1915–65." *Journal of Latin American Studies* 36, no. 2 (2004): 233–65.

———, ed. *Cocaine: Global Histories.* New York: Routledge, 1999.

Karch, Steven B. *A Brief History of Cocaine.* Boca Raton: CRC Press, 1998.

———. "Japan and the Cocaine Industry of Southeast Asia, 1864–1944." In Paul Gootenberg, ed., *Cocaine: Global Histories,* 146–64. New York: Routledge, 1999.

Kennedy, Joseph. *Coca Exotica: The Illustrated History of Cocaine.* New York: Cornwall, 1985.

Mann, Michael. *The Sources of Social Power*. Cambridge: Cambridge University Press, 1986.

Martindale, William. *Coca, Cocaine and Its Salts*. London, 1886.

McAllister, William B. *Drug Diplomacy in the Twentieth Century: An International History*. London: Routledge, 2000.

Meyer, Katherine. "Japan and the World Narcotics Traffic." In Jordan Goodman et al., *Consuming Habits: Drugs in History and Anthropology*. London: Routledge, 1995.

Mintz, Sidney W. *Sweetness and Power: The Place of Sugar in Modern History*. New York: Viking, 1985.

Mortimer, W. Golden. *History of Coca: "The Divine Plant" of the Incas*. New York: J. H. Vail, 1901.

Musto, David F. *The American Disease: The Origins of U.S. Narcotics Control*. New York: Oxford University Press, 1973.

———. "International Traffic in Coca through the Early Twentieth Century." *Drug and Alcohol Dependence* 49, no. 2 (1998): 145–56.

Painter, James. *Bolivia and Coca: A Study in Dependency*. Boulder: Lynne Reinner, 1994.

Paz Soldán, Carlos E. *La coca peruana: Memorandum sobre su situación actual*. Lima: SNA, 1936.

———. "El problema médico-social de la coca en el Perú." *Mercurio Peruano* 19 (1929): 584–603.

Pilli, Emile. *The Coca Industry of Peru*. Rahway, N.J.: Merck, 1943.

Pomeranz, Kenneth, and Steven C. Topik. *The World That Trade Created*. Armonk, N.Y.: M. E. Sharpe, 1999.

Reens, Emma. *La coca de Java*. Thesis. Paris: Université de Paris, 1917. Abbrev. trans. (chapter 4) in Steven Karch, *A History of Cocaine: The Mystery of Coca Java and the Kew Plant*. London: Royal Society of Medicine Press, 2003.

Rusby, H. H. *Jungle Memories*. New York: McGraw-Hill, 1933.

Schivelbusch, Wolfgang. *Tastes of Paradise: A Social History of Spices, Stimulants, and Intoxicants*. New York: Pantheon, 1992.

Searle, William S. *A New Form of Nervous Disease Together with an Essay on Erythroxylon Coca*. New York, 1881.

Spillane, Joseph F. *Cocaine: From Medical Marvel to Modern Menace in the United States, 1884–1920*. Baltimore: Johns Hopkins University Press, 1999.

———. "Making a Modern Drug: The Manufacture, Sale and Control of Cocaine in the United States, 1880–1920." In Paul Gootenberg, ed., *Cocaine: Global Histories*, 21–45. London: Routledge, 1999.

Stares, Paul B. *Global Habit*. Washington: Brookings Institution, 1996.

Tamayo, Augusto. *Informe sobre las colonias de Oaxapampa y Pozuzo y los Ríos Palcuzu y Pichir*. Lima: Ministerio de Fomento, 1904.

U.S. Bureau of International Narcotics and Law Enforcement Affairs. *International Narcotics Control Strategy Report*. Washington: Government Printing Office, 2000.

U.S. Department of the Treasury, Federal Bureau of Narcotics. *Traffic in Opium and*

*Other Dangerous Drugs*. Annual reports. Washington: Government Printing Office, 1926–72.

Wacquant, Loic, and Pierre Bourdieu. *An Invitation to Reflexive Sociology*. Chicago: University of Chicago Press, 1992.

Wallerstein, Immanuel. *The Modern World-System: Capitalist Agriculture and the European World-Economy in the Sixteenth Century*. New York: Academic Press, 1974.

CONCLUSION

# Commodity Chains and Globalization
# in Historical Perspective

Carlos Marichal, Steven Topik,
and Zephyr Frank

AS WE WALK TODAY through any university bookstore, the term "globalization" stands out among social science titles. However, as may be judged from the twelve essays in this volume, understanding what globalization means is no simple task. A final comment on the methodological and theoretical contribution of these essays should make clear that their authors consider "globalization" a catchall term and therefore necessarily imprecise. Certainly there exists a justifiable demand for a comprehensive description of the dynamics of contemporary world trends, but this description must be illuminated by a subset of broad but flexible concepts that can help explain how and why globalization has become so pervasive.

We argue that one useful approach is the concept of commodity chains, in good measure because it is sufficiently broad, flexible, and focused to suggest avenues for future research. However, it should be clear that none of the authors represented in this volume is wedded to the world systems concept of global commodity chains. This is an important starting point, for historical case studies oblige us to reshape concepts and adapt them in new ways. According to David McCreery, the idea of commodity chains helps us to understand the production of a commodity on a world scale as well as how chains compete to deliver a given commodity or substitute to market and where and when production or commercial monopolies form; how profits and risks come to be distributed and redistributed within and between chains; problems of adulteration and substitutability; and the role(s) of the state within and between competing commodity chains.

But the concept of commodity chains is not just an instrument to understand economic transmission lines: it also obliges the historian to focus on social history of production and consumption of export products. In chapter 12 Paul Gootenberg argues that "this holistic view helps us to overcome traditional divides between internal and external factors and between economic and noneconomic factors in Latin American history, binaries shared by neoclassical and dependency perspectives." Indeed, the approach adopted in this book aims to redress the balance which has been lost in the din of battle between dependency scholars and neoliberal research advocates. International demand for commodities did not imply that the Latin American economies and governments did not benefit from export booms. As Rory Miller and Robert Greenhill argue in chapter 9, in some cases the commodity chains "may have been dominated by foreign intermediaries as a result of asymmetries of information and access to business networks and cheap finance, but the host economies still obtained substantial benefits and rents from the trades." In other cases, historians continue to carry on strong debates as to costs and benefits.

While all of the essays in this book emphasize the economics of trade, our studies lead us to conclude that the analysis and comparison of commodity chains cannot be limited to one simple purely economic model. Such models are of great use, but if we are to understand the origins and trajectories of the various export commodities, we should also attempt to understand other key facets, including a set of new spheres of research which can help to reestablish old bridges that have broken down between economic, social, and political history as a result of growing specialization. It is for this reason that in these concluding comments, our focus is on three associated fields of research which should attract interest in the future.

## HOW LOOKING AT CONSUMPTION CHANGES
## TRADITIONAL VIEWS OF LATIN AMERICAN HISTORY

An important issue addressed by all the contributors to this volume is the need for future historical studies to pay more attention to consumption. The majority of Latin American economic histories have emphasized problems of supply and have shortchanged demand. In other words, many researchers have studied the production of key agricultural and mineral products of Latin America over the centuries but paradoxically little is known about who consumed the commodities exported to the industrialized nations of the North Atlantic and what buyers valued in the product. One of the central aims of this collection of essays is precisely to establish a two-way bridge between Latin American history and the history of Europe and the United States by paying attention to both production and consumption of the key commodities analyzed, but always to keep in mind the importance of commercial intermediaries. This new approach is facilitated by the fact that the history of consumption has become a major area of pathbreaking research, allowing for studies of changing needs, tastes, and methods of marketing for all kinds of commodities.

Our essays show that a number of things are desired from the same good at the same time, but the desiderata can change over time because of shifts in demand or the emergence of competing products or the rise of new technologies. The first essay in this volume shows that the export of gold and silver (the most important colonial exports) was fueled by the demand for these precious metals as money, as a store of reserve, and as inputs for luxury items. However, from the mid-nineteenth century, silver in particular became an industrial input and hence the demand for it changed substantially at the same time that new sources of production arose.

Other goods which were in demand mainly as hospitality foods or drinks, or as marks of distinction for conspicuous consumption, could also be considered medicinal products. As Laura Náte suggests in chapter 4, from the late sixteenth century in Europe, sugar and tobacco were considered a kind of panacea. The consumption of both was so rapidly disseminated and accepted that they became highly negotiable commodities in European markets. Curiously enough, there are inverse parallels here with the origins of consumption of a major twentieth-century commodity from Latin America, coca—transformed into cocaine—which was initially promoted as a medicine and later sold as an addictive recreational drug which found a mass market, particularly in industrial societies.

The consumption of a given product could change dramatically in respect to the social groups that demanded it. Coffee went from an aristocratic luxury (in the seventeenth and eighteenth centuries) to a mark of bourgeois class (in the early nineteenth century) to a proletarian necessity (from the late nineteenth century). But this did not mean that the beverage would not continue to be drunk by all social classes. While today coffee may be seen in part as a drug to stimulate industrial and office labor, perhaps in the form of instant coffee, it remains a leisure drink for the middle class, as among Starbucks sippers, and is still a luxury, as is demonstrated by Japanese aficionados of Jamaican Blue Mountain coffee. The same name, in this case "coffee," covers products with strikingly different provenances (Brazil, Côte d'Ivoire, Vietnam), different uses (instant and gourmet specialty coffee), and even biologically different cultivars, Arabica and robusta, which are markers of different class statuses.

A number of the exports we study are also industrial inputs that require substantial processing before consumption. Over time the distinction between final products and industrial inputs disappeared as almost all of the goods required ever more processing. Sugar became an essential additive in the food-processing industry just as tobacco became part of an enormous industrial complex. Even the coffee bean has become an ever smaller portion of the end price of canned or coffee shop coffee, so that it is more an input than a final product.

Consumption patterns of cacao and bananas, like those of coffee, moved to the rhythm of the expanding industrial economies of North America and Europe during the nineteenth and twentieth centuries. In both instances, new technologies of transport and processing allowed prices of these commodities to fall to levels low enough to engender mass consumption. The rapid growth of consumption led in turn to the formation of large corporations, which, in the case of bananas, were vertically integrated. According to Marcelo Bucheli and Ian Read, advertising and government regulation also came to play a role in the scope and parameters of commodity chains involving what became basic items in the consumer's food basket.

Rubber consumption grew dramatically, driven by demand for automobiles in the early twentieth century. Zephyr Frank and Aldo Musacchio demonstrate that large firms were created to serve this demand, and some firms attempted to integrate vertically (owning rubber plantations, rubber factories, and tire dealerships). However, the tendency in the rubber chain was for a division between producers, transformers, and final retail suppliers. Changing technology could affect patterns of consumption of rubber goods just as it did those of many other commodities analyzed in this volume. Improved tread wear, for instance, lengthened the life of tires and reduced consumer demand—although rising rates of automobile ownership compensated for this effect on the bottom line.

In all of these cases, there existed a complex relationship among productive capacities, technical developments in processing, the evolution of mass consumer markets, and the creation of large multinational enterprises. Just as consumers experienced sometimes radical changes in their lifestyles or eating habits, their sheer numbers and buying power fed back into producing regions, pushing for greater supplies and encouraging firms to seek lower costs and higher profits in the realms of transportation and distribution, and, most important, at the level of commodity prices, which could be lowered by a shift to substitutes or by a move to regions where wages were lower.

## THE SOCIAL HISTORY OF LATIN AMERICAN COMMODITIES

While the history of consumption offers a new and important angle from which to approach historical trajectories of key export commodities, the social history of production and distribution of commodities is also a major challenge. The social relations of production defined the long-run prospects of rubber and cacao, for example. Scholars have come to a general consensus that rubber workers maintained significant levels of autonomy, and because labor was scarce, the wage structure of the wild rubber industry (in Brazil in particular) was high and fairly rigid. The rubber boom created a dense and ingenious network of rubber tappers, provisioners, and merchants. This network, however, proved incapable of producing sufficient supplies of rubber at low prices and thereby encouraged massive entry of competitors based in European colonies. Social relations mattered because they set the limits of commodity production in the short and medium terms. But other elements also played a part in commodity life cycles on a regional level; for instance, in the long run, environmental factors might have prevented the natural rubber industry in Brazil from continuing to grow.

With cacao the situation was different. Labor shortages and rigid wage structures were less of a problem. What is more, because a range of valuable commodities could be produced in the region where cacao was grown, a varied pattern of production provided for a much more flexible economic environment. Owing to this flexibility, cacao planters in Bahia entered the world market more or less on their own terms. The rise of cacao in this region was therefore much more than the local manifestation of a demand-driven process emanating from the centers of consumption; rather, it represented the culmination of a long period of experimentation. This is similar to Mario Samper's concept of the "coffee complex," the group of plants that have a virtual symbiotic relationship: shade and lumber trees, banana and fruit trees, beans or corn planted between the rows. These plants serve to lower dependence on exports and dampen the damage when coffee export prices fall. Other exports formed parallel complementary complexes.

At the other end of the commodity chain, producers and consumers of automobile tires and powdered hot chocolate experienced social change themselves. It goes without saying that the automobile transformed almost every aspect of modern life, including adolescence, marriage, work, regional mobility, and popular culture. We take automobiles for granted now, and the tires are not even an afterthought. Yet in the initial years of this transformative industry, it was Brazilian rubber that made it possible for the first generation of car owners to ride in relative comfort at relatively high speeds while demanding the building of an extensive network of paved roads. Substitutes for natural rubber were still on the horizon, and other sources were limited in their production. It could be argued that few natural commodities ever had such an immediate and profound effect on social life.

Cacao's contribution was more modest, yet here too the transformation of an expensive, rare commodity into one of mass consumption through industrial processing made lasting changes, this time in eating habits. The explanation may be found in part in the fact that over time the rare commodity cacao was joined with a less expensive one, sugar, to expand its appeal. One would not be the least surprised to find today that the value of annual consumption of products containing cacao exceeds that of the consumption of goods containing natural rubber. The point here is not to suggest direct equivalence in terms of costs of raw inputs or overall market size; rather, it is to show how important and ubiquitous cacao has become in worldwide consumption patterns. Latin American producers largely lost out in the battle to supply these commodities; early prominence has been no guarantee of long-term dominance in the global economy.

## THE STATE IN LATIN AMERICAN COMMODITY POLITICS

The economic and social dynamics of commodity chains are essential to their comprehension, but equally essential are politics and policy. Virtually every essay in this book confronts the fact that understanding the trajectories of commodities also requires political analysis. As David Mc-

Creery argues in chapter 2, "land, labor, capital, appropriate technology, and the rest are necessary but not sufficient for the construction of a commodity chain. Except perhaps in an ideal free trade environment, political decisions are typically key to the constitution and the destruction of commodity chains."

From very early on, tax policies were essential to the management of export commodities. Laura Nater points out in chapter 4 that in the early seventeenth century the fiscal policies applied to tobacco were already important in struggles among European powers to maintain control of their American colonies: "By 1614, James I of Great Britain had established taxes on foreign tobacco in order to favor tobacco from his own colonies. In response, Philip III of Spain eliminated his previous prohibition of planting tobacco in the Caribbean region and imposed capital punishment for smugglers."

Subsequently, during the colonial period practically every commodity in one or another of the American colonies was subject to a set of regulations. These implied incentives and constraints were designed either to increase fiscal revenues or to favor certain groups of producers or traders involved in the commerce of a given international commodity.

Commodity regulations continued to be of great importance in the nineteenth century. As Rory Miller and Robert Greenhill point out in chapter 9, "The Peruvian and Chilean states seem to have been much more competent in organizing the guano and nitrate trades, monitoring foreign intermediaries and producers, and extracting profits than many writers, especially those in the dependency tradition, might have expected." Indeed, both states derived the bulk of their revenues for long periods from these export goods, a fact that demonstrates how the growth of international trade could strengthen states as well as weaken them. Nonetheless, the cyclical trajectory of exports also caused serious problems. In Peru, the demise of the guano boom in the mid-1870s led to private and public bankruptcy and a prolonged social, economic, and political crisis. In Chile, the nitrate age, which ran strong from the 1880s to 1929, was cut short by the Great Depression of the 1930s and provoked enormous tensions in society, economy, and polity.

Another striking example of government regulation and promotion of commodity trade was the case of Brazilian coffee, particularly from the early twentieth century. Although guided by liberal trade theory, Brazilian state officials intervened increasingly in the world coffee market after 1906. As Brazil's coffee industry moved from ad hoc crisis managing by the coffee-growing state of São Paulo to federal government assistance to a permanent provincial and then federal institution, Brazilian state authorities came to oversee and regulate coffee planting, warehousing, shipments to port, exports, financing, grading, and even advertising abroad. This development led to an international accord with other Latin American producers and eventually the International Coffee Agreement of growers and consumers worldwide, which set prices within a politically determined range.

In the cases of rubber and cacao, the role of the state varied significantly. Mary Ann Mahony suggests in chapter 7 that state regulations regarding land use, especially timber policy, affected the pace and location of the development of the cacao industry. The state was largely weak and ineffective in controlling the rubber industry, in providing it with needed public goods (such as transport facilities), and, in the end, in devising a policy that would have protected it against competition. This failure is in stark contrast to the relative success experienced by the Brazilian state (and São Paulo) in intervening on behalf of the coffee industry. With coffee, Brazil held a strong hand. It had market power and relatively abundant supplies of all the key factors of production, and the coffee growers were closely tied to the state. The market power enjoyed by Brazil's rubber industry waned in the 1910s, but its comparative advantage in factors of production was based entirely on a natural endowment of rubber trees. Once plantations took root in Asia, market power was lost, and with it any real prospect of successful state intervention.

Horacio Crespo tells a very different story in chapter 6. The countries that imported Latin America's sugar adopted public policies to favor their own competing agricultural products in order to reduce imports from Latin America. His essay demonstrates that as early as the mid-1850s, various European governments began to adopt policies that favored sugar beets, with the object of reducing imports of cane sugar, particularly from Spanish Cuba, the most productive sugar colony the world has known. Clearly, politics is as essential a factor as economics to keep in mind when we study the commodity history of Latin America.

In summary, this volume offers new approaches to the process of growing world economic integration, arguing that the knowledge of historical origins and dynamics is necessary to achieve a fuller comprehension of the complexities of the contemporary age. All our essays suggest that this challenge must be confronted by a second and related intellectual challenge, which consists in the need to integrate history with theory, for indeed without the application and development of theoretical tools, modern historical analysis cannot be placed on the same level as the other social sciences.

At the same time, our collective work suggests that while the term "globalization" may logically be identified with a worldwide process, this view begs the question of what happens at the local level. In fact, it may be argued that globalization actually consists of processes in which the local becomes embedded in the international, and vice versa. Describing this interaction is precisely the objective of the essays in this book. By analyzing the historical trajectories of twelve Latin American commodity chains in the world, the authors aim to clarify how the development of export commodities in different regions was driven by a complex set of social and economic factors that were both local and international. These factors can be effectively described in terms of a commodity chain, which is the concept adopted here to provide a dynamic framework for a group of complementary case studies ranging over the last five centuries.

The need to explicate more cases studies through the use of theory is evident in the historical literature on Latin America, which traditionally has been heavily empirical. All contributors to this book have made a systematic effort to produce analytical history while avoiding the pitfalls of dogmatism. This effort may be observed in the varied and sometimes eclectic approaches advanced to explain the global commodity chains that have traversed Latin America from the sixteenth century to our own. And let us insist once again that while the economics of trade is our starting point, other social science approaches are also applied to this collective research. Inevitably a comprehensive study of the trajectories of the key export commodities leads to the exploration of related analytical problems: the social history of commodity production and consumption, the roles of labor and key entrepreneurial actors, the importance of state regulations in the respective Latin American regional economies, and the ecology of production of agricultural and mineral products for export.

Finally, it seems only just to suggest that this study is quite simply a first attempt to explore the extraordinarily rich history of the commodities of Latin America and of the world over the course of centuries. Our essays cover important subjects but many more have acquired importance in international trade, including Latin America's wheat, wool, hides, meat, and such mineral products as tin, copper, and the king of modern exports, petroleum. We hope that this volume may stimulate further research on the past, present, and future role of Latin America in world history.

MARCELO BUCHELI spent the 2004–2005 year as a Newcomen Fellow at Harvard Business School. He is an assistant professor of business and history at the University of Illinois. His most recent publication, *Bananas and Business* (New York University Press, 2005), analyzes the shifting role of the United Fruit Company in Colombia.

HORACIO CRESPO was born in Argentina in 1947 and studied at the Universidad Nacional de Córdoba. After obtaining his doctoral degree from the Universidad Nacional Autónoma de México (UNAM), he taught at various universities in Argentina and Mexico and received a Guggenheim research fellowship in 1998. He is currently a professor of history at the Universidad Autónoma del Estado de Morelos and in the postgraduate program of UNAM. He is the author of numerous books, including *Historia del azúcar en México* (Fondo de Cultura Económica, 1989–90), *Estadísticas históricas del azúcar en México* (Azúcar S.A., 1990), and *Modernización y conflicto social: Hacienda azucarera y pueblo campesino en el Morelos porfirista* (INEHRM, 2005).

ZEPHYR FRANK is an assistant professor of history at Stanford University, where he teaches Latin American social and economic history. His most recent publication is *Dutra's World: Wealth and Family in Nineteenth-Century Rio de Janeiro* (University of New Mexico Press, 2004). He is currently researching the geography of urban life in Rio de Janeiro during the nineteenth century.

PAUL GOOTENBERG was a Rhodes scholar before receiving his Ph.D. from the University of Chicago in 1985. He is a professor of history at the State University of New York at Stony Brook, where he was the director of Latin American and Caribbean Studies (2000–2005). His books include *Between Silver and Guano* (Princeton University Press, 1989), *Imagining Development* (University of California Press, 1993), and the edited volume *Cocaine: Global Histories* (Routledge, 1999). He is currently writing a global history of Andean cocaine from 1850 to 1970. Gootenberg lives in Brooklyn and has two children: Danyal (b. 2000) and Léa (b. 2004).

ROBERT GREENHILL was formerly head of the Department of Business Studies at London Guildhall University. His research has focused on Britain's economic links with Latin America during the nineteenth and twentieth centuries. He has published a number of articles on British shipping in Latin America and the commodity trades in such journals as *Business History*, *Accounting, Business and Financial History*, and the *International Journal of Maritime History*, and has contributed numerous chapters to edited volumes. He coauthored (with Edmar Bacha) *150 anos de café* (Rio de Janeiro: Martins and Johnston, 1992). Since his retirement from full-time academic life in 2002 he continues to teach part-time and pursue his research interests.

MARY ANN MAHONY is an assistant professor of history at Central Connecticut State University. She is the author of several articles on Brazilian history; she is currently finishing a book titled "Revisiting the Violent Land: Bahia's Cacao Area, 1850–1937."

CARLOS MARICHAL is a professor of history at El Colegio de México. He has been two-term president of the Mexican Association of Economic History (2000–2004), of which he was one of the founders. He is author of *A Century of Debt Crises in Latin America, 1820–1930* (Princeton University Press, 1989) and has edited many books on the economic history of Mexico, specializing in fiscal history (eighteenth and nineteenth centuries) as well as on the history of enterprise (nineteenth and twentieth centuries).

DAVID MCCREERY is a professor of history at Georgia State University. He has taught and done research in Central America and Brazil. His most recent book is *Frontier Goiás, 1810–1890* (Stanford University Press, forthcoming). Currently he is studying the participation of coastal shipping and commerce in the development of the Brazilian Northeast during the nineteenth century.

RORY MILLER teaches in the Management School at the University of Liverpool, having previously been director of the university's Institute of Latin American Studies. He is the author of *Britain and Latin America in the Nineteenth and Twentieth Centuries* (Longman, 1993) and co-editor of *Business History in Latin America: The Experience of Seven Countries* (Liverpool University Press, 1999). After spending much of his early career researching Peruvian economic history, on which he published a number of articles in such journals as *Business History Review, Journal of Latin American Studies,* and *World Development,* he is now working on British companies in Latin America since World War II and editing a book titled *Consumption, Trade, and Markets in Latin America, 1750–1950,* to be published by the Institute for the Study of the Americas in London.

ALDO MUSACCHIO is an assistant professor at Harvard Business School, where he teaches economic and business history. He completed his dissertation on corporate law and capital markets in Brazil at Stanford University in 2005. His current research focuses on the importance of doing history and detailed country studies in order to understand how the institutions that sustain economic transactions evolve over time. His work focuses on the regulation of corporations and financial markets in historical perspective in Mexico and Brazil, and on the effects of bank privatization and the entry of foreign banks into Mexico in the 1990s.

LAURA NATER is a professor of history in the Departamento de Humanidades, Facultad de Estudios Generales, Universidad de Puerto Rico, Río Piedras. She obtained her doctorate at El Colegio de México in 2000 with a thesis on the royal tobacco monopoly in colonial Cuba, based on archival research in Spain, Cuba, and Mexico. She is currently preparing this study for publication. She has published several essays on the history of the royal tobacco monopoly in the colonial period in Mexico, Cuba, and Louisiana.

IAN READ, a Ph.D. candidate at Stanford University, is completing his dissertation on the conditions of slave life in Santos, Brazil. With Marcelo Bucheli, he is cofounder of the United Fruit Historical Society.

MARIO SAMPER is a rural historian with complementary interests in historical geography and agricultural production systems. Trained at the Universidad de Costa Rica and the University of California at Berkeley, he has been a visiting professor at the University of Wisconsin, Madison, and the Université de Toulouse. He currently works in the history department of the Universidad de Costa Rica as well as in the geography department of the Instituto de Ciencias Sociales at the university. He is the author of *Producción cafetalera y poder político en Centroamérica* and *Generations of Settlers: Rural Households and Markets on the Costa Rican Frontier, 1850–1935*, as well as co-author and editor of a number of books on coffee in Costa Rica and elsewhere in Latin America, including *Coffee, Society, and Power in Latin America*; *La cadena de producción y comercialización del café: Perspectiva histórica y comparada*; *Café de Costa Rica: Un viaje a lo largo de su historia*; and *Entre la tradición y el cambio: Evolución tecnológica de la caficultura costarricense*.

STEVEN TOPIK is a professor of history at the University of California, Irvine. He is author of *Trade and Gunboats* (Stanford University Press, 1996); *The World That Trade Created*, with Kenneth Pomeranz (M. E. Sharpe, 1999); *The Second Conquest of Latin America: Coffee, Henequen, and Oil during the Export Boom, 1850–1930*, with Allen Wells (University of Texas Press, 1998); *The Political Economy of the Brazilian State, 1889–1930* (University of Texas Press, 1987); and editor of several volumes, most recently *The World Coffee Economy in Africa, Asia, and Latin America, 1500–1989*, with William Clarence-Smith (Cambridge University Press, 2003). He is currently working on a global history of coffee.

ALLEN WELLS, Roger Howell Jr. Professor of History at Bowdoin College, is currently finishing a book about a group of refugees who fled Hitler and established an agricultural colony in the Dominican Republic in the 1940s. Among his publications are (with Steven Topik) *The Second Conquest of Latin America: Coffee, Henequen, and Oil during the Export Boom, 1850–1930* (University of Texas Press, 1998) and (with Gilbert M. Joseph) *Summer of Discontent, Seasons of Upheaval: Elite Politics and Rural Insurgency in Yucatan, 1876–1915* (Stanford University Press, 1996).

factories: textile production in, 77; tobacco and, 94, 101–8; closed in Havana, 110; sugar and, 154; steam power and, 187; Peru's cocaine, 328

Faletto, Enzo, 7

FDA (Food and Drug Administration), 332

fertilizers. *See* guano; nitrates

*filière*, compared to commodity chains, 13

Firestone, Harvey, 282

Firestone Rubber Company, 289

Flanders: silver and, 36, 37; cochineal and, 79, 80; fertilizer and, 237. *See also* Dutch

foreign debt, 7

foreign investment, 7, 8; coffee and, 127; fertilizer and, 258–59

France: wars against Spain, 37, 110; merchants and contraband silver, 38; indigo transshipped from, 70; demand for luxury crimson in, 80; tobacco production in St-Domingue, 94; trade disrupted with Spain, 96; colonies encouraged by Dutch, 99; Haitian Revolution and, 110; slaves and coffee in St-Domingue, 118; development of sugar beet industry, 151, 153, 156; as participant in sugar conferences, 157, 164; use of fertilizer, 237; coca mania in, 325

Francia, José Rodrígues de, 4

free trade, 3–7, 358; indigo and, 69; 70, 71; coffee and, 140; sugar and, 154, 156–58; fertilizers and, 236; rubber and, 292

Freud, Sigmund, 324, 327

Fruit Dispatch Company, 208–9, 211, 213

FTAA (Free Trade Area of the Americas), 7

Furtado, Celso, 6

García Márquez, Gabriel, 205, 214

Geneva Conventions, 341

Genoese merchants, 1, 38, 81

Gereffi, Gary, 231

Germany: silver and, 36–37, 47; chemical dyes and, 90; sugar beets and, 153, 155–57, 160, 161–64; fertilizers and, 240–42; cocaine and, 324, 327–29, 331, 337

globalization, 1, 3; commodity trade and, 8; silver and, 25; competitive commodity markets in, 292; as imprecise term, 352; need to connect to local level, 360

gold, 2, 5, 10; in relation to silver, 25–28; as form of money, 30, 354; ratio between silver and gold, 32, 41; flows of, 34–37; abundant in Brazil, 46, 124; drained from Spain, 98; smuggling from Minas Gerais, 179

gold standard, 5, 28

Good Neighbor Policy, 343

Goodyear, Charles, 274

Great Britain: as model for Latin America, 13; gold standard and, 28; war with Spain and, 37, 108; silver and, 38; East India Company and, 42; demand for indigo and, 54; contraband trade and, 55; commerce with South Carolina, 61, 64; merchant houses in Bengal, 62; mercantile system, 67, 123; government intervention in markets, 69; loss of American colonies, 70; luxury textiles and, 80; tobacco and, 95–96, 98–99, 108–9, 358; sugar and, 102, 155, 156, 164, 169; pure food laws, 137; abolitionism and, 152, 183; free trade and, 154; sugar conferences and, 157–59; banana growers and quotas, 217; farming and fertilizers in, 228, 236–37, 239; limited liability companies and, 244; Peruvian reliance on trading houses of, 250; financing of services in Peru, 256; stocks of cap-

trade, 230; Chilean monopoly of, 233; structure of commodity chain in, 235; combinations and, 245, 252; domination by Guggenheims, 236; price volatility and, 236; growing use in Europe, 239; demand associated with sugar beets, 240; Haber-Bosch process and, 241; replacement by manufactured fertilizers, 241, 242; ownership in production of, 244–45, 248; labor force and, 246–47; intermediaries in trade of, 249–50, 252; United States market for, 253; role of trading houses, 255–56; retention of profits by states, 256–57; state structuring of commodity chains, 258, 358; lack of futures market in, 259

North, John, 252–53, 255

Oaxaca: production of cochineal in, 78, 82, 83; peasant communities in, 84, 85, 90

Oliphants (company): guano trade and, 252; failure of, 253

Ortíz, Fernando, 93–94, 98

Ottoman Empire, 27, 39

Pacific War. *See* War of the Pacific

Parke-Davis (company), 327, 329, 330, 335

peasants, 6; communities of, 29, 77, 82, 85–86; Chinese, 40, 77; indigo and, 57; in Bengal, 60; control of resources in Bengal by, 68, 70; Chinese, 77; in Oaxaca, 83; as laborers, 84–85, 118; repartimiento system and, 86; production of cochineal and, 90; sugar and mobilization of, 149; Cárdenas administration and, 316; expansion of coca and, 344

peons, 300, 312–14

Peru, 4, 9; silver and, 28–29, 41–43, 45–46; indigo and, 70; dye trade

and, 84; tobacco and, 97, 100; sugar and, 162, 163, 164; fertilizers and, 229, 233, 236–37, 238, 241, 244–46, 249–51, 254–61; rubber and, 271, 273–74; coca and, 323–25, 327, 328–31, 333, 335–41; U.S. interest in coca from, 343; guano boom and, 358

peso, silver: as money supply, 25, 26, 46–47; coinage, 27–28; mints, 32, 33; exports of, 34–35; surplus of, 37; China and India and, 39; circulation in the Americas, 43; in nineteenth century, 46–47; cochineal and, 82. *See also* silver

pharmaceutical companies, 330

Philip II, 36

Philip III, 36, 99, 358

Philippines: silver and, 27, 34, 37, 41; dye trade and, 70; state tobacco administration in, 106; coffee production in, 123; as major sugar exporter, 162–63; Smoot-Hawley Act and, 165; sugar quotas and, 166–68; bananas and, 215; rubber production in, 291; hard fiber production in, 308–10

plantations, 10–11; indigo, 54, 56–60, 71; tobacco, 97, 99; coffee, 124, 126; sugar and, 151–53, cacao, 175, 181–86, 192, 194; bananas, 204–5, 207, 211–17, 220; fertilizers and, 228, 238, 240; rubber, in Asia, 271–77, 279, 280–88, 291–93, 359; henequen, 302, 304, 309, 311–12, 314, 315, 316; coca, 323, 333, 335, 341; vertical integration in rubber industry and, 355. *See also* planters

planters: indigo, 54, 55, 57, 58, 59, 62, 64, 65, 66, 67, 69; Brazilian coffee, 125, 127–28; Costa Rican coffee, 131, 136; sugar, 154, 156, 157, 164; cacao, 174–85, 191–92, 193–94; fertilizer and, 230, 238; rubber, 284; henequen, 313; gen-

tire manufacturers. *See* tires
tires, 12; in rubber commodity chain, 272; manufacturers of, 272, 274, 278, 282, 285, 289, 293; and demand for rubber, 274–75; for bicycles, 280; pneumatic, 282; demand for, 284–85; tread wear of, 285, 355; profits from, 291
tobacco, 2, 3, 10, 11, 17; silver and, 26, 38; as panacea, 93, 354; spread of production, 94; consumption of, 95–96; sugar versus, 98–100, 110; Cuban factory, 101–2, 107, 110; smuggling, 102, 109; in Iberia, 102–3; monopoly in Seville, 104–5; tax on, 106; monopoly in Mexico, 107; effect of American independence on trade, 108; subsidies in United States for domestic, 166; depletion of soil and, 238; part of industrial complex, 355; battle for control of colonies and, 358
tourists, 214, 300, 318
trade agreements, 149, 166
trading houses, 151; indigo and, 62; fertilizers and, 249, 252, 254, 259–60; German, 327. *See also* merchants
transaction costs, 4, 127, 133
transatlantic trade, 78, 97
transport costs, 56, 57, 86, 133, 330
trapiches, 110
Tropical Radio, 215
Trotsky, Leon, 13

Underwood-Simmons Bill, 210
United Brands, 219. *See also* United Fruit Company
United Fruit Company: origins and image of, 204–5; vertical integration and, 206; relation with United States, 206; sources for study of, 207; growth of, 208; advertising strategy of, 209–10, 211; consolidation of banana industry by, 212; plantations and, 213; monopolis-

tic practices and, 214–15; effect of World War II on, 216; decline of, 217–19; as Chiquita Brands International, 220; changes in, 221; exploitation and, 290
United Nations, 343
United States, 5, 8, 12–14, 17; silver and, 28, 46, 47; indigo and, 67; coffee and, 118, 123, 133, 135, 137, 139–41; sugar and, 147–48, 150, 156, 158, 162–67; cacao and, 187, 190; bananas and, 204–5, 208, 211, 213–14, 219; fertilizers and, 228, 238–42, 244, 252–53, 255, 259–60; rubber and, 274–76, 282, 286, 291, 293; henequen and, 305, 309; coca and, 325, 328–33, 337, 340–41, 343–45; commodity chains and, 354
urban workers, 6, 133

vacuum packing (coffee), 137
Virginia, 94, 96, 99, 101

W. R. Grace and Company, 241, 252–53, 255, 259–60
Wallerstein, Immanuel, 7, 230–31, 260, 290, 322
War of the Desert (Argentina), 13
War of the Pacific, 229, 245, 252–53, 256, 260, 324
wet processing (coffee), 63, 130–31
Wickham, Henry, 279, 283
woad, 53, 67
workers, 6, 7, 13; urban, 6, 133; silver and, 29; indigo and, 58–60, 63; coffee and, 118, 123, 127; sugar and, 149, 163, 165; cacao and, 182, 184–85; bananas and, 204, 212–14, 218; fertilizers and, 243, 246–47, 257; rubber and, 274, 287, 291; henequen and, 300, 302, 312–15, 317; coca and, 323, 325, 328; social relations of production and, 356. *See also* labor
working class, 5; coffee and, 127, 136;

chocolate and, 186, 188–90, 192; banana as food for, 208–9, 216

STEVEN TOPIK is a professor of history at the University of California, Irvine.

CARLOS MARICHAL is a professor of history at El Colegio de México.

ZEPHYR FRANK is an assistant professor of history at Stanford University.

Library of Congress Cataloging-in-Publication Data

From silver to cocaine : Latin American commodity chains
and the building of the world economy, 1500–2000
edited by Steven Topik, Carlos Marichal, and Zephyr Frank.
p. cm. — (American encounters/global interactions)
Includes bibliographical references and index.
ISBN 0-8223-3753-3 (cloth : alk. paper)
ISBN 0-8223-3766-5 (pbk. : alk. paper)
1. Primary commodities—Latin America.
2. Latin America—Commerce—History.
3. Exports—Latin America—History.
I. Topik, Steven.
II. Marichal, Carlos.
III. Frank, Zephyr L.
IV. Series.
HF1040.9.L37T67 2006
382'.098—dc22
2006004882